CHINESE COMMUNIST EDUCATION

Records of the First Decade

COMPILED AND EDITED BY
Stewart Fraser

VANDERBILT UNIVERSITY PRESS
Nashville 1965

8/4/67   Bro-Dart   10.00

To

G.M.F., A.S.F., and B.J.F.

Foreword

The study of any educational system is difficult and hazardous unless the student or researcher has available to him sufficient primary documents and artifacts of the area under consideration. Contemporary educational research into regions where language problems must be overcome or where there are political barriers in gaining material have handicapped all but the most devoted scholar, be they linguists or research specialists. Accordingly, it cannot be denied that the adequacy and competence of detailed research will continue to be based on language skills and a comprehensive knowledge of the primary documents involved. For many students and teachers, however, there are a variety of alternatives available which may afford materials sufficient for introductory study purposes. The continual growth in the number of journal articles and books about Soviet Russian education during the past decade reflects a greater interest in foreign education in general and, more specifically, an increase in the number of specialists competent to deal with Russian educational matters. To a lesser extent, the same may be said of Communist China, an area up to now neglected in comparison with the research already launched into the Soviet Union's educational commitments.

Only a handful of scholars in the United States are presently engaged in analyzing the educational system of the People's Republic of China. Yet, from the commencement of the Korean War to the present, there has been open access to a variety of English-language materials on Communist China, some of them available in English editions of official Chinese Communist government publications. In addition, news broadcasts monitorings and a range of non-Communist translation services operating under both private and governmental auspices have been available. The extent and range of the materials in the English language relevant to Chinese Communist education are such that one might venture to say that it bears favorable comparison with the availability of English-language material on Soviet Russian education during the decade between 1950 and 1960. Its employment by comparative educators for both teaching and research purposes has, however, rarely approached the use made of similar materials available to students of Soviet Russian education.

The problem regarding information from Communist China since 1949 is complicated for American researchers by the nature of the political relationship between the People's Republic and the United States and the fact that educational and cultural contacts during the first decade and even now have been kept to a minimum. This is in contrast to the numerous official and non-official groups of American educators who have visited Russia in recent years and the government-sponsored cultural exchanges promoted between the United States and the Soviet Union.

A second problem is that of the availability of data, statistical, descriptive, or analytical, in English and the use of what may be called "quasi-primary sources," that is, translations of original documents, speeches, and articles on education which appear regularly in the Chinese Communist press.

One of the earliest and most useful summaries of the availability of Chinese Communist material in English is given by John M. H. Lindbeck in "Research Materials on Communist China: United States Government Sources." [1] A brief perusal of the considerable writings of some of the recent researchers on Communist China, such as Robert Barendsen, Theodore Chen, Chester Cheng, Peter Tang, Chang-tu Hu, Leo Orleans, W. W. Rostow, and Richard Walker, will illustrate the importance of these various translation services, as well as of the English-language editions of official Communist Chinese documents. See, for example, in the bibliographical section of this book the thoroughly documented type of more recent analysis on Chinese Communist education undertaken by Chen, Barendsen, Orleans, and Hu. Barendsen's recent monograph on a critical area of Communist education, *Half-*

1. *Journal of Asian Studies*, XVIII, No. 3 (May 1959), 357–363. The bibliography of the book in hand includes references to many of the English-language works on Chinese Communist education in its various phases.

Work, Half-Study Schools in Communist China, is carefully substantiated by documents and articles gathered from the major translation services available. It is backed by the author's parallel review
of the relevant Chinese-language daily press and education journals; in addition the analysis is enhanced by the author's reputation
as a competent Sinologist. Orleans has produced a most significant
contribution to the study of Communist education in his *Professional Manpower and Education in Communist China.* It is
important, not only because of the paucity of worthwhile books
on education in Communist China but because it analyzes closely
one of the key areas of economic viability, namely the adequacy
of training and the employment of high-level trained personnel
by the regime. Orleans' book shows the careful research into and
the painstaking analysis of English-language translations available
to him at the Library of Congress. Something like a quarter of
his book is composed of translated documents supporting the
analytical portions of the text. In addition to the material
emanating from the various translation services, Orleans has had
the undergirding services of Chinese-language specialists at the
Library of Congress to verify the translations and provide supplementary material not normally available in translations. Chang-tu
Hu's latest work, *Chinese Education under Communism,* includes
carefully selected collections of some of the more interesting contemporary essays on Chinese Communist educational philosophy.
The essays were, for the most part, available originally in English-
language translations from both official Chinese Communist
sources in Peking and from United States government agencies
in Hong Kong.

Reference should be made also to the writings of Richard
Walker and W. W. Rostow. Walker states in relation to his own
research that:

> The major source has been the published documents of the Chinese
> Communists themselves. I realize, of course, that most of their claims and
> statistics must be subjected to close scrutiny and analysis. For preliminary
> analysis, as well as screening of the great quantity of Communist material,
> I am deeply indebted to the pioneering work of the United States Consul
> General in Hong Kong. . . . Their English-language productions of im-

portant Chinese Communist documents constitute a basic collection for any study of the Mao regime, and in many cases first-rate scholarly analysis is added.[2]

To support further the suggestion that there has been a considerable volume of accurately translated material available to the non-linguist, it is perhaps useful to quote from Professor W. W. Rostow's important contribution to Chinese studies, written over a decade ago, *The Prospects for Communist China.* In a bibliographical note, it is indicated that:

> The analysis of Communist China from the outside requires certain special techniques somewhat similar to those required for the study of the Soviet Union. Since few relatively objective observers are allowed extensive access to Communist China, the bulk of the data must be that released from official Communist sources, especially the Communist Chinese press. . . . Fortunately, good translations of the Communist press are issued regularly . . . so that a good part of this primary material is easily available to the Western reader.[3]

The compilation of this series of select documents on Chinese Communist education has been undertaken so that some of the more useful statements would be set forth in a unified and readily available form for those interested in both the comparative and political aspects of contemporary Chinese education. The items selected for inclusion in the collection undoubtedly show my own bias; however, a wide range of material is represented in the compilation and may suffice for those requiring background information on Chinese Communist education. For advanced students, particularly those undertaking specialized research, these selected documents will give a general indication as to the type of "primary" source materials already available in English-language translations. They may also provide a framework or incentive for others to undertake extensive and intensive research, not necessarily exhibited in this collection. The documents prin-

2. *China under Communism: The First Five Years* (London: George Allen and Unwin, 1956), p. xiii.
3. *The Prospects for Communist China* (Cambridge, Mass.: M.I.T. Press, 1954), p. 327.

cipally encompass the period from 1950 to 1960, though there is a somewhat greater concentration of items dealing with the period of so-called "intellectual freedom" from 1955 to 1957. Most of the selected documents have been edited, briefly commented upon, and their original source described. In some cases, an alternative source has been suggested, and a comparison of the various texts may indicate some minor differences between official and semi-official translations.

The principal source for these records has been the United States Consulate General in Hong Kong, which since 1950 has engaged in one of the most comprehensive translation services available for private and institutional research. Principal translations of the Consulate include *Survey of China Mainland Press* and *Current Background*. Full acknowledgment is made to the External Research Division of the Office of Intelligence Research of the United States Department of State for its assistance in making the material available to libraries and interested researchers as well as granting permission to use these translations in this compilation. A further important government source of information since 1957 has been the United States Joint Publications Research Service.

In addition, a major source of documentary material, as would be expected, is the government of the People's Republic of China, through its Foreign Languages Press and other publishing outlets in Peking. Nearly a third of the documents in this collection are derived directly from official Chinese Communist sources and have already been translated into English in Peking.

In anticipation of criticisms and queries regarding the editing of the selections themselves or other details affecting them, it should be pointed out that educational content and import were the primary considerations deciding their inclusion, and in turn, this was determined chiefly by the relevancy of the selections for education in a general political context. If the reader suspects injustice has been done to the selections or abbreviations unnecessarily imposed, then recourse should be made immediately to the basic translations, if not to the original documents in Chinese where available. It is perhaps apropos to note that Leo

Orleans used these same translations for his study, *Professional Manpower and Education in Communist China,* as I have used for this collection of speeches and articles on Communist education. On the subject of quotations and sources I would share his viewpoint and approach towards the materials that "it will become immediately apparent to the reader that many of these translations are rather awkward. Only minor changes were made in the often literal translations of the original texts, because by polishing them up, they lose some of the original flavor and color" so often present in the language and special vocabulary of the Chinese Communists.[4]

This collection is a preliminary attempt to place within the reach of non-Sinologists and nonlinguists, among whom this compiler places himself, certain educational material which may assist in a better understanding of the problems and state of education in Communist China. It is perhaps necessary, however, to utter a note of caution with regard to documentary and statistical material emanating from the People's Republic of China: namely, *caveat lector.*

STEWART FRASER

Peabody International Center
Nashville, Tennessee
January 1965

4. *Professional Manpower and Education in Communist China* (Washington, D.C.: National Science Foundation, 1961), p. vii.

Acknowledgments

I am greatly indebted to a number of researchers and scholars working in the field of Chinese Communist studies, particularly in the area of Communist education, for assistance in preparing this manuscript for publication. I have been guided in the selection and presentation of documents in this collection by the interest, correspondence, and careful review of material of many interested colleagues.

First, I would note with appreciation the particular involvement of Robert Barendsen, Asian Specialist of the United States Office of Education. He has taken a keen interest in the progress of the manuscript and has offered pertinent and constructive criticism throughout. Many of his suggestions have been incorporated into the final draft. William Brickman, Professor of History and of Comparative Education in the Graduate School of Education of the University of Pennsylvania; Chang-tu Hu, Professor of Comparative Education in Teachers College of Columbia University; and Theodore Chen, Professor of Education and Asian Studies in the University of Southern California have, through their personal encouragement and interest, promoted the research and compilation of the documents in this collection.

I am also indebted to the longstanding interest, encouragement, and correspondence of J. Chester Cheng, Associate Professor of History in San Francisco State College; Don-chean Chu, Professor of Education in Indiana State College, Pennsylvania; George Bereday, Professor of Comparative Education in Teachers College of Columbia University; Michael Lindsay, Professor of International Relations in American University, Washington; Roderick MacFarquhar, editor of *The China Quarterly*, London; Stephen Romine, Dean of the School of Education, Mehdi Nakosteen, Professor of Educational Foundations, Homer Rainey, Professor of

xi

Higher Education, and Earl Swisher, Professor of History, all at the University of Colorado.

The staffs of the *Far Eastern Economic Review,* Union Research Institute, and *China News Analysis* of Hong Kong and the Chinese Section of the Reference Department of the Library of Congress have kindly assisted in many ways with the bibliographical compilation.

Special acknowledgment is made to the most valuable assistance and correspondence of T. W. Miller, Jr., Chief of the United States Joint Publications Research Service; Theodore E. Kyriak, of Research and Microfilm Publications, Inc., Annapolis, Maryland; and Richard Sorich of the East Asian Institute of Columbia University. In particular, appreciation is noted for use made of the extensive bibliography of JPRS material on Communist China prepared by Dr. Sorich under the sponsorship of the Joint Committee on Contemporary China of the American Council of Learned Societies and the Social Science Research Council.

Full acknowledgment is made to the Institute of Asian and Pacific Studies (International Secretariat of the Institute of Pacific Relations) of the University of British Columbia for kind permission to quote from Professor Michael Lindsay's notes on *Educational Problems in Communist China* (1950); and to the Human Relations Area Files, New Haven, Connecticut, for permission to use educational charts from Chang-tu Hu's *China: Its People, Its Society, Its Culture* (1960). I would also like to acknowledge the use made of translated documentary material from Mr. Hung-fang Wang's Master's thesis, "Higher Education in Communist China" (University of Washington, 1953).

To Mrs. Margaret Walker and Miss Bonnie Randall must be extended my thanks for their careful editorial and typing assistance.

S.F.

Contents

xiii

Contents

UNIVERSITIES AND COLLEGES MUST PROPERLY HELP INTELLECTUALS 400
  ACQUIRE QUALITIES OF LABORING PEOPLE

Education, Indoctrination, and Ideology
in Communist China, 1950–1960

Education, Indoctrination, and Ideology in Communist China, 1950–1960

By Stewart Fraser

FROM CLASSICAL TO REPUBLICAN

The introduction of a modern plan of education into China covers a period of some fifty years, and the establishment of a potentially universal system involves perhaps only a decade. However, China has rightly boasted of having had for more than a thousand years a theoretically democratic and universal system of learning which, in many of its features, was second to none. Yet education was neither universal in practice nor democratic in application when the Chinese Empire collapsed at the turn of this century.

The history of modern China is, to some extent, a history of the formal and informal educational forces at work in that country. The inability of Imperial higher education to cope with the demands of the foreign powers who exploited China is all too apparent today. The introduction of Anglo-Saxon educational models, radically different from those they supplanted, had been only a qualified success. Chinese academic leaders toiled in an intellectual climate which tended to shun the best of the previous thousand years and expected Western science to be China's panacea in the twentieth century. Social and political upsets did not allow for any real consolidation in education during the previous fifty years; they frustrated the patterning of education in a modern, indigenous, and purely Chinese mold.

The mastery of literary Chinese and an understanding of the Five Classics of Confucius were inadequate training for a technical, dynamic, and ever-shrinking world. Chinese scholars ventured abroad in increasing numbers and brought back their conflicting impressions of Western scholarship. It was too little, too

3

late. Unlike Japan, China was not able to stave off the intrusive West.[1] While there were many foreign educators who tried to bridge the gap between the two cultures, their efforts were often misapplied and their motives sometimes misinterpreted. Private and state, missionary and secular, national and provincial, foreign and indigenous conflicts accounted for much of the fragmentation of Chinese education.[2]

Even the development and expansion of education with a slowly modernizing China was not without its problems. Instead of rewarding employment, academic training often meant unemployment after graduation. The displaced intellectual and the perennial student have been found in other cultures in recent years, and China has had her share of this gentry. The fabric of respectability which once was a prerogative of the teacher-scholar-intellectual in China underwent a metamorphosis culminating in final disillusionment when only a Pyrrhic victory was achieved in August 1945 against the Japanese. The teacher was confronted with almost insurmountable problems in reconstructing China. The situation was continually irritated by the debilitating civil war which lasted for another four years.

The revolutionary spirit of the Kuomintang had ebbed, and the idealistic enthusiasm of the twenties, which was tested in the thirties against the Japanese, did not have sufficient impetus to withstand the forces of communism unleashed in China after 1945. The intelligentsia were foremost among those who were disenchanted with the ruling cliques, and the peasants soon gave more than tacit support to the "new wind" of communism, which promised to relieve them of their misery.

The course of Chinese communism originating in 1921 had not entirely bypassed the overwhelming bulk of the intellectuals, though they were unable to evaluate its real direction or anticipate all the connotations it had for them. In the 1920s the May Fourth

1. See Teng Ssu-yii and John K. Fairbank, *China's Response to the West* (Cambridge, Mass.: Harvard University Press, 1954), and Earl Swisher, "Chinese Intellectuals and the Western Impact, 1838–1900," *Comparative Studies in Society and History,* I, No. 1 (October 1958).

2. See C. H. Becker, *et al., The Reorganization of Education in China* (Paris: League of Nations' Institute of Intellectual Co-operation, 1932).

Anti-Western Student Movement [3] and the "literary renaissance" sparked by Hu Shih, one of modern China's outstanding liberal educators, did bring many students, teachers, and intellectuals together, irrespective of their politics. But after the Kuomintang-Communist "separation" of 1927, many of the intelligentsia kept to their so-called "towers of ivory and jade," the educational centers of the major seacoast cities, while the leftwing student element became temporarily separated from their comrades in the Communist armies who were conducting their famous forced Long March into the interior of China away from the Kuomintang.

The excesses of the outgoing Kuomintang regime in 1949 are remembered today instead of the ideals and partial successes achieved by the Chinese government battling against the Japanese. Many of the fundamental farsighted educational programs envisaged by the Nationalists had to be abandoned until the time became more auspicious to introduce reforms. The situation never became truly auspicious and was materially altered by a Chinese Marxism which would not wait. This "new wind" of communism forced the pace and, in the end, won over from the Kuomintang the bulk of the disillusioned students and teachers, who saw a way out of their intolerable situation, though not necessarily through the avenue they might have perhaps chosen if there had been some real freedom of choice.

THE ADVENT OF COMMUNISM

It is a fallacy to interpret the Communist victory as being achieved entirely by default on the part of the Nationalists. Likewise, it is insufficient to see the advent of Marxism in China as achieved by massive Soviet assistance or by centralized planning from Moscow. Furthermore, the Chinese Communists did not "inherit" a nation of over six hundred million souls quite unprepared, though the final collapse of the Nationalist regime

3. For a scholarly and detailed analysis of this "student movement," see Chow Tse-tsung, *The May Fourth Movement: Intellectual Revolution in Modern China* (Cambridge, Mass.: Harvard University Press, 1960).

came quicker than had been expected. During the previous quarter of a century the Communists had been tested in every conceivable manner. At first welcomed as a partner in the "Chinese Revolution" in the early twenties and virtually pronounced the spiritual heirs of Sun Yat-sen, they were ultimately expelled decisively from the cities by the Kuomintang. In an effort to set up Chinese soviets they were forced to march across the length of China. They suffered enormous losses in material and manpower. Spurned by the Soviet Union for the most part, they had to take an "official" second place in the war against Japan. By the end of the Second World War, they faced a Nationalist government backed, seemingly, by the enormous resources of the United States of America.[4] Their initial victory in Manchuria was partially a disillusioning experience. They entered the industrial heart of China, the richest prize of all, only to find that the Soviet Union had systematically looted it and that much of what was left had been demolished by the civil war.

Yet the Chinese Communists persevered. With three decades of political and military experience behind them, including ten years of administrative practice in the northwest portions of China and with three years of rehabilitation and restoration activities in the badly damaged industrial area of Manchuria successfully accomplished, they felt qualified to take their turn at being China's master.

HIGHER EDUCATION IN COMMUNIST-HELD AREAS, 1944–1949

Higher education under the Communists in the areas which they controlled from 1934 to 1945 was limited to a mere handful of institutions, the most significant of which was perhaps Yenan University. One of the best and most widely recognized research studies (apparently the only documented one compiled by a British scholar in the Communist area) is by Michael Lindsay.

4. See *United States Relations with China: With Special Reference to the Period 1944–1949* (Washington, D. C.: United States Department of State Publication No. 3573 [Far Eastern Series 30], 1949).

The source material he used was brought from China at the end of 1945 and is perhaps the only collection available in English of its type. His study is principally concerned with the Shensi-Kansu-Ninghsia area and is a collection of the laws and regulations of the Communists in Shensi, Chahar, and Hopei, published to December 1945.

The story of the Chinese Communist split with the Kuomintang in 1927, the establishment of soviets in South China, and ultimately their Long March to Northwest China is well known.[5] Despite great losses from Kuomintang harassment, some fifty thousand troops reached the new bases in North Shensi and Kansu during 1936. The next few years saw the consolidation of the Communist base, a temporary rapprochement with the Kuomintang, a joint front against the Japanese, and the *de facto* inheritance of much of Northwest China by the Chinese Communists. By 1939 the Communists and Kuomintang were conducting a three-cornered military and political struggle with the Japanese which lasted until the Japanese surrender in 1945, when a temporary truce was effected between the Chinese factions. The failure of General Marshall's mission in 1946 signaled the official commencement of hostilities again. With the ineptitudes of Nationalist generals, the corruption of many officials, and the growing apathy of the masses, it was almost inevitable that the Kuomintang should be expelled from the mainland. This happened in 1949. Whether this was a victory by default or victory by design is again outside the scope of these notes. Irrespective of the causal factors involved, a new revolutionary dynasty had taken over after a long and arduous political march which had begun for the Communists in 1921. Of the earliest forms of Communist education Professor Lindsay interestingly states:

There is almost no information available about the original Chinese Communist educational system in the South China areas of the Chinese Soviet Republic. A great deal of educational work was certainly attempted, and the Constitution refers to the right to education. . . . Later writings usually

5. One of the best accounts of this is given in Edgar Snow's *Red Star over China* (New York: Random House, 1938).

criticize it for being too doctrinaire and for taking too little account of the wishes of the people.[6]

The problem of schools and colleges in the Communist area, which at a moment's notice had to be evacuated or camouflaged, was considerable. Likewise, the recruitment and training of teachers was a problem which bedeviled the Communists throughout their sojourn in the Northwest. These so-called "liberated areas," controlled by the Communists, were without normal contact with the city centers where the universities and colleges had formerly been located, and from 1939 to 1945 the stream of students and young intellectuals attempting to leave Japanese-controlled areas was severely curtailed.[7] Even within the Communist-held areas there was considerable competition for skilled, trained, intelligent personnel, and "administration" competed strongly with "teaching" in the recruitment of satisfactory personnel. Education *per se* could not command an immediate priority in manpower unless it could be rigorously justified. Accordingly, the philosophy of education that evolved in these areas was the result of trial and error and was adversely influenced by such factors as peasant disinterest. When compulsory elementary education was first introduced, there was considerable peasant reaction—so much that Communist educational workers were forced to answer the paradoxical question, "Education was meant to help serve the masses, so why should the masses strongly reject it?" A new educational policy developed, based on the *ad hoc* arrangement of "people manage, public help," whereby schools and colleges met at convenient times and studied what was necessary and utilitarian. Education, for these areas of China, was expected to develop large numbers of capable, vocationally trained people suited for short-term specialized tasks. Accordingly, the structure of secondary and higher education was different from that in the areas held by the Kuomintang or Japanese where, especially in the case of the latter, there was an absence of such a nationalistic and patriotic

6. Michael Lindsay, *et al.*, *Notes on Educational Problems in Communist China, 1941–47* (New York: International Secretariat Institute of Pacific Relations, 1950), p. 35.
7. An interesting account of the student migrations commencing in 1937 is given in Hubert Freyn's *Chinese Education in the War* (Shanghai: Kelly & Walsh, 1940).

educational philosophy undergirded by a need for great practicality.

It is interesting to note the new regulation of Yenan University (May 21, 1944), which stated:

(1) The object of this school is to cultivate and improve new Democratic and Revolutionary Three People's Principles cadres for practical work in political, economic and cultural reconstruction suited to the needs of the war of resistance and the reconstruction of the Border Region . . . (3) . . . the education of this school will be joined up with the practical working department of the Border Region and all kinds of practical activity in order to raise practical experience to the height of theory and to realize the unity of theory and practice and the correspondence of study and use.[8]

This philosophy was carried out in practice, and emphasis was placed on small group study and mutual group assistance teams. The classroom problems were practical ones and could only be solved with on-the-job experience. Accordingly, Communist government administrative organizations allowed students to utilize their facilities and coöperated in breaking down the traditional separation between mental and manual work said to be so characteristic of Chinese higher education. As might be expected, this degree of educational pragmatism led to a wide range of educational institutions—all with greatly varying standards and all accordingly geared to different aims and interests. There appear to be few reliable estimates of the quality of instruction or research carried on in the Communist areas. Lindsay himself makes only passing reference to this point.

There is no information available about the standards attained in higher education except in the case of medical schools which have been visited by a number of UNRRA doctors and other qualified observers. In this case the general opinion seemed to be that results attained were extremely good, considering the extreme shortage of equipment and books.[9]

Libraries were practically nonexistent, and printing presses turned out rudimentary copy suited more for propaganda purposes than for academic research and teaching. With the capture of more

8. Lindsay, *op. cit.,* p. 133; see also Gunther Stein, "A People Goes to School," chap. 27 in *The Challenge of Red China* (London: Pilot Press, Ltd., 1945).
9. Lindsay, *op. cit.,* p. 41.

cities after 1945, library sources were multiplied, but the basic
handicap still remained.

Efforts made by the authorities of the Border Regions to obtain books were
frustrated by the blockade (1945–1947). President Fan of Pei Ta (Northern
University) told us of two of their attempts to bring in books and supplies
purchased outside. The first failed when the supplies were lost in a military
action in North Kiangsu; and the second failed also, when the University
representative, who was bringing in a collection of books, disappeared en
route, presumably captured.[10]

The Chinese Communists, in enlarging the areas under their
control, were concerned with mass education rather than with
advancing higher education at a spectacular rate, at least for the
moment. There were greater gains to be made from expanding
the adult education program and from re-educating the people in
the newly "liberated" areas. The slogans were "re-education for
the newly freed areas" and *cheng feng* ("improvement of spirit")
for the old base areas.[11]

EDUCATIONAL TRANSITION TO THE PEOPLE'S REPUBLIC OF CHINA

The final four years of the civil war saw the Communists emerge
from nominal control of one third of China in 1945 to the total
control of the mainland by the end of 1949. The Japanese surrender led to rapid changes in territorial ownership. Within a
few weeks, most of the countryside in North China was in the
hands of the Communists, while the cities, railways, and communication centers were retained by the Nationalists. South
Manchuria was occupied for the most part by the Nationalists, and
it was not until the end of 1947 that the tide slowly turned in
favor of the Communists. By the middle of 1949 the struggle of
"liberation" for the mainland was nearly over, and there remained

10. *Ibid.*, p. 152. Pei Ta, referred to by the author as Northern University, was
located in the Chin-Chi-Lu-Yu Border Region during 1947.

11. Lindsay comments here that even in the "old areas" the notion of "thought
reform" or ideological reform (*cheng fengism*) was distasteful for many doctrinaire
Party cadres and that it failed because "they were cases for psychiatry, not for
education."

the gigantic task of consolidating the country under a new centralized administration.

During the period of civil war the universities and colleges fared lamentably with respect to their rehabilitation, first under the Kuomintang and then under the disability of military operations.[12] It is important to pause for a moment and attempt to account for the Nationalist debacle and the part played in it by the intellectuals, teachers, and students in general. The Nationalist regime had been unable fully to educate the students and to provide the intellectuals with satisfactory and satisfying employment. Admittedly, conditions in China during the previous fifteen years had been entirely inimical to these aims. The only ideology that the Kuomintang could offer was worn out, tarnished, and highly suspect. Nationalism could not even capture the interest of the intellectuals, at least not in the way it was presented to them by the Kuomintang and certainly not in the way it was presented to the masses of China. Yet there were few educated persons in China who did not feel ashamed that education had been able to do so little in spite of the lip service paid to democracy and the educational opportunities which were to go with it. That democracy was perhaps not the ideological vehicle for China is one thing, but the seeming inability to aid education by the regime was another. The intellectuals tended to withdraw from public office, their consciences unable to cope with the situation. A critical observer commented:

The universities were suffering the heavy hand of the "Te Wu," the special secret police of the regime. Sudden and secret arrests, mysterious disappearances, assassinations, a covert reign of terror prevailed in academic circles. Students were suspect, professors watched, freedom of thought, of publication and of speech suppressed. In so far as the choice between totalitarian and democratic government was concerned, it did not exist; the Chinese people groaned under a regime Fascist in every quality except efficiency. The Kuomintang had long lost the peasants; now they had cast away their only asset, the support of the scholars. The educated no longer feared

12. See the account given in Lindsay's *Notes on Educational Problems in Communist China* by Marion Menzies and Luther Paget of the university transition in the Border Region during 1947. The authors, representing World Student Relief, investigated student conditions in Hopei, Honan, and Shensi Provinces. Lindsay, *op. cit.,* pp. 146–173.

the victory of Communism; what they feared was a continuation of civil war. An end, any end, was what they hoped for. Only one end was now possible.[13]

These views are those of a scholar who was not only antagonistic to the Nationalists but who looked with partiality on some of the Communist reforms. The sentiments of Frank Kierman do approach a higher degree of impartiality, and yet he also says:

As the Chinese Communists took power in 1949 and 1950, the intelligentsia were in every way vulnerable to . . . persuasion and force, and they were few. . . . The Communist approach to the task of taking them over was very much like guerrilla warfare. . . .

The Chinese intelligentsia had a great range of vulnerabilities, and the Communists played skillfully upon them. They had no real hope of a career outside of government; so they stood to starve if they were intractable. . . . The Communists . . . invented the fascinating concept of an intellectual proletariat, and by qualifying for this category the "mental workers" could acquire both jobs and absolution; most grasped at this like a drowning man for a straw. . . . They loved China; and the Communists gave China an international stature far beyond anything the Kuomintang had been able to do. They wanted to help China; and the Communists wanted them to do it. . . . In the final analysis, the Chinese intelligentsia were unable to withstand these multifarious and omnipresent pressures; their tradition was not one of opposition to strong regimes, and they . . . made their peace with this one.[14]

A DECADE OF EDUCATIONAL EXPERIMENTATION

The new regime was outwardly cautious in its pursuit of the control of the government in 1949. In regard to education, it instructed students, faculty, and administrators to carry on, letting "socialistic consciousness" be their guide. Gradual intrusion into academic affairs, especially in higher education, can be first seen in the adjustment of curricula, the thought-reform of professors, and the reorganization of the universities.

In the Communist regime's first period in power, from 1949 to 1952, consolidation, reconstruction, and reorganization were

13. C. P. Fitzgerald, *Revolution in China* (London: Cresset Press, 1952), p. 103.
14. Frank A. Kierman, Jr., *The Chinese Intelligentsia and the Communists* (Cambridge, Mass.: Center for International Studies, Massachusetts Institute of Technology, 1954), pp. 17–19. This quotation and its use were suggested by its initial inclusion in W. W. Rostow, *et al.*, *The Prospect for Communist China* (Cambridge, Mass.: M.I.T. Press, 1954).

paramount. Even in this initial stage of Communist control some of the harshness and dogmatism of Chinese Marxism quickly became apparent. The scientific application of neototalitarian ideas in education, not apparent to the main bulk of the academics previously, at last was fully revealed.

The second period, from 1953 to 1957, of the first Communist decade, is measured in terms of the Five Year Plan, the regime's first. This period, however, is best remembered by the startling upset of the intellectuals, artists, and cultural workers, rather than by the Plan's implementation. The regime in 1956 encouraged the literati to take an active part in commenting upon and criticizing their lot under communism, holding that only beneficial results would come from many contending schools of thought. But the regime became profoundly upset because of the extraordinary enthusiasm with which the "many contending schools" took over the general public's fancy. Perhaps at no other time during the decade to the same degree did the students and their teachers exhibit those tendencies of independent criticism which are anathema to any dictatorship, even one of the "proletariat." The "revolt" of the students, the dissatisfaction of their professors, and the curious interest of the people could not be contained within educational or artistic circles. Instead, the reverberations were heard all over China and were transmitted in time to the other countries of the Soviet bloc. In spite of some initial alarm, the regime was ultimately equal to the task, and the dialectics centering on the themes of contradictions in Communist society and the rectification of errors gradually replaced those concerned with the intellectual ferment characterized by the phrase, "blooming and contending." A lesson in discipline on a national scale had to be learned by the Party, the intellectuals, and the slowly but increasingly literate public. Many Party cadres were reproved for their overbearing attitude towards formal education, and conversely the ranks of the Party were increased by newly recruited members from the intelligentsia. But in time the Party turned the criticism of the critics against the critics themselves, and the result for education eventually led to a degree of regimentation not anticipated before May 1956. Reform through labor was again resurrected, with liberal doses reserved for those who ignored the formula of "criticism, self-criticism, and countercriticism."

The activities of the third and final period of this decade were to be based on the unsettling experiences of "blooming and contending," and to underscore this an old Marxist maxim, "the unity of theory and practice," was rejuvenated and brought into play again. This reflected the perennial concern of Chinese Communist leaders that the educational system did not sufficiently stress the relationship between theoretical studies and practical work.[15] The third stage in the decade (1958 to 1960) bears the title, "the great leap forward," and represents an attempt, by dint of centralized planning, to place China among the leading industrial nations of the world within the next decade. In addition to the "great leap forward" went the concomitant doctrines of "combining education with labor" and "walking with both legs." The notion of "walking with both legs" implied the movement forward on all fronts. In higher education this required an expansion of regular universities as well as an extraordinary development of "red and expert" colleges for the masses. These colleges were dedicated to producing a graduate who was both dedicated to communism as well as being technically proficient. These "red and expert" institutions were part-time schools generally designed for rural workers and farmers who wished to partake of the nationwide demand for further education. The "red and expert" colleges, when integrated with the commune movement, allowed the regime to proceed with its grandiose agricultural plans and provide locally for the modicum of education required to underpin the enormous experiment.[16]

15. The lack of integration between educational as well as political theory and practice was commented upon in 1941 by Mao Tse-tung at a series of political conferences held in Yenan. In discussing the "unity of theory and practice," he said: "We are studying Marxism, but in the very study of Marxism many of us use a method that runs directly counter to Marxism. That is, these people have violated the fundamental principle repeatedly enjoined by Marx, Engels, Lenin, and Stalin: the unity of theory and practice. Having violated this principle, they have invented an opposite one: the separation of theory from practice." (Mao Tse-tung, *Reform Our Study* [2d rev. ed.; Peking: Foreign Languages Press, 1960], p. 5).

16. See Robert D. Barendsen, "The Agricultural Middle School in Communist China," *China Quarterly*, No. 8 (October-December 1961), 106–134.

During this decade, Chinese education has seen, for the most part, the final official abandonment of the Confucian philosophy in education. It has seen the replacement, with few exceptions, of the Anglo-American philosophy and practices in education by a thoroughgoing Soviet system founded upon "scientific Marxist" principles. The foreign, missionary, and private colleges have been closed, and in their place state-supported and state-controlled institutions are now exclusively catering to "New China's" youth. The colleges and universities themselves have undergone continual revision and have been subject to dramatic structural and organizational changes. The specialized institute and the general technical college now dominate, where previously the comprehensive general university held sway. Furthermore, the expansion and transformation of the Chinese Academy of Sciences, again on a Soviet model, has enhanced scientific training to an extent previously unseen in China.

Students in engineering and science, the "intellectual technicians" trained to run the Five Year Plans, have been elevated in importance, relegating the general or liberal arts student in nonscientific or nontechnical fields to a position of much less importance; this partially corrected an imbalance of some fifty years' standing that had been impossible to rectify until the national goal of industrialization could be effectively launched by a strong, determined, and ruthless central government.

The initial Sovietization of several important facets of Chinese higher education was an accepted fact and was fully encouraged by the regime, which rarely failed, until recently, to acknowledge Russia's assistance in educational matters. This is manifest in organization, administration, curricula, and teaching techniques, as well as in the monolithic control of education through both the formal and informal activities of the Party and its members. But to believe that the Chinese Communists are unoriginal, slavish imitators is to ignore the whole history of the relationship between Communist China and Soviet Russia.[17] Acknowledgment

17. Shih Ch'eng-chih, *The Status of Science and Education in Communist China: And a Comparison with That in the U.S.S.R.* (Hong Kong: Union Research Institute, 1962).

of assistance has not meant total acceptance, as events of 1956–1957 and those since 1961 have shown. Discrimination in the acceptance and incorporation of Soviet methods and the gradual reappraisal of certain aspects of Western pedagogy is more in evidence now that the birth pangs of establishing a Communist regime in China have been overcome.

The nature of Chinese youth today, educated in a revolutionary spirit, tempered with political and military successes, is a force with which to be contended. The vast majority of senior professors are still from the "wrong classes" and, though technically competent, are still politically suspect in spite of having given their all to the regime. The graduates of Chinese universities today are brought up on a dogmatic system which, for obvious reasons, cannot provide as complete an objective education as those educated in a Western tradition would perhaps wish to see. This, however, is exactly the weakness of any form of comparative reporting: namely that of seeing others as we would wish them to be seen or casting them entirely in our own mold. The present Chinese Communist regime cares little or nothing for so-called "Western" education and judges itself by standards continually adjusted to suit the Chinese scene; that is, by standards determined pragmatically, though based on formulas propounded first by Marx, then by Lenin, and now by Mao Tse-tung.[18]

The concept of a universal mass system of education, with open access from lowest to highest levels, as believed in and practiced to the greatest extent in the United States, is still lacking in practice in many countries. The Chinese Communists, on the other hand, are looking forward to the time when they can lead the countries of Asia in the universalization of education with the largest percentage of school-age children attending school on a regular basis. But this extensive system of education is being molded in a format of their own choosing and owes less and less each year to foreign models, with the partial exception, perhaps, of those adopted from the Soviet Union. The literacy classes, part-

18. See J. Chester Cheng, "Basic Principles Underlying the Chinese Communist Approach to Education," *Information on Education Around the World*, No. 51, OE-14034 (Washington, D. C.: United States Office of Education, 1961).

time workers' schools, factory-run "universities," and advanced scientific institutes are all major adjuncts to the more familiar primary, secondary, and formal collegiate institutions to be found in "New China." In higher education alone there has been nearly a tenfold increase in the number of students attending college during the decade. The class background of the students is changing, and today nearly half are from the so-called "worker-peasant classes," which will continue to provide, from the Chinese point of view, the more desirable and reliable recruits for college entrance.

The regime is attempting to ensure against any rebellion of the intellectuals such as that of 1956–1957, and accordingly much has been done to promote students with the "correct" proletarian background. Today over half the college students and three quarters of secondary students have a "satisfactory" background of worker-peasant origin. For all students or professors, irrespective of background, physical, practical, and integrated labor has been prescribed. This is necessary to achieve the so-called "new all-round man" destined for leadership in Communist society. The concept of the dignity of manual labor is fundamental to the political awareness of the scholar's new place in Chinese society today. This is not something new in Chinese Communist philosophy; indeed it was a well-established doctrine some twenty years ago, when the Communist "government" in Yenan discussed at length the future role of intellectuals in modern Chinese society. Mao Tse-tung's attitude towards the intellectuals is clearly documented at the famous Yenan Literary Meetings in May 1942, which established the pattern of future relationships between the Communist Party and the artists, writers, teachers, and intellectuals.[19]

Mao Tse-tung's pungent remarks at this conference should have been clear warning later to the old-line academics and lukewarm fellow travelers who accepted the new regime's promises for education unquestioningly in 1950. Mao's warnings to the intellec-

19. For a comprehensive set of Chinese Communist documents relative to this period, see Boyd Compton, *Mao's China: Party Reform Documents, 1942–44* (Seattle: University of Washington Press, 1952) ; and Conrad Brandt, *et al.*, *A Documentary History of Chinese Communism* (Cambridge, Mass.: Harvard University Press, 1952) .

tuals at Yenan in 1942 were more than a diatribe against the artists; they included also a self-confession or self-criticism and a blueprint for future educational and intellectual controls, when victory should be won ultimately by the Communists.

The words, "scholar," "student," "intelligentsia," may soon have little meaning, because of the planned integration of all sectors of the community. The definition of college, university, institute, likewise have become blurred with the multiplication of institutions of higher education during the past few years. The university, as it has been known in the past, may in the future be a generic name for communal part-time adult education centers of the type which sprang up all over China between 1958 and 1961. The so-called "red and expert" institutes may be "only" a school of a high order for training advanced rural cadres in political ideology. The specialist institute may be a well-founded technical college turning out production specialists, all of the type associated with the Academia Sinica, and devoted to national research. While there is still a core of over two hundred higher educational institutes of the "first order," a host of supporting and ancillary ones of varying sorts have come into being on local initiative. But just as the ideological "flowers" withered or were weeded out, so will many of these so-called "universities" cease to exist or be abolished when there is a lack of interest or finance to support them.[20]

The total result, however, of this frenzied expansion of facilities

20. For a listing of the various institutions of higher education and their specialties the following references should be consulted; because of the difficulty in listing and accurately evaluating these "institutions," there may be a number of apparent discrepancies and contradictions, see:

(1) *Current Background* (hereafter cited as *CB*, Hong Kong: United States Consulate General), No. 462 (July 1957).

(2) Joseph C. Kun, "Higher Educational Institutions of Communist China, 1953–1958: A Cumulative List," appendix C in *Selection and Enrollment of Students in Communist Chinese Higher Educational Institutions* (Cambridge, Mass.: Center for International Studies, Massachusetts Institute of Technology, 1961).

(3) Leo A. Orleans, *Professional Manpower and Education in Communist China* (Washington, D. C.: National Science Foundation, 1961).

(4) Chi Wang, *Mainland China Organizations of Higher Learning in Science and Technology and Their Publications: A Selected Guide* (Washington, D. C.: Government Printing Office, 1961).

(5) *The World of Learning, 1963–64* (14th ed.; London: Europa Publications, Ltd., 1963), pp. 227–236.

in 1958 was to place some form of "further" education in the hands of many worker-peasant Chinese who a decade earlier would, in all probability, have been unable to secure any form of education at all. Higher education, on the other hand, has been expanded at a pace hardly equaled in other Eastern countries (or for that matter in the West) in recent years and has been geared to accord fully with the central planning and long-range goals of Chinese communism. The introduction, in 1958, of new designs for higher education was, to say the least, of major importance. The older concepts of "higher education" as we in the West know them have been partially abandoned. Industrial units and factories now purport to offer a "full" range of courses from literacy to the higher levels. A new educational format would definitely appear to be in an evolutionary stage in China at present. It is one, however, that has not escaped severe criticism, and rapid and severe cutbacks have been imposed when economic problems and agricultural failures have made necessary a rapid reappraisal of educational goals. Whether this system is successful will be a matter of history, but for many underdeveloped areas the Chinese experiment will be interesting and, even if it is only partially successful, may well tempt others to emulate it to some degree or other.

POLITICAL CAMPAIGNS: EDUCATION AND THE
INTELLECTUALS

During the first ten years of Communist government in China, a series of political movements or ideological campaigns were launched on the populace on an *ad hoc* basis.[21] In the main,

21. The treatment of academics and the political re-education of the intellectuals in its various phases is well presented in:

(1) Theodore Chen, *Thought Reform of the Chinese Intellectuals* (Hong Kong: Hong Kong University Press, 1960).

(2) Chow Ching-wen, *Ten Years of Storm* (New York: Holt Rinehart and Winston, 1960).

(3) Chalmers A. Johnson, *Communist Policies toward the Intellectual Class* (Hong Kong: Union Research Institute, 1960).

(4) Roderick MacFarquhar, *The Hundred Flowers Campaign and the Chinese Intellectuals* (New York: Praeger, 1960).

these campaigns were applicable to special strata or groups in China and in many cases were truly mass movements designed for consumption by the whole populace. Few of them bypassed education. In fact, the formal educational structure and all those contained within it were intimately bound up in many of the campaigns.

The intellectuals as a group (that is, if it is valid to group them) have received mixed treatment from the regime. Their problem is aggravated by the difficulty in determining who specifically these intellectuals were or are. The Chinese Communists themselves do not entirely help, as they are continually redefining and reapplying the word. Loosely and even erroneously, it has referred to anyone who has had formal education and graduated from secondary school but who takes little or no part in manual labor. More generally, it may include students, schoolteachers, university graduates, and professors, as well as a host of government officials with advanced education, artists, writers, and others who lay claim to the title for what it is worth.

INITIAL CAMPAIGNS

One of the main techniques employed by China's present regime in educating, indoctrinating, and remaking its people is the device of launching a nationwide political advertising campaign. The topics for advertising are drawn from both the widespread experience of international communism and the basic requirements of the Chinese scene, as determined by a skillful and intelligent group of Chinese Communist leaders. It is obvious that an element of pragmatism is present in the waves of major and minor campaigns which have swept China since the new regime was installed in 1949. However, it is quite apparent that also present are the theoretical requirements and fundamental teachings of Marx, Lenin, and Mao which give the relevant underpinning necessary for the various campaigns.

The role of the intelligentsia in China has remained unchanged for such a considerable period of time that it is at first difficult to see the intellectuals as an integral part of the present regime and not as an example of "extreme individualism," as they have often been described in the past.[22] At times the course of the various ideological campaigns has given the appearance of bypassing the intelligentsia and those within the schools and universities. However, on closer examination, the pertinence of each movement to the teacher and academician is there only awaiting proper identification.

As a generalization, it can be said that the essential method of the ideological mass campaign has been an initial trial and testing for one selected stratum in Communist society, then an extension and reapplication for the other members of the community, until the whole nation's attention and interest is brought to bear on it. The movements are further identified by their launching by keynote speeches of explanation or "redefinition." The course and intensity of the movements furthermore indicate a fairly regular progression through various stages until a climax is reached and one campaign wanes, giving way to a new movement.

The campaigns or movements which are briefly reviewed below are those that concern particularly the teacher, educator, and "intellectual worker" in China. The collection of records, documents, and speeches to be found later in this compilation will give various illustrations of the different political movements and indicate the development of an educational and political philosophy.[23]

The Chinese Communist Party between 1949 and 1952 was concerned principally with establishing itself and seizing the main instruments of power. In the first instance only so-called "unregenerate Kuomintang leaders, imperialists, large landlords, and bureaucratic capitalists" were to be excluded from the administration and positions of authority. By isolating recalcitrant groups within the universities or the civil service, it was possible to bypass them and avoid a head-on clash for the time being. Various groups or fronts were formed, many of which found

22. See Kierman, *op. cit., passim.*
23. For the period from 1949 to 1955, see the especially well documented study by Richard L. Walker, *China under Communism: The First Five Years* (London: George Allen and Unwin, Ltd., 1956).

their representatives already well established on university campuses and in higher secondary schools. Mass organizations, such
as the All-China Federation of Labor, New Democratic Youth
League of China, and the All-China Federation of Women were
formed in 1949, prior to the final collapse of the Nationalists on
the mainland. Of these, the New Democratic Youth League is
said to have played no small part in reopening the schools and
universities, as did the All-China Students Federation. By working through these various mass front organizations, the Chinese
Communists sought to generate an atmosphere of general acquies-
cence, if not positive support, at least until the full-scale machinery of control became operative.

The importance of the cadres—the trained Party organizers—
in laying the groundwork throughout the towns and countryside
cannot be overemphasized. In the universities and schools cadres
were to the forefront explaining, cajoling, denouncing, encouraging, and criticizing teachers and students alike. Marxist study
groups sprang up, and intellectuals within or without the colleges
humbly allowed themselves to be cajoled, interrogated, and investigated in order to reveal both their private affairs and "thought
processes." [24] Groups as well as individuals attempted to outdo
each other in confessing their faults, of course thereby making it
patently obvious to all how inadequately suited many of them
were for the teaching profession.

THE INTELLECTUAL CHENG FENG

This period, for want of a more appropriate name, is labelled
the *"cheng feng* era." Though it was in 1942 that the term ap-

24. The government went to some lengths in enumerating the principal traits
which were to be cast out by intellectuals and others; these have been variously
summarized by several writers on Chinese communism and include: feudal mentality
indicating the incorrect attitude of intellectuals towards manual labor; egoism
rather than collectivism; the notion of "face"; family personalism, that is, placing
family and hereditary ties before others; individualism, which was opposed to group
consciousness and true socialism; heroism, or the demand for personal glory;
hedonism; bureaucratic formalism; idealism, which contrasted with Marxist materialism; corruption and low morals; "comprador" mentality particularly prevalent
among the mercantile classes of the former "concession cities."

peared to be coined, its extension or reintroduction, particularly during 1950 and 1951, places it among the foremost of the series of mass education or ideological campaigns. *Chen feng* is variously translated as "ideological remolding" or "reforming," and the application here is to the movement for "the correction of unorthodox tendencies in learning, the Party, and literature." [25] The *cheng feng* movement, while applied in this instance to a particularly intense period between 1950 and 1952, in a wider sense may be applied more generally to all the Chinese Communist mass re-education campaigns. In actual fact, *cheng fengism* can go on indefinitely and can be brought into play whenever Party methods need "rectification." Remolding and rectification are allied exercises and both naturally may appear together or separately.

The purpose of the *cheng feng* movement, especially among the teachers and intellectuals, was to introduce the peculiar vocabulary or jargon of the Communists, particularly Mao Tsetung's version of it, and to make clear what definition of the terms and concepts used would be acceptable to the new regime. The effect in the schools and universities was startling, as the remolding process affected all those located on the campuses, with few if any exceptions. The professors, the students, and even the university workmen were all called upon to take part. The repeated definition and redefinition of terms that were soon to be commonplace in texts and newspapers and heard incessantly over the radio must have sounded strange at first to the academics. From then on, a premium was to be placed on fervor and submission rather than on "merely" critical thinking.

The psychological consequences of public confession and the abject acknowledgment of error forcing conformity made the next step of revamping the curriculum and reconstructing the schools and universities much easier. Mao said of the *cheng feng* movement in 1942:

> If the reasoning is good, if it is to the point it can be effective. The first method in reasoning is to give the patients a powerful stimulus, yell at them

25. See Brandt, *op. cit.*, and Compton, *op. cit.*, *passim*.

"you're sick!" so that the patients will have a fright and break out in an overall sweat; then, they can be carefully treated.[26]

At this juncture it is appropriate perhaps to note Mao Tse-tung's own comments on the intellectuals stated in 1942 at a conference on "Problems of Art and Literature" held in Yenan, Soviet China:

Let me tell you of my own experience; let me tell you how my feelings towards the people changed. I was once a student, and in school I acquired student habits and manners. For instance, I was embarrassed when I had to carry my luggage on a bamboo pole in the presence of my fellow students. They were so refined that they could not stand having any weight press upon their shoulders and disdained the very thought of carrying anything in their hands! At that time I was convinced that only intellectuals were clean, that workers, peasants, and soldiers were unclean. I would therefore readily borrow clothes from an intellectual but never from a worker, or a peasant, or a soldier because I thought that their clothes would be unclean.

During the revolution I began to live among workers, peasants, and soldiers. Gradually I began to know them, and they also began to know me. Then, and then only, did the bourgeois and petty-bourgeois sentiments inculcated in me by the bourgeois schools change fundamentally! Ever since then, whenever I compare unreformed intellectuals with workers, peasants, and soldiers, I realize that not only were the minds of those intellectuals unclean but that their bodies were also unclean. The cleanest people in the world are the workers and peasants. Even though their hands may be soiled and their feet smeared with cow dung, nevertheless they are cleaner than the bourgeoisie and the petty bourgeoisie. That is what I mean by a transformation of sentiments—a changing over from one class to another.[27]

It would not be incorrect to say that few if any of the intellectuals ignored completely the implications of the *cheng feng* movement. This was impossible because of the thoroughness of the Party, using the media of the press and radio, and the cadres in organizing mass meetings. The numerous campus discussion groups, all of which were difficult to evade or ignore, dominated the scene.

The starting point for the ideological remolding movement is placed at September 29, 1951, when Chou En-lai, as Premier,

26. See Mao Tse-tung: "Opposing Party Formalism: February 8, 1942," in Brandt, *A Documentary History of Chinese Communism*, p. 396.

27. Mao Tse-tung, *Problems of Art and Literature* (New York: International Publishers, 1950), pp. 12–13.

addressed at length a group of Peking-Tientsin intellectuals. In the course of his five-hour lecture he made it clear that the professors were to adjust their thoughts drastically, using the process of criticism, self-criticism, and countercriticism. It was apparent that this was the signal for a massive new campaign to be launched on the unsuspecting scholars. During the next month discussion groups were quickly organized by the cadres in the Peking-Tientsin area, which had one of the largest university concentrations in China. Kuo Mo-jo, Chairman of the Committee of Culture and Educational Affairs, remarked:

A basic task in the reform of the schools is the improvement of the quality of the teaching staff. For this work we are preparing to adopt the following steps: (1) to launch an ideological remolding movement among the teachers which will start in Peking and Tientsin (2) and as far as possible to send teachers to take part in agrarian reform and (3) to attend political-training schools and (4) to take other measures to further this ideological remolding movement.[28]

Publicity for the forthcoming campaign was assured by the implication of various scholars identified as Western-orientated and *ipso facto* anti-Communist. One name that was singled out for particular attention was that of Dr. Hu Shih, known abroad for his liberalism and tolerance as well as for his services to China both as an educator and statesman. Hu Shih was denounced by many of his friends and even by his own son.[29] Typical press comment at the time was:

Hu Shih is an intellectual who has sold out to the imperialists and the reactionary ruling class and has helped the enemy as an accomplice. This man who is guilty of the most heinous crimes against the people, still re-

28. Chung Shih, *Higher Education in Communist China* (Hong Kong: Union Research Institute, 1953), p. 37.

29. See Edward Hunter, *Brainwashing in Red China: The Calculated Destruction of Men's Minds* (New York: Vanguard Press, 1951), appendix A.

A complete denouncement of Dr. Hu Shih by his son is reprinted from Hong Kong newspapers which carried it in full. The final paragraph reads: "Until my father returns to the people's arms, he will always remain a public enemy of the people and an enemy of my own class, I feel it important to draw a line of demarcation between my father and myself. Except that I should be vigilant enough not to let sentiments gain the upper hand, I must establish close relations with the working and farming class."

fuses to repent and is even now [1951] taking refuge in America as an imperialist instrument.[30]

The campaign against Western-educated scholars and others
whose orientation was deemed incorrect built up in intensity
during the early part of 1952 and reached peak excitement when
innumerable confessions by academics were made public. As a
rule, the recantation of those accused of imperialistic backgrounds
began with an outline biographical sketch delivered by the
author, giving a detailed historical inventory. The autobiog-
raphies were embellished with references at particular points to
the odious influences of reactionary teachers, friends, and colleagues—particularly American academics—as well as to a mass
of other incriminating information. Included in this sketch there
was often a lengthy description of overseas studies undertaken.
The crux, however, of any confession lay in the complete rejection
of all works and writings undertaken in the decadent mental
framework of pre-Communist China. Irrespective of their merit or
worldwide acclaim, scholarly productions became tainted irre-
vocably because of the antisocial atmosphere in which they were
conceived. The confessional climax was reached when the would-
be penitent indicated that salvation was offered and accepted only
through the grace of Marxist precepts. In the end it was the road
back to "reality" and the complete acknowledgment of Communist teachings that became important, particularly for exemplary purposes. This served to remind others that, in spite of their
totally inadequate background, it was perhaps possible for regeneration to take place, but only if the good offices of the Party
were accepted.

From the reformed intellectuals' point of view, this process of
recitation, recantation, and regeneration was thoroughly unsatisfactory if a first confession was not accepted at face value and
further performances were demanded. It is recorded that although
some leading scholars made as many as three confessions, others
were forced to make five or more published recantations before
they were released from the direct pressure of *cheng feng*. Tsui

30. See "The Campaign Against Hu Shih," *CB*, No. 167 (1951).

Shu-chin, in surveying the plight of the intellectuals caught up in this ideological maelstrom, comments:

> In the eyes of the Reds, the intellectuals are always wrong despite their public confessions and their eulogies of Communist leaders. When a professor shows what the Communists call progress, he is accused of having made "simulated progress." When he admits too many mistakes, he is accused of confessing imaginary shortcomings in order to conceal the real ones, i.e.,— dissembling. And if he becomes too frank at the confession meetings, the Reds censure him for simulating reform for get-it-over-with purposes. On the other hand, if he refuses to confess, they condemn him as a reactionary. No matter what course he takes—right, left, or middle—he is always wrong.[31]

Concurrent with the ideological remolding movement were the "three anti" and later the "five anti" campaigns. The first was aimed at eliminating competition within the Party and at persons who held or were holding administrative positions. The second was wider in scope and found its target among the petty bourgeoisie.[32] While these campaigns in the main passed by the universities, except where inefficient Party cadres were concerned, it was apparent later that an indirect lesson for higher education was being prepared. The anti-waste and anti-bureaucratic elements of the "three anti" campaign was revealed when the universities were urged to reconstitute as well as to reform themselves drastically.

The enmeshing of the campaigns becomes clearer when it is recalled that the problem of the reform of intellectuals was bound up with adjusting their collegiate environment. It was not enough merely to ensure that the professors were rethinking correctly, but it was also necessary to regroup them functionally in "correctly" organized schools and universities. Curricular reform and institutional reform had undoubtedly long been considered, but, although some progress had been made up to 1951, the total

---

31. Tsui Shu-chin, *From Academic Freedom to Brainwashing: The Tragic Ordeal of Professors on the Chinese Mainland* (Taipei, Taiwan: China Culture Publishing Foundation, 1953), p. 20.

32. Essentially urban campaigns, the "three anti-" campaign (anti-corruption, anti-waste, and anti-bureaucratism) and "five anti-" campaign (anti-bribery, anti-tax evasion, anti-fraud, anti-stealing of state property, and anti-theft of state economic secrets) extended central government economic controls, raised substantial funds to finance the Korean War and prepared for the elimination of further private sectors of the economy.

pattern of higher education had not changed drastically. Officially called the "readjustment of colleges and departments," the program forced scores of well-formed and internationally known universities to dissolve completely.

It is impossible to approach this so-called "consolidation of higher learning" entirely as a separate series of reforms devoid of all connection with the *cheng feng* movement. While opportunism, rather than detailed planning, may appear to have preceded the change in status of many colleges, the end result produced a different and apparently formidable functional structure. It was in the latter half of September 1951 that some three thousand teachers from the twenty higher institutions of Peking-Tientsin met to "reform" the teachers' ideology and higher education. It is perhaps significant that six weeks later the Ministry of Education held in Peking a conference of deans of engineering colleges in China.

A plan was produced at this conference for the "readjustment" of engineering colleges in China, and by the middle of 1952 the reorganization was carried out, while the ideological remolding movement was still in full force. Towards the end of 1952 it was obvious, however, that the majority of the universities were being reorganized, not merely those having engineering faculties. *Jen Min Jih Pao* [People's Daily] in September 1952 gave a comprehensive survey of the plan indicating that:

. . . the readjustment of colleges and departments of the institutions of higher learning has been carried on in the whole country, with North China and East China as the focal areas. Peking and Tientsin are the two focal areas in North China where most readjustments are made. After this readjustment, there are forty-one institutions of higher learning in North China. Shanghai and Nanking are the two focal areas in East China where most readjustments are made. After the readjustment there are fifty-four institutes of higher learning in East China.[33]

In actual fact, the reforms resulted in a reduction in the total number of universities, with only seven left as institutions of general studies. However, the number of schools of agriculture, forestry, education, medicine, and engineering was increased,

33. Cited by Chung Shih, *op. cit.*, p. 44.

reflecting the change in emphasis towards the founding of specialized and technical institutes. In an editorial, the influential *Jen Min Jih Pao* stated:

> The general policy of the readjustment which aims at the cultivation of teaching staff and cadres for the industrial construction has been: to develop technical colleges and specialized institutes; to reorganize and strengthen universities for general studies, to establish by gradual steps correspondence schools and night-universities; and to pave the way for recruiting great numbers of students from labor and peasant classes into institutions of higher learning.[34]

By 1953, when a further reorganization took place, many of the older, well-known universities (certainly all the private and all the Christian colleges) had been dismembered and were no longer in existence. This rationalization was no doubt inevitable, particularly in the face of the Russian development of highly specialized courses and institutes successfully utilized for some years. It had been accepted that certain faculties and departments would play a major part in national development, while others would quickly prove to be superfluous.

A short Chinese Communist historical account of higher educational progress is given by one of the regime's leading spokesman, Chang Tsung-lin, who indicates:

> The institutions of higher learning left over by Old China had two kinds of conditions which were not commensurate to each other. On the one hand there were over two hundred universities and colleges which had deteriorated. Of these two hundred schools, scores were subsidized by imperialists and served as the instrument of imperialistic cultural aggression; about one hundred were schools under the monopolistic control of politicians paid by the reactionary government for their mutual struggle for privileges and profits and for their factional strife; and several dozens were "shop-style" (money-making) private universities.
>
> . . . .
>
> Since the liberation of the whole country in accordance with the directives and policies of the Party and the government, higher education departments have taken over, readjusted, and reformed old institutes of higher learning and established new systems at different times and on the basis of different conditions. Generally speaking, they first took over the old institutes and then undertook a series of tasks. As they did not take over, before

---

34. *Jen Min Jih Pao* (hereafter cited as *JMJP*, Peking), September 24, 1952. Cited by Chung Shih, *op. cit.*, p. 46.

1951, tens of institutes of higher learning which had been financed by imperialists, they found it difficult to carry out any task in these institutes where they were even prevented from establishing a Socialist political course. Afterwards, as soon as such institutions were taken over, the hindrances put up by imperialist agents were swept away, and teachers and students immediately roused themselves.[35]

The full significance, however, of the changes was neither foreseen nor felt until the first Five Year Plan, from 1953 to 1957, was scheduled. Here at last it was discernible how important science and engineering were to be, as opposed to "liberal arts" or general studies. The Five Year Plan indicated for the present, at least, how far higher education was to be reoriented in the years to come. It confirmed the specialist and delimited approach to educational administration, organization, and teaching.[36]

It is possible to epitomize and overgeneralize regarding each of the new regime's years in office. Thus 1952 can be called the "year of regimentation," while the succeeding year is often thought of as a "year of retrenchment." As part of the plan to consolidate the hard-won gains of 1952, the regime decided it was feasible and necessary to eliminate many of the non-Communist components of the "United Front." The United Front included several organizations sympathetic to the nationalistic and socialistic aims of the Chinese Communist Party and had been kept on an active status to present some appearance of a democratic multiparty façade.[37] Included among the various parties or organizations in the United Front were various liberal democratic and intellectual bodies. Certain persons in these organizations came under fire, and it was necessary to render them more ineffective

35. Chang Tsung-lin, "Discussion on Achievements and Problems in Higher Education," *JMJP*, September 4, 1956. Translated in *Survey of China Mainland Press* (hereafter cited as *SCMP*, Hong Kong: United States Consulate General), No. 1429 (1956).

36. See Peter S. Tang, *Communist China Today: Domestic and Foreign Policies* (New York: Praeger, 1957), p. 377. For a comprehensive list of colleges and universities and their specialties at this time, see "Institutions of Higher Learning in Communist China," *CB*, No. 462 (1957).

37. The United Front organization allowed the Chinese Communist Party to dominate and control the numerous "democratic parties and groups" which have been allowed to exist in China. The Revolutionary Committee of the Kuomintang, the China Democratic League, and the Taiwan Democratic Self-Government League have been prominent "democratic parties" organized under the United Front.

than previously before a new program of "transition to socialism" could be launched. Along with members of literary and cultural circles, there were numerous academicians who thought that they had made their peace with the Communists. They had aided in the reconstruction of the universities, had abased themselves by publicly remolding their thinking, and had even acquiesced, after some protests, in the amalgamation and reorganization of their universities.

The new general line to be known as the "transition to socialism" facilitated the regime's further condemnation of many important professors, particularly those with the unsavory background of a Western-type education. Mention has already been made of the confessions expected of an intellectual, and it is of interest to quote some of the passages from a document typical of the period from 1951 to 1953.

Aside from the mental makeup of the general run of intellectuals hailing from the capitalist class, I am possibly even more handicapped by capitalist education. In my complete apathy, I thought that, having already discarded the old democratic ideals and individualism, I had only to read up on Marxism-Leninism and the thoughts of Mao Tse-tung and to emulate the Communist style of work in order to improve myself. But I was mistaken, completely mistaken. While it was impossible to acquire the new before discarding the old, it was also difficult for me to single out the old and the undesirable. Following the comparatively penetrating process I went through in the course of actual participation in the revolutionary process of agrarian reform, I realized the mistake of excusing myself on the grounds of such trifling reasons as "through force of circumstances" and out of "good motives" and the danger of overlooking these defects under the false impression that I have made progress.[38]

This part of Ch'ien Tuan-sheng's confession, emanating from no less a person than the Dean of the Law School at Peking National University, was bound to carry considerable weight. It provided a model for other academics to follow. In spite of such confessions, a spate of which were extracted late in 1951 and early in 1952, the intellectual-academic-literary element not already committed to the Communist cause needed further discipline be-

38. *JMJP*, November 6, 1951 *(CB,* No. 169). Originally quoted by Walker, *op. cit.* Walker knew many of the Chinese professors who repudiated their American training when undergoing thought reform.

cause of its resistance to the changing order in education.[39]

THE NEW GENERAL LINE: THE TRANSITION TO SOCIALISM

In November of 1952, a Ministry of Higher Education was established to take over the university, college, polytechnical, and specialized educational institutes. During the next year, when retrenchment was at first the keynote, it was obvious that quality rather than quantity was stressed for both student enrollments and the application of the Five Year Plan. Instead of education for the working masses, it was education for the immediately educable. Although the Five Year Plan called for greater numbers of engineers and scientists, modifications undoubtedly were imposed. In actual fact, although the plan was for 1953–1957, as late as August 1954, production and target goals had not yet been generally announced.

The introduction of the "new general line," i.e., the carrying-out of "Socialist revolution and construction," as an ideological campaign was hampered by the fact that educational reforms were proceeding too slowly. Yet the country was being geared for a series of massive projects based on the "bootstrap principle." Despite the termination of the Korean War, the "transition to a Socialist society" campaign partially cloaked the plans for modernizing the armed forces and maintaining the security and independence of China, which, it was firmly believed, had been decisively won on the battlefields of Korea at great financial, material, and physical expense.

This stock-taking period allowed for some degree of rationalization in higher education. Many students were eliminated from courses and enrollments curtailed, with the result that many colleges found that they were marking time. The overall effect was to introduce a note of austerity. This was coupled with an air of uncertainty as to how far the vague plans for reorientation would ultimately proceed. Retrenchment, uncertainty, and consolidation

39. Some of the most useful documents regarding the confessions of intellectuals are to be found in the *Current Background* series. See Nos. 169, 182, and 213, which cover the three stages of the regime's campaign against the intellectuals.

were the background for the universities in their "transition to socialism." It was apparent that the slogan for the new ideological campaign withheld much but undoubtedly promised more.

The transition or resettlement period was basically concluded at the end of eighteen months. However, during the summer of 1953, a series of crucial conferences on higher education were held, at which high-ranking party officials denounced as deviationism the placing of quantity above quality. These conferences gave the official stamp to the temporary obstructions placed in the way of university education. It is interesting to note that the slogan, "transition to socialism," for the time being implied that means other than those of rapid industrialization were to be used to achieve socialism. An attempt directly through the "products" of the educational institutes was not feasible in the near future.

In December 1953, it was first suggested that "glorious work in the fields and factories should be the goal of the young." Much encouragement was given in the press to students who would forsake their studies until they could be properly accommodated in college, and assurances were given that their consolidation would be fully secured by their participating in hard but dignified manual work. Thus, during this crucial period of retrenchment or curtailment, a practical suggestion was produced and implemented for those who were temporarily turned away from further study. This so-called "new general line" of the Party as a mass ideological campaign differed somewhat from the earlier movements in that its importance for education was not immediately clear. The confusion lay in the carrying-over of the "thought reform or ideological program" and the steps taken to change and redistribute many of the centers of teaching. Superimposed were the vague proposals for implementing a Five Year Plan, which was not generally revealed until its second year.

The message and meaning for education became clear once Peking had laid down the courses and boundaries to be followed. However, to suggest blandly to many thousands of students that they would be better off working in the fields instead of continuing their studies was merely a temporary and dubious expedient resorted to by the regime. The curious aspect of this obvious subterfuge is the fact that "study combined with productive labor" had always been a dogma of Mao, who remembered how, in his own student days, manual labor was regarded with great distaste by most educated Chinese. Yet, in encouraging students to forget their disappointment when places at schools or universities were not available, the regime for the time being was solely interested in a general reorganization, with emphasis on quality rather than on graduating masses of students.

As a radical step, however, the new general line could not compare with the *cheng feng* movement because of this unwieldy admixtures of items left over from other campaigns. Indeed, this "campaign," if it still merits that title, merely masked the real intentions of the regime to wait until constructive plans could be formulated and put into operation. For higher education in particular, this period of consolidation meant the pruning of the development programs. As might have been expected, many of the suspect and tainted intellectuals were ignored temporarily and allowed to continue where they were, undisturbed. Thus, unintentionally, the transition to socialism allowed for the temporary maintenance of the intellectual's status, and in 1954 many of the non-Communist components of the United Front were still politically solvent, although their influence continued to be curtailed.

RECTIFYING AND CONTENDING

It was not until the end of 1956 that a further campaign of inordinate intensity was let loose among the scholars, academics, and intellectuals, both within and without the Party.

The key words and phrases that soon were to be commonplace included "rectification," "internal contradictions," "contending schools of thought," and "right-wing deviationism." Possibly at no other stage in the ten-year period from 1950 to 1960 has such a radical and unsettling influence been unleashed in the various intellectual circles of China. The reaction and surprise of the Communists at the widespread response to the new campaigns were unusual. This is especially so in light of the fact that one would expect the nation to have been at least somewhat conditioned to the Chinese Communist techniques of self-criticism by this time.

The original campaign launched in May 1956 was concerned with the so-called "rectification" of certain abuses which had developed in various Party organizations. Like so many of the other campaigns originating from within the Party for the purpose of removing dead wood or for regeneration, it was applicable first to the cadres within the government and then later directed into the broader spheres of administration, education, state enterprises, and so on. The process of rectification was specifically aimed at such abuses as "commandism," "bureaucratism," and even "mandarinism," of which many senior officials were said to be guilty in their dealings with subordinates.

The campaign in its early and milder stage was merely concerned with criticism and self-criticism; it was even suggested that "the gentleness of the breeze and the shower" should epitomize the campaign and the pace should in no way be forced unnaturally. The small group discussion, rather than the flambuoyantly boisterous exhibitions of previous years, was to be practiced, and student groups were to consult among themselves while the professors and teachers were likewise to be separately closeted.

The colleges and universities in Peking suspended lectures so that activist students would be able to have sufficient time to attend rectification meetings, and in Shanghai schools actually extended their sessions so that discussions could be conducted in an unhurried leisurely atmosphere.[40] Early in 1957, while the rectification campaign was proceeding and following its "natural" pace and before it had entered the second phase, that is, of denunciation and confession, a new movement from earlier months started to assume major proportions. This movement of so-called "blooming and contending" which gradually intruded onto the scene had in fact originated during May of the previous year, 1956, and chronologically paralleled the rectification campaign in origin. However, it took eight or nine months for this parallel campaign

40. Edgar Faure, *The Serpent and the Tortoise* (London: Macmillan, 1958), p. 89.

to build up its own discussion groups and suddenly to cause the Party grave and manifest concern. By that time, the Party belatedly found that it had unwittingly almost fostered a major new campaign, whose legitimacy may have been in doubt initially but whose significance was spectacularly and embarrassingly obvious.

During May 1956, Lu Ting-yi, in a speech addressed to the intellectuals, spoke of the latest Party line for the "cultural workers" of China.[41] At the time, Lu held the position of Propaganda Chief of the Central Committee of the Party. He had been asked to deliver his address by Kuo Mo-jo (one of the foremost intellectuals of "New China" and President of the Academia Sinica). In brief, the pertinent point of his speech concerned the "blooming and contending of ideas within intellectual circles." For the artists and writers, a hundred flowers were to bloom; for the savants a hundred schools were to compete.[42] In explanation he said:

... more than two thousand years ago many schools of thought competed among themselves for supremacy. It was a Golden Age in the intellectual development of China. History has shown that when independent thought and free discussion are not encouraged, academic life stagnates.[43]

"Blooming and contending" were to represent a step forward, and as with the other campaigns, this movement did not admit to any reservations or inadequacies in its makeup.

The possibility of there being more than one constructive school of thought, more than one worthwhile viewpoint for art, literature, and scholarship was an exciting notion. There was an intellectual stir which resulted in multifarious voices being raised

41. Note, however, that the initial credit for this speech was given to Mao Tse-tung. "In May, Mao Tse-tung attempted to encourage greater initiative in the cultural sphere with the slogan 'Let a hundred flowers bloom, let a hundred schools contend.' (Mao's speech was never published, but it was publicly interpreted by Lu Ting-yi, head of the Party's propaganda department." (Roderick MacFarquhar, *The Hundred Flowers Campaign and the Chinese Intellectuals* [New York: Praeger, 1960], p. 8).

42. Faure, *op. cit.*, pp. 119–128. See particularly chap. 14 devoted to "The Hundred Flowers and the Hundred Schools." The campaign has been known variously as a "thousand schools" or "contending and blooming." In May, 1959, there appeared to be a slight revival of the campaign, with further *ad hoc* references appearing in the Communist press during 1960. Thus a movement may never die though a particular campaign may be allowed to wither.

43. *Ibid.*, pp. 119–120.

in a flood of criticism on the widest and, at times, most unexpected range of topics. The pedagogic techniques of university professors came under fire. But they fared little better than the dedicated cadres, for the spirited denunciation of the manner by which young Communist activists dominated and distorted student life became a feature of the campaign in its middle period. It is necessary to note at this point that the flowers came to blossom rather slowly, and for some time the campaign was regarded as something of a fiasco. With characteristic hindsight, critics have endeavored to indicate that the flowers were deliberately cultivated, so that the more assertive of their numbers could be later plucked (or weeded) when the time became auspicious. The suggestion that the Communists deliberately fostered a campaign among the intellectuals in order to identify the "deviationists and rightists" has varying foundations. The Communists themselves may have given the impression that this was in mind when Lu first made his speech to the gathered intellectuals and that in actuality the regime all along had full command of the situation, carefully overseeing each of the various steps. An alternative viewpoint, however, might indicate that, because of the unexpected escalating of the campaign and the evident delight with which it was taken up by many persons other than scholars, the authorities were ultimately convinced of the necessity to introduce "automatic checks." These checks, or the application of the next portion of the Communist campaign methodology, concerned the introduction of the "confession," which would ultimately result in total subjugation, by means of criticism, self-criticism, and counter-criticism (the necessary components of all such movements or campaigns) .[44]

It would appear that there were in reality at least two, if not

44. This analysis is in part both speculative and tentative. The conclusion of Professor G. F. Hudson would suggest that "the . . . Rightists were deliberately encouraged to commit themselves in order that the Communist leadership might have pretext for taking action against them." ("Let a Hundred Flowers Bloom: The Complete Text of 'On the Correct Handling of Contradictions among the People'" [by Mao Tse-tung, with notes and an introduction by G. F. Hudson], *The New Leader* [September 9, 1957], section 2, pp. 4–5) .

For the official English-language text of Mao's speech, see *On the Correct Handling of Contradictions among the People* (Peking: Foreign Languages Press, 1960) .

three, campaigns in force at the same time. That the "rectification" campaign against the three "isms" for Party followers and the "hundred flowers" movement for the scholars and artists were concurrent is quite apparent. However, at times it would appear that there was no clearcut division between these two movements, and the Chinese Communist press aided in confusing the issue by referring to scholars who "required rectifying" and government cadres who "contended unwisely." It is difficult to see how Communist activists, either staff or student members, at the universities could have concentrated exclusively on the "many schools" campaign to the detriment of the rectification campaign. The former resulted in a general critical spirit, while the later continued stodgily along, being based on quite explicit Party instructions. The "flowers" nominally predated rectification. However, the tempo of the two campaigns reached a climax at about the same time. In fact, in his speech to the Supreme Council of State on February 27, 1957, Mao Tse-tung devoted a whole passage to the "hundred flowers," whereas "rectification" was barely mentioned. Mao's reference to the "hundred flowers" also indicated a warning that limits were to be placed on the boundaries of criticism. Mao explained that Marxism is certainly open to criticism but that the format to be followed allows for refutation of criticism and likewise requires that persuasion follow discussion.[45]

It is apparent that the liberal and so-called "truly progressive" trends initiated by the "hundred flowers" movement had been severely dampened, probably by the middle of 1957. However, the Chinese scholar has had a long record of compatibility with the various regimes that he has served. The significant difference

45. The strict limits of criticism as defined by the Chinese Communist Party were: (a) Whatever encourages the union of all the people of our multinational country but not that which provokes division among the people. (b) Whatever encourages Socialist transformation and Socialist edification. (c) Whatever encourages the strengthening of the democratic dictatorship. (d) Whatever encourages the strengthening of democratic centralism and does not sap or weaken the system. (e) Whatever encourages the strengthening of the leadership of the Communist Party and does not lead to erosion or weakening of this leadership. (f) Whatever encourages international Socialist solidarity and the international solidarity of all peace-loving peoples and is not to the prejudice of these two forms of solidarity. See Faure, op. cit., p. 126. For the official English-language text, see Mao Tse-tung, On the Correct Handling of Contradictions Among the People, pp. 55–56.

between the past and the present, however, lies in the fact that today he does not entirely feel that he is under the regime. Instead he is led to believe, and undoubtedly at times feels, that he has an integral, honored, and practical part in it. His position is assured—within limits. He is valuable and necessary to the state, almost "above" others in "Socialist construction," and he has a position of some respect and security, at least equal to, if not considerably superior, to that which he enjoyed under the Nationalists.[46]

This "blooming" campaign, although perhaps not originally intended as a full-fledged movement, developed in such an uncontrollable way as to alarm Peking in no small manner. And yet it was initially designed to fit the restricted literary, artistic, and scientific circles of China in order to release creative ideas that had become somewhat stultified during the preceding years. In tentatively summing up, it is possible that there may be lasting benefits in spite of many who have had their fingers burned. It may be that the dynamics of cultural evolution are weighted against any regime—even a Communist or Socialist one—keeping so far ahead of the aspirations and actions of its intelligentsia, even of its "tame" intelligentsia. The "benefits" of induced liberalism, if they can ever be called this, may remain latent, because of the abrupt and unsatisfactory termination of the campaign.

Within seven weeks of the launching of the "rectification" campaign, its "liberality" was turned, and it was submerged, rather than merged, by an "antirightist" campaign. In fact, by the middle of June 1957, one sees the build-up of the new slogans and the intensification of meetings to identify the latest "paper tigers," that is, the rightists or those who had overstepped judicious bounds, ignoring Mao's warning about criticism. Mao had laid down as Party doctrine that one could criticize and discuss personalities in general, but the sacrosanct cornerstone of the regime, the Party itself, was not to be questioned or criticized, especially

46. A contrast in viewpoints is vividly offered by Kierman's *The Chinese Intelligentsia and the Communists* and C. P. Fitzgerald's penetrating but empathetic account of the "Scholars," chap. 2 in *Flood Tide in China* (London: Cresset Press, 1958).

by outsiders. The time and incident of the merging (if this is the correct description) of the two campaigns, "rectification" and "antirightist," is not clearly discernible. Likewise, it is not entirely satisfactory to identify certain critical incidents of the middle of June 1957 as arising out of one campaign rather than out of the other.

On June 12 and 13, certain disorders occurred in the subprefecture of Hanyang, in Hopei province. A riot by over a thousand students led by a professor caused considerable material damage. In particular the rioters singled out the local headquarters of the Communist Party for destruction. The students paraded in the streets shouting anti-Communist slogans and plastered the city walls with "particularly offensive" posters critical of the regime. The subprefect, Han Mao-lin, barely escaped lynching, and three Communist officials were reportedly kidnaped by the excited students.

In the following weeks more violence broke out, and eventually the press began to report the incidents. A few days after the Hanyang affair, a "bomb" was thrown at the home of the branch secretary of the Communist Party at the Peking Medical School. The secretary, who was also Vice-Principal of the Medical School, was said to have been attacked by a young student teacher of a nearby secondary school. The young trainee-teacher threw a small glass bottle containing, among other things, gunpowder. *New China News Agency*, on June 20, 1957, indicated that damage was negligible and nobody injured. However, some importance must have been attached to the incident by the authorities, for instead of dismissing the affair as the work of a disgruntled former student of the Medical School who had turned to teaching, it was worked up into a *cause célèbre* by the press. The news agency goes on to report:

> Over 1,000 students of Peking Medical College met in the afternoon of June 17 in protest against the explosion. Word was quickly spread around. Thereupon students of various institutions of higher learning in the city unanimously regarded the explosion case as a penetrating class education, which indicated that class struggle was still on, and that all must remain highly vigilant. The students pointed out that the plot to injure the vice-president of the medical college by reactionary elements was not an isolated

incident and that earlier people had shouted, "kill the Communists." They said the bomb was thrown into Chu's house one day and wondered where it would land the next day. They unanimously indicated they would draw a clear dividing line with the reactionary elements, stand pat on their proletarian ground, and deal determined counterblows to rightists and counterrevolutionary elements. The meeting of the students of the Peking Medical College also adopted a message to college students in Peking. The letter made this appeal: "For the sake of the Socialist enterprise, let us unite closely around the Party, strive to smash the fallacious antiparty and anti-Socialist utterances of the rightist elements, and stamp out the sabotage activities of counterrevolutionary elements. Rectification must go on and bombs will not intimidate us into submission." [47]

If this so-called "bomb incident" is taken seriously, then it is possible to suppose that instead of "observing limits," as Mao had instructed, there were certain elements who hoped to capitalize on the disquiet caused by the "blooming flowers" and "rectification." The "liberal" processes initially engendered by the one campaign had soured and were busy poisoning the "good works" first realized under "rectification." Hence instructions were passed along to change the pace and direction of the campaigns, and for all practical purposes they were diverted into the new antirightist movement.

It is of no little importance to appreciate the complex and sensitive problem that the regime faced with respect to the education and discipline of the senior students in the educational hierarchy.[48] From August 27 to September 6 the Subcommittee on Higher Institution of the Chinese Communist Party Peking Municipal Committee held a ten-day conference for teachers of political theories in Peking's institutions of higher learning. If one notes that the date of the conference coincides with the meeting for the reappraisal of the campaigns of early 1957, that it occurs after the student disorders of June and July, and that it is held in Peking, where there are clustered many of the major institutes, universities, and technical colleges, this study conference

---

47. *New China News Agency* (hereafter cited as *NCNA*, Peking), June 20, 1957 (*SCMP*, No. 1959).

48. For one of the best eyewitness accounts of this exciting period as seen by a foreign student in Peking, see René Goldman, "The Rectification Campaign at Peking University," *China Quarterly*, No. 2 (October-December 1962), pp. 138–153.

assumes a status of some importance. The conference's avowed goal was to "understand more clearly how to set up a Socialist ideological education course in the coming academic year." The lessons brought out by "blooming and contending" had been learned by the end of 1957, and the regime at last decided that drastic remedial treatment had become necessary to stem the flood innocuously unleased.

It is of salutory interest to recall Mao Tse-tung's earlier analysis regarding "the Party and intellectuals" in the new order. Mao's speech, "On the Correct Handling of Contradictions among the People," had been delivered on February 27 to the Supreme State Conference, and "edited, official" versions were available in July. Part Five of that speech concerned "The Question of Intellectuals," and the following quotation contains the essence of the Party's attitude to this "class"—an explanation tempered with a warning.

China needs as many intellectuals as she can get to carry through the colossal task of Socialist construction. We should trust intellectuals who are really willing to serve the cause of socialism, radically improve our relations with them, and help them solve whatever problems have to be solved, so that they can give full play to their talents. *Many of our comrades are not good at getting along with intellectuals. They are stiff with them, lack respect for their work, and interfere in scientific and cultural matters in a way that is uncalled for.* We must do away with all such shortcomings.

Our intellectuals have made some progress, but *they should not be complacent. They must continue to remold themselves, gradually shed their bourgeois world outlook* and acquire a proletarian, Communist world outlook, so that they can fully meet the needs of the new society and closely unite with the workers and peasants.[49]

IDEOLOGICAL MOBILIZATION

It would appear that a major problem still confronting the Communists in 1957, after seven years' "success" in reorganizing many aspects of Chinese life, concerned the unsatisfactory caliber and origin of many students enrolled at the colleges and uni-

49. See Mao Tse-tung, "On the Correct Handling of Contradictions among the People," *The New Leader*, pp. 39–40. [ITALICS ARE MINE. S.F.].

versities. While student origins and student activities at Peking do not necessarily act as a mirror for the rest of China, they are nonetheless revealing. The report of the Peking Study Conference of August-September 1957 continues at some length to indicate where students came from and what their social background was. It finally concludes by castigating Party and college authorities for assuming that students in general are automatically adherents of the regime. The conference reported:

In the course of the present discussion, teachers referred to the situation in the antirightist struggle and pointed out that the old viewpoint was not suited to actual conditions. Eighty percent of the higher institution students of the capital came of landlord, bourgeois, or petty bourgeois families. They were greatly under the influence of landlord, bourgeois or petty bourgeois ideologies. This was quite clearly exposed during the "free contention and free blooming." If political classes did not greatly help the students remold their ideology, then those classes would become practically empty talks, and bourgeois ideologies would be allowed to grow freely in the students.[50]

While the social antecedents of many students was thus to be deplored, it was equally apparent that academic staffs would be likewise tainted. The extent, however, to which instructors and professors were tarred with bourgeois backgrounds was quite startling. Writing in the influential Peking daily, *Jen Min Jih Pao,* some months later, Han Ming discussed the question of enforcing intellectual policy in institutions of higher education. He said:

Are the old intellectuals the intellectuals of the bourgeoisie? Are they double-faced by nature? This has to be determined by facts and has to be judged by their class background, their social environment, the education they received, and the philosophy of life and world outlook derived therefrom. According to the statistical materials relating to the 2,474 professors and assistant professors in forty-six institutions of higher education in China, the absolute majority of them came from landlord and bourgeois families and only a few individuals came from the families of working people. More than 98 percent of them received their higher education in old China, which is soaked with the class spirit of the bourgeoisie. A very considerable proportion had also gone abroad to study in European and American capitalist countries. The absolute majority of them have passed their middle age. This

50. *NCNA,* September 11, 1957 (*SCMP,* No. 1630).

is to say that they have spent the greater part of their life in the old society. Social existence determines the social consciousness. The lengthy and intense influence of the bourgeois society, family, and education, as well as the lengthy bourgeois ways of life and study could not but leave the bourgeois brand deep on the body of these intellectuals.[51]

If the figures quoted above—namely that 80 percent of university students in Peking alone at that time were from bourgeois families and that an absolute majority of professors from leading Chinese institutions had similarly "unfortunate" backgrounds— are at all indicative, the problems of the regime can be readily appreciated. Not content with ideological remolding, the effectiveness of which had been challenged during the "blooming and contending" era, the authorities were determined to remedy the faulty social-class structure of the academic staff and the college students as rapidly as possible. Bourgeois origins evidently were all too pervading and, according to the Communists themselves, were of such consequence that remolding and reforming had to be intensified, with the activists becoming more alert and paying greater attention to their duty in exposing fallacious thinkers.[52]

The regime, however, had made strenuous efforts to rectify the imbalance of students from the "less desirable" socio-economic classes. The allocation of scholarships, entrance places at college, and professional employment is to some degree based on class origin. On the Communists' own figures, however, the situation is gradually becoming more "favorable," so that the "number of intellectuals with working-class or peasant backgrounds is steadily increasing in China." [53] The leading English-language periodical, *Peking Review,* published two articles on education within a six-month period in 1958.[54] Both articles dealt at length with

51. *NCNA,* January 18, 1958 *(SCMP,* No. 1705).

52. A fallacious thinker may be equated with any intellectual possessing a bourgeois background. The contention is that background alone, if it can be identified quickly and accurately, may be the best guide for discovering fallacious or incorrect thinkers.

53. See "Education, Training Worker and Peasant Intellectuals," *Peking Review,* I, No. 12 (1958), 16.

54. *Ibid.*

the changing class composition of college students and in identical tables indicated the changes.

Changing Class-Composition of College Students
1952–1958*

School year	College students of worker-peasant origin	Percentage of total college students
1952–1953	40,000	20.46
1955–1956	80,000	29.20
1956–1957	130,000	34.29
1957–1958	160,000	36.42

* "Education, Training Worker and Peasant Intellectuals," *Peking Review*, I, No. 12 (1958), 16.

Political education classes were to some extent a feature of all institutions of higher learning by 1952. Yet it is surprising to find that either Communist Party or Ministry of Higher Education directives had been ignored, circumvented, or misunderstood. The Peking Study Conference of August-September 1957, noted that

. . . the remolding of ideology as suggested [i.e., by higher directives] had been considered as not necessarily applicable in higher institutions . . . so direct systematic theoretical education would be sufficient, it being unnecessary to help the students remold their ideology with reference to their ideological conditions. They had considered that the problem of establishing the Communist concept of the world in students should be solved later on by the students themselves after they had finished with the theories.[55]

This statement barely gives the hint that obviously there had been a high degree of laxity in many universities with respect to the inclusion of political studies in the curriculum, apart from insisting that students should attend such courses if provided. The Conference intended to remedy these defects and provide a more embracing plan to overcome the disadvantages of a growing national student body which was not benefiting sufficiently from the salvation that Communist and Socialist studies would produce. By September 20, 1957, if we take note of the Conference activities going on in Peking, a familiar pattern can be seen unfolding as to how Socialist ideological education was soon to take

55. *NCNA*, September 11, 1957 (*SCMP*, No. 1630).

place. The education was to be

... conducted in three stages, the first of which was mobilization. Mobilization of teachers and students would be necessary so that Chairman Mao's speech, "On the Correct Handling of Contradictions among the People" could be fully discussed. The discussion or great debate was the second stage after the correct elements had been gathered together. The final phase consisted of "mobilizing the masses to launch self-criticisms and summing up the results of the education." [56]

The correct handling of contradictions was to be a lively issue in the universities. However, after the devastating effects of "blooming and contending," it provided some relief and comfort to Party theorists, principally because the campaign's course was soon happily following orthodox lines and did not deviate from the textbook solutions.

From Peking, the campaign to discuss Socialist education and its relevancy for rectification spread southward to the other university and college centers. Under the heading, "Shanghai Higher Institutions Furiously Improve Work," *New China News Agency* on September 24 commented on the political program and discussion topics for the forthcoming academic year. It was anticipated that there would be a redoubling of efforts to make up for ground lost during the summer.

Seriously and responsibly dealing with every suggestion of the masses, leadership personnel of higher institutions in Shanghai have kept on improving work furiously, with the result that the rectification campaign for the new academic year is distinguished from the very onset by great liveliness and fervor.[57]

Even as far afield as Moscow, it was reported that nearly three thousand Chinese students were assembled on September 8 to listen to reports on the rectification campaign. All Chinese students in the Soviet Union were actively and seriously to devote some of their time to reading documents and holding discussion meetings on the problems of rectification in order to "distinguish between very right and very wrong to overcome the inclination toward individualism, liberalism, and nationalism." [58]

56. *Ibid.*
57. *Ibid.*
58. *Ibid.*

One is curious as to whether Russian colleagues of those Chinese studying in the U.S.S.R. could offer sufficient guidance to their fellow Communists from the East in order to solve the latest in ideological conundrums. The spectacle of Russian professors counseling Chinese students in the correct understanding of Mao's speech on internal contraditions would undoubtedly be most illuminating. The converse probably is more accurate; that Russian students first heard from their Chinese foreign student friends the various rumors concerning internal contradictions which had arisen in China's Communist Party. In fact, before the matter was made public in Moscow, Khrushchev was asked to comment on the scope of these Chinese internal contradictions and asked to explain their relevancy for Russia. It is reported that Khrushchev at first dismissed the questions somewhat cursorily, indicating that the matter concerned the Chinese solely and was not necessarily applicable to Communist Party developments within Russia.[59]

After rectification and the antirightist program, it was possible and necessary to turn to fresher fields in order to derive further ideological material. The year 1957 had produced some surprises, and it was apparent that in certain spheres drastic remedial measures were called for. The antirightist program catered to this in part, and "fresher fields" were found by developing some of the more useful and constructive aspects of "blooming and contending." One of the more positive ideological developments

59. "Each socialist or capitalist country has its own course of development and its own stages of development and therefore socialist countries, we, for instance, our country, has been in existence forty years; the Chinese People's Republic has been in existence eight years. Therefore a stage through which we passed does not necessarily have to be repeated in other socialist countries. Then each people have their own habits, customs, its own history, and the Communist Party of the country concerned should take that into account, of course, and our Chinese friends have many original ideas, which they are implementing in the course of socialist construction in their own country. They are giving birth to new ideas, too, which take into consideration the specific conditions in China. We look upon that as perfectly normal, and we lend support to many of these things. We publish these ideas in our Press, but each one has to base oneself on the conditions existing in one's own country. There is no contradiction with any Marxist-Leninist ideas in this respect." (Nikita Khrushchev, in an interview with news correspondent Daniel Schorr on "Face the Nation" [CBS Television and Radio, June 2, 1957]. Reported in *NCNA*, June 4, 1957. See MacFarquhar, *op. cit.,* p. 306.)

of the year resulted in the further weeding-out and identification
of the waverers among the intellectuals. The corollary of this resulted in the critical reappraisal of the effects of several years of
Communist influence and dominance in primary, secondary, and
higher education. As with all other campaigns, there was boundless material for the Party cadres to digest, and the results gave
a valuable indication as to the Party's strengths and weaknesses in
its hold over students and the effectiveness of Party teaching and
controls. The defects revealed were disquieting by the Communists' own admission, and towards the end of 1957, plans were
made for tightening up the teaching of politics and indoctrination
courses at the colleges and universities.[60] It appears doubtful
whether many of the universities had in fact imposed sufficient
compulsory classes in politics, because the wording of a directive
issued by the Ministry of Higher Education in December referred
to the "Opening of Courses of Socialist Education in All Institutions of Higher Education." [61] The principal text for study was
Mao Tse-tung's "On Correct Handling of Contradictions among
the People," as well as certain essential Marxist-Leninist classics
to be stipulated later by the different institutions concerned.
Provisionally the course of study was to last for one school year,
with eight hours each week allocated exclusively to "Socialist education." An interesting, though not unexpected, aspect of the
real import that the courses were to have is revealed towards the
end of the directive which states:

> The students must be guided to learn the documents by heart in a planned
> manner, and free discussion and debate must be organized when engaging
> in discussion and debate, the principle of unity-criticism-unity must be
> firmly adhered to. The method of fact-giving and reasoning must be used
> to set out the different facts and viewpoints, to reason with thoroughness,

60. See H. Arthur Steiner, "The Curriculum in Chinese Socialist Education: An
Official Bibliography of 'Maoism,'" *Pacific Affairs*, XXXI, No. 3 (September 1958),
286–299.

61. Quite obviously ideological or political teachings can be presented in many
forms without specific inclusion in the curriculum, which undoubtedly was the
case in some colleges as revealed by the curricular guides issued by the relevant education authorities in China. For an outline of the earlier curricula, as laid down by
the regime, see Chung Shih, *Higher Education in Communist China*, chap. 5
(Hong Kong: Union Research Institute, 1953).

and to contend over and over again so that all people may talk freely and be able to distinguish the right from the wrong.[62]

As it became obvious that the courses in Socialist education were to be rigidly controlled and directed by Party cadres at the universities, it is understandable why it was necessary to learn Mao's speech on contradictions by heart. This was essential so that an unshakable dogma could be presented, thus introducing the yardstick by which the subsequent discussions could be based and judged. It may appear strange to read that "free discussion and debate must be organized," yet this was in keeping with the overall goal of the course: to weed out rightists and independent thinkers. Free discussion was to be controlled discussion based on the well-known principle of unity-criticism-unity, which in turn could only lead to one interpretation of the problem espoused by Mao in his speech on contradictions.

An explanation is offered by C. P. Fitzgerald of the overall historical implication of the various ideological campaigns and efforts to remake China's intellectuals. It is an explanation which appears to be oversimplified, but it is deceptively so, since it is one which is provokingly pertinent.

. . . China must use all her talents; re-educated, brainwashed, brought to an understanding of where the fault lay, what must be done to remedy it, what sacrifices were required, what efforts demanded, the class of scholars purged of their less desirable members, deprived of their old economic foundations, but still equipped with their brains and skills, could be redeemed and employed. They would soon cease to be a special class, education and selection would bring up the talented poor to their level, would permeate the new ruling group, would take a long step towards the Communist goal, the classless society.[63]

THE GREAT LEAP FORWARD

Apart from the introduction and extension of compulsory courses in political education at the universities and college, the regime had in mind further developments on a national scale for 1958. These would directly affect many aspects of education. Un-

62. *NCNA*, December 17, 1957 (*SCMP*, No. 1683). See also Goldman, *op. cit.*
63. Fitzgerald, *op. cit.*, p. 47.

der the title of the "great leap forward," further target figures
in most fields of endeavor were laid down. One of the goals set
for higher education was the realization of a startling expansion
of facilities for higher education. Efforts were to be made to accommodate an increase of 45 percent in the number of students
expected from 1957 to 1959.[64] The earlier warning that a significant percentage of students were still tainted with bourgeois
backgrounds was well taken, and the number of students of
peasant-worker backgrounds was to be greatly increased. As part of
the leap forward, students were to reorient their study techniques;
a new emphasis was to be placed on "combining education with
productive labor." It is true that practical work and periods of
hard manual labor had already been the lot of students from time
to time under the new regime. This was based clearly on Chinese
Communist tenets which stipulated the necessity for students,
teachers, and intellectuals to identify themselves entirely with the
manual workers.[65]

This basic belief in relating manual work and intellectual
studies has been influenced at times by the practical necessity of
pushing redundant or surplus students out to the country into
physically productive occupations. This occurred particularly in
1953, the "year of retrenchment," when in December the newspaper, *Jen Min Jih Pao,* indicated that the young should be
directed towards "glorious work in the fields and factories."
Again in 1957, it is difficult to resist the temptation of indicating
a casual relationship between the "rectification" campaign and the
sudden uprooting and transplanting to the countryside of nearly
a million functionaries, bureaucrats, administrators, and Party
officials, as well as teachers and intellectuals. On November 23, an
official figure is given simply indicating that 810,000 government
and Party workers left their posts to take up "productive work in
basic sectors of the economy." Of these, over half went into

64. See *Evergreen: A Magazine of Chinese Youth and Students,* No. 3 (1958). Students of worker-peasant origin make up 36 percent of the total enrollment as
against 20 percent in 1952. There were enrolled 441,000 students among 229 colleges
and universities in 1957. According to figures published in *SCMP* (No. 1885), approximately 800,000 students would be enrolled during the 1958–1959 academic year.
65. See Fitzgerald, *op. cit.,* p. 46.

agriculture and industry, with the remainder finding new work and "fulfilling basic-level administrative needs."

If account can be taken of the families that perhaps accompanied the transferred functionaries, it is possible that several million people in all were transplanted or resettled—many of them on a long-term or even permanent basis. At least this was the original intention, whether as a punishment or merely for rectification purposes is not entirely clear. By way of partial explanation, the government admitted that

. . . the reduction of officials helped government departments to simplify their administration and raise their efficiency, so overcoming bureaucracy and subjectivism arising from lack of contact with reality and the masses of people.[66]

It would be expected that, with the removal of so many workers in government departments, those remaining would be threatened or stimulated into working at a sufficient pace to make up for the reduction of staff.

Greatly increased efficiency and increasing returns all around would be the natural corollary of the drastic and immediate dispatch of so many carefully selected cadres destined for a period, of unknown length, of drab, uninteresting work in the provinces. Many of those transferred were said to be members of intellectual cadres who had never undergone the "training of productive labor or actual struggle and who lacked the experience of working at the basic level." Reference is even made to a "very small number of those transferred who, incapacitated by old age or infirmity, have given up office or retired." One wonders how many "a small portion" would number and whether the threat of a transfer was used to rid the administration of its aged and surplus officials? One also wonders what provisions were made for the old age and retirement of these intellectuals and former government functionaries.

66. *NCNA*, November 26, 1957 (*SCMP*, No. 1668). Originally a figure of 810,000 workers was given. However, *Peking Review* of February 10, 1959, p. 10, refers to one million intellectuals who were transferred. It goes on to report the return of some of these to their old positions in 1959. While at first glance the transfers would appear to envisage permanent resettlement, this is not altogether substantiated by these later reports of returning "rejuvenated" government officials.

The course and vicissitudes of the rectification campaign undoubtedly showed up certain weaknesses, and the opportunity to promote, demote, or reward, inherent in the transfer plans, is more than obvious.

The opportunity of re-educating cadres in lowly tasks and reminding them of their transient position in the state would likewise have a widespread salutary and beneficial effect. It would be difficult to discount the very practical benefit accruing to the peasants, cadres, and the government as a whole in having top, bottom, and middle members of the community understand one another (however distasteful the lot of the lower levels appeared to the city-bred intellectuals). The judicious combination of re-education, discipline, and integration for various groups in the community is shown by this massive attempt to transfer so many of the urban intellectual functionaries.

It is probably inappropriate to criticize the regime for the program of resettlement on the grounds that it was effected mainly because of pique, distrust, or outright condemnation of many of its outspoken workers. Instead, the problem is presented so that the *xiafang* (a word often encountered in the Chinese Communist vocabulary, meaning roughly, "one transferred to work at the grassroots level") intellectual must prove himself adaptable and capable of entering into the spirit of the experiment in an impersonal way. Of the *xiafang* intellectual it is said:

. . . quite a few cadres originally could not bear the smell of manure. Since they participated in agricultural production, they have been eager to carry manure. Some of them walk with containers in their hands and pick up manure wherever it is found. Many transferred cadres not only labor with people but also live with them. They have become as intimate as if they were members of the same family.[67]

At first glance perhaps this may appear to be a somewhat facetious quotation. However, this description of a member of a *xiafang* cadre at work in an unusual setting indicates the importance of reconstructing values and how integral to the whole problem is the total identification and transformation of the "mere" intellectual into a glorious peasant laborer.

67. *Ibid.*

The reconstruction of values and the aims of the plan are clearly set out at the Third Plenum of the Eighth Central Committee of the Chinese Communist Party in late November of 1957. The purge of redundant functionaries would further simplify the problem of controlling organs of administration by the Party and at the same time place many of the inept Party workers and pseudo intellectuals in an environment where they could do the least harm. At worst, conservative peasant opposition would continue to isolate them, and at best, if the *xiafang* challenge was accepted, spiritual cleansing would be combined with perhaps an increase in physical productivity. It was anticipated that, with the parallel extensions of educational and training facilities, many cadres would be able, through hard work and further studies, to regain their former positions. The indeterminate time in the countryside or factory would go some way in overcoming the persistent problem of the many intellectual youths and minor officials who were still handicapped by their bourgeois backgrounds.

Allowing for varying estimates, depending on the province or city concerned, the regime has indicated that three quarters of all youths attending universities or graduating from high school into minor administrative positions did not possess the "correct" family background. While it will require at least fifteen years to bring to the desired level the proportion of youths possessing the necessary work-peasant origin, the *xiafang* movement was a satisfactory, though temporary, expedient to lighten the problem.

The Communist Party on various occasions has openly indicated doubt and dissatisfaction as to the sincerity, far less the subordination, of its young elite to the Party and *ipso facto* to the state. Therefore, as it will take time to form an elite of proletarian origin, concentration and pressure must be applied to the large number of youths trained by some form of bourgeois background. They are humbled, made to feel inferior, and placed on sufferance in order to highlight the fact that they are entirely dependent on the state for their existence and future employment.

It is true, as Professor Fitzgerald has indicated, that

... China could not afford a vast purge of the educated and the skilled. ...
There are better ways of transforming a society than by wholesale liquidation
and massacre: more certain and lasting success can be attained by converting
opponents than by persecuting them to death. Persuasion and propaganda,
the techniques of the modern age, are the chosen instruments of Chinese
Communist government. Force is kept in reserve.[68]

Another aspect or extension of the "redemption through labor"
process, aimed primarily at students, had its origin in a desire for
efficiency and economy. It had been pointed out that, apart from
the full-time *xiafang* program, spare-time work and study on the
part of students would save the state sufficient funds to build additional universities. The *Kuang Ming Jih Pao,* commenting on
the decision of the Central Committee of the Young Communist
League to promote spare-time paid occupations for students, indicated that eighty million *yuan* is spent each year on People's
Scholarships to subsidize selected students at institutions of higher
learning. A reduction of 10 percent in scholarships alone would
build a new university, and as the commentary openly reveals:

... promotion of part-time work and study will lighten the duty of the
students' families to pay their tuition and living expenses, thus affording
more workers' and peasants' children the opportunity of entering schools.
... Some students ask: since the state has established Peoples Scholarships,
why should school authorities adopt the system of part-time work and study?
The state has established scholarships to help the students from poor families
to overcome difficulties in meeting school expenses. This is entirely necessary.
However, when the state is concentrating its capital on developing industrial
and agricultural production and when the number of students increases every
year along with the increasing development of educational enterprises, we
must set a definite limit to financial aid given to the students. This will
have to rely on the students to do part-time work while they are studying so
as to make up for the deficiency of state aid.[69]

It would appear that the state had set definite limits as to the
aid it would give and, in particular, that aid was restricted to
students possessing the desired cultural background. It is also
obvious that parents were expected to pay part of the cost of their
children's education in the past and presumably would still be
expected to pay a considerable portion of the necessary expenses in

68. Fitzgerald, *op. cit.,* p. 48.
69. *Kuang Ming Jih Pao,* February 11, 1958 (*SCMP,* 1756).

the years to come. Furthermore, students were expected to make a contribution themselves and not be dependent entirely on the state or on their parents for their maintenance and tuition costs. It is interesting to note that in many Western countries this form of parental aid and/or self-help has altered somewhat during the past decade, with the state subsidizing more and more of the costs of higher education. Yet in China at present, socialization of education does not mean free education by any means, and the onus has been placed on the students to meet some of the educational expenses. The reason for this policy, as given by the Communists, is twofold: economy of finance for national construction and the intrinsic value of labor combined with study.

The view that the parents and/or the students can and should pay for education is put forward in the widely distributed English-language periodical, *China Reconstructs*. Under the heading "New Development in Education" it states:

> Until February this year 1958, there was a tendency among many educational workers to lay overmuch stress on state-financed, full-time, free schooling and to disregard the potentialities that lie among the people themselves. They did not encourage the people to set up their own schools; they overlooked the importance of vocational schools and part-work, part-study schools. They failed to realize that with the improvement in living standards people can afford to and would be willing to pay small fees for their children's schooling.[70]

GLORIOUS PHYSICAL WORK

The prescription of part-time work for students and an open acknowledgment of the necessity for restricting public expenditure on education is somewhat at variance with the overall plans envisaged initially in the "great leap forward" of 1958–1960. Nonetheless, it is possible to acknowledge the value of hard manual work for either students or *xiafang* intellectuals. Likewise it is valid to suggest that a mixture of motives, pragmatically determined, allowed for much of the uncertainty as to the principal reasons for the so-called "joy through labor" strictures issued throughout China in 1957 and 1958.

70. *China Reconstructs*, VII, No. 11 (November 1958), 23.

The subsequent development, during 1958, of a new policy towards Party, government, and university cadres arose from the lessons learned in the rectification campaign. Early in 1958, the Chinese Communist Party Central Committee and the State Council decided that cadres were to take part in physical labor.

The 1958 decision for each of the government cadres to have one month of physical labor training also contributed to a leap forward in government work. With the same amount of work but less personnel, the cadres remaining in government organizations worked exceedingly hard and emulated those under physical labor training.[71]

About 95 percent of all the members of cadres of the central government organization are said to have taken part, and an analysis of the total man-days involved would indicate that a month's physical labor was indulged in by a very high proportion of Party, government, and education officials. In Febraury of 1959, *New China News Agency* indicated that more officials had gone to work in villages and factories: "This is a continuation of last year's practice whereby office workers go in rotation to temper themselves in productive labor."

One of several conclusions that could be drawn from the "back to the farm and the factory" movement is the importance that the Party has placed on acquainting its educated members and the intelligentsia with the realities of the monotony and exhausting effects of manual work. The doubts of many of the inner members of the Party had been revealed, and there was no better way of cleansing their souls as well as maintaining the support of the peasants (many of whom were in line for organization into agricultural communes in the immediate future) than by sending these functionaries to share their lot. Thus, many of the recalcitrants, the waverers, and the redundant were moved out to the country or into the factories. Accompanying these, as would be expected, were more zealous Party members who did not look upon their transfer as a demotion. They were determined to make full use of their organizing skill and special aptitudes on the peasants or in local administration in the remote *hsiangs* (local administrative units comparable to counties).

71. *NCNA*, February 1959 (*SCMP*, No. 1953).

In spite of the report, in *Peking Review* of February 1959, that most *xiafang* intellectuals were back at their desks, it is more than probable that "natural socialistic attrition and wastage" had allowed only the most "productive" to return. The same issue of *Peking Review,* in a lighthearted vein, published a poem euphemizing the *xiafang* movement:

> I was a city man from tip to toe,
> Things on the farm I just didn't know,
> But the peasants gave me a warm hello
> Before I learnt to wield a hoe.
>
> Eating rice was always very nice,
> But when I started on the farm, yes indeed
> I couldn't tell a seedling from a weed.
> Well, it didn't take long, oh no,
> Till the peasants taught me how to make rice grow.
>
> I was there when the commune was born,
> When we doubled the harvest of corn,
> Turned out our first heats of steel,
> And introduced the first free meal
> For commune members one and all.
> My joy is recorded in a painting on the wall.
>
> After ten months I wasn't the same,
> I left with much more than I came.
> I filled in the gap of my school education,
> Learnt that labor makes the nation.
> Today its back to the city once more,
> An intellectual who now knows the score.[72]

An interesting sidelight on the method of grading or appraising the "new peasants" at the "grassroots peasant academy" concerns the part played by the local peasant or factory worker who adjudged the *xiafang* intellectual. If the *xiafang* cadre identified himself entirely with those with whom he worked, he would receive a good report. Many of the city-bred functionaries, teachers, and professors proudly reported that they had been elected to village councils or had been nominated as "model peasants." Accounts from Peking indicate that some intellectuals were so

72. *Peking Review,* II, No. 6 (February 10, 1959).

enamored of and wholeheartedly immersed in their new stations that they even behaved quite boorishly when they returned to the capital. They shocked some of their oversensitive colleagues upon returning to their campuses by continuing to sport their peasant clothes, speaking crudely just as their peasant friends did, and, what was worse, smelling as perhaps only genuine peasants could.

After being rid of many "redundants," the Communist Party would have to take steps to maintain the pruning process and ensure that maximum benefits accrued from the grassroots visitation. As a consequence, instructions went out for a certain period of the cadres' year to be devoted to some form of productive labor. The original *xiafang* movement was designed to make up for the abuses revealed through "rectification"; for many intellectuals it apparently lasted but a year. The new scheme was a watered-down version of the original plan, and, rather than punitive, it was remedial and therapeutic in design. So by rotation, cadres, minor officials, teachers, and students were all scheduled to put in their time at "real productive labor." As a government announcement indicated:

Cadres of Central Government organs have started training in physical labor by rotation for 1959, and appropriate arrangements for work, labor and study have been made for them.[73]

The participation in projects involving physical labor has now become regularized and established as a system. Now, however, instead of exiling hundreds of thousands to remote areas to work out their penance, a monthly quota has been fixed.

Similarly, in higher education, the year's program has now been firmly divided among formal classes, physical labor, and vacations.[74] In order to "walk with two feet instead of one," it is pointed out that there must be a correct relationship between work and study, with the total elimination of the boundary between mental and physical labor. The two are to be integrated so that it is impossible to tell whether one is engaged in mental work

73. *NCNA*, February 1959 (*SCMP*, No. 1953).

74. For a comprehensive analysis of developments in higher education between 1950 and 1960, see Chang-tu Hu, "Higher Education in Mainland China," *Comparative Education Review*, IV, No. 3 (February 1961), 159–168.

alone. Likewise, it is stressed that any physical endeavor will require much thinking and planning.

It is apparent that the displacement of the pure theorist allows the regime to place greater opportunities at the feet of the peasants and indicates to them that the intellectual is somewhat ignorant in many practical spheres. The laborer is given a new status and certainly a new role as teacher and friend to the unfortunate *xiafang* cadre pushed into a tough environment. The displacement of the intellectual, from many points of view, was possibly long overdue in China, where he "used to cultivate an apparent dilettantism, an easy charm, a polished sophistication." [75]

But what is more important than the downgrading of the intellectual is the opening-up of new means of education long denied to the great majority of Chinese peasants and urban workers. The establishment of goals and opportunities common to all classes is obstensibly emphasized, rather than the ridiculing of the professors, however, unsatisfactory their landlord or bourgeois antecedents might have been.

The clarification of the role of education and its integration in the general plan for combining work and labor is further revealed in a State Council directive of September 1958. This is one of the most important pronouncements on education during this decade, and its importance can be gauged from the new relationship to be built between school and factory and eventually between commune and university. The mass campaign of the "great leap forward" has its plan for ideological education in this document.

The Party line in educational work seeks to make education serve the proletariat politically and to unite education with productive labor. In order to implement this line, educational work must be led by the Party. Marxist-Leninist political and ideological indoctrination must be carried out in all schools to indoctrinate the teachers and students with the class viewpoint of the working class: the mass viewpoint, the labor viewpoint, or the viewpoint calling for the integration of mental labor with physical labor, and the dialectical materialistic viewpoint. The future direction is for schools to run factories and farms, and for factories and agricultural cooperatives to establish schools. . . . We will spend about fifteen years to

75. Fitzgerald, *op. cit.,* p. 46.

universalize higher education. After that another fifteen years or so will be spent to enhance the work.[76]

There is no doubting the unmistakably long-term, though confident, approach that is being made to integrate education and make it serve the demands and requirements of the Party. The "new man" of all-round development in Chinese Communist society is "one who has both political consciousness and culture and is capable of taking up both mental and physical labor."

Translated into more practical terms, this meant that many institutions of higher education (and for that matter the bulk of senior secondary schools) were destined to establish ancillary factories and workshops. By the end of 1959, well over seven thousand such establishments had been founded by universities and colleges. In an endeavor to reduce cost by some form of productivity and give valuable practical experience to many students, a host of workshops associated with high schools were reported to have been established.[77]

The policy of fostering a small pilot industrial unit at many educational institutions reflected the growing awareness, on the part of the regime, of the importance of developing, at the earliest opportunity, reverence for things "practical and applicable." Discussing the "Revolution in Higher Education," the President of Tsinghua University, in Peking, stated:

Since the nationwide policy of combining education with productive labor was put into practice, instructors and students in our Tsinghua University, China's biggest polytechnical institution, have been doing a real job in workshops and on construction sites, as well as studying in class. In the formerly quiet laboratories and teaching workshops, over 500 different products were designed and manufactured for the national economy during

76. "Directive of the Chinese Communist Party Central Committee and the State Council on Educational Work," September 19, 1958 (*SCMP*, No. 1883). An article in *Evergreen: A Magazine of Chinese Youth and Students*, No. 6 (1958), indicates that: "Many big enterprises have already set up a complete system of education from primary school to college. Some factories have merged with schools to carry out a half-work, half-study system, so that everybody becomes a worker and student at the same time. In this way young people can go from primary school to college without any family or state support—and for that matter without going out of the factory. Not a few factories have planned to popularize higher education among their workmen in eight or ten years."
77. See "New Developments in Education," *China Reconstructs*, III, No. 11 (November 1958).

six months of last year. Many were up to the best Chinese and international standards and of wide significance to the economy.[78]

The Party line was even stressed in the children's page of *China Reconstructs* for February 1959. Under the heading, "What Schools Can Make," readers were told how many junior schools were forming their own factories. An eleven-year-old child, working at a recent exhibition held in the College of Mechanical Agriculture in Peking, proudly disclosed that "our school is in Kirin province in the Northeast. We each work there from four to eight hours a week." Another student at the exhibition, a fifteen-year-old girl from Kiangsu province, is reported as saying:

I learned to embroider from my mother. When our school set up a workshop last winter, 45 students joined it. Fifteen embroidered bedspreads can buy a ton of steel. That was something to think about, wasn't it![79]

PART-WORK, PART-STUDY PROGRAM

A generally valid criticism often made against many Chinese students has been that "they are too theoretical and need the basic experience of the machine shop." The government, however, does not merely want students to complete practical work as part of their course of study. Instead, it wishes to have the students organizing their studies around particular work projects.[80] In China today, the school, college, or technical institution is expected to make a direct, immediate, and substantial contribution to the national economy. The "great leap forward" was dependent, in part, on the success or failure of the "work while you study" program. Because of the considerable reversals in and adjustments of the "great leap forward" program, especially after 1960, the enormous increase planned for steel and coal production alone today are still greatly dependent on the continual increase in the number of practical technologists forthcoming from

78. *China Reconstructs,* VIII, No. 2 (February 1959) , p. 10.
79. *Ibid.*
80. For a critical and particularly thorough analysis, see Robert D. Barendsen, *Half-Work, Half-Study Schools in Communist China: Recent Experiments with Self-Supporting Educational Institutions* (Bulletin No. 214 [OE-14100]; Washington, D. C.: Government Printing Office, 1964) .

the universities and polytechnical colleges. While the specialists may be limited in their scope and training, they are expected to be eminently practical (that is, if the present bias in the curriculum towards on-the-job study is to proceed successfully, and there is still considerable doubt on this point). The faculties other than the technical ones are certainly not exempt from participating in the new labor designs for education. While few specialized schemes at the college level have been designed to cover the humanities and nontechnical sciences, an *ad hoc* program can be devised as necessary. For instance, in August of 1958, three hundred teachers and staff members of the philosophy faculty at Peking University went to a people's commune in one of the city's suburbs. Mornings were spent in the field laboring, and afternoons were given over to reports and discussions. It may seem fitting that "deep plowing" and harvesting were selected for the Peking philosophers. However, this might suggest either that only a narrow range of suitable practical work was available for them or that this was perhaps the correct activity to offset their theoretical and philosophical studies.

Tsinghua University had gone so far as to lay down a program of studies which required one term out of three to be spent in productive labor, which might be performed either inside or outside school. The developments at Tsinghua may well lead to an overall formalized national plan for combining normal studies and productive labor rather than merely ensuring that theoretical studies are complemented by a practical application. It would seem, from the pronouncements in the Chinese press on education, that there was some divergence of views as to whether "productive labor" was to be incorporated in the curriculum for its intrinsic value or whether, because of its nature, the students' courses would be technically more satisfying. The more direct and efficient use of a student's time in the university workshop would generally result in a straight-out integration rather than alternation of practical and theoretical studies, with the cruder physical aspects of manual labor of secondary importance.

Commenting on the "half-work, half-study" system, *New China News Agency* states:

In Tsinghua University, students spend one third of a term in productive labor without affecting the fundamental courses. The school year is divided into three terms. Each department will divide the time between theoretical teaching and productive labor in accordance with the characteristics of its specialization. Students in the departments of water conservancy, engineering, and civil engineering in general spend one term in concentrated productive labor and two semesters in theoretical study. Other departments spend alternative days in work and in study, or work two days and study four days a week, or work half day and study half day. There is no standard method or sharp division. Some theoretical teaching is also carried out during the period of concentrated productive labor and some work is done during the period of concentrated theoretical teaching.

After the carrying out of half-work, half-study system, politics remains a required course for all students. Every department will use two weeks in every school year for the rectification of thinking and style of work.[81]

From Peking emanate many of the government and/or Party directives which trigger off the so-called "spontaneous meetings" and "mass movements" which have continually occurred throughout the nation. These are often based on conference results or experimentation undertaken in the capital. As a consequence, the pattern set at Tsinghua has been in part followed by other universities and technical colleges, with local variations to suit individual institutes.

As the President of Tsinghua University has carefully indicated in commenting on the new design for university curricula:

The educational institution becomes not just a school but at the same time a research institute, factory, designing institute, and building concern. An end is put to the traditional concept of a school as a consumer unit, an ivory tower torn away from social life. Our policy bridges the gap between educational and producing units.[82]

During 1959 and 1960, a parallel development of the school running a factory was the establishment of means of training and general educational facilities within the larger factories. Many of these factories, especially those constituting a clearly defined industrial complex, have set up comprehensive educational systems covering the range from literacy classes to university-level lectures. The part-work, part-study schools represent a new stage in Chinese

81. *NCNA*, November 1, 1958 (*SCMP*, No. 1889).
82. *China Reconstructs*, VIII, No. 2 (February 1959).

education. Although perhaps familiar in some parts of the Western industrial world, they are still a novel feature for many urban Chinese workers. Taiyuan, one of the fastest-developing industrial centers, illustrates an interesting example of this trend towards "extension" education, with the establishment of an Institute of Iron and Steel Technology at the Taiyuan iron and steel works. Initially started solely as a training school for technicians employed as operators in the iron and steel works, it was converted into a "regular" specialist university. The background of the Institute's first two hundred students is interesting, as it reflects the preference given to Party members and to factory workers. One hundred students were chosen from these two categories, while the other half were graduates of senior middle schools.

The energy and enthusiasm that was centered on "educational reconstruction," as has been mentioned earlier, was part and parcel of the "new general line" launched in 1958. This mass economic and ideological campaign, the "great leap forward," was designed to pull China up by her sandal thongs to rival the Japanese at least in the short run and Britain or Germany within the next ten or fifteen years. With so much ground to make up in so many fields of economic development, any advance would appear to be significant and noteworthy, considering the past developments of this century. However, exaggeration, falsification of production figures, and shoddy accounting have clouded the full evaluation of China's economic achievements under the various Five Year and Seven Year Plans. Work and study was indicated as the necessary corollary to the "great leap forward." It was in capital production rather than in consumer goods that the "fruits of socialistic labor" lay; so believed the regime in 1960. Its attitudes are largely unchanged today.

Thus work is directed towards productive ends, and study becomes oriented towards science and technology. Education for its own sake—divorced from "reality"—cannot exist in "New China." What is required is an increasing volume of production, and if this cannot be obtained, in the main, by superior planning, it may be attempted indirectly by extreme specialization and intensification of courses at the technical schools and universities. Students and staff have been informed of the general requirements, and some initiative is allowed them so that they may devise ways and means of fulfilling their programs. Self-help, where possible, is to be the keynote in financing the cost of education, with parents paying fees and the students working part-time. Socialization in education by no means implies a liberalizing of scholarship provisions, and it was said that the "great leap forward" could only be accomplished by individual and collective effort not necessarily state-organized or state-financed. Thus, universities were encouraged to go into production and made salable items, school children were encouraged to produce handicraft articles to help pay for imports, and factories were urged to found their own schools, without necessarily waiting for specific central government directives.

Prognostications regarding future trends in Chinese Communist education can only be tentative in this summary. The organizational changes effected so far in China are enormous, and the educational plans of the regime are formidable, as far as one can see. Although the educational system of Communist China has been "adjusted" in its entirety during the past few years, the problem still remains as to the political loyalty and reliability of the masses. Likewise, a major problem for the regime is that of how to ensure the wholehearted coöperation of the newly emergent groups of Marxist intellectuals and the adaptability of the old-line Party members to rapidly changing conditions.

The 1956–1957 "intellectual uprising" and the necessity for "education to be combined with productive labor" indicates that education for the masses and the critical scholarly class (even those molded in the Marxist pattern) is a Pandoralike phenomenon. At the same time, it is patently obvious that persistent vigilance is required of the regime's educators in order to harness the intellectual, creative, and laboring efforts of over seven hundred million people.

The succession of bad harvests, natural calamities, and administrative ineptitudes occurring during the "great leap forward" should be a sufficient reminder to account fully for the unexpected while planning for the expected. A satisfied peasantry and a ma-

terially advancing working class will determine the success or
failure of mass education in Communist China for some time to
come. The fruits of universal education are still far off, and the
rewards, though seen by many, are experienced by few at present.
While the regime believes that education underpins the industrial
and political advancement of China, it is unwilling to depend
entirely on education's formal structure to bring this about. Thus
the "multi-multi track" of a part-time and regular school system
of education in Communist China is virtually attempting to
"move forward on all fronts." While the emphasis has changed
from year to year and from one Five Year Plan to another, the
theoretical aim of universal education for all China's people still
remains. The Communist Party and the monolithic political
structure, however, also remain. For the Chinese Communists,
educational advancement is dependent on Party leadership and
not the other way around. In theory, the Communists would
claim that education in its "correct" sense could not exist without the Party. It would become individualistic, chauvinistic, and
antisocial.

SUMMATION

Educational reforms during this first decade of the Communist
regime are perhaps summed up pertinently by Lu Ting-yi, the
Party's foremost educational theorist, in a speech which has much
significance for the future course of education in China. Ideological reforms and controls are the keys to Communist pedagogical
success. Bringing workers and peasants into the higher educational
stream is a monumental change in a traditional pattern. The
"total" integration of practical work and theoretical studies charts
a radical departure from some traditions of Western, non-Marxist
models of education. The role of the Party or the "advanced element in educational circles" is considered a fundamental part of
the educational process, and the Party's contribution to educational direction is considered of unique importance.

Yet the regime recognizes the element of pragmatism and makes
some concessions to experimentalism in education as long as

deviations from the "Marx-Lenin-Mao" general line are not incurred. In gross terms, the Chinese Communist government believes that it has made spectacular advances. Accepting the Chinese government's own figures, an increase in the number of students in higher education from over one hundred thousand students to over one million in a decade is significant, not to mention the three to four million expected to be enrolled in higher education during the next ten years. These expectations have to be tempered and fully weighed against the severe cutbacks in plans for education at the higher levels which occurred between 1960 and 1962. In addition, there is still a drastic shortage of properly prepared teachers in China today, unalleviated by the promotion of primary and secondary teachers to secondary and tertiary positions respectively, without a commensurate upgrading in their skills or preparation periods.[83] In recent years, certainly since 1960, there has been a gradual abandonment of some of the part-time colleges and even of some secondary schools. The emphasis has been on quality instruction rather than on irresponsible, uncoördinated mass education. Yet the regime has to administer the world's largest formal system of education, with an enrollment of over one hundred million primary school pupils and nearly twenty million secondary school students.

The Communist regime has enormous difficulties in educational planning, compounded by the size of the rapidly increasing population and the slow progress in industrialization. But its problems are partially of its own making, as it is handicapped at times by its rigid ideology. Dogmatic, rather than rational, concepts dominate educational thinking, and the ideology of communism dominates all other likely aims of education in China. It is more important to be a trustworthy activist than a competent engineer. When a choice has to be made, political reliability rather than intellectual superiority wins out. Obviously the regime hopes to combine the highest level of technical or academic competence with devotion to the cause of communism. It

83. One of the more comprehensive analyses to date of the training of teachers is to be found in Theodore Chen's *Teacher Training in Communist China* ("Studies in Comparative Education Series," No. OE-14058; Washington, D. C.: United States Office of Education, 1960).

has taken the Communist Party of the Soviet Union something like forty years to achieve this (and even this contention is strongly challenged, both by Western analysts of Soviet Russian society and, more recently, by the Communist Party of China). The schools of Communist China are to be continually integrated within the master grid of overall state planning. The schools and their students are simply an integral part of the comprehensive program for developing a modern China. But the programs of the schools and the specialties of the universities can be quickly jettisoned, if necessary, to suit the ever-changing overall needs of the state. Unfortunately, too many people are involved to achieve this with no more than a modicum of friction. The dogmatism of the Party functionary who forces the pace at the local and intermediate levels of education builds and refocuses resentment against the state. This is only modified if there is a continuing satisfaction of the steadily rising level of educational aspiration. When the increasing demand is not answered satisfactorily, ideological sabotage and intellectual dry rot can quickly set in. The Party attempts to eradicate all such tendencies by a desire to improve the lot of the Chinese masses. A constant thought-reform and indoctrination campaign is waged as a means of perpetual warfare against independent "disorganized" and "ill-regulated" criticism. The problem still remains as to who is being educated by whom and for what purposes.

The final paragraph of Lu Ting-yi's famous speech of April 1960, "Our Schooling System Must Be Reformed," while it is perhaps typical of many Chinese Communist annual summaries of education, contains educational aims of first-class importance. It should not be ignored in ascertaining the regime's attitude towards failure or success in education.

After undergoing ideological reform and after receiving large numbers of new members, our educational personnel have greatly changed their ideological stand and have made much progress. Large numbers of advanced educational personnel have developed skyrocketing work enthusiasm and a high morale. However, it can be understood that a small number of educational personnel may have failed to change themselves completely from the old habit of paying attention only to their private interests to the spirit of bearing in mind only the interests of the society and from their bourgeois education ideology. These personnel are in need of some sympathetic and personal assistance for achieving the change. This is a glorious task to be carried out by the advanced element in educational circles.

We are stepping on a road never traversed by our predecessors. We should step on this road with great courage, because we firmly believe it is the correct road. *However, in spite of our certainty of the success of our program, inasmuch as we are carrying out experiments, we may experience partial and temporary setbacks and even partial failures. For this reason we must not carry out any task in a reckless manner.*[84]

84. [ITALICS ARE MINE. S. F.] See Lu Ting-yi, "Our Schooling System Must Be Reformed" (speech at the second session of the Second National People's Congress), *NCNA*, April 1960 (*CB*, No. 623).

Speeches, Articles, and Documents on Education
from Communist China

Regulations of the Education Department
North China Union University
February 1944

The North China Union University (Lien Ta) was established first in Yenan in 1939, then in the Shensi-Chahar-Hopeh Border Region. After virtually collapsing in 1942, it was reformed in 1944, and after V-J Day it grew rapidly, recruiting many of its students from the Nationalist-held areas. Its three campuses were originally located near Tientsin, Peking, and Kalgan, but because of the civil war were forced to relocate as circumstances required. Ultimately, Lien Ta and Pei Ta Universities were amalgamated to form Hua Pei (North China University), which moved into Peking when that city fell to the Communists. The vicissitudes of war had forced Lien Ta to relocate over much of northwestern China, and its history is of interest, as it was one of the few "institutes of higher learning" successfully operated by the Communists before they came to power in 1949.

QUALITY, DUTIES, AND EDUCATIONAL LINE
OF THE EDUCATION DEPARTMENTS

The character of Lien Ta Education Department is determined as that of a school of cadres. Its responsibility is to raise and cultivate lower- and middle-level cadres for Party, army, government, and people and to train cadres. The raising of the standards of cadres now serving is the main objective. The line of education is to raise the culture of cadres as the main objective. It is also to make a thorough study to serve the needs of building up a new democratic society according to the present environment in the

73

villages behind the enemy lines (carrying on the war and preparing for the counteroffensive). With the principle of intimate unity between theory and practice to cultivate cadres (for the war of resistance) for the work of the construction of a new democratic society, to be the material to serve the masses and having the necessary abilities.

QUALIFICATIONS FOR AND OBJECTIVES IN SETTING UP CLASSES AND PERIODS OF TRAINING

(1) Normal classes should be set up to raise and cultivate qualifications of lower and higher primary school teachers. On the foundation of suitably raising the cultural level, this should do a great deal to give understanding of every kind of policy and law in the Border Region and understanding of the fundamental spirit of new democratic culture as well as of the line of "people manage, public help" education and practical methods of work. The period of training should be established as one and a half years.

(2) Middle-level classes should be set up to raise the level of Party, government, army, and people's cadres, making the raising of culture the main objective and also giving further understanding of the spirit of all sorts of fundamental policies. The period of training should be established as two years.

(3) Political classes should be set up to train and improve the intellectual youth from the cities. The main objectives should be to make them understand all the Border Region policies and to improve their thought. There need be no fixed period of study.

(4) Short-period training classes of a temporary character should be set up, with the main objective of training cadres now serving in the fields of hygiene, economics, coöperative work, accounting, production skills, education, etc. There need be no fixed period of study.

(5) The number of students should, in principle, not exceed six hundred for the time being.

SELECTION OF STUDENTS

To realize the concrete objectives of each class and to guarantee the best results in a comparatively short period, from now on the students selected should have a standard equivalent to the standard of higher primary school. After the plan for receiving students has been drawn up for each term, each leading organization among the Party, government, army, and people should be responsible for selecting students and guaranteeing to send them. The random selection and sending of students should be avoided.

COURSES

Except for the political course and the temporary short-period training courses, the middle-level and normal classes should have the following three main courses:

(a) Study of the reconstruction of the Border Region, including the history and geography of the Border Region, Border Region policies, and Border Region organization.

(b) Training in political thought, including "cheng feng," current affairs, general political knowledge, etc.

(c) Cultural education, including Chinese, mathematics, history, geography, and general knowledge of natural science.

(d) General production knowledge, medical knowledge, military knowledge, etc. The normal classes should also add courses in education.

The relative importance of the different subjects should be different according to the different educational objectives of each class and the different types of students. (Practical decisions should be made about this.) During each year of study, two or three months should be devoted to production.

METHODS OF TEACHING LEADERSHIP

The principles should be: unity of theory and practice, mutual necessity of education and social reconstruction, and coöperation between teacher and student.

(1) Educational methods should be those which arouse interest and not those aimed at forcing knowledge. Every kind of course should make self-study, discussion, and research its main objectives. Such methods as asking for a summing-up report after a lecture should also be used. The democratic spirit of finding out and respecting the general feeling should be developed to make the content of study intimately connected with the students' thought and knowledge. Forcible methods of teaching should be opposed.

(2) This spirit of joining teaching and leadership should use the methods of teaching and leadership which join teaching and doing. Investigation, experiment, lecture, and discussion should be equally important. In principle, the time spent in classes each day should not exceed four hours. If there is some really important work, there should be a plan to organize the students to help and experiment, to make a close connection between teaching and practical activities. The doctrinaire spirit of dead book-learning should be thoroughly corrected.

ARRANGEMENTS FOR ORGANIZATION

The terms, "middle school department" and "normal department," should be eliminated. The college should directly lead each class.

The department under the leadership of the principal should set up an organization office to manage questions of the cadres of the whole school and questions of leadership and teaching. Under it should be a library sub-office, a duplicating sub-office, and a cadres' affairs sub-office, each with two to three people.

There should be a school manager's office to manage all questions of supply and the organization's production. Under this should be a general affairs branch, a production branch, and a medical clinic.

There should be an office secretary and manager, one each, who manage correspondence and telegrams, entertainment, security, communications, and other work.

Every class should have a chairman (besides the teacher) who is responsible for the work of leadership of the education and leadership of the whole class under the leadership of the organization office.

CHOICE OF TEACHERS

Improvement in the quality of teachers is the most important condition for conquering doctrinairism and raising the effectiveness of teaching. The teachers for general cultural courses can be chosen from the present teachers. For reconstruction of the Border Region and political-thought teaching it will be necessary to choose cadres with actual experience to serve as teachers and to ask responsible comrades in all the organizations of the Border Region to give lectures for a certain period on military affairs, governmental reconstruction, medicine and hygiene, engineering, agriculture, and other special questions.

SOURCE: Michael Lindsay, *Notes on Educational Problems in Communist China* (New York: Institute of Pacific Relations, 1950), pp. 112–114.

Yenan University Educational Line and Temporary Regulations
May 1944

Yenan, in Shensi Province, became the headquarters of the Chinese Communist Soviet after the Long March from South China, and for nearly fifteen years it was the "other capital" of China. Communist centers of higher education were established in Yenan for the purpose of training cadres and attracting young intellectuals from all over China. While many students migrated from the coastal regions, which were under Japanese control, to Southwest China, others were drawn to the revolutionary universities of the Northwest and came to Yenan.

The students were taught the "unity of theory and practice" and integration of practical work and theoretical studies, tenets which never failed to be emphasized in Communist higher education during the first decade.

EDUCATIONAL LINE

(1) The object of this school is to cultivate and improve cadres for practical work in political, economic, and cultural reconstruction suited to the needs of the war of resistance and the reconstruction of the Border Region.

(2) This school will carry on education in Chinese revolutionary history and in the present situation to improve the students' knowledge of revolutionary theory and their thought about "new democratic" reconstruction, that is, according to the "people's three revolutionary principles." It will also carry on education in *lebensanschauung* and methods of thought in order to cultivate the students' revolutionary standpoint and a spirit of work based on getting at the facts.

(3) Through the various following forms, the education of this school will be joined up with the practical working departments of the Border Region and all kinds of practical activity in order to raise practical experience to the height of theory and to realize the unity of theory and practice and the correspondence of study and use.

Definite connections in organization or in work should be set up with all departments of the Border Region concerned with practical work. According to the actual circumstances, the responsible people in every department concerned with practical work should directly join in the leadership of the educational work in the respective department of this school.

The policies, directives, and periodic reports of experience of the different phases of Border Region reconstruction should form the main content of the teaching in this school. The technical courses should take as their standard the present needs of Border Region reconstruction.

The research workers of this school should carry on planned and systematic investigation of every kind of practical question in Border Region reconstruction. According to the actual circumstances, they should join for a definite period in the practical work of the respective departments.

The students of this school during their period of study shall be assigned for a definite period to some practical working department for practice.

(4) This school will carry on education combined with production, in order, through organized labor, to cultivate the students' constructive spirit, their habit of labor, and their labor viewpoint.

(5) The foundation of teaching in this school shall be self-study and collective mutual help. Teachers and students should join in study to secure the interpenetration of book learning and practical experience. At the same time, democracy in teaching should be developed in order to encourage the spirit of asking questions in difficulties and of keenness in discussion. The object is to cultivate the ability of independent thought and criticism.

SYSTEMS OF EDUCATION

(1) This school shall consist of a college of administration, a college of natural science, the Lu Hsun art school, and a medical department. Their aim is to produce all types of technical cadres. The college of administration shall be divided into four departments: administration, law, finance and economics, and education. The college of natural sciences shall be divided into three departments: engineering, agriculture, and chemistry. The Lu Hsun art school shall be divided into three departments: drama and music, art, and literature. Each department shall be divided into classes or groups according to the type of study.

Besides this, this school may have all kinds of supplementary training classes according to temporary or special needs.

(2) The periods of study in the various colleges shall be temporarily determined as follows: college of administration, two years; college of natural science, three years; Lu Hsun art school, two years; department of medicine, one to two years. But the periods of study should not be fixed mechanically; what is important is the objective of finishing the study of the prescribed courses.

(3) In the teaching carried on in this school, learning in the school (including lectures, reading, talks, discussion, etc.) and practical work are of equal importance. In the complete period of study, learning in the school should occupy 60 percent, and practice 40 percent. These proportions can be varied by each college according to its actual circumstances.

(4) Both faculty and students of this school must certainly do regular productive labor. The proportion of time spent should be 80 percent for study and 20 percent for production. This production may be increased or decreased for the faculty according to the circumstances of their work.

. . . .

TEACHING METHODS

(1) The first special point in the teaching methods of this school is the alignment of study with use, that is, on the one hand,

study, on the other hand, do. Go from the process of study to action and from the process of action to study. For this reason the faculty of this school and students of sufficient ability should enthusiastically join in every kind of relevant practical work and research into every kind of practical question. In their practical work they should, on the one hand, serve the Border Region and, on the other hand, carry on teaching. To join in practice and to investigate practical questions is one of the main duties of the faculty.

When the students have finished a period of study in the school, they should, in general, then go into the country for three months for practical work, then come back to sum up their experiences, and then do a further stage of study. During this period of study in the school the districts near the school can be used as a field for practical work.

In technical classes practice (or practical experience) is most important.

In the grades and marking of this school, the ability to apply study to use and knowledge to action (with emphasis on realism and willingness to admit mistakes) should be the main standard.

(2) The second special point in the teaching methods of this school is that self-study is more important, and teaching supplementary. On the foundation of self-study, collective mutual help is realized. Mutual study between faculty and students is encouraged. Students of various degrees and various qualifications should be organized for mutual help in study. Teaching should, in general, be carried on in the following ways:

Lectures. The teacher should just teach the main points of the course and emphasize the asking of questions and encourage the research of the students.

Research. Students should carry on research according to the practical materials and under the direction of the teacher and produce memoranda or reports for discussion.

Summing up. When research is finished, the teacher should collect the disputed and difficult points that have arisen in the course of research and explain them in detail, or else he should give a fairly systematic summing-up of the whole course.

(3) The third special point in the teaching methods of this school is the expression of the democratic spirit in teaching. The faculty have freedom of lecturing and of research. Differing ideas can be mutually discussed and mutually criticized. The students can also put forward suggestions and criticisms about the teachers' lectures. In leadership, leadership in thought should be emphasized and every effort made to avoid settling problems by administrative methods.

SOURCE: Michael Lindsay, *Notes on Educational Problems in Communist China* (New York: Institute of Pacific Relations, 1950), pp. 133–139.

Culture and Education Policy
From the Common Program
October 1949

The Common Program of 1949 was the pro tem *constitution of the newly established People's Republic of China. It remained the principal constitutional document of the new regime until a formal one was adopted in 1954.*

CHAPTER V

Article 41. The culture and education of the People's Republic of China are new democratic, that is, national, scientific, and popular. The main tasks for raising the cultural level of the people are: training of personnel for national construction work; liquidating of feudal, comprador, Fascist ideology; and developing of the ideology of serving the people.

Article 42. Love for the fatherland and the people, love of labor, love of science, and the taking-care of public property shall be promoted as the public spirit of all nationals of the People's Republic of China.

Article 43. Efforts shall be made to develop the natural sciences to place them at the service of industrial, agricultural, and national defense construction. Scientific discoveries and inventions shall be encouraged and rewarded, and scientific knowledge shall be popularized.

Article 44. The application of a scientific historical viewpoint to the study and interpretation of history, economics, politics, culture, and international affairs shall be promoted. Outstanding works of social science shall be encouraged and rewarded.

Article 45. Literature and the arts shall be promoted to serve

83

the people, to enlighten the political consciousness of the people, and to encourage the labor enthusiasm of the people. Outstanding works of literature and the arts shall be encouraged and rewarded. The people's drama and cinema shall be developed.

Article 46. The method of education of the People's Government shall reform the old educational system, subject matter, and teaching methods systematically according to plan.

Article 47. In order to meet the widespread needs of revolutionary work and national construction work, universal education shall be carried out. Middle and higher education shall be strengthened; technical education shall be stressed; the education of workers during their spare time and the education of cadres who are at their posts shall be strengthened; and revolutionary political education shall be accorded to young intellectuals and old-style intellectuals in a planned and systematic manner.

Article 48. National sports shall be promoted. Public health and medical work shall be extended, and attention shall be paid to safeguarding the health of mothers, infants, and children.

Article 49. Freedom of reporting true news shall be safeguarded. The utilization of the press to slander, to undermine the interests of the State and the people, and to provoke world war is prohibited. The people's broadcasting work and the people's publication work shall be developed and attention paid to the publishing of popular books and newspapers beneficial to the people.

SOURCE: "The Common Program," *China Digest,* VII, No. 1 (October 1949), 3–9.

See also Liu Shi, "China's New Educational System," *People's China,* IV, No. 11 (December 1, 1951), 5–8.

Education and Culture in New China
By Lu Ting-yi
April 1950

Lu Ting-yi has in this article summarized Chinese Communist educational philosophy and has expressed the regime's general expectations for the next decade. This review is clearly intended for an external audience and for non-Chinese consumption. It is, however, a useful example of an early educational document, though devoid of any real substance or specific details of the first educational reforms which were soon to follow. It has been included in this collection because of its author's importance in the Communist cultural hierarchy. During the 1950s, Lu held the post of chief propagandist for the Communist Party, and by 1960 he had become Vice-Premier of the State Council. His pronouncements on education have been of major importance, and he is today perhaps the leading spokesman of "New China's" educational philosophy.

The great victory of the Chinese Revolution is not only of first-rate significance for the struggle to safeguard world peace, it is also a momentous event for the development of the culture of mankind. One should imagine the effect of the fact that one quarter of the world's population will be liberated from the depths of cultural ignorance and backwardness, that their intelligence and creative power will have an opportunity of developing into a higher level, and that they will play their part in the peaceful and democratic construction of the new world. Is this not a matter of tremendous importance for the development of world civilization and cultural progress?

More than two thousand years of feudal rule and one hundred years of imperialist enslavement have combined to reduce a nation with the oldest culture and history in the world into a nation culturally ignorant and backward, where the intelligence and creative power of the people have been tragically strangled and where it is impossible for a brilliant cultural tradition to develop. But the Chinese people have now stood up. Under the leadership of the political party of the working class, the Communist Party of China, the Chinese people have overthrown the prolonged rule of imperialism and feudalism and have put an end to the dark history of over two thousand years. This is a world-shaking historical event. The Chinese people have built their own country, and they will also build up their own culture. This is completely possible, because once the educational and cultural work is in the hands of the broad toiling masses, there can be no limit to their creative power. This new educational and cultural work of the people not only belongs to China's toiling masses, but it is also an important part of the cultural work of the progressive peoples of the world.

In 1940, Comrade Mao Tse-tung published his famous book, *On New Democracy,* which is the most oustanding work analyzing the history of China's modern culture from the angle of Marxism-Leninism. Comrade Mao Tse-tung in this book predicts the future of Chinese culture. He adds:

In the whole course of Chinese history, the progress made during the twenty years after the May 4th Movement [1919] surpassed not only that of the eighty years before that period but even that of the preceding two thousand years. If another twenty years is allowed, the extent of China's progress could well be imagined.

Yet, in only another ten years' time, the New China as envisaged by Comrade Mao Tse-tung has come into being. Is it not apparent that through the efforts of our people and with the assistance of the progressive peoples of the world, foremost among them the Socialist Soviet Union, China will become one of the most civilized and progressive nations in the world?

THE CHARACTER OF THE CULTURAL MOVEMENT

From the class standpoint and from the standpoint of dialectical relationship between international culture and national culture, Comrade Mao Tse-tung, in the above-mentioned book, has explained the character of China's new cultural movement, its contents and its future, and has refuted all the nonsense uttered by bourgeois idealists and the Trotskyist gang about China's culture. He pointed out that since May 4, 1919, the cultural movement in China has had a New Democratic character. In other words, it has been led by the proletariat and is an anti-imperalist and anti-feudalist culture belonging to the people; and, as such, it is part of the socialist culture of the international proletariat. He defined China's new culture as being national, scientific, and popular in content. That is to say,

it is opposed to the oppression of the imperialists; it maintains the dignity and independence of the Chinese nation; it is linked with the socialist and New Democratic culture of other nations, establishing with them such relations as mutual absorption and mutual development so that each and all may become part of the culture of the new world. . . . It is opposed to all feudalist thoughts and superstitions; it seeks after nothing but facts in the quest of right and wrong; it accepts nothing but the objective truth; and it stands for uniformity in theory and practice. . . . It should serve the interests of the toiling workers and peasants, who constitute over 90 percent of the country's population, so that in time it will become their culture.

These guiding principles, as laid down by Comrade Mao Tse-tung have been clearly embodied in the Common Program adopted by the People's Political Consultative Conference of 1949 and have been written into the concrete policy for building up China's education and culture [see Articles 41 to 49 of the Common Program]. These principles and policy constitute the general directive and general line for educational and cultural development in New China.

After the inauguration of the Central People's Government, which has still to shoulder the great tasks of mopping up the remnants of the enemy and liberating Taiwan and Tibet, the Chinese people are now faced with two important tasks, namely, economic reconstruction and cultural development. When the People's

Political Consultative Conference was in session last year, Comrade Mao Tse-tung predicted that a powerful wave of economic construction would inevitably be followed by a powerful wave of cultural advance. It is a certainty that Comrade Mao Tse-tung's prediction will come true. Nonetheless, if we are to crown our efforts with success, we must of necessity exert gigantic efforts to meet this upsurge of cultural advance. Because of the long years of feudal rule, especially of more than two decades of Fascist Kuomintang tyranny, the toiling masses have hitherto been deprived of their chance of receiving any education, and the overwhelming majority of the people today are illiterate. Cultural and artistic activities had nothing in common with the masses. Research work in natural sciences was so seriously held up that it was virtually dying out. Even the negligible amount of scientific equipment available has been either destroyed or removed by the Kuomintang bandits. As a result, it is in such a deplorable situation and under such difficult conditions that we are going to re-lay the foundations for our education and culture of the New Democracy by counting on the strength of the people.

Face to face with these complex and tremendous tasks, we are proceeding towards two main objectives: first, to shift the cultural and educational work hitherto in the hands of a small number of people onto the basis of the laboring masses; secondly, to make culture and education effectively serve the restoration and development of the production of the country. That is to say, we must successfully link up the popularization and elevation of education and culture and bring about unity in theory and practice. In order to fulfill our tasks, we have to rely on several cardinal conditions: to wit, the correct ideological leadership on the part of the working class and its political party, the support of the broad laboring masses, the consolidation and expansion of the united front of various strata of revolutionary cultural workers, and the assistance and coöperation on the part of international Socialist culture. It must be said that we have already these conditions. We believe that even in the difficult objective circumstances we are capable of carrying on our work with confidence.

.   .   .   .

FOR WORKERS AND PEASANTS

In view of the above-mentioned conditions, the Central People's Government regards the development of education for workers and peasants and the turning out of new intelligentsia from among the workers and peasants as its foremost cultural and educational task. The significance of this is that it is not only meant to meet the cultural demand of today's workers and peasants, it is also meant to pave the way for China's socialist reconstruction of the future. We hope that in seven or ten years, there will appear in China tens of thousands of highly educated persons from the worker and peasant class, playing an indispensable role in China's economic, cultural, and national defense construction, together with the intelligentsia from other social classes who are likewise determined to serve the country, the people, the workers, the peasants, and the soldiers. The Ministry of Education of the Central People's Government plans to set up a Chinese People's University in 1950, the students of which will be workers and peasants. The educational system and the courses offered in this institution will all be on new lines based upon the experiences of the Soviet Union and adapted to the needs of China's economic construction. In this work, we are especially grateful for the great assistance given us by our Soviet friends.

Next, the government is drawing up a plan which provides that beginning in 1950 all educational institutions, factories, and military units throughout the country will help in the popular establishment of three-year short-term middle schools for workers and peasants. Cadres with worker or peasant background, as well as officers and men of the People's Liberation Army, will be offered a chance to finish in three years the basic subjects of middle school by attending such short-term schools. After graduation, they may continue their studies in universities or colleges.

In addition to the above-mentioned measures for opening the school doors to workers, peasants, and soldiers, steps must be taken to change the policy of the past, which was completely divorced from the tasks of national reconstruction. Educational departments must keep in close touch with industrial, agricultural, communication, and financial administrative organs in order to turn out systematically the kind of personnel required by various construction works, to wipe out the phenomenon aptly described as "graduation meaning unemployment," and to assist or guide the various organs to establish senior or junior polytechnical schools to replenish the personnel they need.

REFORMATION OF INTELLECTUALS

To reform the old-time intelligentsia by giving them political education is another part of our work. The people's cultural and educational construction of China requires a common effort on the part of the intelligentsia from all revolutionary social strata.

Old-time intellectuals and technicians must be properly educated so that they may serve the cause of the revolution. The declared policy towards the intelligentsia, as decided by the Central Committee of the Chinese Communist Party, is to win over, unite, educate, and reform them. For this purpose, instructions have been given to inaugurate various short-term political colleges or training classes for helping the intelligentsia to build up a revolutionary outlook on life and an ideology of dialectical materialism and historical materialism. Over 200,000 persons attended such schools in 1949. After having completed their studies, they were assigned to various work. Politics is now being widely and most enthusiastically studied by our people. The study of politics has been regarded as an indispensable part of their daily life by all working cadres, professors, teachers, artists, scientists, and, especially, the young intelligentsia. Their usual curriculum includes the history of the development of society, political economy, the principal works of Marx, Engels, Lenin, and Stalin, and the works of Comrade Mao Tse-tung. Meanwhile, with the same enthusiasm they discussed current events.

The breaking up of their past illusions about American imperialism and of their ignorance regarding the Soviet Union demonstrated that their re-education gave tangible results. The majority of the intelligentsia has come to understand the value of labor, and they themselves are brain workers and as such ought to line up together with workers, peasants, and soldiers. Yearnings for the highly developed science and culture of the Soviet Union have led the Chinese youth and the learned to study the Russian language with enthusiasm. There are many Russian classes in all big cities. And in Peking and Mukden, Russian is being taught on the air. In Peking alone, there are no fewer than seven thousand listeners to the Russian lessons.

Source: Lu Ting-yi, "Education and Culture in New China," *People's China*, I, No. 8 (April 16, 1950), 5–7, 26.

Resolutions of the First National Conference
on Higher Education
July 1950

This conference on education led to the first major steps undertaken by the Chinese Communist government in drawing up nationwide plans for the regulation and control of higher education. The two resolutions below indicate clearly the role of the state and the Ministry of Education in relation to the administration and enforcement of curricula in institutions of higher learning.

RESOLUTIONS CONCERNING THE LEADERSHIP OF

INSTITUTIONS OF HIGHER LEARNING

This act was passed on July 28, 1950, at the forty-third administrative meeting of the State Administrative Council.

In principle, all of China's institutions of higher learning are uniformly under the leadership of the Ministry of Education of the Central People's Government. However, in order that higher education may more effectively serve the country, the simplification of administrative procedures, facilitation of the school work, and the relationships in higher leadership are to be as follows:

Article 1. The Ministry of Education has the responsibility for leadership for all the higher institutions of the nation (except military schools). The Education Departments of the various People's governments and the Departments of Education and Culture of the Military and Political Committee of the various administrative districts have the responsibility of leadership in the higher institutions within their respective districts.

(a) All the higher institutions of the nation are expected to carry out the decisions made by the Ministry of Education regarding supervision, policy, and system; laws and regulations; instructions in the principles of educational affairs; the establishment, change, or closing-down of higher institutions; the appointment and dismissal of presidents of a university or professional college or the principal of a professional school; teacher-remuneration and student allowance; and school-expenditure standards. In cases of expediency, because of special conditions in a certain district or school, the decisions may be made and examined by the Education Department of the administrative district and submitted to the Ministry of Education for approval.

(b) The Ministry of Education, in order to understand the actual situation, studies the problems and sums up experiences and may ask a certain school to submit directly a special report. The Education Departments of the various administrative districts have the same authority over the higher institutions within their respective districts.

(c) Before nationwide plans are made by the Ministry of Education for the reconstruction of higher education and for the distribution of subsidies for higher education, the Education Departments in the various administrative districts are responsible for making these plans for their respective districts and submitting them to the Ministry of Education for approval.

Article 2. The institutions of higher learning in the North China District, except those which are already subject to the leadership of the provincial governments, are under the leadership of the Ministry of Education. The institutions of higher learning in the other administrative districts are temporarily under the direct leadership of the Education Departments of the various districts as authorized by the Ministry of Education. The Ministry of Education shall systematically take over the direct leadership of those higher institutions according to plan, when conditions allow. The higher institutions in the various areas must stay in close association with the local, provincial, or municipal People's governments; these governments are expected to give active assistance to the local higher institutions in connection with students' political study, field trips, practical work, school policies, and general personnel affairs.

Article 3. Universities which are comprehensive in nature and professional colleges which are connected to several establishments of the government or industry are under the leadership of the Ministry of Education or the Education Department of the various administrative districts. As to professional education, field trips, and practical work, the Ministry of Education must keep in close association with the various related establishments of the government or industry in consultation and operation; these establishments are expected to be actively responsible for substantial assistance and guidance of the students. In those institutions which are related to a single establishment of the government or industry or directly connected to a single establishment, the affairs of ordinary administration, teaching staff arrangements, equipment, and financial management are subject to the direct leadership of the related departments in the Central People's Government, the People's Governments of the administrative districts, or the Military and Political Committee. In those related establishments of the government or industry, personnel and offices must be set up for education and be responsible for carrying out the aforesaid leadership duties. But in addition, they must also carry out the regulations under Article 1 of this resolution.

Article 4. According to the above principles, if it is necessary to make changes in the relations of higher institution leadership, a plan, systematic steps, and careful preparation shall be laid out for the change, and all parties concerned shall be properly consulted before the change is made by order of the Ministry of Education.

Article 5. These resolutions are to be promulgated for enforcement by the State Administrative Council of the Central People's Government.

RESOLUTIONS ON THE ENFORCEMENT OF CURRICULUM REFORM IN THE INSTITUTIONS OF HIGHER LEARNING

Article 1. According to the cultural and educational policy of the Common Program of the Chinese People's Political Consultative Conference, the aim of the institutions of higher learning of the People's Republic of China is to educate workers for national construction who will have a higher cultural level, will possess modern scientific and technical accomplishments, and will serve wholeheartedly the people, by means of the teaching method known as "the unity of theory and practice."

Article 2. A majority of the curricula in the existing higher institutions are still not "new democratic"—that is, not national, scientific, and popular, and not in conformity with the needs of new China's reconstruction work; therefore, the curriculum-reform of the higher institutions throughout the nation must be planned and systematically carried out according to Article 46 of the Common Program, in order to obtain the unity of theory and practice.

Article 3. All the higher institutions of the nation, according to Articles 41 and 47 of the Common Program, must abolish politically reactionary curricula and offer "new democratic" revolutionary curricula, in order to eliminate feudalistic, comprador, and Fascist ideas and to develop the ideal of serving the people.

Article 4. Institutions of higher learning shall take each department as an instructional unit in educating professional personnel. The curriculum in each department must be so arranged as to conform to the immediate and long-term needs of national economic, political, defense, and cultural reconstruction. It must also enforce proper specialization on the basis of systematic theoretical knowledge. According to the principle of curriculum simplification, the necessary and important curricula must be emphatically organized and strengthened; duplication and unnecessary curricula and their concepts must be deleted; at the same time, the interrelationship and connection between various courses must be carefully worked out.

Article 5. In order to strengthen the unity of theory and practice, a close association between the higher institutions, on the one hand, and the professional departments of the governments and their affiliated establishments and organizations, on the other, must be set up. Teachers in institutions of higher learning must conform to the work, production, and scientific study of said departments; they must organize field trips and practical work for the students in a planned manner and consider these field trips and practical work as an important part of their teaching. To educate national reconstruction workers effectively, the professional departments of the government must give assistance through the Ministry of Education to the higher institutions in the matters of teaching, practice, and study and must consider these matters a part of the make-up of their own operation; they should share the responsibility for leadership of the students doing practical work with the Ministry of Education.

Article 6. Because of the need to produce a large number of reconstruction workers, the various higher institutions, taking into consideration the essential conditions, and under the leadership of the Ministry of Education, must assist the departments of reconstruction work and consult with these related departments in opening professional courses, training classes, or correspondence classes offering proper curricula.

Article 7. The period of study in the various departments of the higher institutions must be stipulated, with three to five years as a basis. In principle, the actual time spent in class instruction each semester is seventeen weeks; the actual time spent by the students in learning (including independent study and experiment) is forty-four hours, with a maximum of no more than fifty hours; the time spent in extracurricular activities in a week is limited to six hours.

Article 8. The raising of the quantity and quality of the teaching staff and the training of new teachers are crucial in enforcing curriculum reform. Therefore, teachers in the higher institutions of the nation must make efforts to strengthen their own political study, professional study, and research work; and must organize themselves in "groups of teaching, study, and guidance" for the improvement of instructional method and content, by helping each other. The work of the research departments or the research institutes in the higher institutions must be strengthened in a systematic and planned manner; these institutions must be the principal location for educating the teaching staff of the nation's institutions of higher learning. Work and guidance for the assistant instructors in colleges and for graduate students must be strengthened, so as to encourage them to have a spirit of active study and research and to educate them to become good teachers in New China's institutions of higher learning.

Article 9. The compiling of teaching materials suitable in scientific viewpoints and methods for use in New China's higher institutions is an essential condition of the enforcement of curriculum reform. Therefore, under the leadership of the Ministry of Education, a committee shall be set up for the compilation and examination of teaching materials in higher institutions. On the basis of the spirit indicated in Articles 41, 42, 43, 44, 45, 46, and 47 of the Common Program, plans shall be made to translate systematically and to edit various suitable teaching materials and reference books. Hereafter, the teaching materials of several departments and courses shall be written in the Chinese language, except those of the foreign language departments and courses.

Article 10. All higher institutions of the nation shall make drafts of curricula and teaching plans in accordance with the above principles, with reference to the various curriculum drafts discussed in the First National Conference on Higher Education and in consideration of the actual conditions of the respective institutions, and then submit the drafts to the Ministry of Education for approval.

Article 11. These resolutions will be promulgated for enforcement after they have been submitted by the Ministry of Education to the State Administrative Council for approval.

SOURCE: *People's Education,* I, No. 5 (September 1950), 67–68. Translated by Hung Fan Wang and cited by him in "Higher Education in Communist China," unpublished M.A. thesis, University of Washington, 1953.

The Disposal of American-Subsidized Schools Is the Foremost Task on the Cultural Front Now

By Tseng Chao-lun

February 1951

Tseng Chao-lun was Vice-Minister of Education when he issued this statement in February 1951. He had earlier, since December 1950, filled the position of Director of Higher Education in the Central Ministry of Education. A scientist, prominent atomic physicist, and onetime professor of chemistry at Peking University, Tseng was also well known for his political activities as a member of the Democratic League. His attack on "foreign colleges" culminated the regime's campaign to do away with private institutions in China. Like many others who had been educated overseas (Massachusetts Institute of Technology), he found it necessary to join in the diatribe against "American cultural aggression." The Korean War and the "resist America" campaign undoubtedly gave the government "just" cause to terminate the religious and foreign colleges and thus put to an end one of the "offensive anachronisms" inherited from the previous regime.

For the past hundred years, American imperialism has not only been carrying out the most blatant sort of military, political, and economic aggression against us, but, what is far more pernicious, it has always employed a small part of the spoils derived from the Chinese people for the establishment of missionary schools in China in order to carry out cultural aggression in conformity with the statement that "it is more dependable to further trade by spiritual means than by the military banner" (as contained in a memorandum addressed by President James of the University of

98

Illinois to President Theodore Roosevelt). In these schools, American imperialist elements used to exercise absolute control over the school administration, either in the open or by devious means, in an attempt to achieve the spiritual enslavement of Chinese children and youths through the dissemination of poisonous pro-America, revere-America, and fear-America sentiments; further to ally themselves with the Chiang bandits to harm and persecute progressive teachers and students; and even to make use of the school as camouflage to engage in espionage activities against the interests of the Chinese people. All these facts have been thoroughly exposed to the eyes of the world through the Chinese people's "resist U. S. and "aid Korea" movement, together with the movement, staged by the entire body of students and personnel of American-subsidized institutions of higher education, against the slanders of Warren Austin. With the truth of the so-called "traditional American friendship for China" thus exposed by the people, nobody shall further be made the dupe of such nonsense.

On being frustrated in its bloody attempt at aggression against China, American imperialism forthwith resorted to freezing the Chinese people's funds and property in America in an effort to create difficulties for the educational activities of the People's Government and to threaten the livelihood of the students and personnel of missionary schools. But the mighty people of China shall never be cowed by such a paltry trick. In conformity to the wish of the whole nation, the Government Administration Council of our Central People's Government promulgated the "Decision on the Policy of Dealing with American-subsidized Cultural, Educational, and Relief Institutions and Religious Bodies" so as to rally the people of the country in a determined effort to eradicate all traces of American imperialist influences of cultural aggression from China.

In the wake of the string of military and diplomatic victories scored by the Chinese people, the above should be taken as another of our important political tasks.

With a view to carrying out the decision of the Government Administration Council correctly and making a success of the important work of recovering our sovereignty, it is my belief that the teachers and students of American-subsidized schools should first of all consider the campaign as a political struggle against American imperialism. During this struggle, it behooves us to realize to the full that American imperialism is our deadly enemy, and it is up to us to sever all relations with it, not only financially but ideologically as well. Only thus shall we be able to stand firmly on the side of the Chinese people, to distinguish between our friends and foes, and to give the American imperialists no opening.

Apparently, in refusing to take their defeat lying down, the American imperialists will leave no stone unturned in the attempt to sow dissension by bribery or threat. When the conference on foreign-subsidized institutions of higher education was convened by the Ministry of Education on January 16, 1951, the United Board for Christian Colleges in China in New York cabled various university presidents concerned expressing the wish for them to proceed to Hongkong in February for consultations on the matter of funds. This obvious attempt to sabotage the Government Administration Council's decision by bribery has already been exposed. This is but one example—and depend upon it—the American imperialists will exhaust all possible means to carry out their conspiracy. However, provided that we are able to stand resolutely by the side of the people and embrace the principle of "to remain unmoved in spite of riches, poverty, or force," no intrigue on the part of the American imperialists will be of any avail.

Our fatherland is expecting much of us, and we should resolutely sever all relations with American imperialism to remain true to the glorious tradition of the Chinese people.

In the course of dealing with American-subsidized schools, it is imperative for us to consolidate and develop the anti-America patriotic outlook. Without a single exception, the "resist U. S. and aid Korea" movement should be well promoted in all these schools in order to expose the crimes of American imperialist cultural aggression, to raise the students' understanding of the aggressive nature of American imperialism, and to increase their hatred against the American imperialists. In the past, this movement scored successes throughout the country in the initial establishment of sentiments of hatred, scorn, and disdain for American imperialism amongst the students and personnel of American-subsidized schools. For instance, the labor union of Yenching University, while conducting discussions on ways and means of gaining a true understanding of John Leighton Stuart, succeeded in establishing, through irrefutable facts, that Stuart is the agent of American imperialist aggression in China. Similarly, Nanking University exposed their former President Ferguson's criminal attempt to ally himself with the feudalistic force of the Manchu dynasty in the persecution of Chinese revolutionaries. Hwa Chung University brought charges against Margaret Sheets for the dissemination of pro-America and revere-America sentiments and for slandering the Chinese people. These irrefutable facts are further proof of the truth of the statement made by James and will serve to rectify the views of those who still harbor certain illusions about American imperialism. Nevertheless our efforts are still insufficient, and it is up to us to exert ourselves further.

At the same time, we should emphasize the systematic implementation of education on patriotism, not in political classes alone but in all phases of pedagogical activities, so as to enable our youths to realize that the Chinese people are known in the world for their diligence and bravery and that they love freedom and are in possession of both a revolutionary tradition and a glorious history; and to understand the importance of the People's Republic of China in the entire world and in the world's democratic camp of peace. Thus shall Chinese youths be led to love their fatherland, love the people, support the Central People's Government, support Chairman Mao, eradicate their mistaken blind respect for Europe and America, rectify their sentiments of inferiority, establish their self-respect and self-confidence, and become active members for the reconstruction of New China.

Provided with a clear aim of struggle, it will then be possible to consolidate and extend, on the basis of our anti-imperialist and patriotic outlook, the anti-imperialist united front, so as to rally all patriotic teachers, students, and working personnel under one banner in order to increase our strength and to isolate and defeat our enemies.

In view of the historical background of American-subsidized schools, it is necessary to emphasize the union between Christians and non-Christians. On the part of the Christians, there can obviously be no contradiction between loving our own country and opposing American imperialism and our religious convictions. Historically, the glorious patriotic deeds of the famous Catholics, Paul Hsu and Ma Hsiang-po, are still in our memory, and at the moment we have further examples of the self-sufficiency, self-government, and independent propagation-of-faith movement of the Catholic Church. All these are definite proof that it is only by freeing ourselves from imperialist shackles that there can be true religious freedom, that our churches will be prevented from being turned by the imperialists into their bloody implements of aggression against China and that our patriotic spirit will be given full play in conformity to the wishes of the people. On the part of non-Christians, it is up to them to abide strictly by the stipulations of the Common Program to respect and unite with the Christians as well as to assist them in their patriotic movement in a joint effort to eradicate all traces of American imperialist cultural aggression.

It can thus be seen that the work of dealing with American-subsidized schools is not a simple administrative job, nor a matter of funds, but a most important political undertaking.

In these schools certain students in their anxiety may clamor to have their schools turned into state institutions, and certain directors of school boards and administrative personnel may wish to remain in private institutions. These opinions, if truly based on the interests of the people's educational enterprises, are all above reproach. But the key to the whole problem obviously does not lie in the question of whether the institutions should be state-owned or privately operated but rather in the attempt to gain a victory in the cultural front by defeating the American imperialists' efforts to intimidate us.

No matter whether these institutions are to be operated by the state or by private individuals or organizations as schools established by the Chinese people, the fact remains that they have finally been returned to the fold of the fatherland to become true educational institutions of the people. I am absolutely sure that the People's Government will accord them the same love and care it gives to all other schools, as well as giving them all possible assistance, not only for the maintenance of these schools but further for their future development and improvement.

Under the leadership of Chairman Mao, the Chinese people are absolutely invincible. Let us put our shoulders together to put a final, complete, and lasting end to over a hundred years of American imperialist cultural aggression against the people of China and write a new page of glory in the educational annals of the new China.

SOURCE: *Current Background,* No. 107 (Hong Kong: United States Consulate General, August 15, 1951). Originally published in *Hsin Kuan Ch'a,* February 10, 1951.

U. S. Imperialist Cultural Aggression as Seen in Yenching University

By Lu Chih-wei

February 1951

During 1951–52, the regime concentrated on the rectification of "undesirable elements" in higher education—namely, the "foreign-controlled private" colleges and the "foreign-educated and politically backward" professors. Both elements were slated for removal or reform, and the private institutions of higher education were totally eliminated by 1952. The regime believed that this signaled "the end of aggression by foreign elements against Chinese education."

Yenching University in Peking was one of the leading private universities in China and since its founding in 1919 had attracted a faculty of international repute. The campaign against foreign institutions, especially American and religious colleges, built up in intensity during the early part of 1951, and on February 12, Yenching was taken over by the Ministry of Education.

Lu Chi-wei was President of Yenching University, having assumed his post in April 1949, shortly after the capture of Peking by Chinese Communist forces. His confession of cultural crimes against the University and its student body is reproduced here in part. It represents only one side of the picture, and the student rallies that followed his removal from office give a fuller account. It was made complete when his own daughter, Lu Yao-hua, denounced him at a student rally in March 1952.

It is rather difficult to relate in a short article how Yenching University has suffered in the past from the effects of American imperialism. My students, Kung Li-chia and Lu Nien-kao, have already written a fairly complete report, which appeared in the January 24, 1951, issue of *Hsin Min Pao*. Young men, not so encumbered with the old as I am, see things more clearly than I do in certain aspects. In that report numerous instances of cultural aggression were cited for the readers' reference. I shall make no further accusation here, as I believe my self-criticism is not thorough enough. For the many personal grievances, some concerning my own interests or the matter of "face" of the intelligentsia in the old society, which is irrelevant to the national stand, I dare not blame imperialism. However, I am definitely no "yes" man; I have never stooped to the Americans nor have I ever in the least doubted that the Chinese people are an elite race. I am only stubborn, being unable to connect my own distress with the people's, and therefore I fail to see through the danger of American imperialist cultural aggression to the Chinese people. I despise but do not hate U. S. imperialism, just because I never hate anybody of any class. A scholar's training teaches me not to rave at people. This means I am still backward in political ideas.

The Americans I have met are of many types, but nine out of ten are low in political level and can very easily be made tools of the reactionary influence. Many missionaries to China have been tools of aggression throughout their whole lives without realizing it. Some are truly secret agents, large or small, while others are not so. From their upbringing, it is difficult to find why none of Yenching's American teachers is completely in sympathy with the Chinese revolution. But to be fair, Leighton Stuart thirty years ago was not entirely a secret agent accomplice of the State Department.

The history of the development of Yenching is virtually a record of Leighton Stuart's gradual collaboration with the reactionary influences. Yenching was established in 1919, just after World War I, through which America suddenly got rich. At that time, Stuart was merely a capable missionary. He was made President of Yenching after he had left his post as professor in the Nanking Seminary. He began his relations with the reactionary clique and a few years later became successful in getting American contributions for Yenching. In 1926, Yenching moved to a new site, absorbed a large number of students of fairly high cultural level, who had returned from America, and virtually became an institute of reputation. (I joined Yenching at that time, before which I was a "noted professor" of a certain national university. To say that I am not a patriot, I will not admit. But I admit I do not quite understand the world situation, although I came into contact with Marxism-Leninism as far back as 1918 and quite admired the revolution of the proletarian class.) Yenching owed its funds mostly to the contributions of the middle-class after the war. Some donated a building, others scientific apparatus and books. The largest amount of donations by big capitalists was the half-million U. S. dollars donated by the Oil King [Rockefeller] as the funds of the College of Science, as Yenching had been commissioned to open a premedical course for the Peking Union Medical College [a Rockefeller-endowed institute]. Other funds came later, such as those for the Harvard-Yenching Institute, supported by the annual contribution of sixty to seventy thousand dollars to the College of Political Science from the daughter of the Oil King. Since that time, Stuart established his relations with the U. S. State Department but still remained unknown in the political arena. Being a Democrat himself, he was unable to get close to the Republicans. He left no stone unturned to get donations in China. His relations with the Peiyang warlords and Chang Tso-lin were close.

The Kuomintang's victory in the Northern Expedition brought Yenching to a new situation. Relations with the new officials had to begin anew. Shortly afterwards, the 1929 American crash ensued, and this dealt a serious blow to Yenching. The large but empty shell faced the threat of imminent collapse, and Stuart had a real time of it. Ho Lien (Franklin L. Ho) of Nankai University, James Y. C. Yen of the Mass Education Movement, and Stuart all wrangled for donations from the Oil King. Short of hands, Stuart asked me to help, but I was no good at wrestling. At his wit's end, Stuart suggested to Yenching's Chinese authorities to ask James Yen to be the President, which almost brought Yenching to an end. However, Stuart was quite resourceful, and his popularity with the Kuomintang suddenly increased that time. As an old China hand, his reputation in American political circles also rose. As to how he managed upon Japanese occupation of Peking to travel between Washington and Chungking, how he was put into prison for three years by the Japanese, how he manipulated the old Political Consultative Conference, and how later he openly conducted aggression work, I had better leave alone, as I, a bookworm, do not know the inside story.

To tell of U. S. imperialist cultural aggression in Yenching, I have to begin with how I came to join Yenching's administration. In 1933, when Wu Lei-chuan suddenly resigned from his presidency as a result of conflict with Stuart, internal discord prevailed, and it was necessary to get some "pure" but incompetent person to be the figurehead. Upon repeated requests, I, allegedly respected by all, had no alternative but to promise a three-month provisional service. In the summer of that year, I left Yenching for America to do a year's research work. Dr. Chou Yi-chun then became the formal President, only to find himself unable to get along with Stuart not long afterward. In the spring of 1934, Stuart had everything set for me to resume the title of Acting President upon my return in the fall. As I had no liking for the presidency, it would be to the convenience of all for me to assume the title. I was known to be stubborn but not interested in administrative work, and could therefore easily be deceived. Surprisingly enough, I really behaved like a president, and looked into matters I was not asked to, especially those about the Americans. I remained for two years as the "real President" until June 1937, when I definitely decided to quit the post. Several weeks afterwards, the Japanese entered Peking, and the problem solved itself with Stuart as the President both in name and fact.

During my tenure of office, things which happened might explain how different was the U.S. cultural aggression in Yenching. The Chinese in missionary schools look at U.S. cultural aggression differently but mainly in two ways: (1) the Americans carry out directly political and economic aggression under the cover of cultural and educational affairs, and (2) they create the opportunities for Americans to teach in missionary schools and thus promote the

American way of life. In Yenching there were seen both of these strategies, especially the latter. Putting trivial things aside, take the University's administrative power for instance. The power of ratification of the budget estimate, of course, rests with New York, and the budget is drawn up as designated by various sinking funds and donations. Once passed, the budget cannot be altered by anyone in the University, including foreigners, even by Stuart himself. The treasurers of missionary schools are usually foreigners. For years, Yenching's treasurer had been a foreigner who knew nothing about accounting but was a rather arrogant spinster. She got on my nerves, and I had to dismiss her. She left for the States. On the surface, it seems the Chinese were quite influential in administrative affairs, but one year later, Stuart told me that she was wanted by the Women's College. The so-called "Women's College" comprised both foreigners and Chinese and the then head of the College was on very bad terms with Stuart. Here I had to take into consideration the internal "conflict of imperialism." Furthermore, in the several years I spent in America, I learned the way the "civilized people" respect "women's rights." So I agreed to the return to Yenching of this spinster, on the condition that she repent. Verily she behaved upon return. On second thought, I realized what a great failure it was on my part. It was an imperialist aggression against me. I accepted the American way of life without realizing it. I cite this instance just to illustrate the complex nature of the internal situation in Yenching, which has so many hidden springs. Any Chinese with backbone need not fear the foreigners, nor need he flatter the foreigners. Highhandedness and kowtowing are not sins of which people in Yenching are guilty, but the real problem lies with what Acheson and Austin call the "American way of life." The way of life is naturally varied. Some unconsciously made his daily life Americanized, but I personally do not consider it anything serious, though other Yenching people are rather skeptical about it, as they believe trifles reflect upon things important. For instance, the use of half Chinese and half English in speech can be considered as a foreignized way of life. People who speak in this manner never learn to speak foreign languages well. Although they actually may not expect to get anything out of it, they gradually and naturally form such habits. I despise them, but, frankly speaking, this sort of people are not uncommon in public schools either. In Yenching, one cannot say that such people are exactly slaves to foreigners. Around the Americans here are numerous small cliques, the most conspicuous of which may be called the "Stuart clique," the nucleus of which may be called the "my-dear-Stuart clique." Almost every American has a group of his followers who form the outer ring of the "Stuart clique." Stuart sometimes became very elated in his chats with me, and he once said, "People all call me Leighton. Why don't you?" During the past twenty-five years, he always called me "C.W.," and I called him "Dr. Stuart." To be frank, this might be the stubbornness I had hatched in the old feudal society and in no way represent any accuracy of political concept.

Let me mention one more difficult job I was up against. An American professor, not now in China, was known as a progressive. He was on very good terms with the progressive students. Foreigners called him the "red professor." When he left last year, he said, "You just see, in the not-too-distant future, the Chinese would take me as a secret agent." Later, in the anti-U.S. and aid-Korea discussion forums, some students criticized him. This not only made it difficult for me to handle but made me feel very bad. But Americans are Americans. Upon his return to America, he would have to wrestle with a frenzied aggressive situation. Even the American Communists' working methods are not the same as those of the Chinese Communists. I mention this because in 1951 we will push the anti-American imperialist movement and strictly enforce education on patriotism. We should be vigilant, especially since the Ministry of Education directed us to differentiate between our enemy and friend and between American imperialists and Americans. In principle and in stand it is absolutely clear, and in the matter of how to distinguish between American imperialists and Americans, we Yenching people are not without experience. The only way to avoid mistakes is by coöperation between students and teachers through the weapon of criticism and self-criticism.

Here, I must pay my tribute to the guidance and leadership of Yenching Students' Union, the Party organ, and the students. I feel they will not doubt my innocence and patriotism. But in revolutionary enterprises I am really a child. Since I have promised the People's Government to carry on the administration, I will strive to learn. While I have always refused to be president of any missionary school, despite repeated requests, I shall this time assume administrative responsibilities as I dare not reject any title Chairman Mao gives me, even though research work is alluring me with ever-greater attraction. In the past, Yenching's contribution to the revolution was made by the students, but in the future both students and teachers will have their definite part to play. Up to now we have had to depend upon America financially and ideologically, but in the future we will definitely sever our financial relations with America, although the thin thread of thought still connecting cannot be completely cut all at once. However, this is a problem common to all educational circles, concerning not just missionary schools alone and especially Yenching. Our "origins" are not so good, and this will perhaps make the reform of our thought all the more difficult. Only by redoubled efforts can we make a more rapid progress than others. We must clear out, with the greatest determination, the influence of American imperialist cultural aggression in China.

SOURCE: *Current Background,* No. 107 (Hong Kong: United States Consulate General, August 15, 1951). Originally published in *Hsin Kuan Ch'a,* February 10, 1951.

For additional readings, see Chiang Yin-en, "Yenching—the Rebirth of a University," *People's China,* III, No. 10 (May 16, 1951), 19–20.

Two Years of Advance in People's Education
By Liu Shih
October 1951

October 1, 1951 is the second anniversary of the founding of the People's Republic of China. In the past two years our country and our people have won great victories and made rapid progress. With the victory of the Chinese revolution and the ensuing basic changes in political and economic life, there have been notable advances in the field of people's education. China is, in fact, today experiencing a great educational revolution, embracing over 475,-000,000 people.

The imperialists called the old China a backward country without culture. For over a century the working people of China, oppressed by imperialism and feudalism, were deprived of the right to culture and education. Even their right to live was challenged. The old educational system, built on semifeudal and semicolonial lines, had nothing to do with the working people. It served only the landlords and the bourgeoisie. Others who were kept outside the school gates regarded the schools with hostility and disdain, sarcastically labeling them "foreign halls of learning."

The term "foreign halls of learning" exposes clearly the semicolonial nature of this type of educational institution. As the political and economic life of our country was semicolonial in nature, the national industries of China, of course, had no chance to develop. All a semifeudal and semicolonial country needs is a few agents to control and rule the people. There is no place or need for a large number of people with scientific training and constructive talent. Indeed, the reactionary regime regarded the raising of the cultural standard of the people as a burden and a threat to its existence.

Consequently, though the old China had talked about public education for over fifty years, statistics on the eve of liberation

111

showed that more than 85 percent of the people were illiterate and less than 40 percent of the school-age children were at school. Secondary schools and universities, even more than the lower schools, existed for the benefit of the few. In the semicolonial society of the old China, the colleges and universities actually became mere preparatory schools for students planning to study abroad in Britain, America, or elsewhere. The imperialists, moreover, established their own schools in our country—colleges, secondary schools and even primary schools—the more effectively to carry out their cultural aggression against China.

Sons and daughters of many wealthy families went abroad to study after graduating from college in China. When they returned home, what little scientific training they had acquired was of very little use to the people. It qualified them only to become officials. Educational institutions above secondary school level were very few; but even so, graduates faced unemployment. As to the nature of education provided by the reactionary Kuomintang in pre-liberation days, it was feudal and Fascist. The children and youth of China had no freedom in these schools.

The roots of education for the people, however, go back to the period of the revolution of 1927. The peasants established their own schools. From 1927 until liberation, there were in fact two Chinas. One was ruled by the Kuomintang, and the other was the people's China (the various revolutionary bases during the different revolutionary periods). Thus, there were also two types of education; one was semifeudal and semicolonial, and the other was for the people.

During more than twenty years in the Chinese people's revolutionary bases, a great deal was accomplished. Archaic traditions and the outmoded system of oldstyle Chinese education were eliminated, and an independent and new type of education geared to wartime conditions and serving the revolution was introduced. The chief characteristic of this new type of education was that it belonged to the working people and served their interests. It was the system of education which Comrade Mao Tse-tung describes in his *New Democracy* as "national, scientific, and popular." It gradually grew in strength over the more than twenty years when the flames of war swept our country. It produced tens of thousands of cadres for revolutionary work. Raising the political consciousness of millions of people, it accumulated rich experiences in its own field and stood in shining contrast to the old, decadent education in Kuomintang areas which worked against the interests of the people.

Only with the liberation of the entire mainland was it possible to carry out an educational revolution on a nationwide scale. Schools in both the countryside and cities, liberated from Kuomintang control, required a thorough housecleaning and reorientation. The schools in the revolutionary bases (known as the old liberated areas) also required changes; wartime education had to be transformed into normal education based on a regular system. New China has an urgent need for millions of people with constructive talents. The working people themselves, politically and economically liberated, called for educational facilities, and so did their sons and daughters. The old type of intellectuals wanted to be re-educated. The People's Republic of China called for a thorough revolution in education. With the founding of the People's Republic, this great and difficult task in the field of culture and education was entrusted to the Ministry of Education.

In the past two years, with Mao Tse-tung's teachings as a guide, and in accordance with the Common Programs of the Chinese People's Political Consultative Conference, the initial stages in the program for developing a people's educational system have been completed. This work is very complicated. But, with the educational path mapped out by Mao Tse-tung, with more than twenty years of experience in education in the revolutionary bases, and with the aid of the Soviet Union's advanced educational experiences and the help of Soviet educators, we are going forward with great strides.

In December 1949, less than two months after the Ministry of Education was set up, the first national educational conference was convened. Policy for education on a national scale was formulated. Emphasis was laid on the requirement that education must serve the construction needs of China and that schools should be open to workers and peasants. New directions were set for education which had formerly been divorced from national construction and been basically against the interests of the people. This change was of fundamental importance. This conference also outlined a policy for the reformation of the old educational system and the various steps which must be taken.

During the past two years the Ministry of Education of the Central People's Government has convened many other important conferences, such as the national conference on higher education, the national conference on workers' and peasants' education, the national conference on primary and normal education, the national conference on education of national minorities, etc.

In line with the general direction of our national education, resolutions were passed detailing directions and systems for the various levels and types of education, so that all schools could proceed step by step along the new path of reorientation and development. At these conferences, the Ministry of Education called together specialists on various subjects from all over the country. Experts and educators actively participated in the discussion, and resolutions were passed on many important and complicated problems. At present, more than a million educational workers of various levels are working wholeheartedly to carry out the Ministry's directives.

, ...

The educational workers of China take pride in their accomplishments in the service of the people. In the past fifty years no one ever dreamed that these accomplishments were possible. Today they see with their own eyes that education, once it unites with the revolution and with national construction, plays a tremendous role in the consolidation of the people's democratic dictatorship. In two brief years the prospect of unemployment after graduation from college and secondary school has been swept away. Graduates happily accept government assignments that provide for their most useful employment in national construction. Indeed, in the admission of new students, the colleges now face the problem of insufficient candidates, for the demand for secondary school graduates is great.

After land distribution, peasant parents, their eyes shining proudly, lead their children to schools and demand admission for the youngsters. Many primary schools are packed and cannot admit all the applicants. Emancipated peasants on their own initiative organize new schools in large numbers. This thirst of the people for education inspires the teachers and makes them realize both the bright future ahead in the field of people's education and the glory attached to being people's teachers.

To meet the demands of these new conditions, the Government Administration Council of the Central People's Government, on August 10, 1951, passed resolutions on the reform of the school system and set in motion the new school system for the first stage of the People's Republic of China. This new system will guarantee that all working people and their children have the opportunity to enjoy educational facilities, thus enabling the country to cultivate more effectively every type of constructive talent from among the people.

SOURCE: Liu Shih, "Two Years of Advance in People's Education," *People's China,* IV, No. 7 (October 1951), 32–34.

For additional reading, see Yu Chi-tung, "Three Years of Cultural and Educational Work in New China," *People's China,* V, No. 18 (September 1952), 29–35.

Political Study Movement of the Faculty of Peking University

By Ma Yin-ch'u

October 1951

The importance of President Ma's speech lies in its significance for the intellectuals who in 1951–52 were to have their "minds reformed and ideology corrected." September 1951 saw the "ideological remolding movement" launched, with Premier Chou En-lai delivering the keynote speech to more than three thousand teachers in twenty institutions of higher learning of the Tientsin-Peking area. The theme was the reform of the intellectuals, the abandonment of bourgeois ideas in education, and the refutation of American pedagogical practices. Ma has indicated below how important it was for the professors to "sacrifice individual freedom for collective interests." The performance of the intellectuals at Peking University became a model for other institutes of higher education. The "brainwashing" of the professors left them cowed and submissive. It was merely one phase of the overall plan to "adjust, dismember, and reconstitute" China's colleges and universities according to the "needs of national construction."

On June 1, 1951, I became the President of National Peking University. The university is like home to me. (I taught there between 1914 and 1927.) When I came and saw the Red Building, my heart was filled with an indescribable feeling. Peking University was, after all, Peking University, where the minds of the students and the majority of teachers had been greatly improved, where everyone wanted the university to keep on making progress

116

so as to become a university that belongs to the people of New China.

Peking University, however, is not without its defects. One of our defects is liberalism and the lack of organization. This may partly be accounted for by the fact that living quarters of teachers, employees, and workers are scattered about, but such a liberal and unorganized atmosphere has deeper origins in general outlook, which must be overcome. Among these, the most obvious is that most clerical employees have a low level of political thought and are little aware that they are now masters. To remedy this, a study reorientation course, which lasted for more than forty days during the summer vacation, was provided for the employees. The results were most satisfactory; efficiency showed considerable improvement when the school term began. We gained experience from this undertaking, and our colleagues fully appreciate the importance of reorientation.

The fifty-three-year history of Peking University has been inseparable from the revolutionary career of the Chinese people. The University played a prominent part in the May 4th Movement; the earliest Marxist study group in China was established in Peking University. At that time Li Ta-chao, pioneer Communist and one of the founders of the Chinese Communist Party, was the librarian of Peking University. He led a large number of young people to study and disseminate Marxism-Leninism. At the same time, Mao Tse-tung, the great leader of the Chinese people, also did research work on Marxism-Leninism in the University and started his revolutionary work there. Such a close relationship as existed between Peking University and the Chinese Revolution is rare, not only in the histories of Chinese universities, but also in those of universities in other parts of the world. This is the greatest glory and pride of Peking University.

Having such a glorious revolutionary tradition, the professors in Peking University are of course ready and willing to accept new trends of thought. Hence they have been able to transform an old-fashioned university into a new people's university. In the two years following the liberation, we have consistently striven in the new direction. To achieve this end, we must fundamentally reorganize the colleges and faculties in the university, make changes in curricula, and improve the substance and methods of teaching. In order to realize this object, the most important thing to do is to make all teachers and students in the University truly aware of the necessity of reform, so that they will voluntarily undergo mind-reform and be better able to serve the people.

Although in the past two years Peking University has accomplished some reform work, yet considering the national requirements and the tasks confronting us, these results still fall short of expectations. We decided, therefore, to initiate a planned and systematic study movement among teachers and employees of the University. At the same time, in pursuance to Premier Chou En-lai's appeal, we must strengthen mind-reform and bring it to the level of our specialized training, so that we may be equal to the new task.

The aim and purpose of the current reorientation is to reform the University through the medium of individual mind-reform. The method of study is attending lectures, studying documents, and launching criticism and self-criticism, so that we may arm ourselves with Marxism-Leninism and Mao Tse-tung's teachings. But in what ways should we arm ourselves?

The aim and purpose of new democratic education is to train for the country large contingents of competent, virtuous, and physically healthy cadres with high Communist spirit. In other words, the responsibility of teachers is to train large numbers of revolutionary youths for the country. Those who are not themselves political-minded will never be able to train large numbers of revolutionary cadres. This is one reason why political study is important for teachers.

If the teachers' political consciousness is gradually raised to the same level as their professional training, greater accomplishments will be attained in various national construction work to be carried out henceforth. Only thus will "personal standpoint" be changed to "the people's standpoint" and the face of China be completely transformed.

Mind-reform will not only train large numbers of revolutionary cadres but will also strengthen the unity among teachers. The study-movement in Peking University was mobilized by the teachers themselves. When Teacher A helps Teacher B in a co-operative spirit to undergo mind-reform, his assistance will most certainly be appreciated. Where there is agreement of minds, work will be pushed a step further.

Although in the past two years higher education has been considerably improved, yet judging from the people's demands, the improvement in higher educational institutions is still far from sufficient. Various construction projects are at present in progress. One of the decisive factors of construction work is personnel, or cadres, but there is a general shortage of them at the moment. The country is in need of a larger number of talents for its construction. The task of higher educational institutions is to train advanced technical personnel and principal cadres for national construction. How are the higher educational institutions able to discharge this duty bestowed upon them by the country and the people? First of all, the number of advanced technical cadres required for national construction is so large, and yet the number of skilled personnel that higher educational institutions have been able to train is so small. Although objective conditions may impose limitations, yet have there been enough subjective efforts? For instance, if we overcome "self-centerism," make reasonable allocations and adjustments of available personnel and material supplies, and sacrifice individual freedom for collective interests, we should be able to avoid waste and make the best use of latent potentials. Thus a small number of teachers will surely be able to train a large number of skilled persons for the country.

What the country needs is cadres who have technical skill and scientific knowledge, who do not falter in class standpoint, and who can truly serve the people. The educational purpose of higher educational institutions is to combine theory with practice. Yet are those graduates trained by higher educational institutions equipped with scientific teachings that have a practical bearing on actual conditions in China? We know that even today individual professors in some universities are still lecturing on American domestic-relations law and the capitalist banking system! These are exceptional cases, but some college graduates have in fact come back to tell me that the theories they had learned in the university were often inapplicable to actual conditions outside and that when they went to work, they often found it difficult to bring their theoretical knowledge to bear on practical problems. Students studying in the university have often made representations to university authorities, pointing out that a certain course of study needs changes in substance and that a certain teacher's method of teaching is unsatisfactory. Some departments have simply stated that university-trained people today are far from meeting their expectations. In short, considering the requirements of national construction and the people, higher educational institutions stand in need of more thorough reform.

We realized the importance of reorientation and made a request for it, which was granted by the Central People's Government. In order to organize teachers of other higher educational institutions in Peking and Tientsin to take part in the program and to avoid the inconvenience of having leading officials take turns to give lectures at various universities, the Ministry of Education decided to widen the scope of this reorientation course. On the afternoon of September 29, Premier Chou En-lai was invited to deliver the first lecture. Premier Chou talked for five hours. Although the lecture was long, the audience did not feel tired.

Premier Chou's lecture discussed seven topics: namely, (1) standpoint; (2) attitude; (3) whom we serve; (4) problems of thought; (5) problems of knowledge; (6) problems of democracy; (7) criticism and self-criticism. The deeper he went into the problems, the more eloquent he became. Coming to the last part of the lecture, Premier Chou spoke frankly in a spirit of self-criticism of his own social relations. The audience was deeply impressed. I think that it is most effective to guide the intellectuals in mind-reform by such a method. It not only arouses their desire for study but also consolidates the learners' confidence, enhances their enthusiasm for study, and steps up the process of mind-reform.

Premier Chou will be followed by a number of leading government officials, whose lectures will be arranged by the Ministry of Education, which leads the reorientation. I hope that our colleagues in various universities all over the country will be determined to go a step further to reform themselves in the course of orientation, so as truly to become people's revolutionary teachers of the New China.

SOURCE: *Current Background,* No. 169 (Hong Kong: United States Consulate General, April 2, 1952). Originally published in *Jen Min Jih Pao* [People's Daily], October 23, 1951.

For additional reading, see Fei Hsiao-tung, "Educating the Educators," *China Weekly Review,* July 29, 1950, p. 157.

The Key to the Reform of Higher Education
By Ch'ien Chun-jui
November 1951

Ch'ien was Vice-Minister of Education in 1951, when he de-
livered this speech. The reform of the universities meant the
initial reform of the professors, all of whom underwent varying
degrees of "thought control" and "mental rectification." The in-
tellectuals were singled out early in the new regime's history, and
great importance was attached to the "ideological remolding" of
the academics to cleanse them of their bourgeois habits.

The experiences gained during the past two years serve to prove
the fact that if the teachers in institutions of higher education persist in adhering to the reactionary thoughts of the British and
American bourgeois class, if they persist in sticking to their personal individualism, objectivism, and sectarian point of view, and
fail to carry out true reform, then all phases of the reform of
higher education, the reorganizing of faculties and departments,
curriculum-reform, the reform of teaching methods, and the like,
will flounder, and it will be impossible to carry out the complete
reform of higher education. Decisions and regulations on the reform of higher education must inevitably remain a dead letter.
This point has been amply borne out by the slow rate and limited
scope of change attained by the great majority of professors during the past two years.

As stated by Chairman Mao, "Ideological reform—first of all
the ideological reform of intellectuals—is one of the important
conditions for our country's all-out complete democratic reform
and gradual industrialization." The correctness of Chairman
Mao's directive in this respect has been fully proved by our work

122

in the reform of old education during the past two years. It is thus obvious that the key to the reform of education lies in the ideological reform of the teachers.

. . . .

First of all, in the past two years, especially since the launching of the "resist America, aid Korea" movement on a nationwide scale, political consciousness has generally been improved among the teachers, and their pro-America, worship-America, fear-America mentality has been greatly weakened. We cannot deny, however, that not a small number of teachers in higher educational institutions are still preserving strong European-American reactionary capitalist-class thoughts, especially a tendency to worship the American capitalist class. Even now they still stubbornly worship the mode of living of the Anglo-American capitalist class, especially the so-called "American way of life." They admire America's wealth (they do not see the poverty of the American working people); the "political freedom" in America (they do not wish to believe that Truman is practicing a Fascism which deprives the people of all lawful rights); and American "civilization" (they yearn for the degradations of the British and American capitalist classes and ignore the miserable position of the broad laboring masses in America and Britain who are denied access to culture). They are impressed by Anglo-American science and technique to the extent of being superstitious, and they cast a contemptuous look at advanced Soviet science and technique. Needless to say, they have little understanding or faith in the creative and inventive power of the Chinese people.

. . . .

In the course of this study movement, we should adopt the Marxist standpoint, approach, and method; fall back upon revolutionary patriotism, internationalism, and collectivism; follow the working class basic viewpoint of union of theory and practice to eliminate with determination the above-described influences of the Anglo-American reactionary capitalist class; and overcome the erroneous trends of individualism, objectivism, sectarianism, and dogmatism.

What are the principal tasks most urgently to be accomplished in the reform of higher education?

(1) Reform of system, including readjustment of colleges and departments. In order to meet the requirements of national construction, higher educational institutions should adjust and reorganize universities and technical colleges and technical schools under a centralized government scheme according to the stipulations in the Government Administration Council's "Decision on Reform of the Educational System." We should especially try to meet the urgent need of national defense and economic construction and strive vigorously to promote short-term specialized education. On the one hand, we should strengthen and reorganize various universities; on the other hand, we should lay special emphasis on strengthening and developing specialized courses and training classes.

(2) Reform of substance of education, i.e. changes in curricula and revision of textbooks. Although in the past two years certain changes in curricula have been made, they still fall far behind the practical requirements. The colleges have not been able to provide many courses, whether in political science, law, literature, education, the natural sciences, engineering, agriculture, or medicine, that are truly needed in national construction. Many of the existing courses are not only useless in national construction, but some are even unfavorable to national construction. We must continue to strive to maintain close contact with various quarters, revise our curricula earnestly, and re-edit our textbooks according to the nation's present and future requirements.

. . . .

It is hoped that as local circumstances permit, teachers in various higher educational institutions all over the country will follow in the footsteps of teachers in Peking and Tientsin to launch a mind-reform study movement in the same planned and systematic manner, so as to realize the goal of fundamentally reforming the system, substance, and teaching methods of higher education in the whole country and successfully training a large number of advanced personnel for national construction.

SOURCE: *Current Background,* No. 169 (Hong Kong: United States Consulate General, November 1951). Originally published in *Hsueh Hsi,* V, No. 1 (November 1, 1951).

China's New Educational System
By Liu Shih
December 1951

The first attempt to modernize the educational system of old feudal China was made in 1903 during the Ching dynasty with the issue of an Imperial edict which attempted to adapt the educational practice of the capitalist countries to China. The new system was in fact copied from that of the Japanese. Reforms of the educational system were again decreed in 1913 and 1922. The first was still patterned after the Japanese system, while the second was adapted from the American. The system introduced in 1922 remained fundamentally unchanged throughout the Kuomintang regime. There was no essential difference, however, between those three systems. They were all designed to suit the needs of the ruling classes in old China. They ignored the needs of the broad laboring masses, the overwhelming majority of the population. In the semifeudal and semicolonial condition of the country before liberation, education was a weapon in the hands of the feudal landlords and the bureaucratic capitalists. It was used to rivet the chains of imperialist domination more firmly on the nation. It was this educational system that left 85 percent of the people illiterate and provided schools for less than 40 percent of school-age children.

On October 1, 1951, the Government Administration Council of the Central People's Government issued the *Decisions Concerning the Reform of the Educational System* and thereby set up the system of education of the People's Republic of China. This has brought about a fundamental reform of the old educational system of China. It differs completely in principle from the reforms in the past. It demonstrated the fact that education had to be taken from the hands of the feudal landlords, bureaucratic capitalists, and imperialists and put into the hands of the people

126

of China, led by the working class, and that it must be used as an instrument for the advance of all the people.

This new system, as made clear in the *Decisions Concerning the Reform of the Educational System,* naturally reflects the character of our present state of social development as a period of transition from the old semifeudal and semicolonial conditions to the new democracy. In order to understand its fundamental spirit, it is important to appreciate its transitional nature and its social character, which are determined by the conditions and demands of this initial period of the Chinese People's Republic. This is in accordance with one of the basic principles of the teachings of Mao Tse-tung—that everything should be considered according to the actual conditions of the Chinese revolution and the demands of the Chinese people. This new system of education takes into consideration the present conditions of China in the midst of vast revolutionary changes and opposition to foreign aggression and also of the present needs of the people engaged in great constructive tasks. This conforms with the New Democratic educational policy as laid down in the Common Program, the basic law of the People's Republic of China. It is based upon the educational experiences of more than twenty years in the old revolutionary bases. It has been devised after making a critical review of the old educational system of China and studying the experiences of the advanced countries of the world.

POLITICAL TRAINING SCHOOLS

The role specially assigned to the political training schools by the new educational system is to guarantee that both young and old intellectuals will have equal chances to acquire a revolutionary education. On October 23, 1951, Chairman Mao Tse-tung emphatically pointed out at the People's Political Consultative Conference National Committee session that "ideological remolding, first of all, of the different types of intellectuals is one of the most important conditions for completing our democratic reforms in various fields and for the gradual industrialization of our country."

This session of the People's Political Consultative Conference National Committee decided to launch the movement for ideological reform and for systematic study of Marxism-Leninism and the teachings of Mao Tse-tung which integrate Marxism-Leninism with the practice of the Chinese revolution and to make this movement one of the three great national tasks. This kind of revolutionary political study movement has already gone on for two years. Especially during the last year, it has educated hundreds of millions of the people of China, raised the people's political consciousness, and roused their patriotism to an unprecedentedly high degree through the three great movements: namely, the movement of resisting American aggression and aiding Korea, the land reform, and the suppression of counterrevolutionaries. The political training schools, such as the revolutionary colleges in various areas, organized in the regular system of education, are only one of the types of institutions offering political study to the people of China. They provide a place where the people can take up a more systematic study of Marxism-Leninism and the teachings of Mao Tse-tung to apply these to their own thoughts and work, to practice criticism and self-criticism to rid themselves of thoughts which are unscientific and reactionary, so as to be able to advance themselves continually. Such schools are in great demand by all the progressive young intellectuals, as well as the old intellectuals in China today. They are the newest type of schools in the world brought into being by the people's revolution. Therefore it is necessary to include such institutions in our system of education. Needless to say, Marxism-Leninism and the teachings of Mao Tse-tung will be studied not only in such institutions but in all other schools as well.

Under the new regulations, the activities of schools of all types and grades, ranging from kindergartens to universities, have been carefully coördinated into one system. On the one hand, short-term training is emphasized because of the present-day demand; on the other hand, an adequate standard of education is prescribed in view of the needs of the development of our country.

.   .   .   .

COÖRDINATED EDUCATIONAL SYSTEM

The new educational system has assigned definite roles to the various schools and types of educational organizations, but at the same time it allows a certain amount of flexibility because of the very uneven political, economic, and cultural development of the various areas of the country.

Schools of various types and grades throughout the whole country, however, all follow the general educational line pointed out by Mao Tse-tung to fulfill the common tasks. All the children and youth must be given an all-round education. All secondary schooling and higher education should be closely related to the construction needs of defense and production. They must train the personnel to carry out the tasks of national construction with a clear understanding of Marxism-Leninism and the teachings of Mao Tse-tung and of the various branches of knowledge. Schools of the same grade and of the same type must work according to a uniform curriculum. All the various types of schools should be brought into this new coördinated system. Those that have not yet been brought into the regular educational system completely and those that cannot be so reorganized without special difficulties will have to be reorganized gradually and conditions created to that end. However, it must be borne in mind that the organizational forms of education need to be extremely many-sided and should be suited to the special habits and customs of the various races and of the different localities. This is inevitable because of the vastness of China; its large population; the unevenness in the political, economic, and cultural development among the different races and different parts of the country; and also because of the various needs of the moment, the various qualifications of the teaching staff, and varying economic conditions.

The adoption of the new system will be brought about as opportunity arises in each place, having regard to the actual conditions throughout the whole country, and will be effected step by step according to plan. The standards of teaching staffs must be gradually raised also, according to the actual existing conditions. In short, uniformity and flexibility must be appropriately combined in the future. Education throughout our country will be developed more uniformly in all respects as local differences gradually diminish in the course of economic and cultural advance.

The central and local people's governments in China are making all necessary preparations to carry through this great reform in the educational system. The Ministry of Education of the Central People's Government is training teaching staff on a large scale and is taking steps to bring uniformity into educational plans, teaching methods, and textbooks. By 1957, there will be available no less than one million primary school teachers and school facilities for eighty percent of the children of school age. The five-year system of the primary schools will begin in 1952, starting from the first class. Reform of the succeeding classes will follow as each year passes till by 1957 the whole system is completely adopted throughout the country. All the various forms of vocational classes, spare-time schools, short-term schools, and other adult educational classes will be gradually brought into the regular system. First of all, schools that are of the same type and have courses of the same duration should devise a uniform plan of education. The next step is to bring the rest into conformity.

Efforts must very soon be made to solve the problems of finding the most advantageous location for the institutes of higher learning and determining how they are to coöperate in their educational tasks. The problem of reforming study courses must also be solved. The new, democratic educational system of China has thus been launched. The difficulties still to be overcome are by no means small, but the educational workers are confident of success. After two years of political study they have made definite advances; they have become a well-organized force; they know that they have the experienced guidance of Chairman Mao Tse-tung and the Central People's Government.

SOURCE: Liu Shih, "China's New Educational System," *People's China,* IV, No. 11 (December 1, 1951), pp. 5–8.

Successes of People's Education
By Ma Hsu-lun
1952

Appointed in October 1949, Ma was the first Minister of Education of the new regime. In this report he describes educational progress effected during the first three years under the People's Republic. From 1949 to 1952 it was the task of the Ministry of Education to activate schools, reform the curricula, and instigate a nationwide reallocation of colleges and higher educational facilities. This early period was one of essential reorganization, and the groundwork was laid for the first Five Year Plan, which was to follow (1953–1957). This period saw the elimination of private and missionary colleges in China, the general nationalization of higher educational facilities, and the ideological remolding of the intellectuals. All three were regarded as necessary by the regime before further massive attempts to reform Chinese education could be contemplated.

The founding of the People's Republic of China ushered in a new era in Chinese history. The yoke which foreign nations and native feudal oppression had laid upon the Chinese people for a long period caused excessive sufferings. What the putrid, venal Kuomintang regime left us was an economically and culturally backward state. In education its legacy was negligible. Workers and peasants were deprived of the right to education. In consequence, 90 percent of the population were illiterate, and the young people who received education, an education permeated with feudal, comprador, and Fascist ideas, soon lost all their self-respect and self-confidence. In areas controlled by the Kuomintang reactionaries, our young men were frequently put in posts where they could not turn to good use what they had learned in school.

131

Graduation usually meant unemployment for college or university graduates, compelling them to lead a hopelessly depressed, insecure life, full of misery beyond description.

LARGER ENROLLMENT SINCE 1949

In the winter of 1949, just after the establishment of the People's Republic of China, there were throughout the country 191 institutions of higher learning with a student enrollment of over 130,000; about 5,200 secondary schools with over 1,270,000 students; and about 346,700 primary schools with 24,200,000 pupils. During the past three years, all types of schools have expanded their scope. If we compare the number of students in 1951 with that in 1949, the number of primary school pupils had increased 77 percent; after this year's summer vacation (1952) the figure was 101 percent higher than in 1949, i.e., more than double, with a total enrollment of 49 million. By 1951, the number of students in secondary schools had increased 57.9 percent over 1949 and after this year's summer vacation (1952) 142.2 percent, i.e., one and a half times, with enrolling students numbering 3,078,000. In 1951 the number of students in institutions of higher learning was 34.8 percent higher than in the year of liberation; after this year's summer vacation (1952) the increase was 69 percent, with an enrollment total of 219,700. Compared with peak year (1946) figures, the number of primary school pupils has increased 107 percent; students in secondary schools, 63.9 percent; students in institutions of higher learning, 69.9 percent.

. . . .

EDUCATIONAL REFORMS

The development of a people's education is unthinkable without reforming the old educational system. During the past three years, the People's Government has resolutely and systematically carried out such reforms in all the aspects of the old educational system according to plan.

First came the general reform of the educational system. The decision on reforming the educational system promulgated by the Government Administration Council of the Central People's Government in October 1959 provided for a new system in education to accord with realities in the preliminary period of China's construction. The key to the new educational system is the important position given the education of working people and of government cadres of worker or peasant origin in schools at all levels, so as to guarantee them the opportunity to receive education; the new educational system also gives an important place to education in special fields and to training classes, continuation schools, political schools of various fields and grades, so as to maintain the supply of the personnel needed in national construction. Primary schools will be based on a thorough five-year system, so as to enable the children of the laboring people both in the cities and in the countryside to receive a complete primary education. Besides, schools of all types and grades are so coördinated and channeled that they will eventually all lead to a college education. Whoever is willing to exert himself will thus have the opportunity of a college education.

Second, all educational facilities are placed at the disposal of the laboring people, i.e., workers and peasants. In order to make education really serve the masses, all schools at varying levels are carrying out the directive to open their doors to workers and peasants, giving them all facilities for schooling. Short-term primary schools and secondary schools for workers and peasants, a workers' political academy, and the Chinese People's University have all been set up especially for workers and peasants. At the present time, workers and peasants constitute over 80 percent among primary school students, 60 percent among secondary school students, and 20 percent among college students. This is unprecedented in China's history.

Third came the ideological remolding of teachers. All teachers wishing to contribute their best to the laboring people, in keeping with education in the Mao Tse-tung era, responded to Chairman Mao's call for ideological remolding through self-education. They studied the new theory, examined the new method and viewpoint of education, and criticized their old ideology, viewpoint, and method. They learned to seek for truth, to correct errors by mutual- and self-criticism, to draw a clear demarcation between enemies and friends, and to define the ideological boundary between the working class and the bourgeoisie. Through this movement, the teachers' ranks were purified, and teachers now display much greater enthusiasm in their work. They are also studying with great interest the advanced experiences of Soviet education, so as to draw up educational plans based on China's situation and needs for improving curricula and revising textbooks. Achievement is also registered in making changes in the content of education and in methods of teaching and learning. All these measures are to ensure that the people's education will continue to improve in quality.

Fourth, in the reorganization of colleges and the different departments of institutions of higher learning, the People's Government has aimed to do away with the anarchic state and the divorce from practice existing in the arrangement and distribution of educational institutions in old China, so that the people's education should serve national construction all the more effectively. The reorganization of colleges of engineering and agriculture, of normal schools, universities, and technical schools is to be completed within 1952. The number of higher technical schools will be increased from thirty-one to forty-seven; of agricultural and forestry colleges from eighteen to thirty-three; normal schools from thirty to thirty-four; and medical colleges from twenty-nine to thirty-two. The proportion of engineering departments among institutions of higher learning will after reorganization be much higher. Under the Kuomintang reactionary rule, in 1946 for instance, students in engineering colleges were only 18.9 percent of the total number of students in institutions of higher learning. However, by the end of the summer vacation of 1952, their number had increased to 35.4 percent, coming first among the various colleges. Among special secondary schools, the enrollment in technical secondary schools is the highest, constituting upwards of 38 percent of the total. Such changes create conditions most favorable for the industrialization of our Motherland and for the training of technical personnel.

Fifth, raising the political status of teachers and students and improving their living conditions. In New China, all teachers willing to serve the people are respected by the government and loved by the people. Young students are regarded as the hope of New China and are given great consideration by the government. Both teachers and students are organized in mass organizations— e.g., the teachers' union and the students' union—whose representatives take part in the people's governments and the people's representative conferences on all levels. They also play their part in social and political life freely as masters of the nation. With finance and economy of the country taking a radical turn for the better, the salaries of teachers and living allowances for students have been revised and raised. Compared with 1951, the salaries of teachers in institutions of higher learning have this year increased 18.6 percent; of secondary school teachers, 25.5 percent; of primary school teachers, 37.4 percent. At the same time, subsidies for students of secondary schools and colleges have been greatly increased. All students in technical secondary schools, normal schools, and institutions of higher learning receive annually a "people's subsidy" from the government, while students among the industrial and agricultural government workers' ranks, as well as worker-students coming from their benches, receive even higher allowances. Thus, not only are boarding expenses defrayed by the state for all students in technical secondary schools, normal schools, and institutions of higher learning, but these students receive also pocket money for miscellaneous expenses. Now students and teachers can be free from financial worries and work wholeheartedly for the build-up of our country, for the good of the people, towards a splendid future for all mankind.

Source: *Culture, Education and Health in New China* (Peking: Foreign Languages Press, 1952).

For additional reading, see "Report of Kuo Mo-jo on Cultural and Educational Work [at the] Third Session, First National Committee of the People's Political Consultative Conference" [October 25, 1951], *Current Background*, No. 140 (Hong Kong: United States Consulate General, 1951).

I Denounce My Father, Lu Chih-wei
By Lu Yao-hua
March 1952

The President of Yenching University, Lu Chih-wei, was re-moved from office shortly after the Communist regime took over the University. His daughter, a graduate student in the Depart-ment of Biology, denounced her father to the Communist authori-ties and assisted in forcing his dismissal. Her speech should be read in conjunction with one of her father's confessions and "self-criticisms" made in February 1951. [See earlier document.]

Now I want to denounce my father, Lu Chih-wei. He did all in his power to deceive me and make loose my stand as a Chinese and to make me disloyal to the masses during the "three anti-" movement. Lu Chih-wei, I have in the past considered you a "noble scholar," clever and capable. I felt that, although you have been seriously affected by the influence of the cultural ag-gression of U. S. imperialism, you still sought to improve yourself and, in addition, that you always pretended to expect me to be progressive. I have always taken you as an example for study, be-cause I felt that you are learned and politically more conscious than I. You are the president as well as a representative of the People's Political Consultative Conference. Because I respected and admired you, all that you have done has a direct bearing on me.

When the Korean war first began, you often told me, "If the war goes on, we will have to evacuate to the countryside. Large cities might be occupied by the U.S., and our life will become very hard." What you said made me doubt the military strength of the fatherland and even fear America.

I remember once I mentioned to you the fact that in the U.S. a daily average of seventeen million workers were unemployed. You said that the figure might be incorrect and could not be so large unless the housewives were included. When I heard your remarks, I felt that our news report about the U.S. might be too "leftish" and began to doubt the reports of the *Jen Min Jih Pao* [People's Daily].

In the several days before you made self-criticism in front of the entire University, everyone of our family tried to help you, in the hope that you would perform a good job. As I trusted you too much and really thought that you could not remember clearly many of the things, I went to all the trouble of finding out the materials for you. My brother even did not sleep for a few days just to help you out. For instance, I remember that Stuart did send somebody to see you and that Chao Tzu-ch'en also came over to see you to rescue six prisoners of war. I knew that I should report these matters to the austerity check-up committee, but to enable you to make a self-criticism, I disclosed them to you. Today, it would seem that what I did is tantamount to helping you "pull through the pass" and deceive the masses.

When you made your self-criticism, I acted as one of the recorders. I thought that the way we helped you would enable you to make a more frank confession. When I saw the audience handing in 900-odd slips to the stage, I felt extremely unhappy, thinking that the masses were too "leftish." During the discussion held following the meeting, I, as your daughter who should understand you better, tried all that I could to argue in your favor, stressing that your contact with the American Consul-General, O. Edmund Clubb, was due to personal relationship. I thought the masses purposely sought to deal you a blow. My schoolmates told me that under the leadership of the Communist Party no good people would be injured. This means that they wanted me to know your problems, but I felt that you could not have deceived me and that wrong had been done to you. I also felt that despite all the misunderstanding people had of you, the day would eventually come when things might be straightened out.

When I read of the numerous facts exposed in the extra newspaper the following day, I began to realize that you are no longer my respectable father but a claw of imperialism. I have always thought that what you have done before and after liberation in collaboration with the U. S. imperialist policy of cultural aggression was merely a coincidence, but, in fact, you were "designated to stick to your post." I thought you had the "backbone" and "the dignity of the race," but you have, in fact, depended upon the benevolence of U. S. imperialism for livelihood all your life without feeling disgusted. I thought you a "noble," "supra-politics" scholar, but you actually are a "Christian with no political sympathy for the Communist Party." All of us feel thankful to the bright happy days brought us by the Communist Party, but to you such good days have become a "difficult test." I thought you liked all Chinese people and under the party guidance cut off close relations with the U. S. imperialists, but you have hoped that in the recent few years you could be more closely related with them.

In my later conversation with my schoolmates, they cited facts to prove the lie you told in your self-criticism. I began to realize that this is a struggle to sever our relations with imperialism and also an unusually severe class struggle. Our victory will make imperialism shiver before us. I want to be progressive. I have already applied for my membership to the Youth League, and it is my duty to struggle against imperialism. I want to use all my strength and stand on the side of the people to bring the struggle to an end.

I have thought previously that you had exposed all your problems and the rest you have forgotten due to advanced age. But I now realize that, crafty as you are, it is impossible for you to forget completely what you have carefully planned in the past two or three years. Have you really forgotten all the things you have done with a guilty conscience? I know that you are fooling me. The masses have given you so many chances, but you repeatedly deceived us. Since you can cheat all the people, why can't you cheat me? The reason I have not been firm in my stand and take you into consideration is because of the love between a father and a daughter. Even if this love is true, it is definitely insignificant as compared with the love among the masses, not to mention that your love is not love but deceit. Why must I be deceived by you and revolt against the people? I want to be with the broad masses and struggle hard for the sake of communism. I will struggle to the last against anyone acting against the interest of the people.

I have always fully supported all policies of the People's Government but why I began to suspect you is that I realized from my past education under the Party that, if anyone should still cherish pro-American thought at a time like this, it would be intolerable. You are not only pro-American but a 100 percent collaborator of imperialism. The reason why I did not see this before and I still admired you is because you have been a hypocrite and I have been cheated by you, with the result that I have tried to shelter you and argue for you. Most serious is that my stand has not been firm under this severe test. It is to save the fatherland from aggression that the Chinese volunteers have been fighting the enemy hard on the Korean front. They have suffered great cold and hunger and made valorous sacrifices there just to win happy days for our people and fatherland. But here in Yenching it is just because of you, Lu Chih-wei, that imperialist influence is still making such a ferocious attack on the thought of every schoolmate. Against you, Lu Chih-wei, as the claw of the deadly enemy of the people, why should I not wage a bitter struggle like that of the volunteers on the front. Why should I shelter you, argue for you, and believe in your lies, instead? Do you think that those few drops of false tears can buy over my heart?

Now I know you full well. You are a 100 percent claw of imperialism and a tool faithful to U. S. imperialism for its cultural aggression. You would not hesitate to betray the interest of the entire people just to satisfy your political ambition. Although you have not the power, you have been thinking of dragging us to the path of Titoism. You have kept this bastion for cultural aggression and continued to do harm to China. You have poisoned many youths and made politically obscure their vision about the future, close as they are to Chairman Mao Tse-tung. You have trained many pro-American elements for imperialism, and you have directly given shelter to the secret agents of U. S. imperialism. For this act of yours no Chinese will ever pardon you.

We want to progress towards socialism and communism and will never allow people like you to destroy the future of our fatherland and pull us back to the colonial society. I definitely will not permit the remnant influence of U. S. imperialism to exist in the land of China, in the vicinity of the capital, or even by the side of Chairman Mao Tse-tung.

SOURCE: *The "Hate America" Campaign in Communist China* (Washington, D. C.: Office of Intelligence Research of the United States Department of State, 1952). Translated from *Hsin Yen Ching* (Peking), April 14, 1952.

Criticizing My Decadent Bourgeois Ideology
By Chou P'ei-yuan
April 1952

The "ideological remolding" movement, which reached a peak in 1952, was highlighted by countless confessions and recantations by university teachers and scholars throughout China. This particular campaign was aimed at reforming the intellectuals. Few academic institutions escaped the "thought-investigations" instigated by the regime. Some professors did not make a good enough showing in their initial confessions and were sent back time and again to rectify their style. The following extracts from the confession of the scholarly Dean of Studies at Tsinghua University is typical of the minimal recantation effort expected of intellectuals.

The great "three anti" movement gave me courage to face the serious mistakes I committed in the past. I had hitherto been in the habit of making use of my position as a specialist and scholar to enhance my social status, to flatter the reactionary government, and even to propagandize for it in an honorary capacity. Because of my worship-America and pro-America ideology, I forfeited my national stand during the anti-Japanese war and fell into the embrace of American imperialism. I became scientifically and technically the accomplice and tool of American imperialism in its aggression against the peace-loving people of the world. The "three anti" movement made me realize that I was so contaminated by the decadent ideology of the bourgeoisie and the cultural aggression of imperialism that for a long time after the liberation, I still harbored a contempt for the cultural and educational policies of the Party, thus seriously obstructing the reform and prog-

141

ress of the school, to the detriment of the people. I want now to tear down my mask to expose my ugly look, to confess my mistakes before the masses, to criticize my decadent bourgeois ideology, to cleanse the contamination of the cultural aggression of American imperialism, and to start afresh with a clean slate.

[The writer then goes on to give an account of his family background and education.]

When I spent my first four years in the United States, I was able to see only the superficial things, like the skyscrapers, the motorcars, and the shamelessly dissolute and free-spending life of the exploiting class, but not the tragic oppression of the toiling people by the monopolistic capitalists. I did not realize that the exploiting class had to squeeze the broad masses of the American people and to steal their fruits of toil before they could afford to lead a free-spending life. I read of the maltreatment and slaughtering of Negroes by imperialists in the newspapers, but I did not realize that the manufacturing of racial hatred was a consistent policy of the imperialists to oppress the people. I tried to think that the slaughtering of Negroes was indulged in by a small number of bad whites but that the good whites were against it. I erroneously believed therefore that the "democratic" system in America was still "good" and that the people there had freedom of speech. Were not the American newspapers free to criticize their President? I did not realize at the time that the American President and the so-called "government officials" were simply lackeys of the monopolistic capitalists and that the controversies in the newspapers represented but the dissensions between the various dominating groups. In short, when I returned to take up a teaching post at Tsinghua in 1929, my entire being was infested with the ideological germs of the bourgeoisie. I was a peddler of American imperialistic culture and education. I forfeited my national sense of self-respect and was ready to contaminate the youths of China.

.   .   .   .

By the end of 1941, when the Pacific war broke out, my pro-America and worship-America ideology went into action. Since the outbreak of the war of resistance, I had acquired the mentality to depend on imperialism in general and on American imperialism in particular, always indulging in the base subjective hope that a change in the international situation would help the Chinese people to find their way out in their sacred war of resistance. My trip to the United States in 1943 fully demonstrated my selfish and ugly ideology. In my vain hope to become an international scholar, I was willing to forfeit my national stand during the most arduous period of the anti-Japanese war. I dropped into the lap of imperialism to participate in the research on military science which American imperialism was sponsoring for the purpose of slaughtering the peace-loving people of the world. Under the grandiose pretext of serving the anti-Fascist scientific research of the democracies, I shamelessly applied to the American physicist, [Robert Andrews] Millikan, for an appointment. I adopted a slick and disgraceful way to achieve my end of going abroad. I relied on the influence of American imperialism to exert pressure on the reactionary government to issue passports to me and my family, and I made use of the official position of my old schoolmates from Tsinghua University in the puppet Foreign Ministry to expedite the issue. I also made use of the American Consul in Kunming and my personal connection with the special agents of the U. S. State Department to obtain the necessary visas for the United States.

My trip to the United States at the end of 1943 was the most disgraceful page in my life history. Although I was proceeding there under the pretext that I was an anti-Fascist scientific worker seeking to help the democracies, yet when I actually participated in the work at the beginning of 1945, the Soviet Red Army was already triumphant in the Eastern European theater of war, and the collapse of Fascist Germany was imminent. As a consequence, the research of military science had lost its progressiveness. At the time, American imperialism had gradually unveiled its fierce looks and was actually conducting research in military science for the purpose of developing new war weapons in the footsteps of Hitler. When one wanted to join such a research organization, one had to answer insulting questions: "Are you a member of the

Communist Party?" "Are you willing to fight for the U. S. Government?"

. . . .

In the autumn of 1948, I was attending an international conference on dynamics in London when Tsinan and Chinchow were both liberated. I anticipated that the liberation of North China and the whole of China would be a matter of time. At the time, my heart was with Peking, although my physical self was in England, and there was a great deal of fluctuation in my ideology. Because of my consistent anti-Soviet and pro-America ideology, I was suspicious of the Communists, not knowing whether China would have freedom of scientific research when she came under Communist rule. But I was unwilling to lead the life of a "white Chinese" and be despised by the whites. I longed for Peking, so I hurried back there to await liberation.

. . . .

Because I was deeply contaminated by the "above-politics" and "above-class" ideology of the bourgeoisie, I preposterously believed that intellectuals needed only technique and could do away with politics. I had therefore a preposterous slant on the matter of study. I compared the self-remolding of intellectuals to the compulsory indoctrination of the reactionaries and remarked: "If study serves the purpose of getting ideology straight, then the intellectuals can be classified into four categories: (1) those who study and get their ideology straight; (2) those who get their ideology straight without study; (3) those who study but cannot get their ideology straight; (4) those who make no attempt to study nor to get their ideology straight." I shamelessly classified myself into the second category. As the Dean of Studies of the University, my adoption of such an antagonistic attitude towards ideological remolding certainly did not help to lead the school on to the new path. I hated myself intensely for allowing the contamination of the bourgeois ideology to blind me to the brilliant sun which lit our path of progress.

. . . .

As a captive of the bourgeois ideology, I subjected the youths

of the rising generation to similar contamination, even after
the liberation. I demanded that they follow in my footsteps and
become scholars isolated from politics and the people. I showed
no interest in the political studies of the students and gave them
no help in political activities. Instead of welcoming the demand
of the students for progress in politics, I used the "business"
promoting method to pull them back. Since working personnel
of a high degree of political consciousness are needed by the
fatherland, my intolerable act is bound to endanger gravely the
future construction enterprise of the fatherland. When, in response to the call of the government, my second daughter wanted
to join the southbound working team, I used every method to ob-
struct her from becoming a member of a revolutionary cadre. I
tried to pull her back and wanted to send her to a university after
she finished her middle-school education, so that she might adopt
my simon-pure "business' viewpoint and sever herself from politics. I adopted the most base means to stop her from joining the
army. In return for my promise to serve as Dean of Studies, I required the North China Higher Education Committee of the time
to admonish her to come home. When this failed, I took advantage
of her health to send her to the Peking University hospital for
medical examination. Superficially, I said grandiosely: "But for
her illness I would not have stopped her from going south."
Actually, my sending her to the hospital was itself a conspiracy.
I knew that the working team for the south was about to leave
Peking, and I hoped that if I could keep her in the hospital for
several days the working team would have departed and she would
not be able to join it. But my plot failed. The evening when she
was discharged from the hospital, fearing that I would stop her
again, she avoided taking the school bus and braved the rain to
go on foot along the railway track into the city to rejoin her
revolutionary ranks. Her fervent love for the revolution formed
a vivid contrast to my opposition to the revolution. She was a
youth of the epoch of Mao Tse-tung, while I was saturated with
the decadent ideology of the bourgeoisie. My ill behavior of obstructing her joining the army was against the interests of the

people. I was unable to face my daughter, much less Chairman Mao and the People's Liberation Army.

. . . .

Thanks are due to the Party and to Chairman Mao, for the education of the Party has enlightened me. I have determined to rid my ideology of all bourgeois contamination, to discard resolutely the burden of my interest in "research above all," to take up conscientiously the teaching work entrusted to me by the people, and to submit myself firmly to the allocation of work by the organization, so that I may serve the people. I sincerely hope that the comrades will help me continually and incessantly to keep me perpetually in the wake of the Chinese Communist Party. I must remold myself to conform with the standard of the people's teacher and be forever on the alert against the corrosion of the bourgeois ideology.

SOURCE: *Current Background,* No. 213 (Hong Kong: United States Consulate General, October 1, 1952). Originally published by *New China News Agency,* April 1952.

For additional reading, see *Current Background,* Nos. 169 and 182 (1952).

Criticizing My Decadent Bourgeois Ideology
By Chin Yueh-lin
April 1952

The confession of Professor Chin Yueh-lin was made during the "thought-reform" campaign of 1951–1952. It complements the previous confession document of a fellow professor at Tsinghua University. Professor Chin was Chairman of the Department of Philosophy at Tsinghua and was regarded as China's leading scholar on formal logic. He was educated in Europe and in America, at Harvard University.

Born of a bureaucratic landlord family, I have always led a life of ease and comfort. I went abroad at nineteen and stayed there for eleven years to absorb the way of life and the predilection for pleasure of the European and American bourgeoisie. The principal source of my various pleasures lay in the decadent philosophy of the bourgeoisie, and for thirty years I played a game of concepts. I was engrossed in this game of concepts because it was the only way for me to feel happy and free and to escape from the restrictive realities of society. I thus cultivated the habit of running away from realities, despising realities, and leading a life isolated from realities. However, since I still had to live in a society of realities, the only way for me to maintain this life isolated from the realities was to gain certain privileges. I needed those privileges, and I thus fell victim to the ideology of special privileges.

My life in school served to form this outer crust of mine which can conveniently be divided into three phases:

My decadent bourgeois philosophy. While in school, I incessantly disseminated the trivialities of metaphysical idealism; in

147

particular the inanities of metaphysical philosophical methods. As I gradually assumed a position of leadership within the Philosophy Department of Tsinghua, all sorts of injuries to the people's enterprises inevitably resulted. (1) I obstructed the development of the philosophy of materialistic dialectics in Tsinghua's Philosophy Department. Though I never actually tried to stop the discussion of materialistic dialectics among teachers and students, I nevertheless throttled the development of materialistic dialectics in Tsinghua's Philosophy Department by subjecting it to attacks by a circuitous system of philosophical debate. (2) I trained those who concerned themselves only with the game of concepts, were not interested in politics, and were even reactionary. As for instance, Yin Fu-sheng, one of the reactionary elements for whose training I was responsible, is now serving the Chiang bandits in Taiwan. I was further possessed of the bourgeois viewpoint of the education of the talented. I was thus very much struck by Professor Shen Yueh-ting's powers in playing the game of concepts. As a result of my evil influence, Professor Shen is even now seriously isolated from the realities. (3) I disseminated the purely technical viewpoint in logic. For twenty years I taught logic to numerous students. All the time, however, I only tried to teach logic from the formalistic viewpoint. For instance, I was only concerned with the correctness of the reasoning, without caring about the truthfulness of the premises. My mistaken viewpoint of education for the talented led me to think highly of Wang Hao, who even now is serving the interests of American imperialism by being connected with an American university. (4) I encouraged the development of sectarianism within Tsinghua's Philosophy Department by stressing the highly involved analysis of concepts and the formulation of circuitous systems of philosophy as the most important aspects of philosophy. I then thought that the Philosophy Department of Tsinghua was very good in these respects. This sort of sectarianism was inevitably one of the facts which obstructed the regulation of the departments and colleges.

My decadent "above-politics," "above-class," "out-of-the-world," and "above-humanity" philosophy of life. Before the liberation, having absolutely no idea of the truth that the human world is created through labor, I mistakenly took the human race to be insignificant and the history of the human race to be but a minor episode in the main stream. I therefore tended to despise the world and to become above politics and above class. My preoccupation with this decadent philosophy of life led me to despise administrative work. I consequently tried by all means to minimize my personal affairs and adopted an attitude of absolute indifference toward all things. When I was charged with administrative work after the liberation, my mistaken attitude inevitably resulted in idiotic bureaucratism. Though a member of the University Administration Committee, I spoke up only once in all its meetings, and I honestly had nothing to talk about; and though the Dean of the College of Arts really had very little to do, what little there was I neglected altogether. For instance, I never seemed to remember that I was actually the Dean of the College of Arts when handling such matters as the resumption of publication of the *Tsinghua Journal,* the maintenance of proper relationship between the different colleges and departments, etc. As Chairman of the Philosophy Department, I left the affairs of the department to take care of themselves, and I never bothered to do anything about personnel appointments within the department.

My ideology of special privileges. In order to maintain my way of life, I had to have special privileges. I felt the need for these privileges, I enjoyed these privileges, became obsessed by the ideology of special privileges, and I became one of the privileged few of Tsinghua. Though I was privileged, I yet refused to shoulder the accompanying responsibilities. Thus, while I enjoyed special privileges in Tsinghua, yet I never burdened myself with administrative work.

The three above-mentioned phases constituted the main ingredients of my crust. The scope of the crust represented my individual self, one crust the Philosophy Department, while another represented Tsinghua. My personal crust being the "core" of this miniature universe, I accordingly remained completely indifferent to things which had little to do with my personal interests. Whenever the matter in question was in conflict with my personal crust, I always sallied torth to give battle. As for instance, when the son of Professor Liang Ssu-ch'eng wanted to change his registration from the History Department to the Architecture Department, I, as an old friend of the family who knew him when he was born, tried to help him, in the thought that he was more suited to the study of architecture. Though there are certain rigid restrictions in connection with the change of registration from one department to another, yet I made use of my special privileges to work on his behalf which resulted in a series of serious mistakes. This is but one example of a situation which conflicted with my personal crust. I opposed the reform of curriculum because I wanted to maintain the crust of the Philosophy Department in Tsinghua. When the regulation of departments and colleges started in 1950, I was dead against it, for my most outstanding crust was Tsinghua University. Motivated by departmentalism, sectarianism, and the educational ideology of the bourgeoisie, I was of infinite harm to the program for the regulation of departments and colleges. Had the regulation of departments and colleges been carried out in 1950, then Tsinghua alone would have turned out another five to six thousand cadre members, and a far larger number would have been turned out throughout the country. Incalculable harm has thus been caused the democratic construction program of the entire country. For this I now hate myself beyond measure.

My crust is based on the past prevailing economic and social foundation, that is, the capitalistic social system. In order to protect this crust, I had to give my political support to the old system of democracy. As a confirmed individualistic liberal, I have always based my political attitude upon this point of view. Only now have I realized that the old democracy is but the dictatorship of the bourgeois class, and the so-called individual freedom is but the "freedom" for the bourgeoisie to exploit and oppress the laboring people. My numerous criminal deeds of the past should thus be attributed to my acceptance of individual liberalism.

With regard to my attitude toward American imperialism, as a result of long years of studying in America, the evil influences of bourgeois education, my large number of American friends, and my constant contact with Americans, I became instilled with pro-American thoughts which prevented me from realizing American imperialism's plots of aggression against China during the past hundred years, and I was turned into an unconscious instrument of American imperialistic cultural aggression. I cried bitterly over the Twenty-one Demands but took no notice of the Sino-American Treaty of Friendship, Commerce, and Navigation. While I was highly indignant at the time of the Tsinan incident during the Northern Expedition and was all for resisting Japan when the Mukden incident and the Luguochiao incident took place, I nevertheless remained blind to the misdeeds of American soldiers in China. In 1943 I was one of the Chinese professors who went to America on the invitation of the American State Department. There, totally deprived of my national standpoint as a result of my pro-American thoughts, I even tried to persuade the American State Department to force the bandit, Chiang, to practice democracy.

With regard to my attitude toward the Soviet Union, in always looking at the USSR from the viewpoint of old democracy, I consistently distorted and slandered the Soviet Union, and right up to the liberation I thought that individual "freedom" does not exist in the Soviet Union. I considered both the October Revolution and the purges within the Party to be "going too far," and I thought that the Soviet Union made use of the Communist Parties in other countries to interfere in those countries' internal affairs. All these ideas were of course mistaken and reactionary. My principal mistake lay in thinking of the Soviet Union as devoid of individual freedom. At that time, in failing to take the October Revolution as an epoch-making event of history, I only tried to antagonize the Soviet Union on the basis of my individual liberal, pro-American ideology. It was only after the liberation that I succeeded gradually in gaining an understanding of true freedom and thus changed my attitude toward the Soviet Union.

With regard to student movements, I nearly always maintained a negative and double-faced attitude toward all of them that I came across in my teaching career. On the one hand, I "loathed" the Kuomintang of the Chiang bandits, while on the other hand,

I opposed the Communist Party of China. I say "loathed" advisedly, because I never tried to oppose them by any positive effort. Before I left for America in 1943, I had to go through five days of Kuomintang training in Chungking before I could get my passport and had to write a short essay of two hundred words on the advisability for local officials to visit the central government. This was really a shame. Though I honestly loathed the Kuomintang, this was not what mattered. The important thing was that I opposed the Chinese Communists. This dualism in my make-up was best shown at the time of the December First incident [a student movement which occurred in 1945 in Kunming]. Though I was highly enthusiastic at the start of the movement, when I followed the footsteps of the progressive elements, I later lost my interest, and finally I stood for the resumption of class. This was because I opposed the Communists. Soon after the end of the movement, I quarreled with Professor Chang Hsi-jo, and I told him in the sternest manner and in tears that, "It is you people who made such a mess of China. After depriving China of 'freedom,' it will take I don't know how many years to have it restored."

As viewed from the three above-mentioned aspects, my political attitude was truly intolerable. How was it possible that, though early in life I loved my country and wanted to save her from the fate of partition, yet I turned out to be such a fool later? On this point I have to charge the American imperialists who made use of a mission school, that is, Tsinghua College, and of the education I received while in America, to turn me into an instrument of American imperialistic cultural aggression, deprived me of my national standpoint, prevented me from making a distinction between our friends and our enemies, and led me to do things detrimental to the people.

My preliminary understanding of the People's Liberation Army and the Communist Party. The miracles of the People's Liberation Army demanded my wholehearted respect. I never thought such discipline possible, and they love the people so much. In the early days after the liberation, I was highly moved by an episode involving the son of my maid Liu. When her son, who was working in a certain factory, misbehaved himself, certain soldiers of the PLA stationed in that factory tried to reform him by education. When this failed, two comrades of the PLA approached Liu to request her to go and reform her son. In the end, the two soldiers treated the mother to a meal and finally saw her home. I consider such a fighting force unique in history. In the spring of 1949, I was fortunate enough to have the chance to listen to a series of reports rendered by members of various senior Party cadres. Their attitude was so very honest and sincere, and they were always prepared to practice what they preach. Though all occupied senior positions within the Party, they yet were always ready to admit their mistakes publicly before the masses. Such a party I consider unprecedented in China. However, this kind of recognition was only the preliminary stage of cognition through emotion, something within the capability of all Chinese.

My change in philosophical ideology. Generally speaking, this change can be divided into three periods. During the first period, I was still unable to link up the actualities of the revolution with Marxism-Leninism. Though I had already acquired a preliminary understanding of the Communist Party and the PLA, this did not mean that I was ready to accept materialistic dialectics and historical dialectics. When Comrade Ai Ssu-ch'i lectured in Tsinghua, I even tried to argue with him. Starting from the months of March and April 1949, I began to attend various meetings for the exchange of philosophical opinions. Even at that time I still held two mistaken points of view: in the first place, I still looked upon materialistic dialectics and the old philosophy as equals and, under the illusion that our Communist comrades were ignorant of the old philosophy, had the wish to initiate them in the mysteries of the old philosophy; in the second place, in the mistaken idea that materialistic dialectics and historical dialectics were not well systematized, I thought of putting them to order by means of my trivial system of analysis. My unbelievable arrogance and ignorance were the result of the fact that I was still looking at materialistic dialectics on the basis of the old philosophy. As I took part in the first attempt at curriculum-reform in the above mentioned spirit, naturally nothing was accomplished.

The Philosophy Department was thus prevented from making any progress.

The second period lasted roughly from the start of the second attempt at curriculum-reform in 1950 to the spring of 1951. From the very start of this period I had already accepted the leading position of materialistic dialectics and rectified my two abovementioned mistakes. I then considered materialistic dialectics as a piece of red string linking up all different branches of knowledge. Yet, though I admitted its importance in an abstract fashion, my real interests were still focused on philosophy as one of the branches of knowledge linked up by materialistic dialectics. In this manner I was still trying to oppose the new philosophy by the old. Both on the basis of my mistaken views and in compliance with the then prevailing conditions in Tsinghua's Philosophy Department, I proposed to divide the departments into three groups: history of philosophy, logic, and history of art. Since this amounted to change in name only but not change in substance, I again succeeded in preventing Tsinghua's Philosophy Department from making any progress.

In the spring of 1951, I went regularly into the city to make a study of *On Practice*. It was during this period that a radical change began to take place in my ideology. For almost two years before this, I had been going to the city regularly every Sunday to take part in the study activities of the Chinese Philosophy Society. Whatever I gained in the course of these two years, coupled with my study of *On Practice,* enabled me to realize the fundamental difference in nature between materialistic dialectics and the old philosophy. The old philosophy, being metaphysical, is fundamentally unscientific, while the new philosophy, being scientific, is the supreme truth. It was during the curriculum-reform campaign of 1951 that I succeeded in realizing that the mission of the Philosophy Department lies in the training of propaganda personnel for the dissemination of Marxism-Leninism. This time the curriculum reform was carried out in a comparatively thorough manner. However, insofar as my understanding of materialistic dialectics was still based on abstract concepts, it inevitably brought serious consequences to Tsinghua's Philosophy Department.

Idealism and bourgeois pedagogical ideology have always occupied a leading position in Tsinghua's Philosophy Department, and I have all the time been an outstanding representative of this decadent ideology. This situation has remained more or less unchanged right from the liberation up to the moment. This naturally resulted in huge losses. In the main, our principal defects lay in our low level of political consciousness and the dislocation of theory from practice.

To deal with materialistic dialectics by means of the analysis of concepts really amounts to the exposition of Marxism-Leninism by means of idealistic metaphysical methods. For instance, should we try to carry out in class a conceptual analysis of "necessity and contingency" and "relative truth and absolute truth," we would inevitably fall into the trap of running around in abstract circles of concepts, with the students getting more and more confused. To teach Marxism-Leninism in such a manner can only result in the distortion of Marxism-Leninism. Marxism-Leninism, which in itself is concrete, militant, and should serve as the guide for our action, has, in our hands, been turned into a lifeless and abstract heap of concepts.

Under the influence of this kind of idealistic bourgeois pedagogical ideology, certain students naturally fell victim to idealism. A student by the name of Li Hsüeh-chin is, in this respect, an outstanding example. Li entered Tsinghua in 1951, and within half a year he managed to read up on Wang Yang-ming [idealist philosopher of the Ming Dynasty], the Buddhist philosophy of Hsiung Shih-li, Moslem philosophy, and various other obscure books. When certain students felt they were unable to study the subjects they needed, they naturally changed their registration to other departments. Of the thirteen students of the class of 1949, nine decided to enter other departments; of the seven students of the class of 1950, five changed to other departments; and of the eight students of the class of 1951, two are going to change their registration to other departments.

Another undesirable manifestation in pedagogy lay in the dogmatic attempt to stuff the students with various theories, without taking pains to solve the ideological problems of the students. Inasmuch as materialistic dialectics is one of the subjects taught in the general political course attended by the entire school, I only tried to deal with materialistic dialectics in a supplementary manner, in the mistaken idea that the responsibility for the solution of ideological problems lay with the general political course, while in teaching materialistic dialectics in the Philosophy Department we only had to deal with the theoretical aspects. I thus erred in idealistically divorcing the problems of ideology and theory to cause the students great confusion.

Though Marxism-Leninism is designed to solve practical problems, yet in our hands it is fundamentally unable to solve the ideological problem of the students. To cite three graduates of the 1950 class of the Philosophy Department as examples: one by the name of Tang entered the graduate school of the Philosophy Department, but he was all the time more interested in mathematics; another graduate by the name of Chou gave up all his former training to enter the Physics Department of Peita; still another graduate by the name of Shui, though he had already qualified for the graduate school of the Philosophy Department, yet chose to enter Peita to study chemistry. Though all three students had ideological trouble, yet neither I nor the other teachers of the Philosophy Department succeeded in giving them timely assistance. Of this year's freshman students in the Philosophy Department, eight have already signified their wish to change their registration. With the situation in our department even as serious as it was, we still failed to notice it, not to say remedy the situation. It is entirely due to the fact that we were so badly poisoned ourselves that we failed to notice the seriousness of the situation and to rectify it.

In the bourgeois pedagogical method there is fundamentally no relationship between the teacher and the student. I myself only went to class to lecture, without caring whether the students understood me or whether they had any problems. I often missed classroom discussions, and I had no concern for the life, ideology, and state of health of the students. In adopting a liberalist attitude towards the students' studies, the teachers of the Philosophy Department always left everything to the individual efforts of the students. For instance, we remained ignorant of the fact that a certain student studies for as many as seventy hours a week, and we certainly would not have done anything had we known it.

Though the mission of the Philosophy Department lies in the training of cadres for the dissemination of Marxism-Leninism, yet as a result of the predominance of idealistic philosophy and pedagogical practice within the department, we inevitably failed to carry out this task, thus bringing about the above-mentioned harmful effects. Whereas this responsibility should be borne by all the professors of the Philosophy Department, the greater part of the guilt should be attributed to me, for I led them to become estranged from politics and isolated from realities.

As stated above, it was in the spring of 1951 that I began to realize the scientific and truthful nature of Marxism-Leninism, though this realization was even then abstract and conceptual. Before the start of the study movement for the teachers of Peking and Tientsin and the "three anti" campaign, I failed to link up Marxism-Leninism both with the realities in general and with my personal case. Though I took part in numerous activities in and out of Tsinghua, these activities never influenced me to any appreciable degree. It was only at the start of the teachers' study movement that I succeeded in linking myself up, criticizing my old democratic individual liberalistic ideology, and taking the first step in gaining a correct understanding of the Soviet Union and of American imperialism. I was still unable to gain a correct understanding of my former ideological self. It was only at the start of the "three anti" campaign that I began to understand my former self, my crust of selfishness, and my ideological shortcomings. Late in the spring of 1951, I began to try to become a good teacher of the people. However, I never was able to succeed in this. Not only did I fail, but I even committed the gravest mistakes. With the assistance of others and following my own preliminary analysis, I now consider the fundamental ideological source for my personal crust of selfishness to be the extremely depraved, epicurean, liberalist, and bourgeois ideology of striving after individual freedom. The philosophical manifestation of this ideology was found in my preoccupation with the completely impractical and extremely abstract game of concepts. In personal philosophy of life, this ideology was manifested in my decadent "above-humanity" viewpoint. In actual life at school, this ideology was manifested in my attempt to maintain my life of ease and comfort and to build up a crust of special privileges. This kind of ideology was the ideology of the exploitative class, or rather the exploitative ideology of the "shareholders" and "behind-the-scene-boss" of the exploitative class. It was owing to this ideology that I was led to become estranged from the social realities and prevented from gaining a correct understanding of the people even after the liberation. I shall smash my personal crust and eradicate the bourgeois ideologies which have for years dominated my life.

He who loves New China well must know that in New China the people are on their feet and have come into their own. There are 470,000,000 Chinese in New China, and I am one of them. This New China is working for the interests and welfare of the people of China as well as of the world. I have no wish to be an onlooker both in connection with the revolution and with the people's construction enterprises. I want to take part in the glorious and mighty enterprises which should be participated in not only by the young but by people of all ages, including the old. I am now close to sixty, and I am a criminal for having sinned against the people. From now on, however, I shall strive to become a new man and a teacher of the people in substance as well as in name. I shall exert myself to study, as well as to work, for one year, two years, three years, or even five or ten years. Provided I am able to keep up my efforts, I shall ultimately succeed.

SOURCE: *Current Background*, No. 213 (Hong Kong: United States Consulate General, October 1, 1952). Originally published in *Kuang Ming Jih Pao*, April 17, 1952.

Reform Ideology, Maintain Standpoint, and Be Determined to Become a Teacher of the People

By Wu Mi

June 1952

*Professor Wu Mi, chairman of the Western Languages Depart-
ment of Southwest Normal College in Chungking, undertook
graduate studies in the United States at Harvard University in
the early 1920s. His confession, although somewhat restrained,
represents the typical self-degradation of a scholar and illustrates
the extent of abject humility expected of professors in "remolding
their ideologies."*

I belong to a family of feudal landlords, and early in life I was
interested in reading old books, both the classics and all sorts of
miscellanies. I never experienced any hardships in my childhood,
and as I left Shensi for Shanghai when I was seven, I knew nothing
about the actual living conditions of the peasants and the laboring
people, nor about the actual conditions of society. I was so much
engrossed in bookish studies that I lived in a world of empty
imagination, completely divorced from the realities. I consciously
overlooked the violent, ruthless, and ugly aspects of China's feudal
history as clearly depicted in the old books but chose to look at
the aspects which pleased me. I thus idealized China's feudal
history and culture by empty fancy, false emotions, and idealistic
objectivism. In concrete matters I prized the beauty of the Chinese
language most, though I also loved Chinese paintings and various
Chinese handicraft objets d'art, which I considered to be our
historical heritage and cultural accomplishments, not knowing,
however, that these are all the fruits of the blood and sweat of the

159

Chinese laboring people during the course of thousands of years. In a word, I considered Chinese culture as good but Chinese politics as bad; and our responsibility as consisting of trying to preserve and develop the better aspects of Chinese culture, under all conditions and under any kind of rule, without bothering to overthrow the rule of the reactionary elements; while believing that the bad aspects of Chinese culture would vanish by themselves without our having to do anything about them. On this question I went so far as to declare that even if China were conquered by Japan or any other country, the Chinese people would, within two to three hundred years, drive out the invaders and regain their independence; but all would be lost should our culture be destroyed. This feudal respect for native Chinese culture, so deeply rooted in my mind, has remained one of my principal ideologies. All the time, while editing the periodical *Hsueh Heng* and the literary supplement of the *Ta Kung Pao,* and on numerous other occasions, I did my best to advocate the feudal ideology of respecting the old native culture. It was after the May 4th Movement that the *Hsueh Heng,* under my editorship, advocated the literary language and the classical Chinese poetry, as well as the preservation of the old ethical and moral standards. At that time, this undoubtedly gave moral support to the diehard reactionaries and obstructed the progress of the revolutionary cause. The *Ta Kung Pao* being then a capitalist paper forcefully taken over by the reactionary Kuomintang government, I did no less than serve the interests of the reactionary ruling class when I edited its literary supplement.

I received the education of the European and American bourgeoisie. I studied for six years in Tsinghua University and then for four years in America, followed by one year in England. I then taught for nearly twenty years in Tsinghua University (including the period of Southwest Associated University). As a school founded on the Boxer Indemnity Funds returned by America, Tsinghua was under the indirect control of the Americans, and at the time when I studied there, the classes were conducted in English, songs were sung in English, and American history and citizenship were taught. When in America, I became a disciple of Irving Babbitt, the great master of the New Humanism, whose theories I considered to be the embodiment of all the past and present cultural attainments of both the East and the West. Though Babbitt castigated American politics as "decadent and weak imperialism" doomed to annihilation, yet I was only interested in those aspects of Babbitt which corresponded to my conservative love for the ancient, idealism, feudal ideology, and love for native culture. Thus during my studies abroad I only succeeded in absorbing the conservative reactionary bourgeois ideologies of the West, which are precisely those theories made use of by the contemporary European and American bourgeoisie for the maintenance of their exploitative rule and by the imperialists for cultural aggression. Aside from the above, I also imbibed various English and American political theories on socialism, all based on the reformism of the capitalist economy. All these I propagated in the *Hsueh Heng* and the literary supplement of the *Ta Kung Pao* when I got back to China. Thus, though I had always considered myself to be "above taking sides" and neutral and not belonging to any party, yet both ideologically and in actual work I had undoubtedly worked consistently and hard for both domestic and foreign reactionaries and for the imperialists and for the propagation of idealism, liberalism, and reformism, and thus held up the progress of the revolution. In posing as a scholar versed in the ideas of both the ancient and contemporary periods and the Eastern and Western countries, my vicious influences have been deep-rooted and extensive in scope. To cite only two examples: (1) Readers frequently wrote letters to various publications which I edited at one time or another to express their agreement with my views and announce their willingness to be my followers, thus unconsciously forming a clique and establishing a style of work. (2) In the course of nearly twenty years of teaching in Tsinghua, few, if any, of the numerous students who graduated from the Department of Western Languages and Literature, who attended my classes, or who knew me well, later turned out to be famous Communists or sacrificed their lives in long years of revolutionary work. Is this not definite proof of my criminal deeds?

I returned to China in 1921 (in total ignorance of the Chinese Communist Party, which was founded in the same year), and for thirty-odd years I taught Western literature at different universities. In my professional capacity, I erred in entertaining the technical viewpoint and the viewpoint of the employee. Realizing that I was both responsible and capable of hard work, I prided myself on being an untainted scholar, earning my living by honest hard work. But looking back at the same question now, I ask myself, who founded these so-called "national universities," and whose money supported those universities; for whom was I working; and whether I was truly "above politics"? I now see the truth that, for thirty years the Chinese government had been a reactionary regime made up of the feudal landlord class, the bureaucratic bourgeoisie, and the comprador class, which are but the lackeys of the imperialists. When I was teaching in the universities founded by these people, I was only serving the interests of these reactionary ruling classes, contented to be their accomplice and slave. Furthermore, my pedagogical method and contents have always been completely patterned on the European and American practices (especially the American); that is, the pedagogical method and contents of the bourgeoisie. I have concentrated my attention on the "talented" students to the utter neglect of the common students. In constantly admiring the ancient times of China and the Middle Ages of the West and praising the political freedom and social orderliness of England, I succeeded in drugging the minds of the youths and consolidating the reactionary rule. I advocated all through the reformism of the bourgeoisie, that is, the old democratic political theories of England and America, and repudiated the violent sanguinary struggles of the revolution. While teaching in Tsinghua before the start of the Sino-Japanese War, I was neither for nor against the students' movement but adopted a self-styled "neutral" stand. I was all for combining the ideas of universal love and humanitarianism of Shelley, Tolstoy, and Romain Rolland; the benevolence and virtue of the Confucian, and the sympathy and commiseration of the

Buddhist. I thus opposed killing and struggling, and I indiscriminately condemned wars and advocated peace.

.   .   .   .

When I carried out my self-examination and discussion on June 5, 1951, at a meeting of the third study group, my fellow group members favored me with numerous correct opinions and critical ideas. I shall endeavor to deal with these opinions and ideas under the following three general headings:

(1) I shall hereafterwards read more, in order to make a study of the new philosophy of materialism, get at the sole truth, and gain a thorough understanding of Marxism-Leninism and the thoughts of Mao Tse-tung, so as to enable me to make a thorough criticism of my past, to discover the source of my mistakes, and rectify and avoid commiting these mistakes. As far as my pedagogical work is concerned, my students expressed the opinion that, in my lectures on the history of English literature and on the history of world literature, I was inclined to overemphasize the importance of facts to the neglect of ideological criticism. This was quite true. Inasmuch as I had only read a very small number of new books, I was unable to make use of the theories of social development and the class viewpoint to interpret the events of the history of literature, the lives of the authors, and the contents of the literary works. In the further thought that the students were ideologically more advanced than myself, I also erred in leaving the work of criticism to the students. Hereafterwards I shall try to study more, adopt a more critical attitude, and read up on Soviet works on the history of literature. (I have already been reading Shakespeare in this manner.)

(2) I shall resolutely maintain the proletarian standpoint and look at the men and the events from the class point of view. Politically, I shall make a clearcut distinction between our enemies and our friends; and I shall draw a clear ideological line of demarcation, in order to keep my personal emotions under good control and avoid mistakes both in thought and in action. Parallel with the presence of class opposition in political and economic fields, literary ideology should also be built upon its class foundation. Thus, in classroom lectures on the history of literature, clear

distinctions should be made in the interpretation of every single event and word, so that we may not lose the class viewpoint.

(3) I shall further heighten my sense of responsibility towards our fatherland and our people and in all matters stick to the right principle, without adopting an attitude of compromise and vacillation or following the middle road. I shall never make the mistake I did in the summer of 1948, when I told my third daughter, Hsueh-ch'ao, to "do as each of us sees fit." Insofar as the right must be distinct from the wrong—and should this be right then the other must be wrong—I must hereafter always base myself on: Marxism-Leninism, proletarian ideology, and the interests of the people.

Besides the above, I would like to reiterate my determination to reform my ideology thoroughly in order to try to become a true teacher of the people. Ideologically, I shall make a study of dialectical and historical materialism, uproot idealism, accept Marxism and Leninism and the thoughts of Mao Tse-tung, discard all reactionary theories, uphold the proletarian ideology, and repudiate the bourgeois ideology. In action, I shall follow the leadership of the Communist Party, which represents the working class, abide by the laws and orders of the People's Government and the instructions of Chairman Mao, love the Soviet Union, oppose America, oppose the bourgeois ideology of reformism, and support the Communist attempt to reform the world completely, in order to advance from socialism to communism and bring the benefits of "one world" to all the people. As far as my personal life and professional work are concerned, I shall always keep an eye on the interests of the people and devote the rest of my life to serving the people.

SOURCE: *Current Background*, No. 213 (Hong Kong: United States Consulate General, October 1, 1952). Originally published in *Hsin Hua Jih Pao* (Chungking), July 8, 1952. Later published in *Ta Kung Pao*, August 10, 1952.

For additional readings, see *Current Background*, Nos. 169 and 182 (1952).

Speech before the Study Group
of Research Members of the Academia Sinica
By Chen Po-ta
July 1952

This speech was made during a critical period, when the "intellectual reform" program occupied the attention of most scholars, scientists, and teachers. The Chinese Academy of Sciences, like all other institutions of its kind, was "destined to be in the vanguard of reform." Chen Po-ta, at the time he gave his speech, was a member of the Central Committee of the Communist Party of China and concurrently Vice-President of the Institute of Marxism-Leninism in Peking. It was significant that, as a vice-president of the Academia Sinica and a leading Party member, he gave this speech explaining in theoretical and historical terms the relationship between the different social elements to be found in modern Chinese Communist society. Particular reference is made to the development of better relations between the older "traditional" (and often foreign-trained) scientists and the "new" Marxist scholars. Chen concludes his address by stressing the then-current theme of "emulation of the Soviet Union," by suggesting that "the good things in British and American science have already been absorbed by the Soviet scientists; hence, the quickest and best way is to learn from the Soviet Union."

Some comrades from the Committee on Studies in the Academy of Sciences [Academia Sinica] asked me to come here to give a talk. Before doing so, I asked President Kuo Mo-jo and the vice-presidents of the Academy for their advice, and I discussed certain problems with the comrades from the Committee on Studies.

165

However, I myself should be held responsible for any error I may make in my talk.

Today I shall speak on three points: (1) the relations between Communist Party members and scientists outside the Party in the work of the Academy, and between scientists of the old and the new type; (2) the orientation of the Academy's work; and (3) scientists and patriotism.

THE RELATIONS BETWEEN COMMUNIST PARTY MEMBERS
AND SCIENTISTS OUTSIDE THE PARTY

There are a number of Communist Party members working in the Academy. What should be their relations with the scientists? Party members have their role to play in the Academy. Our Party is the leading political party in our people's State power, enjoying the highest prestige among the people of the whole country. Consequently, our Party members can also play an important role in the Academy. If they do their part well, they will render great service to the Academy; otherwise, much harm will be done. And whether or not the Academy will be able to do good work, the Party members will have to bear a great share of responsibility. How can Party members carry out their task? Can they abuse the Party's prestige, assume a self-important attitude, issue orders in their capacity of Party members, and claim that scientific workers cannot do anything without previously obtaining their approval? To adopt such an attitude would be a mistake. The fundamental task of the Party members in the Academy is to learn with modesty from the scientists and to help them do their work well. Comrade Mao Tse-tung has consistently taught our Party members, no matter what position they may hold, to be modest and to avoid being arrogant, so as to unite more effectively comrades inside and outside the Party in any common endeavor. Now that our Party has attained power throughout the country, Comrade Mao Tse-tung's instruction is unquestionably even more important than before, and it is particularly important to the Party members working in the Academy.

In this connection, let me quote from Lenin's article entitled "A Single Economic Plan," written in 1921. With respect to the relations between Communist Party members and non-Party scientists, Lenin said:

It has long been noted that for the most part people's shortcomings are bound up with their merits. Such are the shortcomings of many of our leading Communists. For decades we have been working in a great cause, preaching the overthrow of the bourgeoisie; we have been inculcating distrust of the bourgeois experts, exposing them, depriving them of power, and crushing their resistance. It was a great cause, a cause of historic importance. But one has only to exaggerate ever so little, and the truth that there is only one step from the sublime to the ridiculous is confirmed. We have convinced Russia; we have won Russia for the toilers from the exploiters; we have crushed the exploiters. Now we must learn to administer Russia. And to do that we must learn to be modest and to respect the efficient work of the "experts in science and technology"; to do that we must learn to analyse in an efficient and careful way our numerous practical mistakes and to correct them, gradually but persistently. Less intellectual and bureaucratic conceit, more study of what our practical experience, both in the centre and in the localities, is giving and of what science has already given us.[1]

Herein Lenin spoke on the proper attitude which the Bolsheviks, after they had attained power in Russia, should adopt towards scientists and scientific work. It is exactly this kind of attitude that the members of the Chinese Communist Party must adopt. True, the character of our revolution at the present stage is different from that of the Russian revolution at the time mentioned by Lenin, which had overthrown the bourgeoisie. Under the conditions in China, we at the present stage have only overthrown the reactionary rule of imperialism and its lackey, the Kuomintang, which represented the feudal landlords and the bureaucratic bourgeoisie. However, the course which Lenin pointed out then for learning how to administer Russia is the same course we should now follow in order to learn how to administer China. It is, therefore, imperative that Party members working in the Academy learn with great modesty from honest and sincere scientists and assist them earnestly in accomplishing

1. Citations omitted here and below; see original document.

their task. Otherwise, such Party members will be unequal to
their task.

In order to explain fully why Party members must correctly
handle their relations with the scientists, I shall quote more
from the above-mentioned article by Lenin:

It is the duty of the Communists within the "Goelro" to do less bossing,
or rather not to boss at all, but to observe an extremely cautious and tactful
attitude towards experts in science and technology ("in most cases they
are inevitably imbued with a bourgeois outlook and bourgeois habits," as
the program of the Russian Communist Party has it), learning from them
and helping them to expand their outlook on the basis of the achievements
and data of the particular science concerned, remembering that an engineer
will come to accept communism not as the prerevolutionary underground
propagandist and writer came to accept it but through the data of his
science; that the agronomist will come to accept communism in his own
way, the timber expert in his way, and so on.

According to Lenin, a scientist or an engineer will come to accept communism through the data of his science and in his own
way. This is an important revelation to us.

The October Socialist Revolution has opened a broad path for
the development of science in the Soviet Union, enabling the
scientists to unite with the masses of the people. The work of the
scientists is highly respected by the Communist Party and the
people and has been given ample opportunities at all times for
widespread application. Thus, conditions are constantly being
created for honest scientists to accept communism through the
data of their science. The situation in China is just the same following the victory of the people's revolution.

Prior to the nationwide victory of the Chinese revolution, Comrade Mao Tse-tung frequently pointed out that the victory of
the revolution would be impossible without the participation of
the intelligentsia. Having attained victory in the revolution, we
now are on the road to large-scale national construction. We need
more than ever large numbers of intellectuals and scientists to
participate in our work, so that we may accomplish our tasks. In
time to come no doubt qualified scientists will emerge in large
numbers, but, for the present, we must develop fully the potentiali-

ties of the scientists we now have. We must help them to do their work well and to expand their outlook; we must lead them on step by step to Communist ideology. Party members, in their contact with non-Party scientists, must bear in mind the fact that many non-Party scientists have certain definite scientific achievements to their credit and that since the liberation they have, in the course of their work, come in touch with practical problems of economic construction and have made certain contributions. These contributions, though not too many, mark a good beginning and serve to prove that once they are on the side of the people, they will be able to demonstrate their ability as never before. All these conscientious and hard-working non-Party scientists will render a multitude of services to the State in the future. In the past, various kinds of historical backgrounds and social environments prevented them from having an opportunity to accept Marxism-Leninism. Quite a number of them had all along shut their eyes to what was going on in the world and devoted themselves entirely to the study of the writings of the sages." However, they are not much to blame for these things. We cannot judge scientists of the old type by merely considering the time when they accept Marxism-Leninism of their own will. The important thing is to see whether or not they are carrying on work in their respective scientific fields with a realistic attitude. It is very important for Party members to understand this point.

On the other hand, if the scientists, seeing that the people and the Communist Party think highly of them, should adopt an arrogant attitude towards the people, should not strive to reform their old ideology and old style of work, and should not desire to make progress, then they likewise would be extremely mistaken. On this point, Comrade Mao Tse-tung also told us long ago that intellectuals and scientists must associate themselves with the people, if their work is to be crowned with success. Otherwise they will be unable to accomplish anything. Experience of the last one hundred years teaches us precisely that only by joining the masses of the people and by coöperating with the Communist Party will the scientists be able to find their future. It is also exceedingly important that earnest scientists understand this point.

Hence, such relations should be mutual. Party members should coöperate with the scientists, learn from them, and assist them in solving difficulties in their work. On the other hand, the scientists should, on their own initiative, coördinate their efforts with the common cause of the popular masses, as well as with the work of national construction.

To be sure, this does not mean to say that Communist Party members and non-Party scientists should not criticize one another. Mutual criticism is absolutely necessary. Many scientists have carried over from the old society certain old things which cannot possibly be eradicated at one stroke—for instance, carrying on scientific work with a bourgeois world outlook, preserving habits of the old society, taking an impractical, lighthearted, and careless attitude towards work, etc. May Party members criticize these things? Certainly they may do so, and they must do so. This kind of criticism will help the scientists to broaden their outlook and do their work well. In the case of certain Party members in the Academy (including Communist scientists who, though few in number now, will increase as time goes on), may non-Party scientists also criticize them when they have made mistakes? Yes, absolutely, and they must do so. If some Communist scientists, just because they are Communist Party members, should treat the scientific work and scientists rudely and claim to be 100 percent Marxists in any problem, without making any serious study, such Communist scientists will not easily win the confidence of others. Obviously, severe criticism should be given by all concerned to such Communist scientists as have mistaken views and a wrong style of work. They cannot be considered 100 percent Marxists as a matter of course and therefore immune to criticisms just because of their Party membership or their long standing in the Party. Some of the criticisms may be wrong, but even so, it does not matter. Problems need to be discussed. Precisely as Stalin pointed out in his outstanding work, *Concerning Marxism in Linguistics:* "It is generally recognized that no science can develop and flourish without a battle of opinions, without freedom of criticism."

Comrade Mao Tse-tung said: "The enemy of learning is self-complacency." This truism is useful to everybody. Once a person becomes self-complacent, be he a Communist of long standing or a non-Communist of high distinction, he is bound to fall behind the times. Kang Yu-wei, a landlord-bourgeois reformist, who was once active in the reform movement under Emperor Kuang Hsu, said he had perfected his education by the time he was thirty and that after that he made no more progress as no more progress was needed. He claimed that he had learned all the truths in the world. At first, he was a progressive and was considered a rebel by the older generation. The chief reason why he changed from being a progressive at that time to a die-hard conservative must be explained from the viewpoint of historical development of his class background. Nevertheless, from the point of his self-complacency alone, it was inevitable that he should change into a die-hard conservative.

An old Chinese saying goes: "Learning is like sailing against a current; if you do not progress, you retrogress." All things move forward. Even if you are correct today, you will fall behind if you cannot understand and grasp the new things appearing on the morrow. This is still more true of the situation at present, when the achievements of the people are proceeding by leaps and bounds and a multitude of new things are emerging. If you are unrealistic to a slight degree, you will be quickly swept behind by the current of times. Hence, who dares to declare arrogantly and arbitrarily that he is 100 percent correct in all cases and at all times? Communist or non-Communist, if he has not made strenuous efforts to study concrete subjects and yet claims to be 100 percent correct on any question, then the only way to make him improve is to criticize him. Criticism should be particularly severe towards the Communist Party members.

Communists may criticize non-Communists for their bourgeois world outlook, their decadent habits, and other erroneous things brought over from the old society. Non-Communists may criticize Communists for their mistakes. By so doing, they will encourage each other in making improvements. The building-up of such criticism and self-criticism will improve the work of the Academy immensely.

In the work of the Academy, we should pay attention not only to the relations between the Communists and non-Party scientists but also to the relations between the scientists of the old and the new type, that is, between the older and younger scientists. Some older scientists have a poor opinion of the younger scientists, and vice versa. Why? Older scientists have their merits and demerits; so have the younger scientists. A problem naturally arises when one party judges the other party's demerits by its own merits. We all know that the merits of the older scientists lie chiefly in their having more experience and knowing more things. But, they also have demerits precisely because they consider themselves to have studied more and understood more than their younger colleagues. They are inclined to remain where they are and rest content with the accomplishments already obtained. I used to study in a private tutoring school. There, the aged tutor had ideas quite different from those of youngsters. If you did not obey him, he would give you a box on the ear. He thought that he knew all the truths in the world and that there were no others. He would become furious at any young man who knew more than he did. He did not realize that there were a good many things he did not yet know. Many older scientists are comparatively less sensitive to new things. Here, I say "many." I do not mean all older scientists, since some of them are more sensitive than the younger scientists; their receptivity to new things is even quicker. It need hardly be said that the old habits and bourgeois viewpoints and ways not infrequently retained by the older scientists, such as individualism, sectarianism, the habit of working exclusively by and for themselves, etc., are serious defects.

The good points of the younger scientists are mainly that they have a keener sensitivity to new things, have a progressive and forward spirit, are not content with what they have attained, are less subject to the influence of the old, and are more inclined to take in new things. Of course, there are scientists of the new type who are proudly satisfied with what little accomplishments they have made. Their shortcomings lie in their insufficient experience and their unsound foundation in science. They are apt to take a rude attitude towards the defects of the scientists of the old type and are not careful enough. If the young and old scientists understand each other's merits and defects, they should criticize each other's defects and learn from each other's merits. If this is done, old scientists will no longer remain old, and young scientists will become much more experienced. Old scientists should take loving care of the younger generation, while the young should respect the old and particularly should stress their good points, learn from them, and ask for their advice.

THE ORIENTATION OF THE ACADEMY'S WORK

With respect to the orientation of the work of the Academy, the problem is crystal clear. The large amount of work of the Academy should meet the urgent demands of the people and serve the immediate task of the State and the planning of national construction. Such being the case, it is necessary for the scientists to associate themselves in practice on the most basic and broadest scale. Such association in practice is real association with the great masses of the people. Obviously, only from the viewpoint of working for the people's well-being and only on the practical basis of associating with the masses will science in our country make progress in big strides. In the past, some conscientious natural scientists in our country were practical and hard-working. In spite of that, they failed to make any outstanding contribution. In modern China, no natural scientist of first-rate world distinction has yet appeared, and no contribution of a conspicuous and creative character and of a worldwide significance has yet been made to natural science. Is it because we are especially incompetent? Decidedly not. It is because under reactionary rule and imperialist domination it was impossible to develop our industries and to meet the needs of the people. Although a certain number of persons took up the study of science, they were not given due respect. Consequently, some of them gave up their work in the midst of their efforts, while others shut themselves up in their own small rooms and worked all by themselves without receiving any assistance whatsoever. During such a period, how could science have developed and made big contributions? Obviously, we cannot put the entire blame for all these defects on the old scientists. The causes should be found in the historical conditions of society. But, now, epoch-making changes have taken place in China. We are within sight of the industrialization of our nation. How can industrialization be realized? In addition to the strength of the people, the efforts of the scientists are needed. It is the sacred responsibility of the scientists to assist in industrialization. Here, all roads lead to science, and all roads open up boundless vistas for the development of science. If a scientist has eyes but sees not and ears but hears not such epoch-making changes and gigantic industrialization, if he still considers science as something to be enjoyed exclusively and still feels that it is better to shut himself up in a room and work all by himself, such a scientist is surely divorcing himself from the most fundamental realities and doing harm to himself. I cannot imagine a scientist indifferent to the national welfare and the people's livelihood who can still accomplish anything extraordinary in science. Take for example such great scholars as Ivan Petrovich Pavlov and E. V. Michurin, who were both great patriots. They were infused with enthusiasm towards the national welfare and the people's livelihood. Their accomplishments were, therefore, no accidents.

What Comrade Mao Tse-tung said about the necessity of associating with the people means the necessity of meeting the needs of the people. Today, the needs of the people are: through magnificent economic construction, to strengthen the defense of the motherland and of peace, to elevate continuously the material and cultural life of the masses, and to accelerate our country's progress from new democracy to socialism and communism. If our scientists hope to raise the level of science in China and advance it to as high a peak as was ever reached in the world, they must follow the path of actually meeting these needs of the people. Such is the fundamental orientation of the Academy's work. There is and there can be no other orientation.

Having defined the orientation, I shall try to explain the following questions:

First, we are opposed to a one-sided understanding of the problem of connecting theory with practice. Some people suspect that in speaking of connecting theory with practice, we only want practice without theory. This is not so. When we speak of "connecting theory with practice," we surely imply two sides. If there is only one side, it will be impossible to speak of connecting one with the other. What we mean to say is that neither should be isolated from the other but that they should be connected. Theory without practice and practice without theory are both wrong. Stalin said: "Theory becomes purposeless if it is not connected with revolutionary practice, just as practice gropes in the dark if its path is not illumined by revolutionary theory." Comrade Mao Tse-tung often used this quotation to oppose the two extremes of one-sidedness; theory without practice and practice without theory.

To connect theory with practice is the demand which Marxism-Leninism makes on any branch of science. Stalin said: "Theory is the experience of the working-class movement in all countries taken in its general aspect." This refers to the theory of social revolution. In the field of natural science, of course, theory is likewise the generalized experiences in man's observations of the movement of things in the realm of nature and in man's practical activities positively carried out towards nature. As it is understood in the Marxist-Leninist way, theory explains the law of the movement of things; it explains the multifarious and multilateral relations between things. This holds true with social science as it does with natural science. A theory is not worthy of the name if it fails to explain a thing itself or its relations to other things. It will be an absurdity if, in an attempt to explain the law of the movement of things and the relations between things, no effort is made to study real things or to rely on practical experience or a large amount of data. Comrade Mao Tse-tung has clarified all these questions in his writings, *On Practice* and *On Contradiction*. He has constantly pointed out, particularly in *The Reform of Our Study*, that we should possess data in detail, analyse them systematically and minutely. This is because theory consists in the analysis and synthesis of a multitude of facts—the analysis and synthesis of internal and external relations of things as understood in the light of a multitude of facts instead of fragmentary data and isolated instances. Fragmentary data and isolated instances cannot constitute a theory, nor can a theory be derived from separate, trifling facts. It is, therefore, clear that connection with practice is not connection with one aspect of a practice but with all aspects of that practice, its embodiments and its relations. The objects of study of a particular branch of science are, of course, things in that particular field. But the internal and external relationship of the objects of study is many-sided. It would be wrong to draw an arbitrary conclusion after seeing only a certain aspect of an object. We must observe and practice on many sides and take the object as a whole. That is to say, to connect theory with practice is to grasp many-sidedly the sum total of the actual relationship. We must always bear in mind Comrade Mao Tse-tung's warning against one-sidedness.

It is necessary to iterate with emphasis that we must not depart from practice and prate about theory independently; likewise, we must not study practice one-sidedly in isolation from the abundance and richness of actual life. To single out an individual matter without taking into consideration its surrounding conditions and circumstances, its relations with other matters and to carry on one-sided experiments in a laboratory is tantamount to studying practice in isolation from actual life as a whole. For instance, it is reported that a certain scientist carries out research in fertilizers independent of the soil problem. Such effort, I am afraid, will be inappropriate for working out an overall solution to the practical problem. Although what he studies is a specific thing, a specific subject matter, yet, since he separates the object of study from its surrounding conditions, it will be very difficult to arrive at a valid theory, because theory serves to explain the law of the movement of things, and any law of the movement of things is interrelated with their surrounding conditions.

Concerning the problem of connecting theory with practice, some people still doubt whether some theoretical work in natural science, which is not directly but only indirectly connected with the practice of production today, is really wanted. Of course it is. For instance, it is possible that certain research work in astronomy and mathematics may not have a direct connection with practice of production at present, but many things studied, discovered, and explained in astronomy and mathematics can help the progress and development of scientific research work in many other fields and broaden scientific outlook, thereby producing effects upon the development of agriculture and industry. The same is true of certain research work in other branches of natural science. Therefore, some theoretical work in science may have direct connection with the practice of production today, while other theoretical work may have no direct but only indirect connection or no connection for the time being. As some research work is just begun, we cannot demand that it should have extensive and all-round connections with the practice of production and the people's livelihood immediately. In fact, the connection of a good deal of scientific research work with the needs of the great masses of the people always grows from the insignificant to the significant. We should adopt an attitude of respect and active helpfulness toward all these kinds of scientific work. It would be a mistake not to give them direct help, thus causing their abandonment.

A question has been raised as to the connection between certain research work in social science (such as the study of ancient history and archaeology) and the practice of production at present. I am of the opinion that such research work has no connection with the practice of production at present. However, this kind of research helps man to understand historical events and things and is useful for broadening scientific outlook. It is, therefore, also entitled to necessary assistance.

Second, we should place our scientific research on a wide horizon and should not confine it to trivial side issues. I have heard that some scientists want to reach and exceed the world level on certain trifling items and to accomplish something "sensational" on certain odd, narrow little topics. I think it is not for us to prevent certain scientists from making such attempts, or treat them rudely and say to them: "Do not make such research." The attitude we take towards them can only be one of trying to convince them. If they do not agree, let them try. When they come up against snags and fail to obtain any result, they will come to understand that our opinion is right, and they will correct their mistakes. As a matter of policy, as we have said before, what we ask for is that scientific work should contribute to the needs of the people and to national construction. What scientists have to pursue should, therefore, be chiefly what the people need in great quantities and what is important and of a mass character in a certain scientific field. In other words, research work must serve definite purposes and lead to the solution of important problems of a mass character. Do not pursue trivial side issues only, nor carry on research work only for research's sake. Marxists used to criticize the opportunist, Bernstein, a leader of the German Social-Democratic Party, who, in the words of Lenin, became "notorious" for blaspheming Marxism. Bernstein said: "Movements are everything; purpose is nothing." Marx said that the purpose of our proletarian revolutionary movement is to overthrow the bourgeois rule, carry out proletarian dictatorship, and establish socialism and communism, but Bernstein most preposterously called the movement purposeless. When we Marxists do any work, it must serve a clearcut purpose, as purposeless work is useless. Do not do research work for research's sake but for the sake of the people, for the sake of important problems in science. Some people would say: "Ah, this is what I am personally interested in!" We Marxists would say that we do not lightly brush aside personal likes, personal aims, and personal interests, but we ask that personal likes be integrated with the likes of the masses, personal aims with the aims of the masses. We have a definite standard here for judging how personal likes, personal aims, and personal interests should be respected, and that is that they must be subordinated to the interests of the masses as a whole. It is utterly wrong to separate personal likes, personal aims, and personal interests from those of the masses. It has often happened that nothing came out of a lot of research work some hard-working scientists did merely on the basis of their personal likes. If a student of history wishes to make research in the genealogy of a family, he may be considered as working on a definite thing, an actual object, and he may do it for life. But what is the use? It will be of no use to the family concerned nor to the people of China as a whole. So, do not take up any research which is without aim and for which you can give no reason. It will simply be a waste of energy.

It is also necessary to explain that certain things to which nobody pays much attention may look insignificant at first but would engage the attention of some thoughtful scientists who perceive the possibility of explaining some important problems and drawing important conclusions from the results of research in those things. We should not ridicule these scientists who are carrying on such research; we should not oppose them. On the contrary, we should respect them. It is quite possible that the results of their research work may make outstanding contributions. What we ask for is that scientists should be in a position to account for their research plans and the aims of their research.

Third, in the preface to the French edition of *Das Kapital,* Marx said: "In science there are no high roads, and only he will get to its shining summit who is not afraid of tiredness and who clambers up its rocky paths." Marx is the most outstanding genius in history, but in the work of science, he went through strenuous efforts. No person will be able to make any great achievement if he has not studied hard and long enough. That is true of Marx, Engels, Lenin, and Stalin; and in China, it is also true of Comrade Mao Tse-tung. We should all of us learn from Marx. I think our scientists will do well to learn how Marx went about his scientific work. For reference, we may read Lafargue's and Liebknecht's *Reminiscences of Karl Marx.* From these two reminiscences, we will understand the reason why "genius is diligence." Genius does not come down from heaven but turns up on earth. Why can one become a genius? Because one stands on a very reliable and solid ground on the earth. The airplane flies in the air, but it takes off from the ground. It starts from the ground and lands on the ground. There is no airplane base in the air. In China, many persons bloomed in youth, early and quite beautifully, but up till now only a few of them have borne fruits. The reason is that aside from social conditions, they, on their part, think that genius flies all over the sky, and they have not found a reliable base on the ground. So, when they fall, they come crashing down in pieces. There is an old Chinese saying that "a clever child may not be clever when he grows up." Why is it that a clever child does not remain clever when he grows up? Simply because no sooner has he shown a little wisdom than he becomes conceited and stops doing hard work; and so his wisdom dies young. In our scientific work, therefore, we must cultivate a style of perfect simplicity and of going forward with great exertions. This is what Comrade Mao Tse-tung asks of us.

We cannot separate the style of simplicity and of going forward with exertions, the style of working hard and never stopping midway unless the aim is reached, from the style of constant self-criticism. If a scholar does not review his shortcomings and correct his mistakes from time to time, he cannot be said to have the style of simplicity; nor can he expect to make any scientific achievement. Let us consider Marx. Engels said:

> Marx thought his best things were still not good enough for the workers, and he regarded it as a crime to offer the workers anything less than the very best.

Lafargue, in his *Reminiscences of Karl Marx*, also said:

> He [Marx] never relied on any fact of which he was not absolutely sure, and he would never discuss any problem unless he had made a thorough study of it. He was unwilling to publish anything before he had revised it again and again until he felt quite satisfied even as to its form. He would never express any half-baked idea to the public. He would feel very uncomfortable if he had to show his manuscript to other people without a chance of going through a final checking.

We can see that Marx integrated the style of practical realism with the style of self-criticism. It is highly important to nurture such a Marxist style of work in our Academy. It must be clearly understood that any carelessness in scientific work will unavoidably result in errors. Scientists should work with practical realism and exert tireless efforts with great prudence. We should not be afraid to correct our own mistakes. We should welcome criticism from other people and at the same time earnestly practice self-criticism.

Fourth, in the Academy, we should consider scientific work a common enterprise of the people as well as a common enterprise of the scientists. Our work should be built upon the basis of mutual help. We should gradually establish a method of collective research. We should not work singly, each one by and for himself, unwilling to help others. The old working style of minding one's own business should be discarded in this new era. Contact should be established between different research branches and between the research institutes, and concrete methods of mutual assistance should be worked out. Scientists need unity and coöperation; they also need criticism and self-criticism. These two aspects are completely coherent.

On the basis of the above-mentioned orientation and various problems explained thereunder, we should be able to map out some research plans. Each person and each institute should formulate his and its own working plans and submit them to the leading body of the Academy for consideration. The leading body of the Academy will then discuss the plans with the different institutes, draw up an overall plan and present it to the state in the name of the Academy. In preparing these plans, we should ask for opinions from the various departments of industries, agriculture, communications, water conservancy, and others in the Central People's Government to solicit their assistance and suggestions for assignments, so that our plans may become comparatively practical plans to meet more adequately the demands of the State. Of course, such plans are subject to revisions, according to changes in actual conditions. Mr. Li Sze-kuang has put forth a very good idea in suggesting that the leading body of the Academy should help the different institutes to work out topics for research. I think this should constitute the core of the leading body's work in the Academy.

SCIENTISTS AND PATRIOTISM

Scientists should be patriotic and should serve their motherland and the people. For us, patriotism is combined with internationalism.

As is generally recognized, China has a long history of civilization and has made important contributions to the world, such as printing, gunpowder, the compass, etc. However, it would be folly to become conceited on account of these things. We have still less reason to be so, since these contributions were made by our fore-fathers and not by us. Of course, it would be wrong to forget our forefathers in reviewing history, but it would be still worse to live on the reputation of our forefathers and forget to make our own efforts. We shall have no perspective for the future if we ever forget that China lags behind in science in this modern era. We must understand that today we are backward and that we must catch up with the advanced. To be able to catch up we can-not rely on bragging but on sustained efforts.

We must have self-confidence in making creations. Foreign im-perialist aggression and domestic counterrevolutionary rule dragged China into a dark abyss. Consequently, there was a lack of self-confidence on the part of a certain number of people, who thought that there was no hope whatsoever for things Chinese. Some intellectuals of the comprador type even said that "the moon over the United States of America is brighter." People of this type can also be found in the midst of the scientists. They think that everything in the U.S.A. and Britain is good, while nothing in China is good. This national inferiority complex is a result of imperialist oppression. The Chinese people now have stood up and overthrown the oppression by world imperialism. Our revolu-tionary cause was once in grave danger, but, under the leadership of the Chinese Communist Party and Comrade Mao Tse-tung and through a long period of struggle, we have finally achieved victory, confirming the statement of Stalin, who pointed out quite early that "the forces of the revolutionary movement in China are in-calculable." That the Chinese people have such mighty and in-calculable forces explains why we have a boundless future. Since our scientists are the offspring of the great Chinese people and they are under the leadership of Comrade Mao Tse-tung, there is no reason why they should not be able to render magnificent services to the motherland and the people. It is true that, generally speaking, our science is still young, but youth has its advantages, since it is not tied to old traditions and is more ready to accept new things. In science, we can find unexplored virgin soil everywhere. Anyone who is willing to make serious efforts and devote his energy will meet with success in science, and the objective conditions for achieving success do exist. In 1945, Comrade Mao Tsetung wrote in his book *On Coalition Government:*

The industrialization of China is impossible without first establishing an independent, free, democratic, and united China. To annihilate the Japanese aggressors is to achieve independence. To abolish the Kuomintang's one-party dictatorship, to form a democratic coalition government, to realize freedom for the people, to achieve unification by the people, to organize an army of the people, and to carry out agrarian reform and liberate the peasantry—to do these things is to achieve freedom, democracy, and unity. Without independence, freedom, democracy, and unity, there cannot be any large-scale industry of national significance. And without industry, national defense can not be consolidated, nor the welfare of the people promoted, nor the prosperity and power of the nation ensured.

This important point has been made clear to the Chinese people by the history of the past one hundred and five years since the Opium War of 1840, especially of the eighteen years since the Kuomintang came into power. A China that is prosperous and strong and not poor or weak has to be a China that is independent instead of colonial and semicolonial, free and democratic instead of semifeudal, united instead of divided.

To develop industry, build up national defense, promote the welfare of the people, and turn the semifeudal, semicolonial, and divided China into a prosperous and powerful country—all this has been for years the fond dream of numerous people. But their dream did not come true, and they have all been disillusioned. Many well-intentioned educators, scientists, and students who have stayed away from politics and dreamed that they could serve their country with their learning have equally been disillusioned. This is a good sign, for the awakening from such childish dreams marks the beginning of a prosperous and strong China.

The Chinese people have learned a great deal in the war of resistance to Japanese aggression. They have come to understand that, after the Japanese aggressors are annihilated, it will be necessary to build a new democratic China that is independent and free, democratic and united, prosperous and powerful. And they know that these conditions are interrelated, and none of them can be dispensed with. Such being the case, there is hope for China. The productive forces of the Chinese people can be liberated and fully developed only when the political conditions of new democracy are fulfilled throughout China.

The above passages described how the development of events disillusioned many a person who dreamed of developing industries and building a prosperous and powerful state under the rule of feudalism and foreign imperialism and proved that without overthrowing the imperialist and Kuomintang regime, without establishing a people's democratic dictatorship, there can be no industrialized China. And now, such political conditions already exist. In the not distant future, we shall be able to build an industrialized, powerful country. This is no longer a dream but a reality within sight. Our scientists are fortunate, for our motherland is such a great country, and in the scientific field, it is up to us to make explorations. In other words, our scientists will have vast opportunities to play their part everywhere. Indeed, great things await our scientists.

Since the founding of the People's Republic of China, no large-scale movement for rendering meritorious service has yet appeared in our scientific circles. Some contributions have been made, but they are too insignificant in merit. From now on, we should more energetically render service to the people and the motherland and really accomplish something. Some scientists have taken a passive play-safe attitude of desiring no merits but only trying to be free from mistakes. That is not right. They should and must render meritorious service. To desire no merit is a mistake in itself. How is it possible for anyone to be free from mistakes if he does not work for merit? True, in working for merit, one may not be able to avoid mistakes. It is, therefore, necessary that we should, in a spirit of criticism and self-criticism, do our best to avoid, reduce, and correct our mistakes.

It is very important to study Soviet science, which, under the banner of great Lenin and Stalin, stands at the forefront of world science and has made great and numerous contributions to the world. The contributions the Soviet scientists have made and their methods of work are things we must learn. President Kuo Mo-jo calls upon us to learn the Russian language. I think this is an expeditious way to learn Soviet science. Many in this audience know English, French, and German. They can learn Russian very quickly. Of course, when we advise studying Soviet science, we do not mean to say that the works of British and American scientists may not be used as reference. They may and should be. However, generally speaking, the good things in British and American science have already been absorbed by the Soviet scientists; hence, the quickest and best way is to learn from the Soviet Union.

The Central Committee of our Party and Comrade Mao Tse-tung attach great importance to and are greatly concerned with the work of the Academy. In the last three years, on account of multifarious affairs of the State which must be attended to, our Party and the Central People's Government have not been able to pay more attention to the Academy's work. But we can foresee that in the future our Party and the People's Government will gradually give more attention to the work of the Academy because the people need it. In carrying out economic construction on a large scale over a long period of time, the State will have to rely on the efforts of the scientists.

Finally, I fully support the speech made by President Kuo Mo-jo on ideological re-education. The importance of such re-education is clear to all of us. No doubt, ideological re-education of scientific workers is a long-term affair. Moreover, as I have already quoted from Lenin, scientists will come to accept Communism step by step through their own work. Nevertheless, an intensified movement for ideological re-education will enable our scientists to throw overboard all kinds of pernicious and decadent things with much greater rapidity and draw the scientists closer to the people. I am confident that when the present ideological re-education movement is over, a new atmosphere will prevail in the Academy and our work will gradually proceed on the right track.

SOURCE: Chen Po-ta, *Speech before the Study Group of Research Members of [the] Academia Sinica* (Peking: Foreign Languages Press, 1953).

Rally the Youths of China to Forge Ahead in Great Columns for National Construction
By Hu Yao-pang
June 1953

This speech was given at the Second National Congress of the New Democratic Youth League (NDYL) on June 24, 1953, by its new leader, Hu Yao-pang. During this Congress, a revised constitution was adopted by the League, and progress was reported for the four years the League had been in existence. Membership in 1953 was placed at nine million, with 380,000 cells or branches; a year later, membership had risen to 12 million, in over 470,000 primary organizations, while over half a million League members had joined the Communist Party of China during the period from 1949 to 1953.

Comrades, the youth movement in modern China has always developed under the leadership of the Communist Party of China. The Communist Party of China and Chairman Mao have considered the Chinese youths to be an important front army in the revolutionary struggle of our country ever since the May Fourth Movement. Upon its establishment, the Party took charge of the work of the Socialist Youth League of China. The Socialist Youth League of China, later renamed the Communist Youth League of China, played a big part in the first and second revolutionary wars. During the last phase of the second revolutionary war and during the anti-Japanese war, the National Liberation Vanguard of China and the Anti-Japanese Youth Vanguard were formed under the leadership of the Party. All these advanced units of the Chinese units performed their magnificent deeds during

186

the long-term hard revolutionary struggle. Carrying on with the cause of all these advanced units of the Chinese units, the NDYL fostered by the Party continues its march forward.

· · · · · · · · · · · · · · · · · ·

THE TASK OF NDYL IN SCHOOLS

The NDYL has over 1,300,000 members in schools and has become a core of uniting the masses of students. It is incumbent upon us, under the Party and government policy on schools of "reorganization and consolidation, key-point development, raising of quality, steady progress," to assist the Party and government in making a good job of school work in order to train fellow-students into construction personnel, virtuous, talented, healthy and strong.

In order to attain this objective, the NDYL organizations in schools should, first of all, teach the NDYL members to observe the school discipline, to fulfill pedagogical plans, to study their lessons, and use concrete actions to influence and help their fellow students in study. Next, in the course of study the NDYL organizations should promote and develop students' ability of free thinking and practical way of doing things and should, after full discussions, clarify the various and different views of the students and seek progress in order to help them genuinely master knowledge and form the habit of seeking the truth. Further, under the centralized plans of the schools, provided normal study is not handicapped, the NDYL organizations should unite the students to take part voluntarily in the necessary social activities and public welfare work in the schools, thereby to cultivate students' disposition to labor for the public cause and contact with the masses. The NDYL organizations in schools should also show constant attention to the health conditions of the students and assist the schools in developing physical culture and cultural activities, thereby to enable every student to have proper rest and the required physical training.

We youths should respect, show concern to, and help the

teachers in their work. Young teachers, who are fairly large in number in various schools, are a new force for educational work; NDYL members who are teachers should unite the other young teachers and grown-up teachers to play an active role in teaching work.

At the breast of our great motherland are growing millions of children who are heirs to the great revolution and construction cause of our people. It is for the Party and the People's Government to foster them to be a new generation, healthy both physically and mentally, and to be builders of new life in the future. Entrusted by the Party, our NDYL built up the organization of Young Pioneers with membership now reaching 7,000,000. This organization is playing a good part in instilling patriotism into the minds of children, in enhancing their interest in study, in arousing their love for labor, and in cultivating their initiative and discipline. In consideration of the nature of the Young Pioneers and the aspirations of its members, the Party has decided to rename the Young Pioneers as Young Vanguard. We should show concern to the children like our own brothers and sisters. At present, some activities of the Young Pioneers are still not suitable to the children, as they impose upon them too much social work. This should be corrected. Those evil practices left by the old society which destroy the mental and physical health of children should be criticized and combated by effective means. In the noble cause of fostering children comrades, teachers and tutors assume an honorable responsibility. They should ceaselessly improve their work, patiently enrich the knowledge of children according to their physical and mental conditions as well as use their exemplary acts for setting a good example to the children and train the children to be a new generation of high moral quality. The NDYL organizations should pay attention to the work of primary school teachers and tutors, support and praise their achievements, and try to satisfy their reasonable demands.

SOURCE: *Current Background,* No. 257 (Hong Kong: United States Consulate General, July 24, 1953). Originally published by *New China News Agency,* June 6, 1953.

Higher Education in New China
By Tseng Chao-lun
June 1953

Tseng's article is one of the earliest overall summaries on high-er education, and it represents a survey of the regime's progress during the four years following 1949. It is couched in descriptive terms, more generally designed for consumption overseas. He out-lines the educational reforms effected to date which resulted in the complete reorganization of the pattern of higher education in China. Tseng, one of the leading non-Communist intellectuals utilized by the regime in educational administration during the early part of the 1950s, was attacked as a rightist and deviationist and was ultimately replaced.

One of the prerequisites for the successful realization of the first Five-Year Plan of national construction which the People's Re-public of China launched this year is the training of an adequate number of cadres in all key branches of activity. This has necessi-tated the radical reorganization of the old educational system, which served only the interests of the upper classes, and could naturally not cope with the gigantic new tasks of modernizing China. Reorientation has been no easy matter. This was especial-ly the case with higher education, which was more or less a copy of the educational systems of the occidental capitalist countries and was totally unsuited to the needs of the people. However, with the wise guidance of Chairman Mao Tse-tung and the Com-munist Party of China, the enthusiasm of educational workers, and the support of the people, a firm foundation has already been laid for a new educational system able to produce the personnel needed for the work of building China's modern industrialized

189

economy and new democratic social system, to answer the pressing needs of the day.

COMPLETE REORGANIZATION

In the brief period of three and a half years since liberation, higher education in China has made big advances. Besides a great increase in the number of students, there has been a marked improvement in the quality of work. The irrational features of preliberation education have been eliminated. For instance, in the old days, colleges, institutes, and universities were concentrated in a few big cities. One city would often have several institutions offering almost identical courses. This was typical of the chaos of the old society. It resulted in wasteful overlapping of faculties and equipment and the training in certain subjects of too many students, which inevitably led to many of them being unemployed. A common saying in old China was "to graduate from a university is to become unemployed." The universities, ill-planned and uncoördinated, could not cater to the needs of the people. While there was a surplus supply of graduates for certain fields of work, other fields, equally or even more important, were in dire need of new personnel. The logical result of such duplication of study courses was a scarcity of teaching staff and equipment. Consequently, some departments could offer only a meager range of courses, and students graduated with unforgivable gaps in their education.

Many teachers, unfamiliar with actual conditions outside the university campus and with only a hazy understanding of the real needs of the time, passed on knowledge from antiquated textbooks or based their lectures mainly on facts relating not so much to China as to some occidental country where they may have happened to take up their postgraduate studies. Education, especially higher education, in preliberation China was thus in a hopeless plight. It had become totally disassociated from the real needs of the country and, like so many things imported from the capitalist West, had taken on a semicolonial and semifeudal character. One of the basic tasks of New China was, therefore, completely to reshape education, to make it truly Chinese, and to answer the needs of our people. A complete reorganization of higher educational institutions has been undertaken.

Institutions of higher education are now divided into several distinct groups, each with its own special function. Thus there are universities for education in the liberal arts and sciences and higher educational institutions for various branches of technical knowledge. There are now thirteen universities in different parts of China. In big cities like Shanghai and Peking, the old universities which were similar in nature have in some cases been divided up and in others combined so that each region has only one university for the arts and sciences. There are two in North China, at Peking and Tientsin; one in the Northeast, at Changchun; four in East China, at Shanghai, Nanking, Tsingtao, and Amoy; two in Central South China at Wuhan (Wuchang and Hankow) and Canton; two in Southwest China, at Chengtu and Kunming; and two in Northwest China, at Sian and Lanchow. This has brought about a better concentration of personnel and equipment, and the universities have been immensely strengthened by this change.

Twenty polytechnic institutes have been formed by recombining and rearranging the technical colleges of the old universities. One of the prominent features of the new educational system is the addition of twenty-six newly established special technological institutes, such as the steel institute, the mining institute, and the geological institute, each of which is designed to give the specialized engineer training needed for industrial and economic construction. Then there are twenty-nine agricultural forestry colleges, seven institutes for finance and economics, four for politics and law, etc. Finally, the government has founded two special colleges in the Northeast and in Sinkiang which train students from the national minorities as personnel for the national development and promotion of culture in their own areas. The Central Institute for Nationalities in Peking and those in the Northwest and other areas are not included in these totals, which are, of course, subject to increase.

TEACHING METHODS REFORMED

This basic reorganization has also brought about fundamental reforms in teaching methods. In place of the colleges or schools which formed the units of the old institutions of higher education and their subdivisions of departments, each institution now has departments subdivided into one or more "specialities." In some cases a specialty may again be divided into two or more "specializations." This system of specialties and specializations is adopted from the Soviet educational system. The guiding principle of this system is that institutions of higher learning should aim at training cadres for specific jobs in the highly complex fabric of economic construction. The whole educational procedure reverses the preliberation process, which, by trying to turn out jacks-of-all-trades, aimed at lessening the chances of their being unemployed if their own particular "specialty" was already overstaffed.

Each specialty or specialization has a detailed study-plan drawn up, with a very concrete and definite aim in view. For example, the specialty, "internal combustion engines," has a study-plan of its own, different from the study-plans of all other specialties. This study-plan for each course makes provision for practical work in factories in three periods during the four years of college life. A student graduating in this specialty is thus able to step into his work as a mechanical engineer with concrete knowledge and practical experience in the design and construction of various types of internal combustion engines.

Each study-plan embodies a list of courses offered in the particular specialty, and each course has a carefully worked-out program of study which gives the concrete aim of the course and lists the various items to be taken up for study in the academic year or term. It also specifies the time allotted for each item and the exact material to be handled within each hour of instruction. Textbooks are written and compiled according to this program. In this way, standardization and uniformity have been brought about in methods and content of instruction throughout all institutions of higher education in the country.

TEACHING AND RESEARCH GROUPS

Within each specialty there are one or more teaching and research groups, or *kafedras,* to use the Soviet term, whose responsibility it is to see that the study-plans and program are actually put into execution. They also ensure that the best and most advanced methods of instruction are used, giving the best knowledge available, and that new teaching experiences are exchanged between the teachers. Each *kafedra* also has the task of directing research work in its particular field and training postgraduates and assistants so that they can take up teaching posts.

HIGHER EDUCATION EXPANDS

The scale of higher education has greatly increased during the past three and a half years. To date, 219,700 students are enrolled in institutions of higher education. This figure exceeds the pre-liberation 1946 peak of 129,000 by 69 percent. Arrangements have been made so that every single graduate of the middle schools or person with middle-school-graduate status, unless he is already working, can continue his education in an institution of higher education. Before liberation, there were 185 institutions of higher education; this figure rose to 210 in 1951. Now, after the radical reorganization and reshuffling, the figure is 218. The total number of teachers in institutions of higher education, including professors, assistant professors, instructors, and assistants is 26,482, which is a 20 percent increase over the preliberation record. A breakdown of these figures indicates the new trends and nature of our education. For example, students majoring in technology in preliberation days numbered only about 18.9 percent of the total student enrollment. In 1952, this figure rose to 35.4 percent.

There has also been a rapid increase in buildings and equipment. The present Tientsin University, for example, a polytechnic institute which has grown out of the old Peiyang University founded in 1896, has a student enrollment several times larger than that of its predecessor. The new university had to be moved to a more spacious site, and buildings had to be erected almost overnight. In 1952 alone, the total area of construction of this university amounted to 62,000 square meters, a figure which exceeds all the construction work (covering 46,000 square meters) undertaken in the course of Peiyang's long history of fifty years. Of course, such building projects, imposing as they are, fall short of the mark, when compared to the rate at which new institutions of higher education are being established to serve the increased student enrollment. This handicap of space is partially offset by a more efficient use of classrooms, laboratories, and equipment. Instead of having the laboratories open only part of the day and only partially utilizing equipment, everything is made fullest use of by a system of shifts. In this way much of the wastefulness of preliberation times has been eliminated.

OPPORTUNITIES FOR ALL

One of the basic principles of education in the People's Republic of China is the provision of equal opportunities for all young men and women in institutions of higher learning. Formerly, higher education was the exclusive privilege of the wealthier classes. Since liberation, the gates of the institutions of higher education are thrown wide open to the sons and daughters of the working people.

As most workers and peasants and their children at the present moment are unable to take regular university courses because of inadequate preliminary education, the government has founded many schools for workers and peasants to overcome this difficulty. Here students take intensified training courses. Graduates from these schools have proved themselves to be apt candidates for university education and have in some cases won high honors in scholastic work. In order to remove the financial difficulties that might bar the way to higher education, the government has, since the autumn of 1952, exempted all students in institutions of higher education from payment for tuition, board, and lodging. How important this is to youths from the working class and peasantry needs no explanation. The Ministry of Higher Education was inundated with letters from students and their parents expressing gratitude for this measure, which has made it possible for many youths to acquire a university education which would otherwise have been beyond their reach.

NO MORE UNEMPLOYMENT

The saying, "to graduate from a university is to become unemployed," is now only a memory. In New China, the worry is not that students might be jobless on graduation but that the universities are not turning out graduates fast enough to fill the gaps in our gigantic economic construction. Shortened courses have been devised to answer to this urgent need, and in some cases students have begun their practical work while completing their regular school training.

In New China, each student knows exactly what role he is going to fill in the whole splendid edifice of national construction. Upon graduation, each student is alloted the work best suited to his ability. The committee charged with the assignment of students to work handles this delicate job with great deliberation and care. In this matter, besides the students' specialty, many other factors are taken into consideration, such as personal interest and preference, family conditions, and health. Where it is later felt that the assignment has been wrong for any reason, the student is encouraged to request the Ministry of Personnel for a reconsideration. Since the basic principle in the assignment of posts is to make students happy and useful in the positions they occupy, the committee in charge will try to set matters right.

Teachers are also naturally everywhere in great demand. To overcome this shortage of teachers, most institutions of higher education are giving much attention to the training of postgraduate students and assistants, so that they can take up teaching as soon as possible. Even so, the number of teachers still falls far short of the demand caused by the rapid expansion of the educational system since liberation.

It is understood of course that further changes will be necessary to suit the rapidly developing conditions of New China. The stress on quality will become more pronounced in the future.

One of the most remarkable results of New China's revolution in education is the birth of a new atmosphere in all institutions of higher education. Students, teachers, and staff have all come to realize that the people are indeed masters of the country. All feel that they are part and parcel of the institution to which they belong and that the well-being and proper functioning of that institution is something inseparable from their own well-being and the success of their work. Therefore everyone watches over his institution with care and does not hesitate to voice his opinion on its democratic functioning. Where, under the old regime, students were careless of university property, students today love and take care of university property, because it is public property, their property. In the sanitation campaigns, they help clean up the campuses. In the big removals during the reorganizations, they have helped in the work of sorting, arranging, and stacking books and specimens, carefully removing precious apparatus. This keen and active participation in the various great national movements and campaigns and in what goes on around them has built up a strong community feeling among students and teachers.

The government has done everything within its power to make the students and teachers better fed and better lodged. The recent increase of teachers' salaries makes their average pay 18.7 percent higher than in 1951. Furthermore, starting from the fall of 1952, all the teachers and staff in institutions of higher education are entitled to free medical treatment in hospitals and clinics in case of sickness. Since 1952, the government has tried to organize for both teachers and students vacation excursions at greatly reduced rates, so that they can get a real holiday and see with their own eyes the gigantic scope of national construction. In the summer vacation of 1952, over four hundred university teachers went on a visit to Tsingtao; from Peking alone, ten thousand students went on various excursions.

THE HAPPINESS OF SERVICE

Visitors to China since the liberation have constantly remarked upon the buoyant vigor of the men and women students of our university campuses. They have often asked why it is thus and have found the answer in the fact that true happiness comes in the service of one's fellow beings. Our men and women students know that they are free to work wholly in the service of the people. Each of them knows that he is contributing his share to the creation of an ideal state, in which there will be no exploitation and no unemployment and where all shall live in freedom, in plenty, and in peace.

SOURCE: Tseng Chao-lun, "Higher Education in New China," *People's China,* No. 12 (June 16, 1953), pp. 6–10.

See also Tseng Chao-lun's article on higher education in Communist China in *Current Background,* No. 238 (Hong Kong: United States Consulate General, 1953).

Constitution of the New Democratic Youth League of China

Adopted at the Second All-China Congress of the New Democratic Youth League
June 1953

The New Democratic Youth League was organized in 1949 to direct the activities of young Communist activists, and it is today one of the principal "informal" control agencies operating within institutions of higher learning. The League (its title was changed in 1956 to Communist Youth League) comprises adolescents and young adults between fourteen and twenty-five years and constitutes a select reservoir of trained, indoctrinated cadres from which Party members are recruited. Membership of the League is over twenty-five million, while its auxiliary, the Young Pioneers (for students under fifteen) numbers fifty million. The League's 1953 constitutional revision was deemed necessary in order to bring it under closer Party supervision.

GENERAL PRINCIPLES

The New Democratic Youth League of China is a mass organization of progressive youths, led by the Communist Party of China and is also the lieutenant and reserve force of the Party.

The League shall assist the Party to educate youth in the spirit of communism, so that they may become a young generation with a deep love for their motherland, being loyal to the people, educated, disciplined, brave, industrious, lively, and ready to face any hardship. They will follow the direction pointed out by our great leader, Chairman Mao Tse-tung, for the gradual realization of national industrialization and the gradual transition to socialism.

198

The entire members of the League shall be required faithfully to carry out the decisions of the Party and the Government, to be exemplary in observing the state law, to increase the friendly tie between the various nationalities of the country, to consolidate our people's democratic dictatorship, to learn all kinds of knowledge and technique, to participate actively in national construction, and to be prepared for the defence of our great motherland. The Youth League, faithful to the principle of internationalism, will undertake to unite all democratic youths of the world and consolidate the Soviet-led democratic and socialistic camp to safeguard world peace.

Organized on the principle of democratic centralism, the League shall allow ample democratic life within itself. Members of the League will conscientiously observe the discipline and constantly maintain the uniformity of thought, organization, and action of the League. The practice of criticism and self-criticism shall be a powerful weapon of the League to improve its work. The League shall pay constant attention to the life of the masses, listen to their views, learn from them attentively, and, through persuasion and exemplary action, rally the masses of youth closely around the Party.

The entire work of the League shall be conducted under the direct leadership of the Communist Party of China, and the local organs of the League shall accept the leadership and supervision of the Party organs at the same level.

CHAPTER I: MEMBERSHIP

Article 1. All youths, irrespective of sex, above the age of 14 and under the age of 25, who recognize the constitution of the League, participate and work in one of its organizations, implement its decisions, and pay membership dues, shall be members of the League.

Article 2. A member of the League shall have the following duties:

(1) To study Marxism-Leninism and Party politics and propagate them among the masses of youth.

(2) To achieve the mission given by the League and the Party.

(3) To take an active part in the national construction with a patriotic labor attitude.

(4) To engage in cultural, scientific, and technical studies to raise his professional level.

(5) To learn military affairs and take up physical training to be prepared for the defense of our great motherland.

(6) To observe the state law, protect public property, and struggle against any acts detrimental to the interest of the people.

(7) To pay constant attention to the masses, consult with them, make friends with and set an example for the youth.

Article 3. A member of the League shall have the following rights:

(1) To discuss freely and actively any problems concerning the work of the League at conferences and in publications.

(2) To elect and be elected to office.

(3) To criticize any working personnel and leadership organs of the League at meetings.

(4) To make complaints, suggestions, and statements to League organs at all levels up to the Central Committee of the League.

Article 4. The admission of a member to the League shall be made in accordance with the following stipulations and upon the completion of the procedures for admission:

(1) All young workers, peasants, servicemen, intellectuals, and other laboring youths, in applying for membership in the League, shall be required to be introduced by two League members or by one Communist Party member, and to fill out an application form for examination of a League branch committee for the decision of a League branch congress and for the ratification of a district work committee of the League or a committee of equal status before they shall become formal League members.

(2) When a Young Pioneer applies for membership to the

League, he shall be required to be introduced by a Young Pioneers committee at the intermediate level, which may be considered as an equal to a League member.

(3) Those introducing a youth to the League for membership shall be required to make a true statement to the League as to his thought, character, and experience and explain to him beforehand the constitution of the League.

(4) The age of a member of the League shall be determined at the time he is passed for membership at a League branch congress.

Article 5. When a member of the League is transferred from the League to another organization, he shall be required to complete the procedure for transfer.

Article 6. Members above the age of twenty-five desiring to withdraw from the League may state their wish to the League branch committee to which they belong. Those who wish to remain in the League may do so, with the right to speak and to be elected. Before they are elected or appointed cadres of the League, they retain the right to elect and the right of decision.

Article 7. Any member of the League not living the life of the League, nor carrying out its work, nor paying any membership dues for a period of six months, without good reasons upon investigation by a League branch committee, shall be considered as voluntarily withdrawing from the League and shall be reported to the upper-level League committee for his name to be removed.

A member of the League has the freedom to withdraw from the League at any time.

. . . .

CHAPTER V: BASIC-LEVEL ORGANIZATION OF THE LEAGUE

Article 23. Forming the foundation of the League, basic-level organs may be set up in any factory, mine, enterprise, farm station, village, government group, company of the armed forces, school, or street with over three League members.

With over three and under one hundred League members, a League branch shall be set up—where necessary, with small teams under it.

When the number of League members is above ten and under three hundred, a general League branch shall be formed. If need be, such a branch may be set up even with more than fifty members. League branches shall come under general branches.

Enterprises, organizations, and schools with over three hundred League members may set up a League committee. If the work requires, such a committee may be set up even if there are fewer than three hundred and more than one hundred League members. Under the League committee, a League branch or, if necessary, a general League branch, shall be formed.

The setting up of a League branch or a general League branch shall be first ratified by a *hsien* League committee, a municipal League committee, or their equivalent; while that of a League committee by a provincial League committee or its equivalent.

The League branch members' congress shall be called once a month. The general League branch members' congress and the League committee members' congress or the members' representative conference shall be held every three to six months.

Article 24. The basic-level organs are the basic units for the League work and activities and are responsible for the close relations between the League and the masses of youth. The responsibilities of a basic-level organ are:

(1) To educate the youth on the spirit of communism, to strive to carry out the decisions of the Party and the upper-level League committee, and to take an active part in the national construction.

(2) To mobilize the League members and the youth in active political, cultural, scientific, and technical studies.

(3) To organize the League members and the youth for constant participation in athletic, cultural, and recreational activities.

(4) To pay attention to improving the labor and living conditions of the youth and improving their material life and cultural level.

(5) To educate and supervise the League members in fulfilling their duties and protecting their rights.

(6) To accept new League members and educate them on the constitution of the League.

The basic-level organs of the League should take a responsible attitude towards and make suggestions relative to the improvement of the work of their respective units.

The League organs in all units of national construction, especially where there are no basic-level Party organs, should be responsible for the propagation and active implementation of Party decisions.

Article 25: The basic-level organs of the League shall elect basic-level committees to perform their daily functions. No League branch committee shall be set up with any League branch with less than seven members, but a branch secretary or one secretary and one deputy secretary shall be elected.

The tenure of office for a League branch committee, a general League branch committee, and a League committee shall be six months to one year.

CHAPTER VI: REWARDS AND PENALTIES

Article 26. Commendation shall be given to those members and organs manifesting a high degree of loyalty, creativity, and efficiency in fulfilling their duties for or making special contributions to the cause of construction of the motherland, in order to arouse the patriotism and heroism of the League members and the mass of youth.

Article 27. Members not carrying out the decisions of the Party and the League or violating the constitution of the League shall be given due penalty by the League organs at all levels, according to the actual circumstances.

Penalty to an organ shall be: censure, abolition of the leadership organ, the dispersion of the whole organ, and the reregistration of League members.

Penalty to a League member shall be: advice, warning, serious warning, relief from duty, detention in the League for observation, and expulsion from the League.

Article 28. The purpose of the League organization to mete out penalties to its members is to tighten the League discipline and educate League members and youth. Before the League organ at each level decides on and ratifies the penalty to a member, especially the deprivation of League membership, it should maintain a solemn and careful attitude and permit him to participate in the meeting held therefor, so that his opinions may be carefully heard. If he should have a different opinion about the decision, he might appeal to the upper level. The League organ should then take into careful consideration his viewpoints and cause a reconsideration to be made. The appeals of such a member should be transmitted immediately without any delay.

. . . .

CHAPTER VIII: THE YOUTH LEAGUE ORGANIZATION IN THE PLA

Article 34: The work of the Youth League in the People's Liberation Army of China is an important part of the political work of the Party and must be conducted directly under the leadership of the political organ and the basic-level organ of the Party, in accordance with the instructions of the Party committee and the military leaders.

Article 35. The work of the Youth League in the PLA must be conducted in accordance with the special stipulations of the Central Committee of the League and the general political department of the People's Revolutionary Military Council of the Central People's Government.

Article 36. The Youth League organs in the PLA should maintain close contact with the local Youth League organs, constantly take part in the work of the latter, and participate in the election of leadership organs of the League.

CHAPTER IX: FUNDS

Article 37: The funds of the League shall come from the membership dues and other incomes of the League.

Article 38: The amount of membership dues shall be fixed by the Central Committee of the League. A League member who is also a member of the Communist Party of China shall not be required to pay any membership dues.

SOURCE: *Current Background,* No. 258 (Hong Kong: United State Consulate General, September 10, 1953).

For additional readings, see "Constitution of the China New Democratic Youth League" (April 17, 1949), *Current Background,* No. 7 (1950); see also "Third National Conference of Youth League," *Current Background,* Nos. 453, 454, 455, and 456 (1957).

Constitution of the People's Republic of China
September 1954

Article 94. Citizens of the People's Republic of China have the right to education. To guarantee enjoyment of this right, the state establishes and gradually extends the various types of schools and other cultural and educational institutions.

The state pays special attention to the physical and mental development of young people.

Article 95. The People's Republic of China safeguards the freedom of citizens to engage in scientific research, literary and artistic creation, and other cultural pursuits. The state encourages and assists creative work in science, education, literature, art, and other cultural pursuits.

SOURCE: *Documents of the First Session of the First National People's Congress of the People's Republic of China* (Peking: Foreign Languages Press, 1955), pp. 160–161.

Rules of Conduct for Middle School Students
June 1955

The rules of conduct outlined below, though promulgated for middle school students, have relevance for students at all levels throughout Communist China. The regulations which were issued by the Ministry of Education were intended to apply throughout all China on a uniform basis, so that all middle schools ". . . should carry out education on Communist morality, raise political consciousness of the students, develop the spirit of collectivism, and cultivate good character and habits in the students through these rules." The implementation of the rules was to be the specific responsibility of the Youth League, Young Pioneers, and the Student Association.

1. Endeavor to learn; learn to be good in health, good at study, and good in conduct. Prepare to serve the motherland and the people.

2. Respect the national flag. Respect and love the leader of the people.

3. Obey the regulations of the school. Obey the instructions of the principal and teachers.

4. Arrive at the school punctually and attend the classes punctually. Never be late; never leave school before the time; and never miss a class without reason.

5. When attending school everyday, bring all the textbook and stationery required. Before the class begins, prepare all the things required for the lesson.

6. During the class, assume a correct posture; listen to the lecture attentively; do not talk unless when necessary; do not do anything else besides your class work. When desiring to leave the classroom, ask the teacher's permission first.

7. Stand up when answering the teacher's questions. Sit down when the teacher permits you. When you want to ask the teacher a question, raise your hand first.

8. Perform your self-study carefully. Finish your work in all the subjects in time.

9. Respect the principal and the teachers. Stand up and salute your teacher when the class begins and again at the end of the class. When you meet the principal or the teachers outside the school you also salute them.

10. Be sincere and friendly with your schoolmates, unite with them and help one another.

11. Respect and love your parents. Love and protect your brothers and sisters. Help your family do house work.

12. Respect your elders. Respect the aged. Love and protect the children; take care of the sick and infirm; give them your seat on a carriage; give way to them on the road.

13. Be honest, sincere, modest and polite to people. Do not tell a lie. Do not curse people. Do not fight. Do not disturb people's work, study, or sleep.

14. Do not smoke. Do not drink. Do not gamble. Do not take away other people's things without their permission. Do not do anything that may be harmful to yourself or to others.

15. Take plenty of exercises and make your body strong. Keep your body, clothes, quarters, and all public places clean and hygienic.

16. Obey public order. Take care of public property.

17. Value and protect the reputation of the class and of the school.

18. Always have your student identity card with you, and see that you do not lose it.

Source: *Survey of China Mainland Press*, No. 1094 (Hong Kong: United States Consulate General, July 22, 1955). Originally published in *Kuang Ming Jih Pao*, June 18, 1955.

Strive to Improve the Low Quality
of Higher Education
By Chang Chung-lin
June 1955

This statement by the Director of Planning of the Ministry of Higher Education has special significance in the light of the regime's first Five-Year Plan. The Plan, launched in 1953, had been retarded in its educational aspects because of the inferior students enrolled from secondary schools and the inadequate performance of its college graduates. Deficiencies were seen in the "poor physique, doubtful politics, and inferior specialist knowledge" of many students.

Curricula revision and administrative reforms on the part of the institutes of higher education, combined with improved leadership on the part of the Ministry, it was hoped, would alleviate the difficulties revealed by the first years of the Plan's operation.

In particular, three reforms were introduced in 1955 to improve higher education; the first required a five-year system to replace the four-year course of many universities; the second allowed for the eventual abolition of short-term special college courses; and the third indicated that the teaching of Marxist-Leninist theory and political ideology was to be extended further.

The State Council has recently instructed that in future, higher education should concentrate all its strength and adopt all effective means to strive for the enhancement of quality throughout the country.

Since the liberation, the workers in the field of higher education throughout the country have met with certain success in initially reforming the higher education of a semicolonial and semifeudalistic nature taken over from old China in accordance with the line laid down by the Central Government, which gives emphasis to the cultivation of construction personnel for the nation. From 1949 to 1952, close to two hundred large and small institutions of higher education were taken over. Also taken over were several scores of institutions of higher education which were formerly run with subsidy grants from agents of American imperialism or were operated as secret-agent institutions of a reactionary nature. Through the media of different kinds of movements, the teachers were ideologically remolded. The reactionary training systems and the reactionary curricula were abolished. Marxist-Leninist political and educational curricula were introduced, and the teachers and students were made to think in terms of serving the people and of internationalism.

During the three years after 1952, college reorganization was carried out on a nationwide scale, and specialization courses were set up. The institutions of higher education left over from old China were rationally reorganized for the first time, and over two hundred new specialization courses were set up. Units to guide pedagogical researchers were also universally established. This was followed up by the work of pedagogical reform. During these three years, the consolidated pedagogical plans for the departments of engineering and science were basically completed, and five hundred kinds of pedagogical programs were drawn up. Over eight hundred kinds of Soviet teaching materials adaptable to the new pedagogical plans were translated, and pedagogical methods and administrative systems were promulgated.

During these several years, however, the quality of the students in schools and of the graduates was not high enough. The physique of many people was weak. Their political quality was inferior, and their specialization knowledge and techniques were inadequate to satisfy the need of their work. During the school year of 1953 to 1954, for example, over seven thousand of the students in the institutions of higher education had to suspend their studies because of illness, inferior academic attainment, and other causes. The figure was a staggering one, for in actuality, there was quite a number of students who, instead of dropping their studies outright, managed to retain their seats without promotion or by demotion. In certain classes, students of this category amount to 30 percent of the enrollment.

. . . .

The business capacity of an individual is inseparable from his political quality and state of health. In recent years, political education in institutions of higher education has been brought to a higher plane. But in many institutions, especially those of an engineering, science, and medical nature, the trend for the students to estrange themselves from politics is still predominant. A small number of undesirable students still manage to infiltrate into the institutions of higher education. As a result of this, certain factories and mines are reluctant to have students taking up fieldwork in their establishments. They are afraid that this would lead to leakage of national secrets and the sustaining of unnecessary losses. Some factories and mines find it difficult to deal with the politically unreliable graduates from institutions of higher education and are reluctant to give them work. The general health of the students is also far from satisfactory, and every year many students were forced to drop their studies because of illness. In short, although the quality of the personnel cultivated by institutions of higher level in recent years is of a higher level than those graduated from universities before the founding of New China, their quality is still not up to the mark needed by New China for construction purposes.

Because the quality of the students fostered by institutions of higher education is not high enough, and because the various business establishments are not sure of the number of technicians needed by the various enterprises for replenishment purposes, a way out has to be found by compensating for inferior quality with quantity. As a consequence, the number of graduates described to be essential to many business establishments every year is far in excess of the actual need. In the case of some establishments, the number of technicians they plan to recruit is more than 50 percent in excess of their actual need. Although the practice of the various establishments to compensate for quality with quantity is not a good way to have things done, they are obliged to take such a course by force of circumstances. "Since a man cannot do what is usually expected of a man, two men perhaps can do that job." Because the quality of the students from the institutions of higher education is poor, the business establishments have to ask for more graduates, and because of this, the institutions of higher education have in turn to enroll more students. As a consequence, the quality of the graduates is bound to become worse. If no means is devised to eliminate the deterioration of this cycle, a large amount of manpower, material, and money will have to be wasted by the state for the cultivation of senior construction personnel, to the detriment of the Socialist construction enterprise.

.   .   .   .

Although there are such objective causes as the failure of the departments to name the accurate number of cadres needed and the wanting of rigid balance on the part of the National Planning Commission, the Ministry of Higher Education should have made a full estimation of its own strength and given the demands put forward by the different departments a careful study. It should insist on this principle when problems are met. It should not try to have "every request met," thus causing the one-sided shortcoming of pursuing quantity in negligence of quality. Strictly speaking, the Ministry of Higher Education has these several years the subjective shortcoming of avarice for quantity and speed and of aggrandizement. There is a steep climb in the aggregate number of students in the country. Every school boasts of an enrollment of eight or ten thousand. Schools with an enrollment of three or four thousand are looked upon as small schools.

Apart from this, the contents of curricula have also a direct consequence on the quality of the students. During these several years, the pedagogical reform has not been without success, but the demand is inclined to be set on the high side, and the pace set also calls for too much speed. This causes the occurrence of deviations. The curricula for institutions of higher education should have their contents stipulated in the light of the knowledge and technique needed by the graduates for taking up their work with the existing cultural and scientific standard of the students and the quality of the teachers also taken into consideration. The hundred-odd kinds of specialization plans and the several hundred kinds of pedagogical programs, which are being centrally experimented with throughout the country presently, adopt in the main the pedagogical plans and pedagogical programs enforced by the Soviet institutions of higher education before 1954 as blueprints and have been rendered into a more compressed form. To learn the pedagogical contents from the Soviet Union is no doubt a necessity, but the deviation lies in the inability to have this linked adequately with the realities of China. The institutions of higher education in the Soviet Union usually have five-year courses, and certain courses and faculties last even longer. In China, the institutions of higher education last no more than four years in general, and only a small number of specialization courses last five years. Even if the quality of the students in our institutions of higher education were not as low as it has been in these past several years, the requirement of the students to complete in four or five years what usually takes the Soviet student five or more years to complete would prove to be difficult enough.

Since 1952, the number of graduates from senior middle school has proved to be insufficient to fulfill the enrollment need of the institutions of higher education every year. The number of cadres on active duty and intellectual youth of the community seeking to enroll with the institutions of higher education has also proved to be limited. As a consequence, the institutions were obliged to enroll new students who were not up to the standard in general health, in political quality, and in cultural and scientific attainment during the past several years. The poor foundation of the students, the onerous curricula and the inability of the teachers to adapt themselves to the objective demand are all important factors responsible for the poor quality of the students. The inability of the Ministry of Higher Education to align its improvement of the leadership method and its enhancement of the administrative efficiency of the institutions of higher education with the speed of development scored by the higher education enterprise during these years is, of course, also one of the causes responsible for the low quality of higher education.

SOURCE: *Survey of China Mainland Press,* No. 1088 (Hong Kong: United States Consulate General, July 14, 1955). Originally published in *Jen Min Jih Pao* [People's Daily], June 30, 1955.

Higher Education
By Yang Hsiu-feng
July 1955

Yang's speech, delivered at the plenary session of the First National People's Congress, represents one of the first statements on higher education delivered to that body. He reviewed developments in higher education from "liberation" to that time and discussed the more obvious contrasts between Nationalist and Communist ideas concerning education.

Yang echoed in this speech the universal complaints made against the quantity and quality of college students which were being voiced in official quarters in 1955. During this year, political education was intensified in order to rectify the shortcomings of many students whose political reliability was still questionable. For reasons of economy and to further control students, 1955 saw the demise of an overall, national, and free system of higher education. Instead of receiving free board and tuition expenses, students were now to receive a "people's education subsidy," if approved by college authorities, and only under Party and League supervision. While 1955 was to see an improvement in the quality of students (politically and academically) the regime was preparing to overhaul drastically its supervisory function and further regiment its student population in order to ensure the success of the first Five Year Plan.

Because of the attention paid by the Party and the state to the cultivation of cadres, the institutions of higher education were developed to a greater extent and have carried out a series of reorganization and reform work during the past several years. But speaking in terms of the need of the state, our work is still not up

215

to the mark, and the implementation and enforcement of policies is still beset with a number of serious shortcomings. Many problems have not been satisfactorily solved.

First, the quality of the cadres cultivated is still inadequate to meet the need of construction.

Second, the establishment of different kinds of specialization majors by institutions of higher education and their proportionate development are still unable to comply fully with the needs. Speedy steps should be taken to find out the need of the various establishments for cadres for the second Five-Year Plan in order to have the requirements suitably readjusted.

Third, the institutions of higher education are not established and distributed in compliance with the arrangements for the development of state economy. Hereafter, when building new schools, we must, on the basis of the national economic construction plan, link these schools with the newly established industrial bases as far as possible.

Fourth, not enough attention has been paid by us towards sparetime education for the cultivation of workers and staff members on active duty. Hereafter, sparetime education should be vigorously boosted as an important component part of the cadre cultivation plan.

Fifth, the phenomena of irrational usage, extravagance, and waste are still found in expenditures incurred by schools in capital construction, personnel establishment, pedagogical equipment, and other administrative expenses. Hereafter, we must firmly enforce the directive of the Central Government and implement the policy of simplification and economy.

For the sake of implementing the materialization of the Five-Year Plan, the above-mentioned problems must be solved in a planned and systematic manner before the important task of cultivating qualified senior construction cadres can be fulfilled.

. . . .

The cadres cultivated by us must be capable of loyalty to the fatherland and the Socialist construction. They must be sound in physique and capable of mastering the knowledge of modern science. This is to say that the personnel fostered must be able to comply truly with the requirement of "good in physique, good in learning, and good in work." Measured by this yardstick, it is obvious that there are grave shortcomings in our work.

Although different kinds of historical and social cases are responsible for the low quality of the cadres presently cultivated by the institutions of higher education, the principal cause lies in the existence of shortcomings in our work and the implementation and enforcement of our policies. In the course of development during the past several years, we failed to consider soberly the fact that both the supply of students and the number of teachers were seriously inadequate. We set out arbitrarily to pursue quantity, and not enough attention was given to ensuring quality. In cultivation work, we also failed to implement correctly the educational policy of overall development. We were negligent with education in the field of physical culture, and our work in the field of political ideology proved to be most fragile. In addition to this, in learning from the Soviet Union and in carrying out pedagogical reform, because the foundation was poor in the past, everything had to be learned afresh. This would naturally make the teachers and students feel hard pressed.

Due to these causes, the quality of the caders cultivated by us was too low in learning to meet the requirements of national construction. What is more, because their academic attainments were not up to standard, their state of health was poor, and their political quality was inferior, the rate of transfer and attrition ran very high every year. An example can be given here. During the school year 1953–1954, when the school session in the institutions of higher education came to an end before the annual examination, over seven thousand students, equivalent to 3.5 percent of the aggregate enrollment, had to terminate their studies or were expelled from the schools. More than half of this number were unable to carry on with their studies on the ground of ill health, while some of them were expelled due to the inferiority of their political quality. Such a state of affairs adversely affected the smooth fulfillment of the state plan for the cultivation of cadres. It also incurred heavy wastage in manpower material and financial resources to the country.

In the following, I am going to make a special discussion of the political quality of the students. It should be said that the social consciousness of students in our institutions of higher education has been considerably elevated these last several years. They have a fervent love for the fatherland, exert strong efforts in learning, abide by discipline, and yield to the needs of the state. But this is only the principal side of the picture. On the other side, there is a small number of students whose political quality is so inferior that useful personnel can hardly be made out of them. This is also something that cannot be neglected.

Some students are seriously corroded by the bourgeois way of thinking. They are morally degenerate and are of a very poor quality. They lead a decadent life and even band themselves together to form vagabond gangs to violate laws and discipline.

Some students are seriously reactionary in their way of thinking. They spread reactionary views to make known their dissatisfaction with socialism. Some even form themselves into organizations. Reactionary cliques of this nature have been uncovered at the Futan University and the Chiaotung University in Shanghai.

Some gangsters have also wormed their way into our institutions of higher education. Recently, it was found that Chong Chien-an, who had posed as a student in the Northwest College of Agriculture for three years, was actually a counterrevolutionary gangster of bully and landlord status. He was responsible for the launching of many attacks against our anti-Japanese forces, the killing of our cadres, the plundering of property, and the oppression of the masses. He had a series of blood debts to his credit.

Some students are sent by the enemy to infiltrate into our institutions for the purpose of carrying out counterrevolutionary activities. In the course of past years, counterrevolutionary incidents of a sabotage nature involving arson, poisoning, document-stealing, sabotage of machinery and equipment, and posting of reactionary bills were frequently discovered.

The number of criminal and politically impure elements similar to those mentioned above is not large, but if steps are not taken at an early date to eliminate them and to prevent their continued infiltration, the possible damage they can do to the cause of Socialist construction can hardly be estimated.

In order to cope with the need of national construction and to produce qualified senior construction personnel, higher education work must in future vigorously improve the quality of the students, with special attention given to the improvement of their political quality. For this purpose, the following phases of work must be carried out.

The policy of ensuring quality with due attention to quantity must be implemented in order to improve the student-enrollment work and to improve the quality of the new students. For the sake of ensuring the quality of the new students for the institutions of higher education, the State Council this spring made a study of the needs of a number of industrial establishments for technical cadres. It considered the various conditions of the institutions of higher education and coördinated the requirements with the possibilities. It readjusted the student-enrollment task of the institutions of higher education for the next three years and laid down the principles for improving the student-enrollment work. In the future, when enrolling new students, the institutions of higher education must rigorously examine the political affiliation and physical fitness of the candidates and adequately raise the standard set on examination subjects as a criterion for enrollment. The new students enrolled must be politically reliable. They must be able to move along with their classes and be physically fit to enable them to carry on with their studies. Attention must also be paid to absorbing the youths of worker and peasant status, the revolutionary cadres, the servicemen demobilized for construction, and the national minority youths into the schools.

We cannot, of course, set our demand on the quality of the new students so high as to make it inconsistent with the actual current conditions. At the same time, quantity is also a factor that cannot be left unconsidered. Consequently, we should correctly coördinate quality with quantity and strive to increase quality on the condition that a certain level of quantity is assured.

Readjustment must also be made of the students already enrolled by the institutions in the light of the current requirements.

Firm steps must be taken to get rid of the students who are implicated by grave political problems or who are so inferior in quality as to make their cultivation not worthwhile. In the case of those whose academic attainment or state of health is so poor as to make them unable to catch up with their classes or to carry on with their studies, they should be dealt with adequately in accordance with their individual circumstances. This will prove to be of benefit to both the country and the students themselves.

The carrying-out of such reorganization is naturally work of great complexity and delicacy. It must not be carried out perfunctorily. First, ideological work must be satisfactorily conducted, and the reasons must be explained. Not only the teachers and students in the schools but also the people of all circles in society must be made to understand the cadre-cultivation policy of the state and the necessity of ensuring quality. Only then can the above-mentioned measures be smoothly implemented. Consequently the work cannot be done with administrative force alone. A good job can be made of the work only when unanimous efforts are made by the various democratic parties and people's organizations, the people of all circles, and all the teachers and students of the institutions of higher education, under the leadership of the Chinese Communist Party and the Party committees of all levels. I implore, therefore, all deputies to accord their concern and support to the above-mentioned measures.

The elevation of the standard set for the enrollment of new students; the reorganization of the students already enrolled by those institutions; and the measures to change the school system of the institutions of higher education, to prolong adequately the length of the courses and to eliminate step by step the two-year and three-year specialization courses in a planned and systematic manner as laid down by the State Council will undoubtedly provide the institutions of higher education with more advantageous conditions for fostering cadres of a higher quality. But the crux of the matter of ensuring quality still lies in the ability of the institutions of higher education themselves to improve effectively their different phases of work, particularly teaching.

Because our higher education has a very inferior foundation, and New China has a pressing need for a very large number of senior construction personnel of a high quality for its construction needs, all people (including both the teachers and the students) are striving to learn advanced science and techniques from the Soviet Union, in the hope that they may catch up with it in the shortest possible time. This causes certain demands to be set too high and certain measures to be of too hasty a disposition. As a result, the teachers and students find the pedagogical burden so heavy as to be harmful to their health and, to a different extent, to their concern for the study of politics. This calls first for the reviewing of the shortcomings of the leadership work on the part of the Ministry of Higher Education, but the exertions made by the teachers and students should receive encouragement.

Recently, we and the institutions of higher education have been in the process of positively implementing the educational policy of overall development. In line with the principle of "learning less but learning it better," the pedagogical plans and outlines have been suitably revised. With a firm grip laid on the work to improve the pedagogical method and teaching material and to enhance the pedagogical efficacy, many institutions have met with initial success. In order to strengthen the physical training, the Ministry of Higher Education is contemplating a change in the system governing the issue of people's subsidy grants to institutions of higher education, with the object of improving the food and nourishment for the students without increasing the financial burden of the state.

SOURCE: *Current Background,* No. 351 (Hong Kong: United States Consulate General, August 29, 1955).

Chinese Communist Party Session
on the Question of Intellectuals
By Chou En-lai
January 1956

The subject of "unity and reform" of Chinese intellectuals was of such importance in 1956 that Chou, in his capacity as Secretary of the Central Committee of the Chinese Communist Party, gave a lengthy report on the correct handling of intellectuals. Six years after the establishment of the Communist regime, the Party was still concerned with the incapacity of a large proportion of the scholars and professors to accept the revolution and Party in their entirety. The question of suitable employment for intellectuals and their integration within the Party was in part responsible for Chou's speech. Four months later, the sensational "Let Diverse Schools of Thought Contend" campaign was instigated in order to promote a more "permissive" atmosphere for intellectuals to develop a fuller understanding of their place in New China.

The intellectuals have already become an important factor in every aspect of the life of our state. To deal with the question of the intellectuals correctly, in a way that will stimulate their activity and enable them to apply their energies more fully to serve our great work of Socialist construction, has therefore become an important factor in our efforts to fulfill the fundamental task of the period of transition.

. . . .

Certain unreasonable features in our present employment and treatment of intellectuals and, in particular, certain sectarian attitudes among some of our comrades towards intellectuals outside

222

the Party have to some extent handicapped us in bringing the existing powers of the intelligentsia into full play. It is imperative that we give better leadership, overcome the weaknesses, and take a series of effective measures to mobilize and fully apply the powers of the intellectuals by ceaselessly raising their political consciousness, training up new forces on a large scale to add to their ranks, and raising their professional skills as much as possible, so as to meet the growing demands raised by the state on the intellectuals. This is now the fundamental task for our Party on the question of the intellectuals.

. . . .

Our Party has always attached great importance to the question of the intellectuals. Back in 1939, the Central Committee of the Party passed the decision draft by Comrade Mao Tse-tung on the large-scale absorption of intellectuals, and this decision was being effectively carried out in the various anti-Japanese bases. Since the liberation of the mainland, the Party has applied the policy of uniting, training, and reëducating them on a nationwide scale.

. . . .

The Central Committee of the Party further considers that the intellectuals of the past age in China were under the various influences of imperialism and the Kuomintang, so that a portion of them joined the revolution, another portion sympathized with the revolution, the majority adopted a neutral attitude of waiting-and-seeing towards the revolution, and only a very small number opposed the revolution. Facts are increasingly proving to China's intellectuals that, apart from joining the lot of the working class and the Communist Party, there is no outlet for them. Accordingly, unity with the intellectuals is necessary and completely possible.

. . . .

The overwhelming majority of the intellectuals have become government workers in the service of socialism and are already part of the working class. While uniting, training, and reëducating the old intellectuals, the Party has made a very great effort to foster the growth of new intellectuals in large numbers, and there are already a considerable number of laboring-class origin. Because of this, a fundamental change has taken place among Chinese intellectuals in the past six years.

In regard to the current political conditions of intellectuals, statistical data have been compiled in many units. These statistics show that among the higher intellectuals, about 45 percent are progressive persons who actively support the Communist Party and the People's Government, actively support socialism, and actively serve the people. Another 40 percent are the middle-of-the-road sort who support the Communist Party and the People's Government and generally can fulfill the tasks assigned them but who are politically not sufficiently progressive. Together the above two groups constitute 80 percent of all. Apart from them, a little over 10 percent are backward persons who lack political consciousness or who ideologically oppose socialism. Only a few are included among the counterrevolutionaries and other bad elements.

. . . .

In the past six years, there has been a very rapid growth in the number of intellectuals. At the moment, it is estimated that there are about 100,000 higher intellectuals in the whole country engaged in scientific research, engineering, public health work, education, and the arts. According to statistical data available, one third of the figures represents postliberation increases. In some departments, the increase has been especially rapid. For instance, in the first stage of the liberation, there were hardly two hundred geological workers, but in 1955, according to statistical returns from the Ministry of Geology, Ministry of Heavy Industry, Ministry of Petroleum Industry, and Ministry of Coal Industry, the number of geological engineers alone had been increased to 498, while the number of technicians graduating from higher institutions reached 3,400.

In the six years after the liberation, 217,900 students graduated from higher institutions in the country. Though not all of them have reached the standards of higher intellectuals previously referred to, they nevertheless constitute a new force in the intellectual world and the reserve force for our experts. It must be pointed out that many youths, though not yet reaching the status of experts, are already shouldering the tasks of experts and are doing well. Of the teaching staff of 42,000 in the higher institutions, only 17.8 percent are professors and associate professors, 24 percent are lecturers, and 58.2 percent are assistants. Some of the assistants have already taken up teaching work. The same situation is to be found in the engineering world. There are in all some 31,000 engineers of all grades in the whole country, while technicians who have graduated from higher institutions number 63,600. Among them many are actually performing the duties of engineers, and some of them should have been promoted to engineers. In addition, as reserves for higher intellectuals, there are also a large army of other intellectuals who, in the course of field work and sparetime study, are continually raising their knowledge levels.

There is really no definite boundary line between the so-called "higher intellectuals" and general intellectuals. According to available statistics, there are now in all 3,840,000 intellectuals engaged in scientific research, engineering, public health work, education, and the arts. They represent a great force in our Socialist construction. It is an extremely important task of the Party and the state correctly to appraise and employ these intellectuals and help them, in a planned way, to go ahead steadily, both politically and professionally.

. . . .

We cannot overlook the existing forces of the intellectuals, nor can we feel satisfied over them. We cannot indefinitely rely on the Soviet experts, nor can we relax our efforts in the most effective study of the advanced scientific techniques of the Soviet Union and other countries. The only correct principle is to stimulate and bring into full play the existing forces of the intelligentsia so as to carry out the Socialist construction of our country on a large scale, quickly, effectively, and economically. At the same time, we must spare no effort to reëducate them still further, add to their numbers, and raise their level as rapidly as possible, at a speed and scale as really keeps up with the huge pace of development of our state in all its aspects.

. . . .

State secrets must be unconditionally preserved, and any relaxation is not permitted. The problem, however, is the correct demarcation of the boundaries of secrecy, and there should be no extension at random of its scope, to prevent damage to work and difficulties for the workers. At the same time, there must be a correct estimation and understanding of the past history of the intellectuals, so that some of them may not, due to their complex historical record, be subjected over a long period to unnecessary suspicion. Among the higher intellectuals today, many have a complex past history, and this is not to be wondered at. But only a small number of them have political problems. And many intellectuals who still have their political problems unsolved are in that position because the leadership comrades did not assume full responsibility to deal with their problems, so that their solution has been delayed.

. . . .

Many intellectuals feel deeply that they are spending too much time on meetings of a nonprofessional nature and on administrative work. These meetings and many other tasks may not need their participation. It seems that the better known a scientist, writer, or artist, the more of his time will be occupied in meetings, administrative work, and social activities. This is a serious situation on our cultural front. The Central Committee considers it essential to ensure that they have at least five sixths of the working day (or forty hours a week) available for their professional work. The remaining time can be used for political study, attending necessary meetings, and taking part in social activity.

. . . .

Some of the intellectuals have adopted an attitude of reserve towards socialism, or even an attitude of opposition. In our enterprises, schools, and organs, in society, there are still such intellectuals. They make no distinction between the Communist Party and the Kuomintang, no distinction between the Chinese people and the imperialists. They are not satisfied with the policies and measures of the Party and the People's Government; they linger over capitalism and even over feudalism. They oppose the Soviet Union and are not willing to learn from the Soviet Union. They refuse to study Marxism-Leninism and even slander Marxism-Leninism. They belittle labor, belittle the laboring people, belittle the cadres who grew from the ranks of laborers, and are not willing to be together with workers, peasants, and worker and peasant cadres.

. . . .

Generally speaking, there are three ways along which the re-education of the intellectuals proceeds. One is through observation and taking part in social life; the other is through the work in their professions; and the third is through general theoretical study. All three are connected. A person's thinking usually changes under the influence of these three factors. But generally the broadest and most direct education is that received in social life.

To assist intellectuals to seek progress, it is important for the leadership personnel of the Party to have direct contacts with them. Many intellectuals hope that we can give them aid and criticism ideologically and politically and feel that we have given them too little aid in this respect. Not a few intellectuals not only find it very difficult to make contact with members of local Party committees and leadership comrades but they also find it difficult to have opportunities for talks with the members ot the Party committees in their own work units.

. . . .

Plans should also be drawn up regarding the admission of intellectuals into the Party. Already progressive intellectuals have requested admission into the Party. As an example, of the 1,920 engineering and technical personnel in the Non-Ferrous Metals Designing Board of the Ministry of Heavy Industry, 605, or 31.7 percent, have applied for membership in the Party. In the six higher institutions in Tientsin, of the 291 teachers of the rank of lecturer and above, 106, or 36.4 percent, have applied for membership in the Party. Of the 131 research workers in the North China Agricultural Science Research Institute, 53, or 40 percent, have applied for membership in the Party. But in the past few years we have seldom admitted into the Party members of their ranks, and this was a tendency to isolationism. This tendency must be corrected.

.   .   .   .

Comrades! We are convinced that through our work the intellectuals will rally still more closely around the Party and contribute their efforts more enthusiastically to the great cause of socialism. The alliance formed by workers, peasants, and intellectuals all over the country will have new signs of consolidation daily, and it will become more powerful with the development of our work. Relying on this alliance, we can build our country, in not too long a time, into a great industrialized Socialist country that is entirely modern, prosperous, and powerful. In not too long a time, we will certainly be able to realize the great declaration of Comrade Mao Tse-tung: "We shall emerge in the world as a highly cultured nation."

SOURCE: *Current Background,* No. 376 (Hong Kong: United States Consulate General, February 7, 1956) . Originally published by *New China News Agency,* January 29, 1956.

For additional reading, see "Peiping Prepares for General Survey of Intellectuals," *Current Background,* No. 374 (1956) .

Let All Flowers Bloom Together, Let Diverse Schools of Thought Contend
By Lu Ting-yi
May 1956

This document is one of the most interesting and stimulating of the pronouncements made on education during the decade. The announcement of "divergent schools" came after years of enforced intellectual orthodoxy and was eagerly seized upon by countless intellectuals as an excuse to criticize the regime. The speech was initially delivered to a gathering of scientists, specialists in the social sciences, doctors, writers, and artists and was repeated in various forms at later Party gatherings. Lu at the time was chief of the Propaganda Department of the Central Committee of the Chinese Communist Party.

If China is to become wealthy and powerful, apart from the need of consolidating the people's regime, developing the economic and educational enterprises, and fortifying the national defense, it is also necessary to bring prosperous development to literature, the arts, and scientific work. We cannot afford to go without any of these things.

. . . .

To bring prosperous development to literature, the arts, and scientific work, it is necessary to adopt the policy of "letting all flowers bloom together and all schools contend in airing their views." In literary and art work, if there is only one flower in bloom, no matter how good the flower may be, it would not lead to prosperity. Take drama for illustration. Several years ago, there were people who were opposed to the Peking drama. At that time, the Party resolved to enforce the policy of "letting all flowers bloom together and the new emerge from the old" in the phase of drama. Everybody is now able to see that this policy is correct and tremendously successful. Because the different kinds of dramas are free to compete with and learn from each other, rapid progress has been made in the field of drama.

. . . .

This problem is obvious in the literary and art domain. There are among literary and art works things which are obviously harmful. Hu Feng can be quoted as an example. The yellow novels which preach obscenity and lawlessness are another instance. Other instances may be found in so-called "literary" works which preach, "Let us play mahjong and say to hell with all state affairs," and "The moon over the United States is rounder than the moon over China." It is entirely right that all these poisonous literary and art works should be swept away like flies, mosquitoes, rats, and sparrows. This is why we say that there are literature and arts which serve the workers, peasants, and soldiers and that there are literature and arts which serve imperialism, the landlords, and the bourgeoisie. What we need are the literature and arts which serve the workers, peasants, and soldiers, as well as the masses of the people.

. . . .

The Party's policy advocates freedom of thinking in literature, art, and scientific research; freedom of debate; freedom of creative work; freedom to criticize; freedom to express one's opinion, and freedom to maintain one's opinion and to reserve one's opinion.

. . . .

It takes years of hard study and practice for one to become the exponent of a "school" in the true sense and to contend intelligently. This is the minimum knowledge one must possess if the line of letting all schools contend in airing their views is to be understood correctly, and it seems necessary that this point should be pointed out with emphasis. Otherwise, the different research units and institutions of higher education would receive in the future inventions and discoveries from many "schools" which take much valuable time to scrutinize. They have also to explain painstakingly and carefully why such inventions and discoveries are impracticable or to point out that similar inventions and discoveries had been made by some other people before them. In this way, the energy of both the authors and the examiners is wasted in vain. If, however, the line of letting all schools contend in airing their views is correctly understood, this waste of energy can at least be reduced, and useless things can be made to render a useful role.

. . . .

The freedom we are advocating is different from the freedom advocated by bourgeois democratism. The freedom advocated by the bourgeoisie is nothing more than freedom for the minority which the laboring people have no or little chance to share. The bourgeoisie is dictatorial to the laboring people. The warmongers in the United States are presently playing up their so-called "free world." In that "free world," the warmongers and the reactionary cliques have all the freedom. Nevertheless, the Rosenberg couple were sentenced to death because they advocated peace. We advocate that the counterrevolutionaries should be denied freedom. We hold that we must practice dictatorship over counterrevolutionaries. But among the people we take the stand that there must be democracy and freedom. This is a political line. In politics, we must distinguish ourselves from the enemy.

. . . .

The political thought of the intellectuals has undergone a fundamental change, and this situation is now producing further fundamental changes. This was explained in detail by Comrade Chou En-lai in his report on the question of intellectuals. Here, let me recount briefly the latest struggle.

The latest struggle is a struggle against the idealistic thought of the bourgeoisie. In this struggle, the broad masses of the intellectuals have put up a good show and have made great progress.

. . . .

In this struggle, the Central Commitee of the Chinese Communist Party has taught us the need for opposing the thoughts which hamper academic criticism and discussion. These thoughts find expressions in the bourgeois cult of "famous people," on the ground that they are the authority and cannot be criticized.

. . . .

Since the line of "letting all flowers bloom together and all schools contend in airing their views" seeks to mobilize all positive elements, it constitutes the policy for strengthening unity. Upon what is unity to be founded? It is to be founded on patriotism and socialism. What is unity to drive at? To build a Socialist New China and to wage a struggle against our enemies, domestic and foreign.

. . . .

There are still shortcomings in the matter of unity.

What are these shortcomings? First, some Party members have forgotten the teachings of Comrade Mao Tse-tung and the evils of sectarianism. Success leads to a swelled head. This gives rise to arrogance and sectarian sentiment.

When writing his "Rectify the Party's Style in Work," in 1942, Mao Tse-tung said:

> Many of our comrades are much given to swaggering before non-Party people, despising and belittling them, and are unwilling to show them respect or appreciate their good qualities. This is precisely a sectarian tendency. Having read a few Marxist books, these comrades become arrogant rather than modest and habitually dismiss others as no good without knowing that they themselves are really mere tyros and smatterers.

. . . .

On the question of subject matters to write about, the Party has laid down no restriction. It is wrong to entertain the belief that one can only write about the worker, peasant, and soldier, the new society, the new characters, and new deeds. Since they serve the workers, peasants, and soldiers, literature and art should sing the praises of the new society and positive characters as a matter of course. At the same time, they should criticize the old society and negative characters. They praise progress while criticizing what is lagging behind. Therefore, the themes of literature and art should be very broad.

. . . .

Between some intellectuals of our Party, there still exists a certain state of estrangement. We must take the initiative in removing this estrangement. But it often comes from both sides: on the one hand our comrades have failed to approach them, failed to understand them, while on the other hand, some of the intellectuals have adopted an attitude of reservation toward socialism, or even an attitude of opposition.

In our enterprises, schools, and organs in society, there are still such intellectuals. They make no distinction between the Communist Party and the Kuomintang, no distinction between the Chinese people and the imperialists. They are satisfied with the policies and measures of the Party and the People's Government, linger over capitalism and even linger over feudalism. They are opposed to the Soviet Union and are not willing to learn from it. They refuse to study Marxism-Leninism, and even slander it. They belittle labor, the laboring people, and the cadres who grew from the ranks of the laborers, and are not willing to be together with the workers, peasants, and worker and peasant cadres. They do not like to see the growth of the new forces and consider the progressive elements to be speculators. They do not only constantly create disputes and a state of antagonism between the intellectuals and the Party but also create disputes and a state of antagonism among the intellectuals themselves. They are vainglorious, look upon themselves as the best in the world, and will not accept the leadership and criticism of any other. They reject the interests of the people and of society and deal with all problems from the viewpoint of their own individual interests, supporting whatever is in keeping with their own interests and opposing whatever is at variance with them.

. . . .

Fifteen years ago, in May 1941, Comrade Mao Tse-tung wrote his "Reform Our Study." Later, in February 1942, he wrote again the articles, "Rectify the Party's Style in Work" and "Oppose the Party 'Eight-Legged Essay.' " These three articles formed the basic documents of the Yenan Rectification Movement. The Yenan Rectification Movement was an ideological movement launched against subjectivism, principally against dogmatism. This was China's greatest ideological movement after the May Movement. Dogmatism nearly lost our revolution during the period of the democratic revolution of China. It is the great enemy of Marxism-Leninism. We should firmly bear in mind this painful experience. We must be highly vigilant, for if a doctrinaire attitude is adopted in conducting research for knowledge or in leading the work of literature, art, and scientific research, the end would be certain failure, because such an attitude runs diametrically counter to the realistic attitude of Marxism-Leninism.

. . . .

We should learn from the Soviet Union, the people's democracies, and the people of all other countries.

Learn from the Soviet Union! This is a correct slogan. We have already learned something, and in the future there are many things we should learn. The Soviet Union is the first Socialist state in the world and the leader of the world camp of peace and democracy. The rapidity of the development of its industry is the quickest. It has rich experience in Socialist construction, and many major departments of science have reached or exceeded the most advanced capitalist countries. Such a country and such a people are of course worthy for us to learn from. It would be a fundamental mistake if we did not learn from the Soviet Union.

However, our method of learning must not be a doctrinaire, mechanical adoption but must be adapted to the actual situation of our country. Attention must be paid to this point. Otherwise, our work would suffer.

. . . .

Following the advancement of the policy of "letting all flowers bloom together and all schools contend in airing their views," many problems would gradually be brought up for solution. It is hoped that everybody would give more consideration to problems in this field. I talk only about questions of principles today. All are requested to favor me with guidance and correction.

SOURCE: *Current Background*, No. 406 (Hong Kong: United States Consulate General, 1956).

See also Lu Ting-yi, *Let a Hundred Flowers Blossom, Let a Hundred Schools of Thought Contend* (Peking: Foreign Languages Press, 1956).

A Comprehensive Plan for Scientific Research and the Policy of "Letting Diverse Schools of Thought Contend"

By Kuo Mo-jo

1956

Kuo, Vice-Chairman of the Standing Committee of the National People's Congress and President of the Chinese Academy of Sciences, detailed the proposals of the Chinese Communist Party for planned scientific advances during the next decade. There were to be three Five-Year Plans for general construction, and the selection of twelve years for a scientific plan merely placed science prognostications on a par with other sectors of the economy, culminating when their plans did. In fact, a year later, much was made of the rapidity of educational developments, and the regime claimed that objectives of the second of the Five-Year Plans had been virtually accomplished for education in two years.

Kuo refers to a Scientific Planning Committee established directly under the State Council as the body responsible to draw up the plans, under the guidance of the ubiquitous Chinese Communist Party.

I have heard the report by Vice-Premier and Finance Minister Li Hsien-nien on the final account of state revenue and expenditure for 1955 and the state budget for 1956. It drives home the fact that our economic and financial condition is stable and our national construction has made rapid progress. This is certainly a matter for rejoicing.

235

MORE SUPPORT FOR SCIENTIFIC DEVELOPMENT

From the sum alloted for scientific research under the head of social, cultural, and educational expenditures, we can see how sound is our country's financial system and how ample the material conditions for the promotion of scientific research. Outlay for scientific research in the 1955 final accounts came to only 85.96 percent budgeted for the year. The same condition prevailed every year since the founding of the People's Republic, and this means that in the last six or seven years we did not spend all the money allotted for scientific research. Now the state budget for 1956 provides considerable increase in the outlay for scientific research. The increase in the budget of the central authorities is 127.17 percent; and, if the funds provided in the budgets of the local authorities are included, the increase amounts to 153.27 percent. Only in the 1956 budgets have the local authorities for the first time put aside outlays for scientific research. This fully explains how, along with the growth of natural construction, the state is paying greater and greater attention to the promotion of scientific research and how the local initiative has manifested itself.

This gives a bird's-eye view of the whole picture. In my opinion, the final account of state revenue and expenditure for 1955 and the state budget for 1956 are quite satisfactory. I fully endorse and support them.

Fellow Deputies! As a scientific worker myself, I should like to say something, from my own experience and understanding, about the question of how to develop scientific research work in which I am sure you are all interested.

A TWELVE YEAR PLAN

In January of this year, the Central Committee of the Chinese Communist Party called a meeting to discuss the question of intellectuals. To ensure that a Socialist society will, in the main, be built in China in three Five Year Plans, the meeting issued a clarion call to bring out work in the most urgently needed branches of science near to a level with the best of the world within twelve years and to march forward to science. Intellectuals and young students throughout the country are inspired by this call. The leading organs of the Communist Party, the government at all levels, other political parties, people's organizations, fraternal nationalities, and research, teaching, and production units have since given full rein to their enthusiasm and have pledged themselves to make a common effort to fulfill this glorious, though arduous, task.

To fulfill this task, we must first of all understand that it is necessary for us to draw up a twelve year, long-term plan for scientific development. If we go to battle, we must have a fighting plan; and if we build, we have got to have a blueprint, and the twelve year plan for scientific development is our plan to march forward to science and our blueprint for scientific construction.

Twelve years is not a very long period. If we are bent on fulfilling this unparalleled task of construction and research within the time-limit set, we would not reach our goal unless we have a thoroughly considered plan.

Long-term plans for natural sciences, philosophy, and social sciences are being drawn up under the guidance of the Party and the government. A Scientific Planning Committee, directly under the State Council, has been specially set up to direct the work of mapping out plans for the development of science.

Different steps have been taken in the drawing-up of the plans. For natural sciences, planning was started as early as last December. We invited more than two hundred outstanding scientists and technicians from all parts of the country to Peking to discuss the matter. They first defined scores of important tasks for science and technology to perform in the various branches of national economy in the twelve year period and then worked out hundreds of important subjects which must be tackled for the fulfillment of these tasks. Each subject was provided with essential information as to its importance, the international level to be attained, the domestic situation, the contents to be studied, the timetable, the actual measures to be adopted, etc. On this basis, a twelve year national program for the development of natural sciences was drafted. Every organization concerned was then asked to draw up separately its own plans—more specific ones—for research in accordance with this overall plan.

This is a method of proceeding from corporate planning to individual planning; it enables the scientists better to link theory with practice from an overall point of view, properly divide the work, and coöperate within the framework of a master plan.

Planning in the field of philosophy and social sciences started in early February of this year, but the method of gathering together for joint discussion was not adopted. Experts in Peking and a few outside the capital first began making up a list of questions pertaining to the various important subjects to be tackled and catalogued the important works to be written in the next twelve years. On this basis, the general plan for philosophy and social sciences was drawn up. Apart from the important subjects to be grappled with and the important works to be written, many items of important work affecting various fields were also listed. Furthermore, an all-around estimate was made of the training of personnel and the setting up of organizations for research. This draft of the general plan as well as the draft plans for individual subjects will be sent to those doing research in philosophy and the social sciences in all parts of the country for discussion. After opinions have been widely solicited and proper revisions made, the draft plans will be made final. This is a method of proceeding from separate, individual suggestions to a corporate plan, but the same spirit prevails as in the method used to draft the plan for natural sciences. In this draft of the general plan is pooled the collective wisdom of the scientists who, in working out the plan and during the discussion stages, have acquired an all-around view of the situation. They were thus able to integrate theory with practice still better, properly divide the work, and coöperate under a centralized plan.

Although we lacked experience in the drawing-up of plans for scientific research, the scientists who took part did the best they could. They felt honored at being able to take part in the drawing-up of the plans and cherished a great hope for the development of science. Here I must point out in particular that Soviet advisers and experts in China have given us tremendous help. In the drawing-up of the plan for natural sciences, the Soviet government specially sent more than ten of her foremost experts to China, and for two months they plunged into arduous work with their Chinese colleagues. This is an event of historical significance, a milestone in the creative coöperation between the Chinese and Soviet scientists. I must avail myself of this opportunity to express our heartfelt gratitude to the Soviet government, scientists, and people.

By virtue of the efforts of the Chinese experts and with the assistance of Soviet advisers and experts, both draft plans for natural sciences, and for philosophy and social sciences are now approaching the finishing stage. They will be put into effect as soon as they are completed and approved by the government. The scheme of development for some especially important and urgent subjects can be submitted in advance for approval without having to wait for the completion of the whole plan. The plan for scientific development is the collective wisdom of the scientists and, subject to the approval of the government, will become a charter for scientific research in the next twelve years. It is something which they have created together, and they are under obligation to observe it and strive for its realization. This twelve-year plan mainly maps out the basic direction for scientific development. It is impossible to make detailed provisions for methods of tackling key or important questions. Concrete provisions should be made later by the respective units in their annual plans. Needless to say, as we go along the plan itself may be supplemented and revised. But we believe that, having given careful consideration to the basic direction and important measures to be taken, we shall not go far wrong. If we follow the plan in our work, not only can we guard against pitfalls but will be able to fulfill this magnificent task the Party and the government have entrusted to us—to bring our most urgently needed branches of science and technology near to a level with the best in the world and more effectively to serve the building of socialism.

After working out the plans, the next important thing is to

fulfill them. The Communist Party and the government will make a great effort to ensure the fulfillment of the plans; in other words, they will do all they can to encourage the scientists to bring into full play their potential energy, to enlarge the ranks of scientists, to provide all material conditions necessary for scientific research—setting up more institutes, supplying more data, improving the work of publication, promoting international coöperation, etc. Never before had we such excellent conditions for the fulfillment of the plans. We have an urgent task of carrying out large-scale construction in our country. We have also, however, the encouragement of the Party and the government and the disinterested aid of the Soviet Union and the fraternal countries. No matter how numerous are the key subjects and important questions to be tackled and how limited the time at our disposal to tackle these questions and fulfill our task, if all of our scientists give full play to their initiative and creativeness, we are sure we can bring our plans to complete fruition.

THE POLICY OF "LETTING DIVERSE SCHOOLS OF THOUGHT CONTEND"

The question of enabling the scientists to give full play to their initiative and creativeness therefore cannot but become a key question in the fulfillment of the plans for scientific development. Speaking at the Supreme State Conference on May 2 of this year, Chairman Mao Tse-tung reminded us to carry out the policy of "letting diverse schools of thought contend" in academic studies. Later, on May 26, Lu Ting-yi, Director of the Propaganda Department of the Central Committee of the Chinese Communist Party, made a report entitled "Let Flowers of All Kinds Blossom, Diverse Schools of Thought Contend" to the scientists who took part in the making of the plans for scientific development and important cultural workers in Peking. In my opinion, "letting flowers of all kinds blossom and diverse schools of thought contend" is truly an excellent policy of drawing out the best from scientists and cultural workers. We have seen the fine results which "letting flowers of all kinds blossom" has produced in theater. Since Chairman Mao Tse-tung pointed out to the dramatic workers that "Let flowers of all kinds blossom side by side, weed through the old to let the new emerge," flowers of many, many kinds have blossomed, and blossomed beautifully, in the theatrical world over the last few years. Our "flowers" have not only blossomed all over China, but almost throughout Asia and Europe, and recently as far as the northern parts of Africa. Our "flowers" are many; they have blossomed very well, too, and have been acclaimed everywhere. This correct policy we must apply to all departments of literary creation, and the corresponding policy of "letting diverse schools of thought contend" to all departments of academic research.

To draw up plans for raising our scientific and cultural levels in twelve years, so as to serve the cause of building socialism on the one hand and, on the other, to encourage diverse schools of thought to contend and to encourage free research and discussion—these two things, some scholars assert, seem contradictory. Others think that the drawing-up of a plan is bound to hamstring freedom; and conversely, to encourage freedom would lead to belittling the plans. But I think no contradiction exists if we look into the gist of the matter.

"Let diverse schools of thought contend"—this is something that bears the signs of the times. Whenever society reaches an epochal stage, a situation always presents itself in which diverse schools of thought vie with one another in the cultural sphere. During the Warring States Period, over two thousand years ago, which, in my opinion, was a transitional period from slave-owning society to feudal society, scholars representing diverse schools of thought emerged. "Let diverse schools of thought contend" is a saying handed down to us from those times. In the early period of modern Europe, when feudal society passed into capitalist society, there was a "Renaissance," originating in Italy, which is similar in form to the contending of all schools of thought in the Warring States Period. But the stages of development of these two periods are different; the cultural revolutions of these two periods as reflected in their respective ideologies are therefore essentially different. "Let diverse schools of thought contend," as advocated by us today, as I understand it, differs from the emergence of the various schools of thought in the Warring States Period, as well as from the "Renaissance." "Let diverse schools of thought contend," to be more specific, means Socialist emulation in all spheres of academic research, or within a certain field. We do not stand for research for research's sake. Our clearly defined fundamental task is to build socialism. The purpose of letting diverse schools of thought contend is, therefore, to make our academic research flourish so that it will serve the building of socialism better.

So "letting diverse schools of thought contend" means that we must not only contend but contend to advantage. When we say "contend," this implies both competition and struggle. There will be competition between various branches of science, and the scholars will compete with each other to see who have done more, have done it better, quicker, and more economically. At the same time, we will criticize the harmful ideas which are opposed to Socialist construction. This is what we mean by struggle. To carry out the struggle in the academic field, we will adopt the method of free discussion, overcoming ideas with ideas and replacing theories with theories. What we aim at is to wipe out all harmful ideas but not people who harbor those harmful ideas. Provided they are not engaged in counterrevolutionary political activities, those who have harmful ideas not only have the freedom to live the life of an ordinary citizen but the freedom to take part in discussion. If the pernicious ideas are overcome or weakened through free discusssion, it would contribute to the development of scientific research as well as the building of socialism. So it is necessary for us not only to contend but contend well.

To do so, that is to say, to enable our academic research to serve socialism well, directly or indirectly, we must have a better grasp of Marxism-Leninism and apply Marxism-Leninism more effectively to the conditions of China. It is not obligatory for us to study Marxism-Leninism; we do so of our own free will. But if we want to contend and contend to advantage, it is natural that this urge of ours to study Marxism-Leninism should become all the keener. To advocate the study of Marxism-Leninism on a voluntary basis, therefore, does not mean restricting diverse schools of thought from contending; quite on the contrary, it will help them to contend better.

The drawing-up of the plan for scientific development is another flexible application of Marxism-Leninism to the conditions in China. We have studied the laws of development of our society today and the laws of development of science itself. We hold that only when we adapt the development of sciences to that of society can the development of scientific research be safeguarded. Conversely, the same is true. The plan for scientific development is aimed precisely at encouraging schools of thought to contend rather than restraining them. Of course we have set forth in our plan a number of key or important subjects, but this is done mainly from the viewpoint of the development of society and by considering the needs of our country. Those branches of science which are urgently needed for national construction but are at present lacking or rather weak, such as research in the peaceful uses of atomic energy, must be listed as key subjects on which more manpower and material resources will be concentrated. The subjects receiving priority treatment in the plan are, of course, very important from the point of view of national construction and scientific research; but that does not mean that subjects not included are unimportant. No, such is not the case. All branches of sciences are closely connected with each other; the development of a key subject will need the backing of all; and once developed it will bring on the others. A motor or a gear of a machine is of course important, but a small screw is no less important. If a small screw is missing, the machine will get into trouble. Hence, it is obvious that what a research worker should strive for is not whether the particular subject he is working on is listed as a key or important subject in the plan but whether his research will yield fine results and serve socialism fruitfully. Therefore, the making of a scientific plan does not in the least restrict but, on the contrary, provides better conditions for diverse schools of thought to contend. When the gist of the matter is considered, we can see that there is really no contradiction between the making of a scientific plan and letting diverse schools of thought contend.

Fellow Deputies! I have not given a profound and comprehensive opinion on scientific development, but perhaps I may state here that an overwhelming majority of scientists agree with me on the matter. They wholeheartedly support the making of a scientific plan and the carrying-out of the policy of "letting diverse schools of thought contend." They are also of the opinion that there is no contradiction between the two. They are determined to bring their potential energy into full play, show still greater enthusiasm and creativeness, unite more closely, and make greater efforts to train fresh forces.

The Chinese Academy of Sciences, for instance, will enroll six times more research students than last year, and there will be four times more tutors ready to guide them. Scientists and scholars in all fields are looking forward to make their contribution, to take part in the Socialist emulation in academic research. They are energetically applying themselves to the study of Marxism-Leninism and learning what they can from the valuable experiences of the Soviet Union and other Socialist countries, while at the same time rectifying what has so far been a tendency to treat slightingly the useful achievements and experience in cultural and academic work of capitalist countries. With few exceptions, our scientists all share this belief and determination: prompted by the urgent needs of large-scale national construction, correctly guided and vigorously supported by the Party and the government, and with the selfless help of the Soviet Union and the fraternal countries, the scientists are determined to do their best to fulfill the glorious task entrusted to them by the Party and the government —the task of raising the level of certain important branches of science and culture in China on a par with the best in the world within twelve years, so as to support the great cause of building socialism in our country.

Fellow Deputies! Allow me to make a sincere request on behalf of the Academy of Sciences and the scientists: give us constant guidance and advice and exercise supervision over our work, so that the scientific research in our country will advance at a rate commensurate with the progress of our national effort in construction.

SOURCE: *New China Advances to Socialism: A Selection of Speeches Delivered at the Third Session of the First National People's Congress* (Peking: Foreign Languages Press, 1956), pp. 137–148. See also Kuo Mo-jo, "In Refutation of an Antisocialist Scientific Program," *Current Background*, No. 467 (1957).

Higher Education in China
By Yang Hsiu-feng
June 1956

Yang, as Minister of Higher Education, delivered this report to the third session of the First National People's Congress on June 20, 1956. The shortage of qualified teachers, the lack of qualified educational administrators, and the cumbersome central control over higher education led to severe problems in 1955-56. The regime admitted that controls were too rigid and indicated that university and college presidents were henceforth to have greater independence and initiative. Student health and a breakdown of student morale also perplexed the administration, and promises were made that greater care for student welfare would be exercised.

Pursuant to the policy laid down at the national cultural and educational conference last year, the higher educational work has centered on the education policy of higher quality and all-round development during the past year. Much has been achieved in improving the quality of the students enrolled, regrouping the ranks of school students, relieving the students of too-heavy study tasks, improving the students' health, strengthening the connections between theory and practice, bettering the teaching, and developing the scientific research. Since the second half of 1955, in particular, the teachers and students, inspired by the high tide of Socialist construction and transformation, have warmly responded to the "master science" call, and the teachers have generally drawn up long-range plans for self-study, improvement of teaching, and scientific research. Everywhere the schools have a stimulating air of vigor.

246

. . . .

Our efforts to increase the number of graduates during the second Five Year Plan in order to meet the urgent needs of national construction make it necessary to defer appropriately in some schools the original plans for changing the school system and extending the school year. Hereafter, we must gradually change the school system without hindering too much the plans for fostering cadres.

. . . .

The greatest difficulty in rapidly increasing the number of cadres and ensuring a certain quality of cadres is shortage of teachers. Teachers must be increased in large numbers. The demand for teachers has been particularly urgent in recent months and comes into the greatest conflict with the demand of national construction departments and scientific research organs for cadres. In our opinion, it is particularly necessary—in order to foster construction cadres and the reserves of scientific forces—for all sides to assist the higher educational institutions to keep more graduates of good quality to be used as "hens." Otherwise, students enrolled will have no teachers to give them lessons, let alone to provide strenuous development of scientific research and improvement of teaching quality.

. . . .

In our opinion, the leadership relations of higher educational institutions should vary according to the character of schools; higher educational institutions mainly designed to foster cadres for local construction work should be placed under the direct leadership of the local governments; higher educational institutions mainly designed to foster cadres for certain construction work of nationwide character should be placed under the direct leadership of the central government departments, excepting the comprehensive universities and colleges connected with the business departments, which should be placed under the direct leadership of the Ministry of Higher Education. The leadership should be divided in the following way: in respect to schools under the leadership of the central government departments or local governments, the Ministry of Higher Education should check up, direct, and supervise the policies and pedagogical service; draw up and approve unified regulations, systems, and teaching documents; systematically train and transfer teachers; and assist the State Planning Commission in considering the plans for establishing new schools and specialization courses and for balancing the educational service. Other phases of work like everyday teaching work, employment of teachers, capital construction, teaching facilities, personnel matters, and financial affairs should be placed under the direct charge of the competent departments or local governments which are responsible to the relevant departments of the central government. This distribution of graduates should also be appropriately carried out in such a way as to facilitate the activity of various departments and local governments.

The function and power of university and college presidents should be appropriately enlarged. In the past, we carried out the retrenchment policy in the spheres of capital construction, financial affairs, and personnel matters. The policy was right, but in certain cases the restrictions were inevitably made too rigid, making it difficult for the schools to operate flexibly. This was also the case with regulations which handicapped the schools' work in varying degrees. The school administration and teaching work have gradually been brought into the orbit, and some experience has been acquired in recent years. The university and college presidents should have more and flexible power. This will do much good.

.   .   .   .

In the first half of last year, the students of many higher educational institutions had a too-heavy task of study. Following the national cultural and educational conference, the schools concerned took measures to revise the teaching plans, improve the teaching methods, and balance students' assignments, as a result of which, improvement was made in the conditions of study. While their tasks were still heavy, the students were not in such a flurry as before. In the last few months, however, instances have again been reported in a number of schools indicating that the students did not have adequate time to conduct extracurricular study and did not have sufficient time to digest and master the theories and techniques studied, while the students were again too busy in their study and life. The majority of students could not get complete rest on Sundays, and the students in general had to study half a day on each Sunday. According to our information, the percentage of students who failed in the last semester examination was on the increase in a number of schools. While the number of students suffering from tuberculosis and disease of the gastro-intestinal tract decreased, those suffering from neurasthenia and high blood pressure did not decrease in general and increased in some schools. This should arouse our serious attention.

. . . .

Students of the higher educational institutions should take part in certain extracurricular activities and social activities, so as to enrich their life, enlarge their knowledge, and improve their health. But if the activities are too many and confused and if all students are forced to take part in such activities, regardless of their study and rest and regardless of their conditions, not only will the teaching order be disturbed and tension and confusions brought about but students' health will be impaired. Defense and physical culture activities, for instance, are beneficial and necessary to students' health and have achieved the results of improving the students' health, but if we lack preparations and fail to provide the necessary conditions, like medical supervision, and if we require all the students to take part in and spend too much time on such activities, regardless of conditions, then study will be handicapped, and students' health will be impaired.

. . . .

In some schools, the Party and League reports are increased once again. The "class triangle" (class master, class chairman, and responsible person of the League branch) are very busy and attend to many things, including the selection of stipend recipients and management of mess. Under the class triangle, many cadres have to be appointed, numbering more than twenty in some classes. These activities and work put together will inevitably involve many meetings. Student cadres working among the students in particular find themselves lacking both the necessary energy and time.

. . . .

The leaders of many higher educational institutions being accustomed to launching movements while the broad masses of young people being inevitably overzealous and impatient for success, a practice has been developed, under the impact of the upsurge of Socialist construction, to push forward work by means of drives. A number of schools inappropriately stress collective activities and bring about mass pressure, under which the students are obliged to vie with each other in winning collective honors during study of their lessons, during extracurricular activities, and even during cultural activities. In substance, an interclass emulation drive is launched in study and all kinds of activities. To study means a process of painstaking, gradual, and orderly mental labor. The responsibility of schools is to raise the teaching results gradually by improving the teaching system, contents, and methods and should not advance the teaching work and try to achieve immediate success by means of drives and emulations. It is obviously harmful to impose generalized and equal demands on students of different standards and different likings in study, political-ideological education, and social activities and to cause every student to follow others reluctantly under collective pressure.

. . . .

The Ministry of Higher Education and the higher educational institutions should strenuously implement the directive of the Central Committee of the Chinese Communist Party and the State Council on intellectuals by improving the living and working conditions of teachers and seeing to it that each week they can devote five sixths of their time to their professional duties. Teachers distinguished for success in scientific research should be freed from administrative work and provided with assistants, and, if necessary, their teaching tasks should be reduced. Pedagogical research teams should be provided with the necessary auxiliary teaching force (this question is now being energetically solved by this Ministry). All such are important conditions for enabling teachers to set aside more time to improve teaching work, develop scientific research, and take advanced courses.

. . . .

Owing to the weak foundation, inadequate efforts, and many defects in the work, our higher education lags far behind the development of the objective situation. In order to catch up with the demand of the new situation and to increase the number of our cadres and improve the quality of our cadres rapidly and as far as possible, we must make a better study of the advanced experience and advanced science and technology of the Soviet Union and creatively apply such experience, science, and technology in the light of the concrete conditions of China. We must bring into full play the role of the Soviet experts and the strength of our experts and improve teaching and develop scientific research. At the same time, we must pay attention to learning the advanced experience of the people's democracies, critically absorb the best experience and scientific and technical specialties of all other countries, implement the "let all flowers blossom and all schools of thought contend" policy, revive the academic atmosphere, and enlarge upon the cultural legacy of our country. In the past, the leadership of the Ministry of Higher Education had serious defects in these respects, and hereafter attention should be paid to correcting these defects. We believe that, under the strengthened leadership of the Central Committee of the Party and the State Council and with the energetic aid and support of all concerned, our higher educational service will certainly be able to advance, if all higher educational workers develop their activity and creative power and exert concerted efforts.

SOURCE: *Current Background,* No. 400 (Hong Kong: United States Consulate General, 1956). Originally published by *New China News Agency,* June 20, 1956.

For additional readings, see "Problems of Education in Communist China," *Current Background,* No. 447 (1957); and "Guide to Institutions of Higher Education," *Current Background,* No. 462 (1957).

Why Are University Students Tense?

By Chu Wen-pin

1956

During 1956, one of the most spectacular ideological campaigns or political commotions of the first decade occurred in China. It concerned the temporary relaxation of some of the more rigid controls on free speech and criticism of the regime. It gave students a much-needed opportunity to voice their criticism of educational authorities as well as of the Communist Party. University students throughout China were almost universal in their denouncement of the strain placed upon them as they pursued their studies. The physical conditions of the institutions, as well as the professors, teaching methods, and curriculum came under attack. The problem of student unrest is one that the regime has had to face continually, and in 1955, the year before the document below was published, a leading educational authority had warned that some students "spread reactionary views to make known their dissatisfaction with socialism" and even formed themselves into "reactionary cliques." Other university students were said to have been "sent by the enemy to infiltrate our institutions for the purpose of carrying out counterrevolutionary activities." The seriousness of the situation is revealed when students were accused of "incidents of a sabotage nature, involving arson, poisoning, document-stealing, sabotage of machinery and equipment, and posting of reactionary bills." The general situation in 1956 had not greatly improved, but students were invited to speak "freely" and after "deep thinking" write articles on "problems of education." The document below is illustrative of the unrest and disquiet of many students.

252

College students are really too busy. We have no Sunday; it is merely the "seventh day of the week." Many students spend their weekends in the library. Others carry their books or Russian language cards with them in the toilet and in the streetcar or bus. The period of reviewing for the examination is even worse. Due to excessive tension, the students constantly suffer from headaches, fatigue, insomnia, and neurasthenia, and such symptoms become worse daily. It is not unusual for them to talk in their sleep or recite articles or themes. There is a general loss of appetite, accompanied by weight reduction in the case of most of the students. What is more serious is that there are instances of fainting in the dining room, library, or even in the examination hall. Some students become so tense at an examination that they cannot read the questions. During the long-drawn-out examination period, many of them come down sick; sometimes the entire class will collapse. For example, there were twenty-seven students in the first-year preschool education specialization class in the education department, but only nine persisted through the last examination. Almost the entire second-year class failed to sustain to the end. The more advanced they become in academic years, the more deteriorated will become their health. By the time they reach the fourth year, many laughing and dancing young girls show symptoms of old age. By graduation time, many husky and spirited young men acquire more or less the style of the "little old man." Neurasthenia and defective eyesight also grow with the years.

What are the basic reasons for the excessive tension in college students? I feel that there are the following aspects.

TOO MANY COURSES

Some students constantly say: "Our education department is like a variety store in its courses; it has everything there is, but nothing good." For example, in practical training, there are those who have studied education but who cannot write an education project, and others who have studied psychology but cannot make a psychological evaluation. Such a Jack-of-all-trades condition is inseparable from the ponderous and complicated teaching plan and the disability to educate according to the material in conjunction with actual conditions. Take the school education specialization in our department as an example. The first year consists of eight subjects, involving twenty-six hours of lectures a week. Besides the five hours of psychology, which is a specialization subject, the rest are almost entirely political theory and culture courses. Even the teachers do not know the reasons for such courses. For instance, the Modern Literature Selection professor once remarked in the classroom: "I do not know why first-year education requires this course, but anyway, it is good for you." As there is a course, one has to take it, and as one takes it, one has to study for it. Thus, the students do not have time to study more intensively the specialization courses nor the time and energy to participate in the small scientific research teams.

What is worth mentioning is that some culture subjects also exert a high pressure on the students. For example, in Modern Literature Selection and Chinese History, besides classroom questioning and arrangement for preclass study and review problems, there are also classroom discussions. Twenty minutes are devoted to classroom questioning in the Russian language class, and a test is given after the conclusion of each unit of study. What with the preclass studies, postclass review, classroom discussions, in-class questioning, outside assignments, and unit tests of many of the courses, the students can only sit in the library all day and never finish even if they never take a rest.

Of course, the sciences of different departments are related, and it is good for a person to be not unfamiliar with all kinds of scientific knowledge. However, after all, a person's energy is limited, and it will be impossible to learn everything in four years. Furthermore, though all branches of knowledge are organically related, the relations are of varying degrees in regard to a specialization. As the inherent element, interest, and talent of each individual are different and the background not the same, it is not only unnecessary but impossible to become an expert in every subject.

Hence, I would like to suggest to the Ministry of Higher Education, Ministry of Education, and the administrative leadership of the schools to reconsider the current teaching plan in the light of practical conditions, eliminate the courses which are not closely related with the special field, and add some closely related elective courses. I also suggest that the teaching method of classroom questioning and testing on general courses as the means to urge the students on in their studies be abolished or modified. Only thus will the abnormal phenomenon of excessive tension and the obstruction to even development be corrected and the student's independent-study ability be cultivated.

TOO MUCH ACADEMIC WORK

For the past year, I have felt that there seems to be a gap between my current level and the level required of first year of college. Not only there is a lack of general knowledge and independent-work ability, a large portion of the students feel unfamiliar with certain courses. For instance, in Psychology, not only is there a lack of comprehension of terms such as sensing, cogitation, and memory but even the Pavlov theory and the philosophical foundation of psychology are unknown. Thus, the teacher is required to start with the definition of the most basic terms from the level of the students. Certain basic problems will require the teacher's full explanation and analysis. However, as the teaching provided in the teaching outline and the teaching period conflict, only by rushing through, taking advantage of the few minutes between classes, or holding the students over after class can the teachers more or less complete the teaching outline. (If the teacher should go beyond the outline unconsciously, heaven help us!) Thus, in the classroom the students may or may not understand, and at times they do not understand a thing.

Hence, I feel that the Ministry of Higher Education, the leadership of the Ministry of Education, responsible persons of colleges and schools, and the teachers responsible for the courses should formulate feasible teaching outlines in the light of the practical conditions of our country and the academic level, receptivity, and health of college students in general. Only thus will the hurried and confused phenomenon in teaching be overcome and the students' burden lightened.

THE TEACHING QUALITY

Take classroom teaching. The teaching attitude, method, and comprehension of the material of some teachers are not satisfactory to the students. For example, in Logic, for the past year, it has consisted of the teacher reading his lecture notes and the students taking them down like recording machines. Some students, after attending a two-period class, have to spend more than that much time to verify and supplement their notes. The teacher relies on his notes to lecture, and if he should lose a few pages, he will not be able to continue with his lecture. Take the teacher of Revolutionary History as an example. It is more accurate to say that he reads aloud articles and sections of books in class than analyzing the classics. Or the teacher of Psychology cites the classics excessively. To the students, it is like explaining the unknown with the incomprehensible.

The phenomenon of attention to teaching "advance only" and overlooking quality is very serious also. Some teachers concentrate on lecturing and never notice the worried look of the students. Sometimes the fingers ache and the eyes swim in note-taking, and yet the teacher will never let up in his speed and will accelerate even more during the few minutes before the end of the class.

Though incessantly talking about cultivating the students' independent-work ability and coördinating theory with practice, the teachers, in practical teaching, only emphasize note-taking. This not only cannot cultivate the ability and interest of the students in reading reference books but restricts them from so doing. Whoever opens a classic is "charged" with being overambitious and frowned on by others. Our coördination of theory with practice is limited to putting the phenomena and dogmas together. As for participating in small scientific research teams, strengthening observations and training, and entering into liaison activities with middle and elementary schools, they often deteriorate into formalism and empty words.

Hence, I hope that the teachers hereafter will properly master the spiritual substance of the teaching outline, study and understand the material more thoroughly, and turn it into something which they themselves understand before teaching it. There must also be the spirit of "seeking-the-truth-through-the-facts" when lecturing, and they must only lecture on what they themselves understand and must not pretend to understand what they do not. On the other hand, I hope the teachers will not think that it is due to the lack of application that the students do not learn well but will try to understand comprehensively the level and receptivity of the students and help those who have made the effort but still failed, instead of treating them as backward elements. They must be more objective when arranging homework and estimating the time for review, in order to avoid rushing, confusing, and overburdening the students. Attention must be given to turning the knowledge acquired by the students into skill and enabling them to coördinate theory with practice.

. . . .

FORMALISM IN TEACHING

The review-for-examination system must be revised. During the review-for-examination period, a large portion of the students do not consider the acquisition of useful knowledge as the main task, but only worry all day long about how to earn five points. At the examinations, some students, due to temporary tension or other reasons, do not do well and thus feel that all is finished, finding themselves all of a sudden a few inches shorter alongside others. The school and teachers often take the grades alone to measure the academic quality of the students. For example, the first requirement of a superior student is a five-point rating on all subjects, and a four-point rating is required to qualify for participation in the small scientific research team.

I am not saying here that it is not good to make five points in the examinations, but we should oppose the erroneous and dogmatic study method of the simple pursuit for the five points.

During the review-for-examination period, for the purpose of making five points, some students adopt the "short cut." They mechanically memorize the outlines and only "know that it is so without knowing why it is so." They neither cogitate nor study and are neither systematic nor comprehensive. In the examinations, they frequently "give Chang's hat to Li" and transpose irrelevant answers. They know all the themes but not the central problem. However, quite frequently such students earn five points. Just what is the use of the five points?

Some teachers do not have an adequate understanding of the purposefulness and significance of examinations. At ordinary times, they seldom inquire how the students are doing in their studies. They issue the review problems prior to the examinations and give the examination according to such problems. Afterward, when they see that the marks are not bad, they are satisfied and will not try to discover the problems in teaching or seek the way of improvement.

At present, there are problems in the review outlines, examination lots, and grading standards in higher schools.

Take the review outline. Rather than saying that these outlines are for the purpose of helping students review, it is more accurate to say that they are for the purpose of helping the students to face the examination. The subjects in the outlines are merely the big and small themes in the notes. Reviewing according to the outline, the students cannot acquire a systematic and comprehensive knowledge. Some of the subjects in the review outlines cover too wide a field, such as, "the Contents and Historical Significance of the Constitution of the People's Republic of China" or "the Great Achievements in the Process of the Current Construction of Socialism in Our Country and the Reasons for Such Achievements." They are really too expansive for one to cogitate according to the notes. Other subjects are too narrow, such as, "What Is the Essential Attribute?" or "What Is a Concept?" They make one feel that there is no need to cogitate. The purposefulness of such review subjects in the examination review process should be considered.

Take the examination lots. Not only are the quantities of some lots not the same, but they are not representative. In other words, the answers to these do not truly reflect the academic level of the student. The questions in the examination lot are not different from the review outline; therefore, as long as the student can transpose the teacher's ideas in the review outline to his answers, he is all right. Take the first year preschool education of our department as an example. For the examination in Revolutionary History, one student did not study very well at ordinary times and had not even covered a large part of the material on the eve of the examination, but he made four points at the examination. Another student studied very intensively ordinarily and her reviewing was not bad. Her classmates all considered her a better student in class. However, at the examination, she drew one lot with the problem of "the Basic Contents and Historical Significance of the New Democratic Theory" and another with the problem of "the Social Source of the Birth of the Principal Errors of the Three-Time 'Leftist' Line and Their Danger to the Chinese Revolution" (answering time limited to twenty minutes) and ended up with only four points. This type of examination will not only make it difficult to uncover the problems existing in teaching but will often affect the study-enthusiasm in some students and breed opportunist thinking in others.

Some teachers have not given adequate consideration to the grading standards. Some adopt the attitude of "when the water rises, the boat rides high," while the demand of others is too high or too low. This is especially so with some general required courses. There is an even greater lack of uniformity in the teachers' demands at the examinations. Some want the answers more comprehensive, others detailed. The students have to rack their brains to cater to the taste of the teachers.

I feel that it is extremely necessary to reform such a formalistic examination system appropriately.

There are also many problems in classroom discussions. I feel that classroom discussions must be founded on the teaching material to cover further studies of certain themes, so that the students are given the opportunity to express their own approaches and impressions and engage in enthusiastic discussions. However, in our classroom discussions, if it is not a big transposal of notes, it will be a small transposal of notes. A big transposal means that a student transposes all the themes in the notes all at once, and a small transposal is when he transposes the themes in the notes one by one. Hence, if it is not silence in classroom discussions, it will be repeating the themes.

The discussion subjects are too big and too stiff. Classroom discussions are usually held upon the conclusion of one unit, and the subjects will be the contents of the unit concluded. Hence, whether the subjects are announced or not, the students already know what they are. For examples, for Revolutionary History, it will always be "the Background of the Period," "Important Contents," or "Historical Significance"; and for Psychology, "General Concept," "Biological Foundation," "Principal Patterns," or "Method of Cultivation." Such wide problems can hardly be covered by transporting from the notes within ninety minutes, let alone discussed.

There are too many restrictions, and the conclusions are too premature. It is not permitted for the discussion to go beyond the matters in the notes or touch upon matters which the teacher does not consider important. The teacher always has a conclusion for each discussion. The moment a problem is brought up, the teacher will come up with a minor conclusion. When the discussion is in progress, the teacher will wish to make his major conclusion. On this point, the politics teacher is more apparent.

Much time is wasted, but very little gained. It generally takes six hours to prepare for one classroom, at times twelve, and longer with some individuals. But what is the result? During the discussion, some students often yawn with boredom. After the conclusion, they often say: "Ah! It is thus again . . ."

Hence, I suggest that, in classroom discussions, hereafter the subjects should be narrower and more flexible, in order to enable the students to devote more brainwork in writing the statement outline on the foundation of learning the material. During the discussion, there should be more enlightening, and premature conclusion avoided. Meanwhile, the conclusion should be obtained through the discussions and not something written beforehand by the teacher according to the subject of discussion.

The foregoing approaches are merely my individual feelings and the reflections of the students in general. Whether they are correct or not requires further consideration. The defects here are naturally the defects in the advance of academic education, but, still, we should study them properly and solve them.

SOURCE: *Education in Communist China* (Washington, D. C.; Joint Publication Research Service [Scholarly Book Translation Series], 1963). Originally published in *Jen Min Chiao Yu* [People's Education], No. 11 (1956).

An Observation of the Policy of the Overall Development of School Education from the Viewpoint of the Development of History
By Chiang Nan-hsiang
October 1956

This portion of an educational report was one of several given at the National Summer Vacation Study Class of the Youth League of Higher Institutions of Learning. It represents, in abbreviated form, Chinese Communist historical analysis of modern Chinese education and uses the well-known three-stage format of feudalism, capitalism, and socialism. The present stage, that is, the socialistic one, is said to be concerned with overall development, and Chiang refers to Mao Tse-tung's exhortation for youth to "attain the three good achievements," which are "good work habits, good study practices, and a good physique."

If we make a simple observation of history, we can see that under different social systems, different policies are adopted for school education.

In the feudal age before the 1911 revolution, there was also school education. This was given in the so-called "private schools," where there were taught the Four Books and the Five Classics, the eight-legged essay. The educational policy of the time was basically a policy of restraint. There was no physical training, music, or fine arts. There were instead many rules and restrictions: "Look not at what is improper; listen not to what is improper; speak not what is improper; and act not what is improper." In a word, the aim was to foster slaves to serve the feudal ruling class, there being no thought of the development of individuality.

The second age was the capitalist age, the age before the liberation. In this age, school education underwent reform to a certain extent. There were lessons in physical culture, music, and the fine arts. There were also various extracurricular activities. The educational policy of this period was not one of the restraint of individuality, but rather the tolerance and unrestricted letting-loose of individuality, with the result that the individuality of youth could not be normally developed, much less developed on an overall basis. In the *Communist Manifesto,* Marx and Engels stated that in the capitalist society, "between man and man there exist no ties other than stark relationships of interest, other than merciless mercenary transactions." School education of the bourgeois class also revealed this characteristic. Education in this age was characterized by two special features. The first was the lack of a clarified political goal (in fact there was such a goal, namely, service for the ruling class). Study in a school was undertaken with no other objective than that of "winning position and wealth," of "bringing credit to one's parents and making a name for oneself." Those with money could go to school; those without money could not. After graduation, it was still the case that those with money or influence found it easy to get a job, and those without money or influence found it hard to get employment. The standard followed in the choice of a job was also to get a post which paid more money and not to participate in national construction —there was no national construction to speak of at the time.

The second feature was the lack of planning, the state of anarchy which existed in school education. In the higher institutions, the teachers taught what they liked to teach, and the students studied what they wanted to study. Superficially there was great freedom, but in fact the teachers and the students often suffered from the threat of unemployment and lack of schooling facilities. They were trailed and watched over by the gendarmes and the special agents, persecuted in various ways by the reactionary rule. They could not know one day their fate the next day. They could not become masters who held in their own hands their own destiny. In the capitalist society, the policy of the healthy development of individuality and the overall development of education could not be realized, or it was most difficult of realization. In that age, though there were fostered certain outstanding experts and scientists, they were of the absolute minority.

The third age is the age of socialism, that is, the age in which we now live. Socialism has need of talent developed in an overall manner, and it is fully capable of fostering talent that is developed in an overall manner. For this reason, we have produced the educational policy of our age, that is, the policy of overall development with which we are familiar, the policy of the fostering of talent developed in an overall manner. We can come across various forms of this policy. Examples are: "development of wisdom, character, physical fitness, and beauty"; of "having both talent and good character, with a healthy physique." There is also Chairman Mao's call to youth to attain the "three good achievements," namely, "good in physique, good in study, and good in work." There is also the provision made in the constitution of the Youth League calling for "patriotism, loyalty to the people, possession of good knowledge, observance of discipline, courage, industry, vitality, and lack of fear of all difficulties." Though these are different forms, they basically include the same ideological contents.

.   .   .   .

However, certain comrades today have grossly misinterpreted the policy for overall development. They say that "the advocacy of overall development will obliterate individuality and special talent and that "secondary education may be developed on an overall basis, but the higher institutes must seek to develop special talent." The bringing up of such questions indicates that they have misinterpreted overall development as the egalitarian development of the study courses for different subjects. It is obvious that we cannot misinterpret the overall development of individuality as the acquisition of thoroughness of knowledge in every department. "Individuality" and "knowledge" have different scopes and must not be confused. As stated above, overall development and the development of individuality are not contradictory. Whether one is a scientist or a literary figure, one must have a correct political stand, the spirit of collectivism, and a healthy physique, and this does mean that one is expected at the same time to be a scientist, a literary figure, and a physical culturist. When one has for his foundation overall development, the development of his special talent is not obstructed, but rather helped.

SOURCE: *Extracts from China Mainland Magazines,* No. 63 (Hong Kong: United States Consulate General, December 31, 1956). Originally published in *Chung Kuo Ching Men* [China Youth], No. 20 (October 16, 1956).

The Relation between the Party and the Communist Youth League

From the Constitution of the Communist Party of China 1956

The Youth League, organized in 1949, has the primary function of recruiting suitable people into the foremost mass movement designed exclusively for Chinese youth. It has the ultimate goal of selecting suitably indoctrinated "activists" for full Party membership, and its importance can be noted by the constitutional provisions of the Chinese Communist Party.

CHAPTER VIII

Article 55. The Communist Youth League of China carries on its activities under the guidance of the Communist Party of China. The Central Committee of the Communist Youth League accepts the leadership of the Party's Central Committee. The Communist Youth League's local organizations are simultaneously under the leadership of the Party organizations at the corresponding levels and of higher League organizations.

Article 56. The Communist Youth League is the Party's assistant. In all spheres of Socialist construction, Communist Youth League organizations should play an active role in publicizing and carrying out Party policy and decisions. In the struggle to promote production, improve work, and expose and eliminate shortcomings and mistakes in work, the Communist Youth League organizations should render effective help to the Party and have the duty of making suggestions to the Party organizations concerned.

Article 57. Party organizations at all levels must take a deep interest in the Communist Youth League's ideological and organizational work, give guidance to the Communist Youth League in imbuing all its members with Communist spirit and educating them in Marxist-Leninist theory, see to it that close contact is maintained between the Communist Youth League and the broad masses of young people, and pay constant attention to selecting members for the leading core in the Communist Youth League.

Article 58. Members of the Communist Youth League shall withdraw from the League when they have been admitted to the Party and have become full Party members, provided they do not hold leading posts or engage in specific work in the League organizations.

Source: *Report on the Revision of the Constitution of the Communist Party of China* (Peking: Foreign Languages Press, 1956), chap. viii, pp. 47–48.

The Question of Intellectuals
By Mao Tse-tung
February 1957

Mao Tse-tung, on February 27, 1957, as Chairman of the Communist Party of China, delivered one of the most crucial speeches on the problem of "contradictions within a Socialist society." Mao stated that contradictions in capitalist societies can only be resolved by "Socialist revolution," whereas those in China could be resolved by the "Socialist system itself." The speech, "On the Correct Handling of Contradictions among the People," is divided into twelve subheadings, of which Section V, applicable to the intellectuals, is reproduced below.

Contradictions within the ranks of the people in our country also find expression among our intellectuals. Several million intellectuals who worked for the old society have come to serve the new society. The question that now arises is how they can best meet the needs of the new society and how we can help them do so. This is also a contradiction among the people.

Most of our intellectuals have made marked progress during the past seven years. They express themselves in favor of the Socialist system. Many of them are diligently studying Marxism, and some have become Communists. Their number, though small, is growing steadily. There are, of course, still some intellectuals who are skeptical of socialism or who do not approve of it, but they are in a minority.

China needs as many intellectuals as she can get to carry through the colossal task of Socialist construction. We should trust intellectuals who are really willing to serve the cause of socialism, radically improve our relations with them, and help them solve

268

whatever problems have to be solved, so that they can give full play to their talents. Many of our comrades are not good at getting along with intellectuals. They are stiff with them, lack respect for their work, and interfere in scientific and cultural matters in a way that is uncalled for. We must do away with all such shortcomings.

Our intellectuals have made some progress, but they should not be complacent. They must continue to remold themselves, gradually shed their bourgeois world outlook, and acquire a proletarian, Communist world outlook, so that they can fully meet the needs of the new society and closely unite with the workers and peasants. This change in world outlook is a fundamental one, and up to now it cannot be said that most of our intellectuals have accomplished it. We hope that they will continue making progress and, in the course of work and study, gradually acquire a Communist world outlook, get a better grasp of Marxism-Leninism, and identify themselves with the workers and peasants. We hope they will not stop halfway or, what is worse, slip back, for if they do, they will find themselves in a blind alley.

Since the social system of our country has changed and the economic basis of bourgeois ideology has in the main been destroyed, it is not only necessary but also possible for large numbers of our intellectuals to change their world outlook. But a thorough change in world outlook takes quite a long time, and we should go about it patiently and not be impetuous. Actually, there are bound to be some who are all along reluctant, ideologically, to accept Marxism-Leninism and Communism. We should not be too exacting in what we expect of them; as long as they comply with the requirements of the state and engage in legitimate pursuits, we should give them opportunities for suitable work.

There has been a falling-off recently in ideological and political work among students and intellectuals, and some unhealthy tendencies have appeared. Some people apparently think that there is no longer any need to concern themselves about politics, the future of their motherland, and the ideals of mankind.

It seems as if Marxism, which was once all the rage, is not so much in fashion now. This being the case, we must improve our ideological and political work. Both students and intellectuals should study Marxism-Leninism, current events, and political affairs, in order to progress both ideologically and politically. Not to have a correct political point of view is like having no soul. Ideological remolding in the past was necessary and has yielded positive results. But it was carried on in a somewhat rough and ready way, and the feelings of some people were hurt—this was not good. We must avoid such shortcoming in the future. All departments and organizations concerned should take up their responsibilities with regard to ideological and political work. This applies to the Communist party, the Youth League, government departments responsible for this work, and especially heads of educational institutions and teachers. Our educational policy must enable everyone who gets an education to develop morally, intellectually, and physically and to become a cultured, Socialist-minded worker. We must spread the idea of building our country through hard work and thrift. We must see to it that all our young people understand that ours is still a very poor country, that we cannot change this situation radically in a short time, and that only through the united efforts of our younger generation and all our people working with their own hands can our country be made strong and prosperous within a period of several decades. It is true that the establishment of our Socialist system has opened the road leading to the ideal state of the future, but we must work hard, very hard indeed, if we are to make that idea a reality. Some of our young people think that everything ought to be perfect once a Socialist society is established and that they should be able to enjoy a happy life, ready-made, without working for it. This is unrealistic.

SOURCE: Mao Tse-tung, "On the Correct Handling of Contradictions among the People," with notes and an introduction by G. F. Hudson (New York: *The New Leader,* 1957), pp. 39–41.

See also *People's China,* No. 13 (July 1, 1957); and *Current Background,* No. 458 (Hong Kong: United States Consulate General, 1957).

For additional readings, see Feng Ting, "Chinese Intellectuals and Socialism," *People's China*, No. 18 (September 16, 1957), pp. 9–13; and "Let a Hundred Flowers Blossom and a Hundred Schools Contend in Academic Research," *Peking Review*, No. 12 (March 24, 1961), pp. 6–9.

An Analysis of Training Targets and Teaching Plans of Advanced Engineering Schools in China
By Chang Wei
1957

This article presents one of the rarer and more interesting comparative educational studies by a Chinese Communist engineering professor, Chang Wei. The author compares some aspects of engineering training in China with four other countries; the Soviet Union, East Germany, West Germany, and the United States. The review is unusual in that the dialectical diatribe and ideological jargon usually employed by Communist writers is kept to a minimum. Instead, a thoughtful and carefully constructed, though biased, comparative study is made of selected engineering curriculum in two Communist and two non-Communist countries.

Chang utters a note of caution with respect to intercultural borrowing: "When we learn from other countries, we must consider their social background and the conditions of the school." He candidly notes, however, that in certain circumstances emulation may be of use to China: "I have no objection to learning from capitalist countries . . . but . . . not . . . [if] we have no basis for emulation."

Since the educational reforms of 1952, when China adopted the progressive system of the Soviet Union, our country now has a teaching plan with a definite target. This plan correlates theory with practice, politics with work, and trains the student to do independent work. We have added curriculum planning, graduation designs, and field work. This completely altered the preliberation system of aimless and unplanned education. Comrades in education and production have expressed many different

272

ideas on improving the quality of students. This shows the importance of this problem of training targets and plans for advanced engineering schools. I herewith present my views.

To study the teaching plans, we must first decide what kind of people we want to train. In the old days, engineering colleges in China copied the U.S. system and trained people with bachelor's degrees in engineering. There was no aim or question of what these people should or could do. Many of these are now doing good work; but this is due to their own initiative in learning and not to their training. When we went to work twenty years ago, there was very little construction work, and everyone was satisfied with our work. We were taught with examples from U.S. textbooks, so we simply changed the figures in making designs; very much like a mathematician. We did not do graduation designs as students do today. If we were assigned to work immediately on graduation, our weaknesses would be exposed. If our old comrades who are trained in the old school stop and think of this, they will clearly see the shortcomings of the old system. Up to the liberation, there had been little change in the system. Such aimless training to provide a broad knowledge is unsuited to China's Socialist construction.

For Socialist construction, we must train people who have a firm political ideology, are trained in a specialty, and are capable of doing independent work—let us say engineers (we will leave the definition of an engineer for later discussion). China's technology is backward, so we require a student to have training in a special field (this is another problem which we will not discuss now) and will not require field training before he can take up a responsible position and improve himself with experience. In 1956, China graduated a group of four-year students. In the summer of 1957, it graduated the first group of five-year students.

It is difficult to evaluate the group of four-year students, because acceptance standards in 1952 were low in order to provide a large enrollment, and the instructors were unfamiliar with the new system. Nevertheless, these graduates were able to assume their duties; a thing which would not have been possible in old China. Youths can now improve themselves because of large-scale construction throughout the nation, the concern of the government, and their desire to advance. If we of the older generation can improve ourselves, I believe today's youth is able to overcome all difficulties.

The history of engineering schools throughout the world shows that their objective is to train engineers. In Europe, engineering schools began during the Napoleonic era as an instrument of aggression. Artillery schools were established to train engineers in bridge and highway construction and ordnance production. Today, many countries have schools to train engineers for industry instead of military production. Other than in the U.S., the objective of advanced engineering schools is to train engineers. In the U.S., there are engineering degrees in a specialty. This is given after a year of graduate study, on the completion of undergraduate work.

However, there are basic differences between training in the Soviet Union, people's democracies, and China from that in West Germany and other capitalist countries. This is because our students have the correct world and personal outlook gained from a study of Marxism-Leninism. They serve the people and society. In capitalist countries, the engineers are trained to serve the capitalists.

If we adopt the system of the California Institute of Technology and teach only a few highly specialized courses, then the graduates must work a year or two in the field before they can be put to work. Our factories and mines do not need this. From the point of view of the division of labor, this is irrational and uneconomical.

There are many graduates of the old school who were never trained in the new subjects, so they try to audit courses in advanced schools to make up their deficiencies. For example, at Tsinghua University, there were over 1,000 regularly enrolled auditing students last semester in the advanced courses and the not-so-basic courses such as mathematics, science, chemistry, and dynamics. They take these courses so that they can return to their jobs and begin training classes for their fellow workers. This reveals a weakness of the old system; therefore, we should train engineers in the various specialties in our schools.

If we are to reach world technical levels in twelve years, some feel that we should train research engineers in our advanced schools by reducing specialized courses and expanding basic courses, in order to improve the capability of the student in research. This attitude is wrong. An engineer is assumed to be capable of doing research. If we have a research engineer, then the implication is that an ordinary engineer is not capable of research work. In the past, graduates in engineering were immediately assigned to practical work. We need not alter our teaching program to accommodate a small number of offices and thus create difficulties for the graduates and national construction. Since research requires a practical knowledge, then all engineers should have it. If the researcher knows only mathematics, science, and chemistry and has no working experience, he may commit errors by selecting topics which have no relation to production. Such researchers are of no benefit to the nation. The ideal source for researchers is from among working engineers and technicians and not from fresh college graduates. Due to past influences, there is a strong tendency among China's intellectuals not to apply theory to practice.

If we are to build research to serve production, we should not only select researchers with practical experience, but we should give them an opportunity to work when they are doing research. I would say that this even applies to the instructors of the school. Training research engineers is certainly not a target of advanced engineering schools.

Since conditions in the nation demand that engineers be trained in schools (or at least move in that direction), let us study how this training should be done, by analyzing and comparing our teaching plans with those of other countries.

Engineers must be trained to understand current practical problems in production, as well as daily advances in technology, so that they can make new contributions. We must teach students both theory and practice and how to correlate the two, so that they are capable of solving problems independently. Therefore, our reform teaching plan has three parts: class lectures (including practice problems), field work, and graduation designs. Unlike science graduates, engineering graduates must do field work in addition to attending lectures, conducting experiments, and doing practice problems. Field work is to firm up the students' theoretical knowledge and prepare him for further theoretical studies. It will help them with their class work, prepare them for their graduation design, and make them see the importance of field work. The graduation design is a project which the student carries out independently under the instructor. It reveals his grasp of theoretical and practical knowledge in solving a problem. This is an important link in training the student for independent work and a method to improve the quality of students in engineering schools.

From looking at this chart, we can see that Socialist countries like the Soviet Union, Democratic Germany, and China have trained a reserve of engineers and have properly allocated the three segments of class work, field work, and graduation design work. We assign our field work before the summer of the fourth and fifth years, according to the material studied during the year; thus correlating theory to practice. This is an advantage of our teaching plan.

Things were different in old China and in engineering schools in the U.S. Production data were kept secret for profit-making by capitalists and factory-owners, so that an obstacle to progress was created. They could not have our type of graduation designs nor our field work in their teaching programs. Students had no opportunity for practice work before their graduation. Thus we see that in such U.S. schools as the four-year California Institute of Technology and five-year Cornell University, they have teaching programs which include only class lectures.

West Germany requires apprenticeship training, but it only furnishes the factory owner with cheap labor. The student is left to do his own selection, so there is no correlation between theory and practice. In West Germany, the student's graduation design depends on the relations of his instructors with industry and their initiative.

COMPARATIVE CHART OF TEACHING PLANS FOR THE COURSE ON LATHE BUILDING IN THE MACHINE PRODUCTION DEPARTMENT

	Tsinghua University (1957 experimental)		Tsinghua University (1957)		Tsinghua University (pre-liberation)		Soviet Union (1955)		German Democratic Republic: Lei-ssu-teng Advanced Engineering School (1956)		West Germany: Darmstadt Advanced Engineering School (1956)		U.S.: California Institute of Technology (1956)	
Training target	Engineers		Engineers		B.S. in Engineering		Engineers		Engineers		Engineers		B.S. in Engineering	
Course divisions	hours	%	hours	%	hours	%	hours	%	hours	%	hours	%	hours	%
Basic	1177	32%	1130	32%	976	28%	1376	31%	1027	23%	855	24%	1167	36%
Basic technical	821	22%	893	21%	960	27%	1082	25%	1572	35%	1207	35%	921	82%
Major courses	930	25%	1069	26%	1072	30%	1096	25%	1349	30%	1326	38%	367	11%
Average weekly study time	26		31		28.5		33		30		29		26	
Average weekly lecture time	17		17.4		18.1		18.7		16.3		19 (first four semesters)		16	

All this reveals the strength of the Socialist system, where training is planned and objective as well as the weaknesses of the capitalist system.

Let us look at the course material. Most countries have five major groups. These include political science, basic courses (such as mathematics, science, chemistry, dynamics, and drafting), basic technical courses (such as principles of electrical engineering, thermodynamics, and hydraulics), electives, foreign languages, physical education, etc. This is basic training for engineering technicians in any country and is an objective reflection of the historical development of industry. We must therefore study the relative importance of these subjects, as too much stress on some subjects might not produce the desired type of engineers.

Let us first discuss basic, basic technical, and elective courses which are different in each country. China has increased both hours and percentages for basic courses, so that with too many courses, instruction is poor and the students have a poor grasp of the subject. This must be considered after the teaching plan has been worked out.

The 1955 Tsinghua University teaching plan called for an average of 2,223 hours for basic and basic technical subjects. This is higher than the 2,088 hours of the California Institute of Technology or the 2,062 hours of Darmstadt, West Germany. We assign 386 hours to theoretical dynamics and material stresses, while the California Institute of Technology assigns only 93 hours, so we learn much more. We assign 602 hours to physics, theoretical dynamics, and material stresses, while the California Institute of Technology assigns 462 hours and West Germany 407 hours. We give basic courses full weight and do not slight them, as some comrades claim.

Regarding elective courses, other than the California Institute of Technology, all the other schools assign 25 percent, or over 1,000 hours, to them. Elective courses at the California Institute of Technology amount to 11 percent, or 367 hours (which does not explain whether this is sufficient for an engineer), but its graduates have to spend two years of field work in a factory, so, with the work already done in elective courses, the total far exceeds 1,000 hours.

The California Institute of Technology is unusual among U. S. schools. Each year it enrolls only 180 students for its civil engineering, mechanics, electrical mechanics, and chemical engineering courses. In the freshman year, courses are the same for all departments, but students in civil engineering and mechanics must take an additional 199 hours of organic and inorganic chemistry.

When we learn from other countries, we must consider their social background and the conditions of the school. By accepting a portion, we might upset our good teaching plans.

Ch'ien Wei-chang says that our teaching plan is too complex and that this affects the quality of our students. Let us look at the electives in our teaching plan.

In 1956, Tsinghua University opened eight courses in its machine-building, lathe, and cutting-equipment majors; these included machine-designing, principles of cutting, cutting and stamping equipment, and factory organization. An engineer must learn these things while in school.

Engineering schools in West Germany teach engineers more about machine-building and lathes than we do, but they may use a different designation for the subjects. They also have a 34-hour required course on occupational diseases.

The machinery department of Cornell University has required courses on material-processing (cutting and planing), engineering methods (industrial techniques), industrial production (factory organization), and work-safety. In addition, there are courses peculiar to capitalist countries, such as 48 hours of public-speaking, 72 hours of price-control, and 16 hours of reports on job placement.

Comparing the two systems, we find our system of training with an objective has more advantages, and there is no waste in the teaching plan. To include such courses as Cornell's public-speaking and the California Institute of Technology's public utilities and engineering conferences in the plan is adding to the complexity.

Many comrades feel that we should not stress economics, organization, and technical safety. This is wrong. An engineer must not only be capable of solving technical production problems but must also be able to make a factory operate smoothly, as this is essential in modern industry. Each part must be well done, but the whole must also be properly co-ordinated. An engineer who knows only one segment is unable to direct the activities of the whole operation.

We should note that the Soviet curriculum includes only 123 hours for economic organization and work-safety, while the California Institute of Technology in the U. S. and Darmstadt in West Germany assign 240 and 160 hours, respectively (including 60 and 30 hours respectively, for law). Therefore, we need not reduce our hours for these subjects.

Naturally these subjects reflect the capitalist economy and organization of those countries, which are different from the Socialist system of the Soviet Union and China. However, to train an engineer who can serve our Socialist system, advanced schools should teach them economics, business organization and planning, safety techniques, etc. These courses are not superfluous; they are realistic demands on engineering education.

In emulating the progressive educational system of the Soviet Union, we have established the principle of training students for independent work in our advanced schools. We have strengthened the ability of students to do independent work by training them step by step. In the freshman and sophomore years, the students are given limited and simple problems to work out in natural science. Then the students advance into problems which relate basic technology to engineering. For example, in studying the stresses of materials, the student begins by only learning the strength of materials, and he studies construction materials only from the point of view of their qualities and their production. When the student is engaged in specialized studies, then he is taught to look at a problem from all angles. Thus, his ability for independent work is gradually built up until he can undertake the duties of an engineer when he graduates.

Therefore, for the freshman and sophomore years, we should

assign basic courses; the latter half of the sophomore and junior years, basic technical courses; and thereafter, electives. Lower-classmen should have more supervision and classes, and upper-classmen less. In this respect, our countries are more rational than the capitalist countries.

In addition to the above three courses, Socialist countries also have courses on Marxism-Leninism. This political course gives the students a correct revolutionary and world outlook and gives them a scientific mind. (Other courses may do the same.) The political quality of new graduates is better than that of the old ones and far above that of preliberation students. This is a major gain from our reform in education.

Finally, let us take up the question of excessive teaching loads. We can compare our country with others in two respects: the average weekly time allotted to study and to class time. China's teaching plan is lighter than that of other countries. California Institute of Technology assigns fifty hours of study inside and outside class each week. The students attend twenty-six hours of classes, making a ratio of 1 to 0.9 [of study inside class as compared to that outside class]. China's new plan calls for fifty-four hours a week for study, with twenty-six hours in class, which is a ratio of 1 to 1.1. The load in our new plan is light. Like schools in other countries, we have less than seventeen or eighteen hours of class work. In West Germany, class time for the first four semesters is nineteen hours, reaching up to twenty-three hours for the first semester. This shows that we are rational, while the capitalist countries tend to move blindly.

Ch'ien Wei-chang's statement that advanced schools in West Germany have only seventeen hours of classes and that those in the U. S. have a total of twenty hours for class and laboratory work is incorrect. I have no objection to learning from capitalist countries, but if the situation is not so there, we have no basis for emulation.

Thus we can see that by emulating the Soviet Union and reforming our teaching plan for advanced schools, we know the type of engineer we are training for. Our teaching plan calls for a correlation between work and politics as well as between theory and practice and for training students to do independent work. We must implement these steps in well-planned moves. Teaching experiences of the past four years and the quality of recent graduates show that our direction is suited to the needs of national construction. We do not deny that we still have many shortcomings, but we know that we are moving in the right direction. Therefore, there is no question of any change in direction, but we need only to progress along in the same direction and overcome our shortcomings.

SOURCE: *Education in Communist China* (Washington, D. C.: Joint Publications Research Service [Scholarly Book Translation Series], 1963). Originally published in *Hsin Hua Pan Yueh Kan* [New China Semimonthly], No. 6 (1957).

Education Must Be Combined with Productive Labor
By Lu Ting-yi
1958

*Present-day Chinese Communist educational philosophy is suc-
cinctly summarized in Lu's statement concerning the combination
of productive labor and education. The necessity for education
to be directly related to manual labor, or productive enterprise,
has been one of the more stable, long-term goals of the Communist
Party. Many of the "preliberation" Party debates on education
and the intellectuals concerned the practicality of education and
the personal experience of physical labor. The need for both
"red and expert" students—those who are technically proficient
and politically reliable—has been supplemented by this restate-
ment of basic Communist educational philosophy, which requires the complete interlocking of education with productive
skills. The Yenan period of Communist history saw the earliest
development of this educational philosophy. The restated doctrine outlined in this document below is not necessarily the work
of professional pedagogues, who in any case are scorned at times
by the regime, but it is the Chinese Communist interpretation
of Marxist educational tenets brought up to date and integrated
with the "great leap forward."*

*This document represents the codification, reanalysis, and re-
definition of Chinese Communist educational aims in a manner
which suggests that it will remain a fundamental exposition of
the subject for some time.*

Education in our country has developed very rapidly since
early this year. Figures compiled by the State Statistical Bureau
up to the end of June, as yet incomplete, report 1,240 counties

283

with universal primary school education, 68,000 middle schools [1] run by the people themselves, more than four hundred institutions of higher learning newly established by the local authorities, approximately ninety million or more people attending literacy courses, and 444 counties in which illiteracy has been wiped out in the main. The victory in the rectification campaign and the struggle against the bourgeois rightists has given rise to the great leap forward in the industry and agriculture of our country. The leap forward, in turn, has precipitated an upsurge in the technical and cultural revolutions. The great advance in education is one of the signs of the high tide of the cultural revolution.

.   .   .   .

Now this combination of schooling and productive labor has given rise to the campaign to reform school curricula and the efforts to change school systems, as well as to change the composition of the teaching staffs, etc. Our educational work is like a hundred flowers in bloom, like ten thousand horses galloping ahead. Education is now breaking the bounds of exclusive control by the experts and of doctrinairism to become the work of the whole Communist Party and the people as a whole, to become Socialist education suited to the situation in our country. This transformation has been taking place under the leadership of the Communist Party. Such absurdities as: "more, faster, better, and more economical results cannot obtain in education"; "laymen cannot lead experts"; "Communist Party committees do not understand education"; "the masses do not understand education"; etc., are being smashed to smithereens.

Our state is a proletarian dictatorship, a Socialist state. Our education is not bourgeois but Socialist education. Socialist education is inconceivable without Communist Party leadership. Socialist education is one of the powerful weapons for transforming the old and building the new society. The purpose of the Socialist revolution and Socialist construction is to do away with all exploiting classes and all systems of exploitation, including their remnants, and to bring into being a Communist society,

1. In China, the primary schools cover the first six years of schooling. Middle schools account for the years after primary school up to college.

in which the principle "from each according to his ability and to each according to his needs" is carried out, and the difference between town and country and between mental and manual labor eliminated. This is precisely the purpose of Socialist education. Such education can be led only by the political party of the working class, the Communist Party; the bourgeoisie is not qualified to lead education of this type. Only under the leadership of the Communist Party can educational work assume the new countenance that we see it has today.

During the past few years, prolonged debates on educational policy have taken place. Many theoretical and practical problems were settled at the conferences on educational work convened by the Central Committee of the Chinese Communist Party in April and June of this year [1958].

The educational policy of the Chinese Communist Party has always been that education should serve the politics of the working class and be combined with productive labor; and to apply this policy, education must be led by the Communist Party. This is the direct opposite of the educational policy of the bourgeoisie. Bourgeois education is led by bourgeois politicians. It serves the politics of the bourgeoisie, that is, it serves the dictatorship of the bourgeoisie; it is incompatible with proletarian dictatorship. Under the Socialist system, the bourgeoisie dare not advocate directly and openly that education should be led by bourgeois politicians and be a weapon against the proletarian dictatorship; it can only put forward the hypocritical, deceptive propositions that "education should be led by experts" and "education for education's sake," with the aim of preventing education from serving the proletarian dictatorship. In our Socialist country, therefore, the educational policy advocated by the bourgeoisie is embodied in the propositions: "education for education's sake"; "mental and manual work are separate"; and "education should be led by experts."

Education is, first and foremost, the transmission and acquisition of knowledge. But what is knowledge? What is the purpose of transmitting and acquiring knowledge? We Communists interpret these questions differently from the bourgeoisie. Most bourgeois pedagogues hold that only book knowledge is knowledge and that practical experience cannot be regarded as knowledge. They therefore take the view that education means reading books: the more a man reads, the more knowledge he has, and those possessing book knowledge are of a higher order. As for productive labor, particularly manual labor and manual workers, they think all this is humiliating and leading one nowhere. There are other bourgeois pedagogues who maintain that education is life and vice versa. They do not understand life as the practice of class struggle and struggle for production, nor do they stress the importance of theory. So, in the end, they write off education in effect. These two sets of bourgeois views, though they appear to be diametrically opposed to each other, stem from the same root. They imply that there is no class differentiation among human beings and that pedagogy is a branch of learning that stands above classes.

We Communists view the question differently. We believe that pedagogy is a branch of the social sciences. All the social sciences must be guided by politics, and education is no exception. People require education to wage the class struggle and the struggle for production. We believe there are only two kinds of knowledge in the world. One is knowledge of the class struggle. The class struggle is the struggle between groups of men of different economic status, and this has already existed for several thousand years. In the present period of transition in our country, there is still class struggle. In the future, when classes no longer exist, even though there will be no class struggle, there will still be contradictions among the people: Therefore, for ten thousand years to come, there will still be poisonous weeds, that is, there will be a struggle between truth and falsehood, between the advanced and the backward, between those who promote and those who impede the development of the productive forces.

The other kind of knowledge is the knowledge of the struggle for production, that is, the knowledge men gain in their struggle against nature. Philosophy is the summing-up and generalization of the two kinds of knowledge. The importance of philosophy lies in the fact that the philosophy of dialectical materialism provides men with a correct way of thinking. The essential distinction between men lies not in differences of disposition or personality, but, first of all, in their different class standpoints and, in addition, their ways of thinking. Class standpoints and ways of thinking are interrelated and, at the same time, are distinct from each other. Errors often emanate from two sources— class origin and the way of thinking. To avoid making great errors or to commit fewer errors, people must study politics and philosophy.

We Communists also maintain that there are two kinds of one-sided, fragmentary knowledge. One is book knowledge completely divorced from practical activity. Comrade Mao Tse-tung says:

What sort of knowledge is the bookish information of the students? Granted that their information is entirely true knowledge, it is still not knowledge acquired through their own personal experience but only a matter of theories written down by their forefathers to sum up the experiences of the struggle for production and of the struggle between classes. It is entirely necessary that they should inherit this kind of knowledge, but it must be understood that in a certain sense such knowledge is to them still something one-sided, something which has been verified by others but not yet by themselves. The most important thing is that they should be well versed in applying such knowledge in life and practice. Therefore, I should advise those who have only bookish knowledge but little or no practical experience that they should be aware of their own shortcomings and be modest.

. . . .

The purpose of education is to enable students to acquire comparatively complete knowledge and not one-sided incomplete knowledge. It follows that teachers are required to have comparatively complete knowledge.

Our educational workers always say that "education is the people's business." This is good, because in our country this is true. But as the experience of the past nine years shows, there are two different interpretations of this phrase. The bourgeois pedagogues maintain that the masses of the people are entitled to receive education; but as to running education, that is only for the experts, not for the masses of the people. Their slogans are:

"the professors must run the schools"; "laymen cannot lead experts"; "the Party does not understand education"; "the masses do not understand education"; "students must not criticize teachers"; etc.

These myths advanced by the bourgeois pedagogues were even accepted as true by some of our comrades, who forgot that our Party on hundreds and thousands of occasions had been called "laymen," yet, as it ultimately turned out, proved in fact rather more expert than any experts.

Some of our comrades advocated this sort of proposition: (1) only the state may run schools and (2) only one kind of school—general, full-time schools—may be set up. Past experience shows that the bourgeois pedagogues are keenly interested in this proposition, because it ties the hands of the masses and does not permit them to set up schools. The bourgeois pedagogues know that if education were run along these lines, our country would find it very difficult to institute universal primary and secondary education and have no hope at all of instituting universal higher education, because the state has no way of carrying the huge burden of expenditures involved without heavy damage to production.

We Communists do not agree with the bourgeois pedagogues. We think that it is for the Socialist revolution and Socialist construction that the masses of the people need education. As the masses of the people are able to conduct revolution and construction, they are, of course, capable not only of receiving education but also of running education. In running education, it is necessary to rely on a corps of specialists, for without a powerful specialized corps, things will not go well, and at present, this corps of specialists still needs to be greatly strengthened by transferring cadres and establishing teachers' training schools. But the corps of specialists in education must integrate with the masses, and reliance on the masses in running education is the more important. Only by linking the specialized educational workers with the masses, adhering to the mass line of "from the masses and back to the masses," and carrying out the policy of setting up schools by the whole people under the leadership of the Party, is it possible—in fact certain—for our country's educational work to achieve greater, faster, better, and more economical results. And only by fully applying the policy of setting up schools by the whole people under the leadership of the Party is it possible to do all-round planning, duly considering and coördinating all aspects, so that not only does the educational work grow but grows in a way that helps and does not impede the development of production.

Our educational workers always say, too, that educational work must receive leadership from the Party. This is undoubtedly correct. Socialist education must be led by the Communist Party, and educational work in the Socialist People's Republic of China must be led by the Communist Party of China. But there are also different interpretations of what leadership is and what kind of leadership is needed. What the bourgeois pedagogues call "Party leadership" is "Party leadership in political matters and our leadership in vocational matters." On questions unrelated to education they may listen to the Party; but if the Party has something to say about educational principles, policies, systems, methods, and so on, they regard it as unacceptable. In words they want Party leadership, but in practice they do not want it; on minor questions they may listen to the Party, but on major questions they want to have their own way in defiance of the Party. Some of our comrades in the Party who work in the educational field put themselves up as experts in relation to Party committees and fail to respect Party leadership. This is an expression of bourgeois influence in our Party.

In the past few years, the theory that the principal laws governing educational work are to be drawn from the study of the history of education was spread widely in educational circles in our country. From this, it would follow that to run Socialist education it is just necessary to study the history of education, while recognizing Party leadership in the abstract; as for specific Party leadership, this is not needed.

Study of the history of education, provided it proceeds from the viewpoint of Marxist historical materialism, is indeed useful and helps towards an understanding of the laws which governed education for thousands of years in the era of class society. However, it must be understood that the laws governing education in the history of class society are not the same as the laws governing Socialist education, much less the laws governing Socialist education in China. For the past thousands of years, education was in the hands of the slaveowners, the landlord class, and the bourgeoisie. The principal laws to be derived from this history are those governing exploiting-class education. They are certainly a far cry from the laws of Socialist education. Mistakes would be inevitable if these laws were copied as the laws of Socialist education.

What the facts show is that the theory that the principal laws governing educational work are to be drawn from the study of the history of education is in reality a pretense by which the study of the history of education is used to keep bourgeoise educational ideas, policies, systems, methods, and so on, intact under the Socialist system and to palm these off as Socialist.

.   .   .   .

But taking the major aspects, education over the past thousands of years was certainly an instrument in the hands of the exploiting classes, while Socialist education is an instrument in the hands of the working class. This change, from an instrument of the exploiting classes to an instrument of the working class, is a qualitative leap in education and a great revolution in education itself. To study the history of education without seeing this qualitative leap is to depart from dialectics; it is metaphysical. We advocate the study of the history of education but we oppose the view that the principal laws of Socialist education can be found through such a study, because it would lead us to right deviationist mistakes.

Moreover, even the laws of Socialist education, though they are of the same character in different countries, differ in their specific features. Doctrinaire mistakes would be made if the specific features of one's own country are not studied. What are the specific features of our country? First, ours is a Socialist country; second, it has a huge population and covers a vast area; third, its economy and culture are backward; fourth, it is led by the Communist Party and its industry and agriculture are leaping forward rapidly; and fifth and most important, our country has carried out a serious rectification campaign and antirightist struggle, the people are encouraged to air their views, contend, debate to the fullest extent, and publicize their views in *tatsepao*.[2] We must define our educational principles, policies, systems, methods, and so on, in accordance with these characteristics of our own, combining the universal truths of Marxism with the specific conditions of our country.

It is clear, therefore, that the theory that the principal laws governing educational work are to be drawn from the study of the history of education is a most pernicious theory, which divorces education from reality and leads it to right deviationist and doctrinaire mistakes. Not to proceed from the objective realities of one's own country is subjective, anti-Marxist thinking. If we err in our way of thinking, we cannot find out the major laws governing the development of things. If we do not proceed from reality and if we go against the universal truths of Marxism, we will surely make mistakes, either right deviationist or doctrinaire mistakes or both. This is the important lesson we should draw from the educational work of our country.

. . . .

In the final analysis, the debate on education that has been going on in recent years boils down to the question of "what is all-round development?" Marxists believe in producing fully developed human beings and in achieving this through education. It is well that our educationists often talk about all-round development. Yet there are differences of principle in the interpretation of "all-round development." Judging by our country's experience in education in the past nine years, although the bourgeois pedagogues do not directly and openly oppose all-round development and even appear to support the principle actively, yet they interpret it one-sidedly as meaning education through gaining of extensive book knowledge. They do not hold with students studying politics and participating in productive labor. In fact, they vulgarize the idea of all-round development and equate

2. Opinions and criticisms written out in bold Chinese characters on large sheets of paper and posted for everybody to see.

it with the bourgeois educational line which rears "know-alls."

We Communists interpret all-round development in an entirely different way. The essence of all-round development is that the students should acquire comparatively broader knowledge, become versatile people, capable of "going over in sequence from one branch of production to another, depending on the requirements of society or their own inclinations." [F. Engels: *Principles of Communism*] We maintain that workers should be versatile in industrial production and peasants should be versatile in agricultural production; moreover, that workers should at the same time be peasants and peasants should be workers. We maintain that civilians should take up military service and retired military men go back to production. We maintain that cadres should participate in physical labor and productive workers in administration. All these propositions are already being put into practice gradually. Measures such as these, which involve both the division of labor and change of work, conform to the needs of society. They are more reasonable than the division of labor under the capitalist system. They not only increase production but enable the state to carry out reasonable readjustment of the productive forces when this becomes socially necessary, without causing social upheaval.

.   .   .   .

Under our country's present conditions, we can train people to do many kinds of work but cannot yet train people to be capable of undertaking any profession. The essence of all-round development is also that the knowledge imparted to the students must be not one-sided and fragmentary but comparatively complete knowledge. This requires that education should serve politics and be combined with productive labor. Speaking of his ideal of education in the future, Karl Marx referred to "an education that will, in the case of every child over a given age, combine productive labor with instruction and gymnastics, not only as one of the methods of adding to the efficiency of production but as the only method of producing fully developed human beings." That is, he urged that students acquire comparatively complete knowledge and be able to engage not only in mental labor but manual labor as well. Book knowledge alone, however broad, is still partial and incomplete. People with extensive book knowledge alone and without experience of practical work are only what the bourgeoisie call "know-alls." They are not what we regard as people of all-round development. Physical development is necessary in childhood, and this development must be sound. In addition, a Communist spirit and style and collective heroism should be inculcated in childhood. This is the moral education of our day. Both are linked with the development of intellectual education. Both are related to manual work, and therefore the principle of combining education with labor is unshakable.

In brief, the all-round development we stand for is this: students should be enabled to acquire comparatively complete, broader knowledge, grow up physically fit, and acquire Communist morals. In his *On the Correct Handling of Contradictions among the People,* Comrade Mao Tse-tung said: "Our educational policy must enable everyone who gets an education to develop morally, intellectually, and physically and become a cultured, Socialist-minded worker." This is our educational principle of all-round development. "A cultured, Socialist-minded worker" is a man who is both politically conscious and educated. He is able to undertake both mental and manual work. He is what we regard as developed in an all-round way, both politically and professionally qualified. He is a worker-intellectual and an intellectual-worker.

We insist on the educational principle of all-round development. We consider that the only method to train human beings in all-round development is to educate them to serve working-class politics and combine education with productive labor. We say the only method, because there is no other way to achieve this aim. Bourgeois pedagogues do not agree. They consider the only method to train people to have what they call "all-round development" is to read books and learn by rote. They are absolutely against students learning politics and, in particular, students becoming laborers. According to our educational principle of all-round development, we can and must rely on the masses to run education. According to the bourgeois educational principle of so-called "all-round development," they can rely only on experts to run education; they cannot rely on the masses. According to our educational principle of all-round development, education must be under the leadership of the Communist Party. According to the bourgeois educational principle of so-called "all-round development," education can only be led by the experts; it does not need the leadership of the Communist Party, as the Communist Party is "a layman." From this we see that different interpretations of all-round development lead to different and even opposite conclusions. That is why we say that the debate on education in recent years ultimately boils down to the question of "what is all-round development?" This is essentially a struggle between proletarian and bourgeois educational ideas.

If we followed our bourgeois pedagogues' attitude towards knowledge, towards education as the business of the people, towards leadership by the Communist Party and towards all-round development, our educational work would be dragged back to the old bourgeois road. Precisely because of this, it is necessary to give a clear explanation of our Communist interpretation of these questions.

.   .   .   .

The chief mistake or defect in our educational work has been the divorce of education from productive labor. The policy of combining education with productive labor was put forward by our Party early in 1934. Comrade Mao Tse-tung then said:

What is the general policy for the Soviet[3] culture and education? It is to educate the broad masses of the toiling people in the spirit of Communism, to make culture and education serve the revolutionary war and the class struggle, to combine education with labor, and to enable the broad masses of the Chinese people to enjoy civilization and happiness.

In 1954, when the period of economic rehabilitation was over and the first Five-Year Plan already in operation, the Central Committee of the Party raised the question of adding productive labor to the curricula of the schools. But the proposal encountered obstruction and was not carried through at that time. The Central

3. This refers to the Soviet areas in China that existed at that time under the leadership of the Chinese Communist Party.

Committee of the Party repeatedly stressed its policy that education must be combined with productive labor—at the national conference on propaganda work in March 1957, in the editorial of *Jen Min Jih Pao* [People's Daily] on April 8 of the same year, and at the Nanning meeting in January 1958. It is only now that this policy of the Party has been carried out on a nationwide scale. Education must serve politics, must be combined with productive labor, and must be led by the Party. These three things are interrelated. Education divorced from productive labor is bound to lead, to a degree, to the neglect of politics and of Party leadership in educational work, thus divorcing education from the realities of our country and eventually causing right deviationist and doctrinaire mistakes.

The combination of education with productive labor is required by our country's Socialist revolution and Socialist construction, by the great goal of building a Communist society, and by the need to develop our education with greater, faster, better, and more economical results.

The aim of our Socialist revolution is to wipe out all exploiting classes, all systems of exploitation, including their remnants. Basic victory has now been won in the Socialist revolution on the economic front. On the political and ideological fronts, too, the Socialist revolution has achieved decisive victory. As the Second Session of the Eighth National Congress of the Communist Party of China has pointed out in its resolution, our task is "actively to carry out the technical and cultural revolutions, while continuing with the Socialist revolution on the economic, political, and ideological fronts."

The cultural revolution is to enable all six hundred million Chinese people, except for those who are incapable, to do productive work and to study. This means to make the masses of our workers and peasants intellectuals as well and our intellectuals laborers. Only when the masses of the workers and peasants and the intellectuals alike develop along the line of making up what they lack is it possible to change thoroughly the irrational legacy of the old society and eradicate the backwardness of each, i.e., eliminate the cultural deficiency of the masses of workers and peasants and eliminate the bourgeois thinking of the intellectuals. This is, therefore, a very far-reaching revolution, which demands that education must serve working-class politics, that it be combined with productive labor.

. . . .

The future Communist society will be one of "from each according to his ability and to each according to his needs"—a society in which the differences between town and country and between mental and manual labor are eliminated. Our big leap forward in industry and agriculture has made the attainment of communism no longer a far-distant prospect. One hundred and ten years ago, Marx and Engels, in the *Communist Manifesto*, formulated ten measures to establish a Communist society, which "will be pretty generally applicable . . . in the most advanced countries." Of these, the first eight have already been carried out in China, through the adoption of methods suitable to the actual conditions of our country; and the last two, namely, "the combination of agriculture with manufacturing industries; the gradual abolition of the distinction between town and country" and "the combination of education with industrial production," are beginning to be carried out.

It is clear to everyone that because of the application, in the course of industrial development, of the policy "to develop industry and agriculture simultaneously while giving priority to heavy industry; and, with centralized leadership, overall planning, proper division of labor and coordination to develop national and local industries and large, small, and medium-sized enterprises simultaneously," industry has appeared in the rural areas and with it, the phenomenon of workers who are simultaneously peasants and peasants who are simultaneously workers. This phenomenon has the embryo of Communist society.

Because the principle of combining education with productive labor is beginning to go into operation, with schools setting up their own factories and farms, and factories and agricultural cooperatives establishing their own schools on a large scale, the phenomenon of students who are at the same time workers and peasants, and of workers and peasants who are students at the same time is beginning to appear. This, too, has the embryo of Communist society. It can be imagined that when China enters into communism, our basic social organizations will be many Communist communes. With few exceptions, each basic unit will have workers, peasants, traders, students, and militia. In the field of education, each basic unit will have its own primary and secondary schools and institutions of higher learning; at the same time, everybody will have the time to acquire education as both laborer and intellectual. In *The Housing Question* Engels anticipated this situation when he said:

And it is precisely this industrial revolution which has raised the productive power of human labor to such a high level that—for the first time in the history of humanity—the possibility exists, given a rational division of labor among all, of producing not only enough for the plentiful consumption of all members of society and for an abundant reserve fund but also of leaving each individual sufficient leisure so that what is really worth preserving in historically inherited culture—science, art, forms of intercourse—may not only be preserved but converted from a monopoly of the ruling class into the common property of the whole of society and may be further developed.

To attain this prospect, our educational work must not go in the direction of divorcing mental and manual labor but in the direction of combining mental with manual labor and education with productive labor.

.   .   .   .

The principles of running schools by applying the mass line under Communist Party leadership are:

First, to combine unity with diversity. The purpose of the training is unified, that is, to train Socialist-minded, educated workers. But the schools can be run by the central or local authorities, factories and mines, enterprises and agricultural co-operatives, and the forms the schools can take are varied. They may be full-time, or part-work–part-study, or spare-time schools; they may collect fees or be free of charge. As production grows further and working hours can be shortened, the present spare-time schools will be similar to part-time–part-study schools. When production develops considerably and public accumulation rises greatly, the schools that now charge fees will similarly become free.

Second, to combine the spreading of education widely with the raising of educational levels. The level of education must be raised on the basis of popularization, and popularization must be so guided as to raise the level of education. Some of the full-time, the part-time–part-study, and the spare-time schools undertake the task of raising educational levels at the same time that education is being spread extensively through part-work–part-study and spare-time courses. Since the schools that popularize education are part-work–part-study or spare-time schools, they can meet the whole or the greater part of their expenditures themselves and can find teachers locally in accordance with the principle that "every capable person can teach." They can develop gradually by perfecting their curricula, equipment, and teaching staff with aid from the government. In schools where courses in labor are lacking, the stress should be on introducing them, and in schools where the deficiency is in the basic courses, the stress should be on introducing these, so that both kinds of schools go forward to fill in what they lack and apply the principle of combining theory with practice more effectively.

Third, to combine overall planning with decentralization, to bring into play the initiative of both the various central government departments and the local authorities and the masses, so as to develop education with greater, faster, better, and more economical results. In planning educational work, the central and the local authorities, guided by the Party committees, can develop education as fast as possible and enable this development to benefit, not hamper, the growth of production.

Fourth, to apply the mass line in the political, administrative, pedagogic, and research work in the schools. In all such work, it is necessary, guided by the Party committees, to adopt the method of open and free airing of views, *tatsepao,* and the method of the "three combinations" (for instance, in working out teaching plans and programs, the method can be adopted of combining the efforts of the teachers and the students under the leadership of the Party committee and in teaching, the method of inviting people with practical experience to give lectures, in coordination with the teachers in special fields, under the leadership of the

Party committee, and so on) and to establish democratic relations of equality—changing the old irrational relations—between the leadership and the rank and file and between the teachers and the students. Experience shows that remarkable achievements have been made where these methods have been adopted.

. . . .

We must realize that to carry the combination of education with productive labor into effect means a fight with the old traditions that have persisted for thousands of years. Without the Communist style of toppling down the old idols, burying doctrinairism, and daring to think, speak, and do, without the creative spirit of combining the universal truths of Marxism with the concrete realities of our country, we cannot succeed. Today, in our educational work, vigorous efforts are being made to pull down the outdated and set up the new. Bourgeois and doctrinaire ideas are being broken down and new Marxist educational theories, systems, methods, curricula, and school systems suited to our country are being created. This educational revolution has solid economic foundations. The Marxist doctrine of historical materialism teaches that the superstructure must conform to the economic base. The political system is superstructure, the concentrated expression of economic life. Education comes into the category of ideology and is also superstructure; it serves politics. Class society, which has existed for thousands of years, has had ownership by slaveowners, landlords, or capitalists as its economic base. The political systems that conform to these types of ownership are the dictatorships of the slaveowners, the landlords, and the bourgeoisie. The types of education that serve these dictatorships are those of the slaveowners, the landlords, and the bourgeoisie. These types of education differ from each other, but all have this in common—that education is divorced from productive labor, mental from manual labor, and manual labor and manual laborers are despised. The divorce of mental from manual labor is needed by all the exploiting classes, including the bourgeoisie.

Our society has Socialist ownership as its economic base. The political system suited to Socialist ownership is proletarian dictatorship. Our education serves the proletarian dictatorship.

Therefore, contrary to the old traditions that persisted for thousands of years, it must apply the principle of combining education with productive labor, so as to eliminate the difference between mental and manual labor. This also means wiping out the survivals of all the systems of exploitation that have existed in history, so that humanity may enter into Communist society.

The principle of combining education with productive labor is needed by the working class and all other working people. This principle, which conforms to the people's desires, will certainly prevail. On the other hand, the principle of divorcing mental from manual labor, since it does not conform to the Socialist economic base and the people's requirements, will sooner or later be discarded by the people, even though it has a tradition of thousands of years. With politics in command, with leadership by the Communist Party, and the rallying of the entire Party and all educational workers who can be rallied to fight against bourgeois educational policy and for the application of the Party's educational policy, we can so carry through our cultural revolution that all of our six-hundred million people are able to do productive work, and all are able to study, changing them into new men who are both laborers and intellectuals.

SOURCE: Lu Ting-yi, *Education Must Be Combined with Productive Labour* (Peking: Foreign Languages Press, 1958).

See also *Current Background*, No. 516 (Hong Kong: United States Consulate General, 1958).

Educational Work Achievements in 1958 and Arrangements for 1959
By Yang Hsiu-feng
April 1959

Yang, Minister of Education, delivered this speech to the First Session of the Second National People's Congress in April 1959. The new Party line, "the great leap forward," was under way, and developments in education were expected to be exemplary in assisting Communist China to make spectacular economic and industrial advances. The year 1958 had also seen the fuller implementation of a long-cherished Communist tenet—"coördination of education with productive labor." Through practical work integrated with the study programs, students were expected to become better technologists and more "politically advanced" than previously. All institutions of higher learning were expected to establish ancillary factories, and conversely, factories and industrial complexes were encouraged to create "universities."

Emphasis was also placed on the continual development of the "correct" relationship between students and faculty, so that students would make constructive criticisms, though in a humble and disciplined manner.

The tremendous strides made in educational work during the past few years, particularly in 1958, and the future tasks on the cultural and educational fronts have been clearly described by Premier Chou En-lai. I would like to describe some of my personal experiences in carrying out educational work policies during the past year and to present my opinions on education work arrangements for 1959. Fellow deputies, please correct my mistakes.

In 1958, educational undertakings of our country made two outstanding strides. One was successful implementation of the policy of coördinating education with productive labor, which brought about a big and comprehensive revolution in our educational undertakings. The other was successful implementation of the mass line for organizing schools by the entire Party and all the people and adoption of the policy of "walking on both legs," which enabled our country's educational undertakings to make unprecedented strides.

Coördinating education with productive labor is the only method by which all-round development in training can be made. It is an absolute course for training laborers, both in education and Socialist consciousness. In 1958, as a result of their enthusiastic participation in diligent labor-economy study, their high enthusiasm in organizing factories and farms, and their engagement in productive labor and in the mass movements for iron and steel production, autumn harvest, farming, and sowing, faculty members and students of education institutes at various levels not only supported the big forward leaps in our country's industrial and agricultural production but also created material wealth for the state. However, most important of all, they changed the ideology of faculty members and students. Their ignorance of productive labor and their viewpoint concerning the class which exploited the laboring people in the past have been greatly changed, their viewpoints on labor and the broad masses have been strengthened, and their Socialist and Communist consciousness has been enhanced. They summed up their achievements as "broken palms, transformed stand, sun-blackened face, and trained ideology."

.   .   .   .

Since last year, in the course of carrying out the policy of coördinating education with productive labor, we have gained the following major experiences.

Educational revolution should be carried out on the basis of ideological revolution, and on the basis of victories in the rectification campaign and antirightist struggles, including the "double anti-" movement, red and expert great debates, educational policy great debates, and criticisms on bourgeois educational and academic ideology. The extensive implementation of these struggles has provided us with favorable conditions for an educational revolution. If there is no victory in ideological revolution, there will be no victory in educational revolution. In carrying out the Party's educational policy in future, we must—under the leadership of the Party—make efforts continuously to strive for the successful implementation of the policies on two roads and two methods.

In carrying out the policy of coördinating education with productive labor, we must formally include productive labor in our educational plans, with its goals clearly stated. We must also exert efforts to make proper arrangements for productive labor in the daily life of students and to coördinate closely the practices of productive labor with theoretical education so as to enable them to become a wholesome teaching method. However, this is complicated, for it requires overall detailed planning. During last autumn, some of the schools—due to the lack of experience—were unable to formulate their teaching plans properly. As a result of cutting down classes considerably, they were unable to make the necessary improvement in the quality of their educational work. Meanwhile, special efforts have been made by these schools to improve work in this phase.

. . . .

Naturally, as stated by Premier Chou En-lai in his report, for such a thorough revolution on educational undertakings, we have only preliminary work experience. There are still shortcomings in work, and there are also problems that we must solve through further study. Particularly, there are still some general work methods on which we must conduct further study. However, we believe that so long as we have our work direction set properly, after a long struggle, we will be able gradually to establish a new and perfect educational system in conformity with the needs of the Socialist construction of our country.

. . . .

Our country's educational undertakings made unprecedented strides in 1958. In that one year, a mammoth illiteracy-eradication campaign was carried out among the six hundred million people, with results far better than those of the previous eight years. Some thirty million people enrolled in various types of spare-time schools of varying standards organized by mines, factories, and people's communes. We must not deny that this is an event of great significance. Kindergarten education also developed rapidly in 1958. Some thirty million children were enrolled in kindergartens last year, showing an increase of more than twenty-seven times over the preceding year. Enrollment in primary schools in our country last year reached eighty-six million persons, representing an increase of 34 percent over 1957. With regard to intermediate school education, the enrollment in ordinary intermediate schools in our country last year reached 8.52 million persons, an increase of 37 percent over 1957, while 1.47 million persons were enrolled in intermediate vocational schools, an increase of 89 percent over the preceding year. Those agricultural and other professional intermediate schools organized in 1958 had an enrollment of some two million persons. The total number of intermediate school students in China last year increased by 70 percent over the year before; and the number of higher educational institute students was 660,000 last year, an increase of 50 percent over 1957. This unprecedented development of our country's educational undertakings is attributable to the successful implementation of the Party's general line for Socialist construction and the policy of "walking on both legs" as well.

. . . .

Implementation of the full-day, half-day, and spare-time educational systems simultaneously in our country not only can develop our educational undertakings expeditiously in conformity with the guiding principle of more, faster, better, and more economical education but can also satisfy the demand of youths and adults for raising their cultural standards while our country is confronted with heavy production tasks and with a critical labor situation. With the gradual enhancement of labor productivity and the gradual shortening of working hours, the number of schools adopting the full-day system will be gradually increased, and adults will also be able to have time to engage in spare-time studies.

In the development of educational undertakings, we must resolutely adhere to the guiding principle of coördinating the popularization of education with raising educational standards. Neglect of either of these would make it difficult for us expeditiously to change the general outlook of our country's cultural backwardness, as well as to raise our scientific and cultural standards. So long as we implement the guiding principle of walking on both legs in popularizing education and in raising educational standards partially, we will be able to eliminate the contradictions between quantity and quality. We must use the method of developing half-day and spare-time schools together with the organization of educational institutes by factories and mines to meet the needs for popularizing education. On the other hand, we must raise the quality of the full-day schools, as well as raise the work quality of a selected group of these schools to a particularly high level, so as to enable them to become the backbone of our educational undertakings. This way of utilizing reasonably our limited strength will not only popularize education simultaneously with raising standards but will also give equal emphasis to quality as well as to quantity, thus enabling us to have initiative in developing educational undertakings.

. . . .

Productive labor should be listed as a part of the regular curriculum. The time ratio between productive labor and education should be arranged differently by schools of different natures. As for schools adopting the full-day system, education should be their primary assignment, and the time required for engaging in productive labor by their students should be properly arranged in conformity with the ages and other specific features of students and with reference to the practices of other types of schools at various levels and vocational schools. Generally speaking, there are three basic ways for students to participate in productive labor: (a) in factories and farms organized by the schools; (b) in rural areas or factories, through arrangements made by the school; (c) in definitely prescribed social welfare undertakings.

It is demanded that education and productive labor be carried out in a coördinated manner. As for education and productive labor that cannot be carried out directly in a coördinated manner, they should be conducted separately according to schedule. Special attention should be given to prevent the unilateral emphasis on education, which will give rise to the tendency of looking down on physical labor. Bases for carrying out productive labor in schools should be reorganized so as to insure that productive labor will be performed effectively. Efforts should also be made to formulate, step by step, overall productive labor plans according to actual needs and to outline the productive labor tasks of students and the necessary rating systems for their performance as well. Knowledge may be acquired through hard labor. However, a too-heavy educational burden given to students will not only affect the results of their study but will also affect their physical health. Therefore, efforts should be exerted to do away with the tendency of giving excessive assignments to students.

With regard to courses on political theory, along with continuous strengthening of our study of Socialist and Communist ideology and its coördination with current political tasks and events, efforts should be exerted to step up the study of Marxist-Leninist theories in a systematic manner and to coördinate this education with the education on current events and government policies as well as our daily political ideology.

. . . .

In teaching and study, it is necessary to promote the supervisory role of the teachers on one hand and to develop fully the enthusiasm and initiative of the student on the other hand, so that both teaching and study will be advanced simultaneously. For this reason, the teachers are required earnestly to shoulder the tasks of "teaching, giving lectures, and clearing doubts." They should love and protect the students and insist on strict discipline of the students. At the same time, they should listen and accept the opinions of the students so as to improve both teaching and study. The students should respect their teachers and should be humble in their study. On the other hand, they may adopt suitable means or forms to put forward their suggestions and criticisms. Such relationship between the teachers and students is growing among the schools in our country. It is the duty of the educational work-

ers to see that this relationship will be developed more health-
fully.

.   .   .   .

We have learned from experience that the leadership of the
Party is the basic insurance for all our accomplishments. The decisive factor of the enormous achievements we attained in our
educational undertakings during 1958 was in establishing and
intensifying the Party's leadership at the cultural and educational
front. The big forward leap in production has stirred up the cultural revolution. Our powerful and enormous resources lie in
following the correct direction, moving along the mass line, coördinating dissemination and improvement, "walking on two
legs," and developing fully our enthusiasm and initiative.

Our task for 1959 requires us to make a greater step in raising
work-quality. Only by consistently relying on the Party's leadership, relying on the people's masses, summarizing our experiences,
correcting our shortcomings, and improving our work can we
successfully fulfill this task.

SOURCE: *Current Background,* No. 577 (Hong Kong: United
States Consulate General, May 14, 1959). Originally published by
New China News Agency, April 28, 1959.

For additional readings, see Yang Hsiu-feng, "China's Educational Enterprise Goes through the Process of Great Revolution
and Great Evolution," *Current Background,* No. 608 (1960);
"Outlines of Examination for Matriculation to Institutions of
Higher Education for 1959," *Current Background,* No. 587
(1959); and Chang Chien, "Schooling for the Millions," *China
Reconstructs,* October 1959, pp. 54–56.

Our Tasks on the Cultural and Educational Fronts
By Chou En-lai
April 1959

Premier Chou's report was made to the Second National People's Congress. It embodied an analysis of the previous four years of government activity. The first of the Five-Year Plans had been completed, and in 1958 came the second. 1958 saw the start of the "great leap forward" as specified in the plan, the introduction of a new form of social organization, the commune, and the policy of combining education with productive labor. Students were to be both "red and expert," i.e., to be both politically correct and technically competent. While higher education had made significant progress and since the advent of the Communist government nearly five times as many students had enrolled in colleges and universities as had previously attended, Premier Chou felt that it was necessary to warn against the remnants of "old education" which "hoodwinked, paralyzed and corrupted" the worker ideologically. Education in "New China," he indicated, was solely to "serve the people, to put culture into their hands, and to combine mental work with physical labor."

An upsurge of our Socialist culture has started along with the upsurge of our Socialist economy. Through the rectification campaign and after the struggle against the rightists, the leading position of the proletariat was firmly established and strengthened in the various branches and units of cultural and educational undertakings, thus providing the political guarantee for the upsurge of culture and education. In 1958, it was not only the cultural and educational undertakings run by the state which made rapid progress; masses of workers and peasants felt a press-

308

ing need to master culture, and they, too, founded schools on their own, developed the sciences and culture, and engaged in various spare-time literary and artistic activities, altogether creating the panorama of a vast mass cultural revolution. Most of the intellectuals on the cultural and educational fronts, in the course of self-remolding, have enhanced their own Socialist initiative, strengthened their ties with the workers, peasants, and productive labor, and played an energetic part in popularizing culture and raising our cultural level. Our tasks are to continue to mobilize all positive factors on the cultural and educational fronts, to push forward the cultural revolution, to popularize Socialist culture, and to carry out the work of consolidating the positions gained and raising quality on the basis of popularization, so that cultural and educational work can meet the needs of Socialist construction as a whole.

Education in our country has made tremendous progress in the last few years, and especially in 1958. In 1952, the number of students in higher educational institutions was 190,000; by 1957, it was already 440,000, an increase of over 100 percent; in 1958, it again increased by 50 percent, compared with 1957, reaching 660,000. The number of middle school students in 1952 was over three million; in 1957 it was over seven million, also an increase of over 100 percent; in 1958, compared with 1957, it again increased by 70 percent to twelve million. Primary school pupils in 1952 numbered over fifty-one million; in 1957 there were already over sixty-four million, an increase of 26 percent; in 1958 there was another 34 percent increase compared with 1957, bringing the total to eighty-six million. In 1958, spare-time school education for workers and peasants, including general and technical, as well as political, courses, given in varied forms, also made tremendous progress. Much has also been done in wiping out illiteracy.

But these quantitative increases are by no means the only manifestation of our achievements in the field of education. What is more important is the fact that, as the Communist Party has greatly strengthened its leadership in educational work, we have, based on the working-class world outlook and the Socialist and Communist principles of education, carried out the policy of making education serve working-class politics and combining education with productive labor, thereby initiating a great and profound revolution in the educational field.

Serving working-class politics and the cause of socialism is the basic starting point of our education. In our schools, Socialist and Communist ideological and political education must be carried out in the most conscientious way to raise the Socialist consciousness of the students; our children and youth must be educated in cultural knowledge and modern scientific achievements, step by step and in a systematic way, and form the habit of taking part in productive labor in the course of their schooling, so as to fit themselves not only for mental work but also for physical labor. Those who stick to the standpoint of the old society, where education was run by the exploiting classes are, of course, opposed to our policy. In actual fact, the bourgeoisie and other exploiting classes introduce into their own schools political and ideological education aimed at bolstering up their own class interests. Bourgeois society gives the workers only some rough, shallow, and limited knowledge and makes every attempt to hoodwink, paralyze, and corrupt them ideologically and politically. The bourgeoisie consistently train intellectuals serving their system of exploitation in the spirit of separating theory from practice and mental labor from physical labor. Our eductional policy is the very opposite of this policy of the bourgeoisie. Our aim is to arm the workers, peasants, and intellectuals with the scientific and revolutionary proletarian world outlook, to wipe out completely, the ideological influences of the exploiting classes, to make education serve the working people, to put culture into their hands, and to combine mental work with physical labor.

We have already officially begun to introduce productive labor into the educational program of our schools and, in the light of varying conditions, to organize students to take part in productive labor for specified periods of time. Through engaging in productive labor, the mass of faculty members and students have acquired much more practical knowledge of production, and love of labor and respect for the laborers have been fostered. In institutions of higher learning, practical work in production has also given a powerful impetus to scientific research. The facts show that properly integrating education with productive labor can assist in strengthening the ties between school and society, bringing about the integration of theory and practice and the gradual integration of mental and physical labor—turning our schools day by day into a new type, training new men with a Communist outlook. Of course we have only gained a preliminary experience in this far-reaching revolution in education; there are still shortcomings in our work and questions that remain to be studied further and solved. We must continue to accumulate and sum up our experience and constantly improve our work so as to carry out this policy of integrating education with productive labor still more effectively.

In developing education in our country we must adopt the method of combining popularization with a raising of quality. In order to popularize culture and meet the urgent needs of the current development of national construction, in addition to full-time regular schools at all levels, we must also, wherever possible and practicable, continue to set up and improve half-day schools and spare-time schools in the countryside, factories, and mines. The work of wiping out illiteracy must be energetically carried out with the participation of the masses. At the same time, we must also pay special attention to raising the quality of teaching and studying in schools of all types. Last year, schools at all levels made great progress; now it is time to improve, consolidate, and raise their level on the basis of this great development. Full-time regular schools at all levels should make it their constant and fundamental task to raise the quality of teaching and studying. In the first place, we must devote relatively more energy to perfecting a number of "key" schools, so as to train specialized personnel of higher quality for the state and bring about a rapid rise in our country's scientific and cultural level.

In 1958, great achievements were made in both the patriotic public health movement, which centered on wiping out the "four pests" and the principal diseases, and the athletic movement, aimed at improving the physique of the people. We must continue these movements. In our public health work, we must continue to carry out the mass line and have specialists work in coöperation with the masses, so as to improve the health conditions of our people rapidly and effectively. We must get the doctors of the traditional school of Chinese medicine and doctors of the modern school to unite, organize them to make joint efforts in the interests of people's health and develop the medical heritage of the motherland and the medical and pharmaceutical sciences. In the field of athletics, it is necessary, too, to carry out the policy of combining popularization with a raising of quality, to organize mass athletic movements on a wide scale and step by step raise the level of athletics in our country.

In the fields of science and technology, 1958 saw the start of a mass movement for scientific exploration in which thousands upon thousands of people took part. Research work in many fields yielded good results. The ranks of scientific and technical workers greatly increased. In serving the cause of Socialist construction, many scientific workers, engineers, and technicians in scientific research institutes and institutions of higher learning and on the industrial and agricultural production fronts have displayed a very high degree of initiative.

We are still backwards in science and technology, and we will have to work still harder in these fields. Tasks directly serving production and construction must be given top priority. There are a thousand and one technical problems in every sphere of production and construction, and scientific and technical workers should work hard to solve them through a division of labor and coördination of efforts. Attention must also be given to developing the most advanced branches of science and technology; and as regards those branches in which we lack conditions for development, we must make all the necessary preparations now. Basic theoretical research exerts a far-reaching influence on scientific and technological progress, and we must pay sufficient attention to this field as well.

Theoretical studies in the social sciences must also be developed energetically and given better leadership. It is not permissible to ignore their importance. Theoretical workers in the social sciences must be encouraged to make long-term, systematic efforts under the guidance of Marxism-Leninism, to collect sufficient relevant material, and to undertake independent, creative studies.

There is a lively movement on the literary and artistic fronts, both in the work of professional writers and artists and in the amateur literary and artistic activities of the workers and peasants. We must encourage professional writers and artists to work hard to produce works of a still higher ideological and artistic level, which will educate and answer the cultural needs of the people. At the same time, we must give energetic leadership to the literary and artistic activities of the masses and pay attention to training those with literary and artistic talents who appear among the working people.

To achieve a sound development in science and art, we must carry out the policy of "letting a hundred flowers blossom and a hundred schools of thought contend" on the basis of serving the cause of socialism. This policy has pointed out the way of flourishing and development for our science and culture and has given tremendous inspiration to the entire scientific and cultural circles. Soon after the Party put forward this policy in 1956, the bourgeois rightists distorted it. Pretending to be fragrant Socialist "flowers," they attacked the Party and socialism in an attempt to seize the leadership in cultural affairs. Victory in the antirightist struggle smashed this reactionary attempt, and favorable conditions for carrying out the policy were thus created. The leap forward in Socialist construction and the upsurge of the mass cultural revolution have opened up a vast area for a hundred flowers to blossom and a hundred schools of thought to contend in the fields of science and art. Through free debates among different schools and views in science, through free competition between different forms and styles in art, we are confident that before long our scientific and cultural work will enter a flourishing era and achieve great successes.

The creation of an army of working-class intellectuals, numbering tens of millions is a great historic task on the cultural and educational front. It is by training new intellectuals and remolding old intellectuals that such an army will be created.

Happy results have been achieved of late in the self-remolding of the old intellectuals: many of them are not only sincerely willing to accept Party leadership and serve Socialist construction but have begun to go out among the masses and take part in physical labor in factories and villages at regular intervals, have acquired new experience in living and working with the working people, and have raised their ideological level. Some bourgeois intellectuals, after prolonged and serious self-remolding, have begun to transform themselves into working-class intellectuals, and among them, some advanced ones have joined the Chinese Communist Party. These facts show the complete correctness of the policy of uniting, educating, and remolding the intellectuals consistently followed by the Party and the state. By coming over politically to the side of socialism and uniting with the masses, old intellectuals can use their knowledge and skill and give full play to their specialities in serving the cause of socialism and so win the approval of the people. However, it will still take a fairly long time for them to go further and make a complete break with their bourgeois world outlook and really grasp the working-class world outlook. It is wrong to think that old intellectuals no longer need to remold themselves or that they cannot work unless they complete their remolding in a very short time. All old intellectuals willing to take the Socialist road must continue to exert themselves and remold themselves step by step through their work for a long time to come. We must make proper arrangements for them to work, appreciate their initiative, and help them to achieve greater results in their work. At the same time, we must help them study Marxism-Leninism, find more chances to go among the masses, learn about actual conditions and, of their own free will, take part to a suitable extent in physical labor.

Great numbers of young intellectuals are sprouting up pretty fast. They are advancing bravely along the road of being "both red and expert" and have made their first contributions in various fields of work. We must lead them to strive for still greater achievement, encourage them constantly to scale the heights of scientific knowledge, and teach them never to indulge in self-conceit. Young intellectuals too are faced with the task of constantly remolding themselves. Whatever post they may hold, they must, while striving to raise their vocational level, seriously study Marxism-Leninism, to take part in the production and struggles of the masses, participate in physical labor, and be strict with themselves, politically and ideologically, as well as in work. They must learn with modesty from their learned elders, who in turn should also learn from the strong points of the young intellectuals. All patriotic intellectuals should rally under the banner of socialism and work together to build our great motherland.

SOURCE: Chou En-lai, *Report on the Work of the Government* (Peking: Foreign Languages Press, 1959). [Delivered as a speech at the first session of the Second National People's Congress on April 18, 1959.]

See also Chou En-lai, "Report on the Work of the Government," *Peking Review,* No. 16 (April 21, 1959), pp. 18–20.

Regulations Governing the Enrollment of New Students by Institutions of Higher Education in 1959
June 1959

Practices have varied during the decade 1950–1960 in respect to college and university admissions. Annual quotas for enrollment and unified entrance requirements, as determined by the state, are necessary for long-term centralized planning. While some consideration may be given to a student's choice of college and academic specialization, the government-supervised program for the selection and distribution of students remains paramount. The "political qualities" of an applicant are foremost considerations for enrollment; however, candidates with equal examination marks are allocated priorities in terms of their "social, political, and cultural" background. Those of worker-peasant status and faithful Party workers are given the highest priority, followed by former servicemen, children of "revolutionary martyrs," and Chinese applying from overseas, Hong Kong, and Macao.

Following are the regulations governing the enrollment of new students by institutions of higher education in 1959, as promulgated by the Ministry of Education of the People's Republic of China.

The work of enrolling students for institutions of higher education in 1959 must be based on the work of 1958 in giving continued implementation to the principle of recognizing the leadership of Party committees and the class line, in soberly implementing the principle of insuring the quality of the students enrolled according to the conditions of the schools, and in fulfilling the student-enrollment plans of the different kinds of institutions of higher education.

316

According to the above requirement, the following regulations are hereby laid down to govern the enrollment of students by institutions of higher education this year:

I. The institutions of higher education shall adopt the method of combining unified leadership with decentralized handling in the enrollment of students. The different provinces, municipalities, and autonomous regions shall deal with the student-enrollment work according to the expediency of their places in accordance with the provisions of these regulations and the unified arrangements made pertaining to the enrollment of students. The education departments and higher education departments of the different provinces, municipalities, and autonomous regions shall, under the leadership of the People's Councils in their respective provinces, municipalities, and autonomous regions and in conjunction with the establishments concerned, organize the institutions of higher education under their jurisdiction to set up student-enrollment organizations for the purposes of handling student-enrollment work in their respective provinces, municipalities, and autonomous regions.

Schools whose entrance examinations have special requirements may enroll students independently.

All institutions of higher education wanting to enroll students should carry out student-enrollment work under the unified leadership of the Party committees and student-enrollment committees in their places.

II. The Ministry of Education shall consult with the provinces, municipalities, autonomous regions, and institutions concerned in formulating plans to determine the number of students to be enrolled by institutions under the leadership of the different agencies of the central government from the different provinces, municipalities, and autonomous regions and the number of students to be transferred from provinces and municipalities with an abundant supply of candidates to provinces, municipalities, and autonomous regions which are in short supply of candidates. The different provinces, municipalities, and autonomous regions shall consult with each other over the transfer of small numbers of students among themselves.

The student-enrollment organizations of the different provinces, municipalities, and autonomous regions shall, before the registration of candidates, announce the names of the institutions of higher education and their departments and courses (special courses) deciding to enroll students from the different provinces, municipalities, and autonomous regions.

III. All citizens of the People's Republic of China who have a senior secondary school education or its equivalent and are under thirty years of age (the age limit for workers, peasants, demobilized and rehabilitated soldiers, and cadres on active duty may properly be extended in different places) may apply for enrollment in institutions of higher education, provided they are any one of the following:

A. Graduates from senior secondary schools of this year who are in possession of letters of introduction issued by their schools.

B. Graduates from secondary vocational schools of this year who have been authorized by the competent business establishments or local educational administrations to further their studies in a higher school and are in possession of letters of introduction issued by the work units employing them.

C. Personnel on active duty in Party and government organs, business and enterprise units, and mass organizations who have obtained the approval of the work units employing them and are in possession of letters of introduction from such units.

D. Rehabilitated, demobilized, and discharged soldiers who are in possession of letters of identification issued by a government civil affairs establishment of the *hsien* level or above (or of the *ch'u* level in large and medium-size cities) or armed force units of the regiment level or above.

E. Chinese students returned from overseas or students from Hong Kong and Macao who are in possession of letters of identification issued by overseas Chinese affairs organs in China or the Committee to Guide Senior Secondary School Graduates from Hong Kong and Macao to Seek Higher Study in Canton.

F. Other intellectual youth who are in possession of letters of identification issued by People's Communes or People's Councils of the *ch'u* level or above.

IV. The institutions of higher education shall this year divide their examinations into three classes according to the nature of the special courses, and candidates shall be examined in the following subjects:

A. For special courses of all kinds in science and engineering colleges (including the courses in the geography departments in normal colleges and schools and the special course in natural geography in universities); special courses in the mechanization of agricultural production, agricultural minerology, land-planning, farm irrigation, crop-management, agricultural chemistry, agricultural electrification, designing and building of agricultural machines, lumbering and transport, water transport, lumbering machines, manufacture of forestry machines, chemical technology for forestry products, mechanical processing of timber, industrial fishery, and processing of marine products in colleges and schools of agriculture and forestry; and special courses in pharmacology in colleges and schools of medicine, candidates shall be tested in the Chinese language, political science, mathematics, physics, chemistry, and foreign languages.

B. For special courses of all kinds (except those listed under "A" above) in the colleges of medicine, agriculture, and forestry, courses in the departments of biology and physical culture, and the special course in psychology, candidates shall be tested in the Chinese language, political science, physics, chemistry, biology, and foreign languages.

C. For special courses of all kinds in colleges of literature, history, political science, law, finance and economics, and the arts and the special course in economic geography in universities, candidates shall be tested in the Chinese language, political science, history, geography, and foreign languages.

Candidates who sit for the different special courses in colleges of finance and economics, the special course in economic geography, and the special course in philosophy shall be tested in mathematics as well (cadres specializing in finance and economic work who sit for the different special courses in finance and economics may apply for exemption). For candidates who sit for special courses in the arts, physical culture, etc. (departments in courses included), which have special requirements, the additional subjects of examination shall be stipulated by the schools concerned.

The foreign language in which candidates are to be tested may be either Russian or English, according to the option of the candidates. Those who have not studied any foreign language may apply for exemption. Candidates sitting for special courses in foreign languages, however, may not apply for exemption.

V. The joint entrance examinations for institutions of higher education are scheduled to be held on July 20. The dates of examination for institutions of higher education enrolling students independently shall be fixed by these institutions themselves.

VI. The different provinces, municipalities, and autonomous regions shall determine the examination districts and examination centers to be set up themselves and shall announce the same for the information of the candidates.

VII. In enrolling new students, the institutions of higher education shall observe the principle of enrolling candidates with the best scholastic and health conditions, provided their political quality is assured.

The method of recommending candidates for examination shall be applicable to the workers, peasants, cadres of worker and peasant status, and veteran cadres. These recommended candidates shall not participate in the nationwide joint examination but shall be examined independently by the institution to which they are sent. The educational administrations of the different provinces, municipalities, and autonomous regions shall be held responsible for recommending candidates.

Workers, peasants, cadres of worker and peasant status, and veteran cadres who participate in the joint examination because they have not been recommended and candidates who are demobilized or rehabilitated soldiers, cadres on active duty with long service in revolutionary work, national minorities, children of martyrs, overseas Chinese students, or students from Hong Kong and Macao are entitled to enrollment with priority.

VIII. All expenses incurred by candidates of all kinds during the time of the entrance examination shall be borne by the candidates themselves. After their enrollment, in case they are personnel on active duty, rehabilitated soldiers, or graduates of this year from secondary vocational schools, the units (schools) to which they belong shall pay for their traveling expenses to their schools. In the case of other new students, they are in principle required to bear the traveling expenses themselves. In some individual cases, because the candidates have a relatively long way to travel and are really unable to raise the money for traveling expenses due to the straitened circumstances of their families, they may apply to the student-enrollment organizations or to the local educational administrations of their own provinces, municipalities, or autonomous regions for a subsidy grant.

IX. Institutions of higher education should subject the new students to another political and health checkup after their enrollment. If they fail to pass this checkup, they shall be disqualified for enrollment.

X. The student-enrollment organizations and the schools which enroll students independently in the different provinces, municipalities, and autonomous regions shall, in accordance with these regulations and the concrete demands of their provinces, municipalities, autonomous regions, and schools, formulate separate abridged regulations governing the enrollment of students for announcement to the candidates.

SOURCE: *Survey of China Mainland Press,* No. 2041 (Hong Kong: United States Consulate General, June 24, 1959). Originally published by *New China News Agency,* June 10, 1959.

China's Educational Enterprise Goes through the Process of Great Revolution and Great Evolution

By Yang Hsiu-feng

October 1959

Under the leadership of the Chinese Communist Party and its great leader, Comrade Mao Tse-tung, the Chinese people are working with skyrocketing zeal for the rapid transformation of China's "poor and blank" aspect. Inspired by the general line of the Party, which calls on us to build socialism by exerting our utmost efforts and pressing ahead consistently to achieve greater, better, and more economical results, the people throughout the country are bringing their high degree of revolutionary enthusiasm and infinite power of creation into play to win one victory after another.

Like other fronts, the educational front has also gone through ten years of continuous revolution and victory. Over the course of ten years, there have been built on the vast expanse of land in the fatherland close to one million schools of different grades and kinds which give nearly two hundred million people an opportunity to get educated. The broad masses of the workers and peasants are arming themselves with Socialist and Communist ideologies and knowledge of modern science and culture. A vast army of intellectuals, both red and vocationally proficient, is in the course of taking shape. The backward aspect of the old China in culture and education is being rapidly transformed.

During the last ten years, education in China was developed at a rate and on a scale unknown before in history. Compared with the peak year in the old China, in 1958 the number of kindergarten children reached thirty-one million, the increase being 237 times; the number of primary school pupils was in excess of eighty-six million, the increase being 2.6 times; 85 percent of the school-age children were sent to schools, and in many municipalities and *hsien,* the universalization of primary education had in the main been carried out; the number of middle school students reached 10,520,000, the increase being 5.6 times; the number of students in secondary vocational schools reached 1,470,000, the increase being 2.8 times; the number of students in institutions of higher education reached 660,000, the increase being 3.2 times.

A great leap forward was made in education in 1958. During the year the number of children in kindergartens increased by thirty million. The number of primary school pupils increased by twenty-two million, the rate of increase being 34.4 percent compared with 1957. The number of middle school students increased by five million, the increase being 70 percent. The number of students in institutions of higher education increased by 220,000, the increase being 50 percent.

During the last ten years, the institutions of higher education and secondary vocational schools in China trained nearly two million specialized personnel of the higher and intermediate grades for the nation. At the same time, work to eliminate illiteracy and to give spare-time education to workers and peasants was energetically carried out amidst nearly one hundred million young and able-bodied workers and peasants. In 1958, sixty million people took up literacy studies, and some thirty million people joined different kinds of spare-time schools.

Before the liberation, few of the children of the workers and peasants were able to attend schools. Since the founding of the People's Republic, the state has adopted all measures to expand the proportion of students of worker and peasant status among the students in schools in all grades. In 1958, over 90 percent of the kindergarten children and primary school pupils were children of workers and peasants. The students of worker and peasant status made up over 70 percent of the middle school students and 48 percent of all the students in institutions of higher education. In the latter case, the students of worker and peasant status had risen to 62 percent of the new students enrolled in 1958.

The enormous expansion of the educational enterprise in China is the outcome of educational reforms carried out in ten years, and especially of the great revolution and great leap forward in 1958.

After the founding of the People's Republic of China, we took over all the schools in the country and rid them of the system of Fascist administration and the rule of secret agents to which these schools were subject under the reactionary Kuomintang rule. We also recovered the sovereign right of education from the imperialists.

Following this, the Marxist-Leninist type of ideological and political education was carried out in the schools throughout the country. In conjunction with the political campaigns launched at different times, the teachers and students were ideologically remolded, and the feudal, comprador, Fascist, and bourgeois types of thinking were criticized. In 1957, the rectification campaign and a struggle against bourgeois rightists were carried out.

Simultaneously with carrying out these ideological struggles, we inherited the fine traditions of the revolutionary bases in educational work and learned the advanced experiences acquired by the Soviet educational undertakings. In accordance with the Socialist educational principles, a series of reforms were directed against the old forms of education, and the Socialist educational system was gradually set up.

Reorganization of departments and colleges was carried out in the institutions of higher education, and there was a big increase in the number of engineering and normal school students. The number of engineering students in proportion to the total number of students in institutions of higher education rose to over 37 percent, compared with 17.8 percent in 1947. The number of students in teacher-training institutes also rose from 13.5 percent to over 24 percent.

In conjunction with the reorganization of departments and colleges, the method of fostering specialized personnel for different fields of specialization was adopted and used and over three hundred kinds of specialization courses were set up in institutions of higher education and secondary vocational schools. This proved to be highly appropriate for meeting the needs of national construction.

In regard to the establishment and development of schools of different grades and kinds, in accordance with the spirit of handling the whole country like a game of chess, rational arrangements were made in the light of the special features of the different places. The institutions of higher education and secondary vocational schools in the hinterland were greatly strengthened; emphasis was given to the development of secondary and primary education in the industrial and mining districts, the broad countryside, and the minority nationalities areas; and the uneven state of development which characterized the educational undertakings of semifeudal and semicolonial countries was remedied.

Simultaneously with uniting, remolding and educating the existing teachers, new teachers were energetically trained. The ranks of professional teachers swelled to 2,500,000 in 1958, compared with 930,000 in 1949. Because their political consciousness and professional knowledge were raised continuously, tens of thousands of model teachers and outstanding workers emerged on the educational front.

In 1958, on the strength of the great victory in Socialist revolution scored on the economic, political, and ideological fronts by the people of China at different times, illuminated and inspired by the general line of the Party for building socialism, a great leap forward was made in the national economy, and the universal establishment of people's communes was brought into reality in the countryside throughout China. Under the new situation, the broad masses of the workers and peasants urgently wanted to raise their cultural and technological standards.

In order to meet the demand of the broad masses, to carry out the Socialist revolution to the end, to speed up the building of socialism, and to work for the gradual realization of the historical task pertaining to the technological revolution and cultural revolution, the Party Central Committee promulgated the directive concerning educational work and further explained the guideline which called for the submission of education to the political requirements of the proletariat and the combination of education with productive labor and the need to place educational work under the leadership of the Party. It also pointed out with emphasis that for the sake of developing educational enterprise with greater, faster, better, and more economical results, the measure of "walking with two legs" must be adopted, the mass line must be followed, and the establishment of schools by the whole people must be enforced.

As soon as this guideline of the Party was put forward, it at once received the warm support of the broad masses. A great educational revolution with central emphasis given to the combination of education with productive labor and a mass campaign to develop the educational enterprise with greater, faster, better, and more economical results was launched energetically throughout the country. This revolution thoroughly manifested the activism of the masses in the promotion of education, thus enabling China's educational enterprise to enter an entirely new era of development.

Our educational enterprise is one of the powerful tools used by the proletariat to remold the old society and to build up a new one. As early as 1934, Comrade Mao Tse-tung had pointed out that the general cultural and educational policy of the revolutionary bases sought to educate the broad masses of the poverty-stricken people with the Communist spirit, to put culture and education in the service of the revolutionary war and class struggle, to unite education with labor, and to give civilization and happiness to the people of China. The educational policy was observed and carried out in the main by all educational undertakings throughout the country in the revolutionary bases in old days and after the founding of the People's Republic.

Since 1958, the great educational revolution has worked toward the end of making China's educational undertakings serve the Socialist revolution and the building of socialism more satisfactorily, eliminating all exploiting classes and exploiting systems, eventually evolving a Communist society, and eliminating gradually the difference between mental labor and physical labor. In view of this, our educational work must implement and carry out the educational policy of the Party, so that "the educated may be developed morally, intellectually, and physically to become workers with Socialist consciousness and culture," so that new personnel of all-round development with political consciousness and culture who are capable of taking up mental work as well as physical work may be fostered, and so that the goal of making laborers of the intellectuals and intellectuals of the workers and peasants may gradually be realized.

The great educational revolution goes further to solve the problem of relationship between education and politics. The burgeoisie falsely favor "education for the sake of education" and declare that "students should play no part in politics." We maintain, however, that education must serve the political ends of the proletariat, professional knowledge must be combined with politics, and "red and vocationally proficient" personnel must be fostered. Because of this, we look upon the ideological and political education of Marxism-Leninism and the political work of the Party as the soul of all work carried out in the schools and favor the implementation of the principle of "politics in command" in the teaching of all cultural and scientific knowledge. By way of the methodical theoretical indoctrination of Marxism-Leninism, by way of inculcating the political and economic situation and task of the different periods, and by way of participating in different political campaigns and actual productive labor, the teachers and students have gone through in good earnest an extensive course of ideological education in socialism and communism.

In 1958, under the leadership of the Party, the broad masses of the teachers and students employed the methods of contending, blooming, debating, setting out facts, reasoning, and criticism and self-criticism to criticize thoroughly the burgeois viewpoint which divorced work from politics, thus greatly raising their Socialist consciousness. The bourgeois form of individualism in pursuit of personal fame and gain which sought to become "vocationally proficient without becoming red" and followed "the road of the white expert" was held in contempt by the broad masses. Arming themselves with the world outlook of the proletariat, the broad masses of teachers and students firmly aspired to becoming "intellectuals of the working class."

The combination of education with productive labor constitutes the central theme of the great educational revolution. This is a profound revolution of great historical significance. Ever since the entry of mankind into class society, all exploiting classes have had common characteristics in education: namely, the separation of education from productive labor, contempt for manual labor and manual workers, and the teaching of one-sided knowledge to students. Without thoroughly removing this tradition of the exploiting classes in education, without combining education with productive labor, the object of fostering "workers with Socialist consciousness and culture" can never be attained, and education can never be made to serve thoroughly the political requirements of the proletariat.

. . . .

On the eve of the summer vacation, inspired by the call of the Party for "the elimination of superstitious belief and the liberation of thinking" and impelled by the skyrocketing zeal of the workers and peasants, the broad masses of teachers and students glorified the Communist style of daring to think, to speak out, and to take action, and enthusiasm for the establishment of factories and farms swelled in schools at all levels. The teachers and students took action in person to overcome the difficulties and made contacts with the factories for mutual aid and support. When they were short of equipment, they operated in a crude manner. They worked as they learned to make up their technological ignorance. They used actual achivements to show what they could do to those who stood by and jeered at them. In this way, they were frequently able to set up several and even more than ten large and small factories and workshops in a school within several days and nights.

Simultaneously with setting up factories and farms on a large scale, the normal institutes and schools also went to the factories and the countryside to set up spare-time schools for workers and peasants. The medical colleges and schools also helped the workers and peasants to operate hospitals and clinics. Everybody felt it a supreme glory to be able to serve the workers and peasants and to contribute his part towards the development of the national economy.

In the steel and iron campaign carried out by the whole people, the school teachers and students in different places also started steel-refining and iron-smelting campaigns of a mass character. Ninety thousand engineering students and young teachers from institutions of higher education proceeded to the steel and iron front in a planned manner to participate in and to give aid and support to the steel-refining and "late fall" campaigns of the masses. Among them, over two thousand teachers and students from the Peking Institute of Steel and Iron Technology made their way to twenty-two provinces, municipalities, and autonomous regions to take up mining, ore-dressing, steel-refining, iron-smelting, machine-building, equipment-installation, metallographic analysis, metal pressure processing, shaping, and machine-parts-designing work in different places. Refining steel inside the furnaces with personnel by their side, they trained large numbers of steel and iron workers and technological cadres. They themselves were also schooled and disciplined. "Leaving our footprints north of the Great Wall and south of the Yangtze River, we have given our pledge to fight for iron and steel. With the good earth of the fatherland soaked with our sweat, we intend to cast a land of peace in steel. With the country lit by the fire of the blast furnaces, many heroes are hardened." These were the imposing remarks made by the teachers and students sent down to the lower levels for manual labor.

With the schools operating factories, farms, and other social undertakings on a large scale and teachers and students participating in productive labor and in practical work, knowledge was greatly enriched, and wisdom was cultivated. There were encountered in production and practice many scientific and technological problems which had to be solved urgently. So mass campaigns pertaining to scientific research and technical innovation were again launched in institutions of higher education and middle schools, and great achievements were scored in this connection.

The carrying out of educational revolution by the broad masses according to the educational policy of the Party has given a variety of concrete forms to the process of combining education with productive labor. The Party Central Committee has summed up the experiences of the masses opportunely and pointed out in what ways we should direct our efforts. The chief ones are that the schools must operate factories and farms, for they are required not only to foster new personnel but also to carry out the trial and actual production of new products, and that the factories and People's Communes must set up schools, for they are required not only to produce material products but also to foster new personnel.

The schools are divided into three categories: namely, full-day schools, half-day schools (the students there are required to do manual work and study half the time) and sparetime schools. Schools at all levels must list productive labor as a regular subject in their academic plans, and all students must participate in productive labor at the specified time.

As the main business in full-day schools in teaching and learning, the students there must take up some kind of productive labor and do all they can to combine what they take up with their special field of study.

In the half-day schools, the practice of working and studying half time is carried out (half a day of manual work and half a day of study, or the carrying out of work and study on alternate days or on alternate weeks). The students in these schools are students as well as workers and peasants. There are three basic forms of productive labor in which they take part. First, they work in the school factories and farms. This facilitates the overall arrangement of teaching work for the normalization and systematization of productive labor. Second, they coöperate or sign contracts with factories or people's communes and take up work in the factories or the countryside. This enables the teachers and students to get in touch with the workers and peasants and broadens the students' sphere of knowledge. Third, they participate in social welfare work. This benefits in particular the cultivation of the Communist attitude of working without caring for the reward. Overall arrangements should be made for these three forms of productive labor, and none of them may be discarded.

In spare-time schools of all kinds for workers and peasants, study is carried out in the spare time, and teaching must be correlated with production. In this way, both the combination of education with productive labor and the combination of productive labor with education are brought into realization, thus enabling the two to develop by making up each other's deficiency.

The linking of the schools under these three categories will be able to speed up the process of making laborers of the intellectuals and intellectuals of the workers and peasants.

Practice in one year or more has fully proved that the combination of education with productive labor is of great benefit towards developing the teachers and students morally, intellectually, and physically and towards raising the standard of education.

Man's social consciousness is determined by social existence. Because of their participation in the practice of labor and their close contact with the workers and peasants, the students first experience a great change in the spiritual aspect and are taught the class viewpoint of the working class, the labor viewpoint, the mass viewpoint, the collective viewpoint, and the dialectical materialistic viewpoint. They throw themselves into the furnace of productive labor to get themselves tempered and refined. They create material and spiritual wealth for the society with their industrious labor. They test for themselves the truth that society is created by labor. They realize that labor is the most imposing undertaking and that the viewpoint to belittle physical labor is wrong.

Glorification of labor and fervent love for labor have evolved to become the vogue. They adopt an obstinate and self-forgetting attitude in labor to show their contempt for those who love to lead an easy life and hate hard work. Due to the strengthening of their contact with the workers and peasants, the students learn the most vivid lesson from their firm class stand, the vivid contrast between what they like and dislike, and their fine qualities. Their participation in labor makes them realize deeply the greatness of the laboring people and increases their desire to breathe together with them and to share their destiny.

Practice in labor enables them to sense in person the greatness of collective strength and the importance of labor discipline. They have therefore a greater fervor for collectivism and more concern for collective enterprise and discipline. "With hardened hands, they have changed their stand, and with the skin tanned, their thinking takes on a red glow." The broad masses have set out to make laborers of themselves in this way.

Participation in labor gives the students of worker and peasant status a firmer stand and a higher consciousness. The danger of ideological degeneration due to their prolonged departure from productive labor is thus avoided. In the eyes of the workers and peasants, the students of nowadays are no longer "scholars" who "make no diligent use of their limbs and are unable to tell one grain from another" but are intellectuals of the working people. The workers and peasants say: "In the past, we were not sure of your loyalty after you went to school. Now our mind is at ease."

. . . .

In the past, little attention was paid to the outcome of production in the practice of production, labor was not carried out with a sober attitude, and work was incorrectly carried out. Now as production and the finished products are combined whenever possible, there is complete change in the state of affairs, and the labor attitude and technological level are raised greatly.

In the past, most of the curricular designs and graduation designs were based upon hypothetical subjects alienated from reality. The student said: "From books to materials and from materials to drawing papers, formulae are quoted and data are furnished. It is not easy to tell whether the designs thus completed are correct, and they are frequently just a heap of waste paper." Now the arrow is shot with a target to hit, and, whenever possible, the proper kinds of practical problems and projects ready for production are selected. The things to be produced, the condition of the equipment, the technological requirement, the sites of the factories and stations, and the geological conditions are all concrete in form. In general, this is carried out by adopting the method of entrusting the designing work to different people, so that wherever suitable they may interchange their designs, check one another's work, discuss the work together, master the project as a whole, and study the key points intensively.

The different schools are generally of the opinion that this is also one of the best ways to link up theory with reality. It can combine teaching, production, and scientific research closely and is far superior to hypothetical designing.

Engels said: "Production determines the generation and development of science from the very beginning." During the second half of 1958, because of the great leap forward made in industrial and agricultural production throughout the country and the participation of the broad masses of the teachers and students in productive labor, many scientific and technological problems which urgently needed to be solved were raised in the practice of production. This gave the institutions of higher education an impetus to develop their scientific research work.

Under the leadership of the Party, the need to make research serve the building of socialism by linking up theory with reality was made clear to all schools. The masses were urged to discard their superstitious beliefs, to liberate their way of thinking, to think and to take action, to drop their blind worship of a small number of experts, to remove the mantle of mystery from scientific research work, to adopt the mass line by associating the experts with the masses, and to launch mass campaigns. The past tendency for a small number of experts to carry out scientific research work in an isolated manner in pursuit of personal fame and gain and in separation from reality was thus changed, and the appetite for scientific research, inventions, and innovations increased to assume the proportions of a high tide.

Within several months, the scientific research projects accomplished were ten times higher than in 1957, and the quality of these projects was also higher than any of the past years. Many problems in national economy in urgent need of solution were solved. New achievements were also made in such new fields of science and technology as atomic energy, jet technology, computing technology, and radio electronics. It should be pointed out in particular that many outstanding achievements were made possible, thanks to the painstaking research carried out by the young teachers and senior students. In the new society, new personnel who are both red and vocationally proficient have emerged.

The combination of education with productive labor has not

only raised greatly the quality of education. Several hundred thousand university students, several million middle school students, several ten thousand primary school students, and several hundred educational workers have also been organized and led to participate in productive labor. They form a gigantic labor army which possesses culture and is full of vitality and which is capable of contributing immense strength to the development of the national economy. They have completed a large number of prospecting, designing, and work tastes. They have produced over one million tons of iron and several ten thousand tons of steel, over ten thousand lathes and tools of different patterns and designs, and several ten thousand tons of chemical products and manufactured goods. They have forested large areas of land and developed handicraft and subsidiary agricultural production. They have universally taken up social welfare work, rendered unpaid aid and support to the state in different construction projects and people's communes in agricultural production, and created large quantities of material wealth for the nation.

Since 1958, in conjunction with the great educational revolution, we have implemented the Party's guideline of "walking with two legs" to develop the people's educational enterprise and have agitated and depended on the masses to carry out the mass line of leaving the schools to be run by the whole Party and the whole people. This stands for the simultaneous operation of general education and vocational (technical) education, adult education and children's education, full-day schools, half-day schools, and spare-time schools, school education and private studies (including correspondence schools and broadcasting schools), as well as free education and paid education, in accordance with the principle of combining unity with variety, universalization with elevation, and overall planning by the central government with the delegation of power to local authorities.

An active interest in the running of schools was thus fully aroused in different quarters, and as the state promoted education on a large scale, there was also an upsurge of enthusiasm in the establishment of schools on the part of the factories, mines, enterprises, and people's communes. Under the leadership of the Party committees of the different places, for the sake of rapidly raising their own political consciousness and level of cultural and scientific knowledge, the workers and peasants employed the method of contributing labor and materials to solve the problems of school premises, equipment, and outlay for the schools. The method of recruiting locally men of ability to serve as teachers was adopted to solve the problem of teaching staff. In this way, over the short course of several months, there were set up in different places throughout the country several hundred thousand workers' and peasants' schools of all grades and patterns, several ten thousand agricultural middle schools (half-day system), ordinary middle schools, primary schools, and kindergartens.

In the overwhelming majority of the areas in China, the aim of kindergartens and primary schools for all production brigades in the people's communes, junior middle schools for all communes, senior middle schools for all *hsien,* secondary vocational schools, and technical schools for all administrative districts and institutions of higher education of different kinds in all provinces, municipalities, and autonomous regions has in the main been achieved. As a result, there are schools everywhere, and books are read aloud in every household. The educational enterprise in China has really become an undertaking of the masses, an undertaking to serve the people, and an undertaking in the hands of the laboring people.

. . . .

The implementation of the educational guideline of the Party was brought into realization through the sharp struggle between the road to socialism and the road to capitalism, and between progressive thinking and backward thinking. After the question in regard to the relationship between education and politics, and between "red consciousness" and "vocational proficiency" was solved fundamentally, the question in regard to the relationship between education and productive labor formed the focus of the struggle between the educational ideas of the proletariat and the bourgeoisie.

When the campaign to combine education with productive

labor began, those people who insisted on the bourgeois stand and viewpoint brought forward all kinds of data to attack the educational guideline of the Party. Some individual students who came from families of the exploiting class and who firmly adhered to their class stand openly voiced their resistance to the educational guideline of the Party. They firmly adhered to the reactionary viewpoint, professing that "all walks of life are lowly, and only scholars are highly placed." They asserted that the only task of the students was to study and were opposed to their participation in labor. They attempted in substance to preserve forever the difference between mental labor and physical labor and the peculiar status of the bourgeois intellectuals. They were fundamentally opposed to the idea of requiring the intellectuals to take up manual work and of making manual workers of the intellectuals. Under the leadership of the Party, the broad masses of the teachers and students criticized this stand and viewpoint. By way of criticism, they further raised their own Socialist consciousness and marched on with even greater resolution.

When the teachers and students went to the factories and the countryside to participate in labor training, and large numbers of factories and farms were set up by the schools, some bourgeois educators again raised what they described as the "question of quality" and asserted that "the participation of the students in labor would lower the quality of teaching." This was because they thought only book knowledge was knowledge, while experience in practice was not knowledge. They did not understand that the participation of the students in production struggle and their practice of the class struggle were an important form of study and that if a person possessed only intellectual knowledge from books and did not integrate it with sensory knowledge gained in practice, he could not get knowledge which was genuinely complete. There are facts to prove that the participation of the students in productive labor would not lower the quality of teaching but would raise it greatly, provided such labor were satisfactorily coördinated and arranged.

There were some other people who said that, since they always advocated "working one's way through the middle school" and "working and studying half time," it seemed there was nothing new in regard to the combination of education with productive labor. These speakers were in actuality bourgeois pragmatists, whose educational ideas had long ago been criticized. Because they neglected the functions of theories and did not interpert "life" as a class struggle and production struggle in practice, they actually favored the abrogation of education and were therefore antagonistic to the educational guideline of the Party.

There were also some people who once thought that "'labor is study" and book-reading was of no importance. The Party opportunely pointed out and rectified the one-sided character of this idea. Labor can, of course, give us knowledge which cannot be learned in the classroom, but the possession of sensory knowledge is not enough, for it must be combined with book knowledge and intellectual knowledge.

As was pointed out by Lenin, "One must enrich one's brain with the entire mine of information created by mankind before one can become a Communist." The educational guideline of the Party requires the students to learn knowledge from books satisfactorily and to play an appropriate part in production struggle and class struggle in practice. The students must read books and do manual labor, and the two things must be satisfactorily combined. It is wrong for them to read books alone without doing manual labor or to do manual labor without reading books. There is no possibility to carry out this guideline unless imposing mass campaigns are launching to break up the bonds of custom and influences and to replace old things with new things.

Some people leveled attacks against the revolutionary campaign of the masses by saying: "The schools are in such a state of confusion that there is no order to speak of." This was but another distortion of the revolutionary mass campaigns customarily made by the bourgeoisie. Speaking of order, the difference between us and the bourgeoisie does not lie in whether order is wanted but in what kind of order is wanted and how to establish such a kind of order. As is the case with the educational enterprise of the exploiting class, which has a school order compatible with its educational object and guideline, the educational enterprise of the proletariat also needs a school order which conforms to its educational object and guideline. Such an order can only be created with mass campaigns which destroy old things to give place to new things. With the creative experiences of the masses summed up, the Party and the government have laid down general provisions pertaining to the carrying-out of teaching and productive labor in schools and the way of life for students. A new school order fit for the implementation of the educational guideline of the Party has now been established.

. . . .

The leadership of the Party in educational work owes its establishment and consolidation to the gradual conquest of the bourgeois ideology by the proletarian ideology in education. Since 1958, for the sake of strengthening their leadership in educational work, the Party Central Committee and the Party committees at different levels have adopted a series of measures. Conferences were convened periodically to discuss educational work, to publicize the educational guideline of the Party over and over again, to check with thoroughness the condition of the implementation of the guideline, to sum up the experiences, and to solve in good time problems of all kinds encountered in the great educational revolution and the great leap forward. The placing of secretaries in command and the establishment of schools by the whole people were carried out. Large numbers of leaders with long experience in the revolutionary struggle were sent to take up leadership work in schools at different levels. School committees were entrusted with the responsibility of running institutions of higher education under the leadership of the Party committees attached to these institutions. Leadership in political and ideological work, teaching work, and scientific research work was strengthened to insure that the guideline and policy of the Party were implemented and that a great victory would be won in the great educational revolution.

At present, under the illumination of the general line of the Party for the building of socialism, our country is in the course of carrying on with the leap forward on the strength of the great leap forward made last year. The people's communes have stepped onto the road of consolidation and development and are taking another step forward to make their prestige and power felt. In response to the great call for the fulfillment of the principal targets for the second Five-Year Plan three years ahead of schedule, which was put forward by the Eighth Plenum of the Eighth Chinese Communist Party Central Committee, the creative power of our people is being put together into a broad current which is on its way to a new victory, sweeping away all the obstacles in the way. All our educational workers must study the resolution of the Eighth Plenum of the Eighth Chinese Communist Party Central Committee and other relevant documents, examine and overcome all kinds of rightist thoughts and sentiments, and oppose rightist opportunism. They must raise their political consciousness, unify their understanding, strengthen their solidarity, exert their revolutionary efforts to the utmost, and fight resolutely for the implementation of the general line of the Party.

After ten years of revolution, thanks to the great victories won in the great educational revolution and the great leap forward in 1958 in particular, our educational enterprise has acquired plenty of experience. Under the firm leadership of the Party, all educational workers in China examine and overcome the rightist thoughts in educational work, exert even greater efforts, and carry out their work even more satisfactorily. The areas which have accomplished the task of wiping out illiteracy and universalizing primary and junior middle school education must pay attention to consolidating their position, raising the quality of their work, and working earnestly for the successful operation of a number of key schools.

Simultaneously with raising the quality of their teaching work, the full-day schools must not be slack with productive labor. Institutions of higher education should actively carry out scientific research work. In coördination with the situation marked by the continuance of the leap forward in the national economy, the campaign to wipe out illiteracy must be actively carried out, and spare-time schools for workers and peasants must be successfully run and developed.

We must sum up our experiences unceasingly in practice, overcome the shortcomings and obstacles of all kinds found in work, carry on with the leap forward, and consolidate and develop the educational revolution. We must strive to accomplish the task of carrying out the cultural revolution, universalizing education, and fostering ten million red and vocationally proficient intellectuals for the working class at an earlier date. We must work for the fundamental transformation of the "poor and blank" aspect of China to enable our country "to emerge as a nation with a high standard of culture in the world."

Source: *Current Background,* No. 608 (Hong Kong: United States Consulate General, January 8, 1960). Originally published in *Jen Min Jih Pao* [People's Daily], October 8, 1959.

For a different set of enrollment figures and goals of education between 1957 and 1959, see Yang Hsiu-feng, "Educational Work Achievements in 1958 and Arrangements for 1959," pp. 301–307 in this collection.

Constitution of the All-China Federation of Students
February 1960

GENERAL PRINCIPLES

Article 1. This association is named the All-China Federation of Students.

Article 2. The tasks of this federation are: under the leadership of the Chinese Communist Party, to unite the students throughout the country in enthusiastic response to Chairman Mao's call "to have good health, to study well, and to work properly"; thoroughly to implement the Party's policies of "letting education serve the political interests of the proletariat," and "combining education with productive labor"; to make efforts to cultivate ourselves to be both red and expert intellectuals of the working class, so as to struggle to build China into a great and strong Socialist country with highly developed modern industry, modern agriculture, and modern science and culture; to strengthen the unity with the students of Socialist countries; to develop friendship and coöperation with students of various countries; to support the struggle against imperialism and colonialism, so as to exert efforts for the cause of bringing about a lasting peace and the progress of mankind.

Article 3. This federation joins the All-China Federation of Youths as a group member.

MEMBERSHIP

Article 4. Those students' associations of higher educational institutions which agree to the constitution of this federation may join this federation as members.

Article 5. The rights and the duties of members are:

(1) The right to discuss, to make suggestions, and to criticize the work of this federation.

(2) The right to vote and stand for election.

(3) The duties to abide by the constitution of the federation, to carry out the decisions of the federation, and to pay membership dues.

ORGANIZATION, FUNCTIONS, AND POWERS

Article 6. The principle of the organization of the federation is democratic centralization.

Article 7. The National Committee is the highest organ of authority of this federation. The National Committee is formed through election and by consultation among the member associations. The members of the National Committee are elected for a term of four years. Member associations may withdraw and change their own representatives to the National Committee whenever they deem this necessary.

Article 8. The National Committee shall elect one member as the chairman and a certain number of members as vice-chairmen to form a presidium. When the National Committee is not in session, the presidium is responsible for conducting the affairs of the federation.

Article 9. The National Committee exercises the following functions and powers:

(1) To hear and examine the work report of the presidium.

(2) To discuss and decide the work and tasks of the federation.

(3) To revise the constitution of the federation.

(4) To elect the chairman and vice-chairmen of the National Committee.

STUDENTS' ASSOCIATIONS OF HIGHER EDUCATIONAL INSTITUTIONS AND MUNICIPAL FEDERATIONS OF STUDENTS

Article 10. The tasks of the students' associations of higher educational institutions are, under the leadership of the Party and with the assistance of the Young Communist League; to urge fellow students continuously to raise their Communist consciousness, to study hard, and to organize fellow students to take part in social and political activities, productive labor, scientific research, and cultural and athletic activities. Any student now studying in school may be a member of a students' association, irrespective of nationality, sex, or religious belief. The representative meeting of all students in a school (or the general meeting of all students in a school) examines and decides on the work of the students' association and elects a students' committee. The students' committee is composed of a chairman and a certain number of vice-chairmen to be responsible for the daily work.

Article 11. In the municipalities where there are comparatively many higher educational institutions, member associations of this federation may form a municipal federation of students; that is, a joint council of the chairmen of students' associations of higher educational institutions of the whole municipality. Its functions and duties are to assist the students' associations of various schools in carrying out their work and to conduct activities concerning the students of the municipality as a whole. A chairman and a certain number of vice-chairmen are elected by the Municipal Federation of Students to be responsible for the council and its work.

SOURCE: *Survey of China Mainland Press*, No. 2199 (Hong Kong: United States Consulate General, February 18, 1960). Originally published by *New China News Agency*, February 10, 1960.

Close Coöperation between Chinese and Soviet Scientists
By Yen Chi-ts'u
February 1960

Yen Chi-ts'u, the Director of the Technical Science Department of the Academia Sinica, outlines the influences of the Soviet Union in Chinese scientific research. An exchange of personnel between the two countries had been effected during the decade, and Russia's contribution in planning a twelve-year program for scientific research in China was believed to have been of great significance. The estrangement in political relations between China and Russia was soon, however, to negate much of the good will and reduce scientific coöperation between the two countries. The strained relations were reflected in the gradual absence after 1961 of such speeches as the one below.

At the beginning of 1960, our people, with a bright, brave future, are excitedly and cheerfully celebrating the great tenth anniversary of the Sino-Soviet Treaty of Friendship, Alliance, and Mutual Assistance.

The conclusion of this treaty of great historical and international significance has, in the last ten years, played a great role in bringing about the prosperity of China and the Soviet Union, in consolidating and strengthening the Socialist camp headed by the Soviet Union, and in safeguarding peace and dealing blows to imperialist aggression.

In the last ten years, the Sino-Soviet friendly coöperation in science and technology, as in the fields of defense, industrial and agricultural construction, culture, education, public health, and

344

art, has always developed perfectly in an atmosphere of fraternal harmony. At the beginning of liberation, we realized the importance of science and technology in national construction, but our scientific inheritance from the old days is the weakest of all departments of cultural construction. We are very fortunate to have the advanced scientific and technical achievements of the Soviet Union, our great ally, as our example. As early as the beginning of 1953, the Chinese Academy of Sciences sent a delegation, headed by Comrade Ch'ien San-ch'iang, to visit the Soviet Union to find out about and learn from the Soviet advanced experience in scientific work.

Since the signing of the Sino-Soviet Agreement on Scientific and Technical Coöperation in October 1954, this coöperation has developed rapidly, both in scale and in form. In June 1955, a delegation of the Soviet Academy of Sciences, headed by its Vice-President, I. P. Bardin, attended the meeting on the founding of various departments of the Chinese Academy of Sciences. In 1956, the Soviet Union sent a great number of remarkable scientists to help China to draw up a twelve-year program for scientific and technical development.

In the last few years, the Soviet Union has continually sent experts to help our country to carry out Socialist construction and many excellent scientists to give lectures to us and take part in and guide our research work and supply us with scientific data and instruments which could hardly be obtained elsewhere. Many Soviet scientists have accepted our students and research personnel to help China to train cadres. They have also warmly received and sincerely guided Chinese scientists visiting the Soviet Union. Through all this assistance, a foundation has been laid for the development of certain branches of science which were untouched previously, the departments which were formerly short of qualified personnel have gradually formed an army of experts, and those branches of science which were previously developed to some extent have made remarkable progress. All these achievements constitute the crystallization of the profound friendship and common efforts of Chinese and Soviet scientists. Without doubt, Sino-Soviet scientific and technical coöperation has been playing an extremely important role in quickly changing our scientific and technical backward appearance.

It should be pointed out that the Soviet Union has helped our country to conduct research work on peaceful uses of atomic energy, especially to build the first atomic reactor and cyclotron. The latest achievements of modern science such as semiconductors and electronic calculating machines have also been adopted in our country with Soviet assistance.

For the purpose of further strengthening all-round Sino-Soviet coöperation in carrying out scientific research work, our government sent, in October 1957, a scientific and technical delegation to the Soviet Union, headed by Kuo Mo-jo, President of the Chinese Academy of Sciences, to enter into negotiations and signed, on January 18, 1958, an agreement with the Soviet Union, providing for major scientific and technical research projects to be undertaken by the two countries jointly or by China with Soviet assistance. Through the signing of this agreement, the governments of the two countries arranged important research subjects for a five-year period of Sino-Soviet scientific coöperation. At the same time, Chinese and Soviet Academies of Sciences, Ministries of Higher Education, and Institutes of Agricultural Science, respectively, signed compacts on coöperation to ensure the fulfillment of the significant tasks specified in the agreement signed by the two governments. This has also exerted a far-reaching influence on the rapid development of science and technology in our country.

In May 1959, a delegation of the Soviet Academy of Sciences headed by its President, Alexander Nesmeyanov, visited China and signed the 1959 plan for coöperation between the Chinese and Soviet Academies of Sciences. This has greatly encouraged Chinese scientific workers to bring about a bigger, better, and more all-round leap forward in our scientific research and further developed the friendly activities and creative spirit of the two academies.

Through our close contacts with Soviet scientists, their noble communism, their habits of enduring hardships, living a plain life, and studying persistently have given every one of us a very deep impression and a great lesson. We firmly remember the Party's instruction on resolutely learning from the Soviet Union. This is one of the fundamental policies for developing our scientific undertakings and also an important duty of our scientific workers. We should not only study Soviet science and technology but also learn from the Soviet people's excellent qualities.

Of the Soviet Seven Year Plan, which marks the Soviet Union's entrance into the new era of building a Communist society, the first year's program has been victoriously overfulfilled. In man's struggle for conquering space, the Soviet Union has taken the lead and achieved more brilliant and surprising successes every year. In the field of science and technology, the East Wind is also continuing to prevail over the West Wind. Under the brilliant light of the general line, the Chinese people fulfilled in 1959 the second Five Year Plan (i.e., three years ahead of schedule) and are developing Socialist construction at continued high speed. We believe that our scientific undertakings led by the great Chinese Communist Party will also attain remarkable results. The Chinese people will, together with the Soviet people, struggle to the end for the strengthening of the forces and unity of the Socialist camp headed by the Soviet Union and for the complete victory of world peace and the cause of socialism.

SOURCE: *Survey of China Mainland Press,* No. 2233 (Hong Kong: United States Consulate General, April 7, 1960). Originally published in *Jen Min Jih Pao* [People's Daily], February 13, 1960.

For additional readings, see Kuo Mo-jo, "Soviet Scientific Help to China," *People's China,* No. 15 (August 1, 1956), pp. 8–11; and "Tenth Anniversary of the Signing of the Sino-Soviet Treaty of Friendship, Alliance, and Mutual Assistance," *Current Background,* No. 613 (Hong Kong: United States Consulate General, 1960).

Extend the Work of the Young Communist League
to the Spare-Time Universities
March 1960

The slogans, "great leap forward," "combine education and labor," and "walking with two legs," are all exemplified in this editorial exhorting young Communist activists to push back the frontiers of higher education in China. The concept of "regular" universities, in the Western sense, has been blurred, and out of fourteen hundred "higher institutes," possibly two hundred remain as "hard-core, regular" institutions. The realization that the traditional pattern of higher education would be unable to promote China's industrial progress has been more than apparent since 1958. The regime's solution was to "decentralize initiative" and encourage local governments to establish their own institutions, particularly those of a part-time nature. To popularize this plan, the Young Communist League, numbering some twenty-five million youths, has been called in to provide student leadership and maintain the impetus of the drive to produce masses of "trained and ideologically reliable" graduates required for the "advance to socialism."

A wave of enthusiasm is sweeping across the country. The factories and mines in all areas are carrying out work on a big scale for opening workers' sparetime universities. The opening of these universities, which is intended to speed up the training of a technological force for our modern industry, has been a new feature of the workers' spare-time education movement in our country since the beginning of this year.

. . . .

Our Party and Chairman Mao have always attached extreme

348

importance to the education of the laboring people and have always regarded the development of spare-time education as an important task in the cultural revolution of our country and as an important method for training an army of "red and expert" technicians needed in the high-speed building of socialism. Precisely because of this, brilliant successes were achieved in the education of the workers of our country during the past ten years, especially during the big leaps forward.

Recently, the Central Committee of the Chinese Communist Party and the State Council have further decided to establish a spare-time education committee for the express purpose of guiding spare-time education work. Besides, while it has been decided that the existing illiteracy should be wiped out, the opening of large numbers of spare-time universities and secondary technical schools has been made an important program. Things will happen in exactly the same way as is pointed out in the "Notification on Establishment of a Spare-Time Education Committee" of the Central Committee of the Chinese Communist Party and the State Council when it states:

> Several hundred million young and grown-up laboring people (including cadres) will, through spare-time education, gradually raise their political, technological, and cultural levels. There is a great need for the development of spare-time higher education and secondary technical education, and this need will continue to exist for a long time even after the universalization of secondary education, when it will be organized on a still bigger scale.

Never before in the history of our country has there appeared such a situation as that which has appeared today, when thousands and tens of thousands of workers are receiving university educations, and it is precisely under the affectionate care of the Party that such a situation has now been reached.

. . . .

Young Communist League organizations have an important share of the responsibility for opening large numbers of workers' spare-time universities. The League organizations at all the various levels must take stock of the situation, make up their minds to support and promote new things, help the Party actively and on their own initiative, and make a good job of the opening of workers' spare-time universities with regard to the concrete conditions present. The League organizations should educate and encourage the young workers at large to go to a university if they are qualified to do so. As for those who cannot go to a university yet, they should be urged to raise their cultural level quickly and create conditions actively for going to a university.

While helping the Party to open workers' spare-time universities, the League organizations should fully recognize the conditions for the opening of these universities and should look for latent potential that may be exploited in the opening of same. The leadership of the Party is the basic guarantee of success in opening spare-time universities. The ambition of the workers at large to change their "poor and blank" state is a positive factor in the opening of spare-time universities. Apart from this, it should be realized that a large number of university and technical school graduates are working in the factories and mining enterprises, and they will constitute an important source of teachers in the opening of large numbers of spare-time universities. With so many technical cadres, there is no fear that it may be impossible to open spare-time universities. Besides, over the past few years, many of the factories and mines have accumulated rich experience in the opening of spare-time universities. We should therefore say that all the necessary conditions are present for the successful opening of spare-time universities.

Some League cadres feel that "if universities are to be opened at all, they should be opened after the elimination of illiteracy and the universalization of secondary education." Such a view is incorrect. In the factories and mining enterprises, the cultural level varies a great deal from worker to worker. Some workers need to cease to be illiterate, while others need to receive higher or secondary education. It is thus necessary to educate the workers in accordance with their differing cultural levels. In this way, those who should receive higher education will not have to wait, meanwhile spending their spare time in doing nothing. In a number of big modern enterprises, where more young people are working and where the general cultural level is comparatively high, it is all the more necessary to carry out active work for opening spare-time universities or secondary technical schools. Since the commencement of the great leaps forward in 1958, many of the factories and mines have instituted integral systems of education consisting of anti-illiteracy classes at one end and spare-time universities at the other end, as required by different workers with different cultural levels. The institution of these systems is a very good thing where the raising of the scientific and cultural levels of youth is concerned. The League organizations should turn the favorable conditions to account and organize youths with different cultural levels to join different types of spare-time schools.

Some other League cadres argue that "the complicated work of opening universities is under the leadership of the Party and is the business of the trade unions, so there is no occasion for the League to intervene and no point at which it may apply its force." Such a view is also incorrect. Unlike anti-illiteracy work, the work of opening universities is rather complicated. But the League is the natural assistant of the Party in cultural revolution. Now that the Party wants to open large numbers of workers' spare-time universities, the work of the League should be adapted to suit the new situation, should be studied well, and should be carried out satisfactorily. To think that the work is complicated, to fear difficulties, and to refrain from taking part in the work, using the excuse that there is no occasion for one to intervene, are actions which betray that one is looking at the world like a lazy man or a coward. These actions should be given up without hesitation. The tasks of the League in opening large numbers of workers' spare-time universities are certainly worthwhile doing. We must fully promote our organizational role and extend our work to the spare-time universities. As most of the workers studying in spare-time universities are youths, it has become an important task for the League to teach them to form big ambitions and to scale the peaks. Lessons in a spare-time university are more difficult than those in a middle school; the young workers will come across a great number of difficulties while studying in spare-time universities. It should be the duty of the League organizations to encourage and educate them to recognize the situation and their own tasks clearly to study hard and perseveringly and to make up their mind to become "red and expert" intellectuals of the working classes. At the same time, the Young Communist League is also charged with a share in the work concerning the teachers in the spare-time universities. Most of these teachers are young intellectuals graduated from universities and technical schools. Unless they actively and enthusiastically teach and learn, the spare-time universities will not be consolidated easily. Hence, the League organizations should make them realize that, as young intellectuals and technicians in the factories and mining enterprises, they should "combine two duties in one person," that is, they should be engineers and technicians on the one hand and professors and teachers on the other and should make a good job of technical work and management on the one hand and make a good job of the education of the workers on the other. In addition, the League organizations should also assist the Party in drawing up timetables for studies and actively mobilizing the young teachers and students to take part in the reform of teaching and learning.

In short, the Young Communist League has to carry out a great many tasks in the spare-time universities. The League cadres in every factory and mining enterprise must make up their minds to extend their work to the spare-time university of that factory or mining enterprise and must, under the leadership of the Party and by practicing all-out cooperation with the various quarters, make a good job of the running of that spare-time university.

SOURCE: *Survey of China Mainland Press,* No. 2260 (Hong Kong: United States Consulate General, May 18, 1960). Originally published in *Chung-Kuo Ch'ing-Nien Pao,* March 5, 1960.

For additional readings, see "Third National Congress of Youth League," *Current Background,* Nos. 453, 454, 455, and 456 (Hong Kong: United States Consulate General, 1957); and "Communist Education for the Chinese Youth: Chinese Youth March Ahead under the Banner of the Party and Mao Tse-tung," *Current Background,* No. 600 (1959).

Problems Regarding the Education of Returned Overseas Students

By Ch'en Hsu-ching
April 1960

Some fourteen million Chinese live in Southeast Asia, and both the Nationalist Government in Taiwan and the Communist regime have made strenuous efforts vying with each other for their support. High school and college students were offered substantial inducements by the Communists if they would return to mainland China for their higher education.

The Overseas Chinese Affairs Commission was established by the Communist regime under the State Council to encourage political and cultural ties with Chinese communities in countries such as Indonesia, the Philippines, Burma, and Malaysia. The Ministry of Education was responsible for arranging transportation and living facilities as well as the special entrance regulations available to "returning students." Preparatory institutions were also established to overcome language, academic, and ideological problems of the overseas students. Communist educational authorities, however, have encountered a variety of difficulties in administering special programs for Chinese "foreign" students.

In spite of relatively generous provisions in facilities and finances, many "overseas" students have returned home disillusioned with life under communism. Countless others, however, have completed their studies satisfactorily and are now "cultural agents" for the Communist regime throughout southeast Asia. This speech by Ch'en Hsu-ching, a member of the Third National Committee of the Chinese People's Political Consultative Council, reflects the concerns and problems as well as the successes and goals of the government in this, a critical but far-reaching international educational enterprise.

353

THE OUTSTANDING ACHIEVEMENTS OF THE MOTHER
COUNTRY ENCOURAGE THE OVERSEAS CHINESE

To the overseas Chinese, these outstanding achievements are all the more encouraging. We know that the overseas Chinese in Southeast Asia have always been suffering from various oppressions and exploitations of the imperialists. Under the rules of feudal kingdoms and reactionary parties, they have become overseas orphans. Now the mother country is getting stronger and stronger; its constructive undertakings keep leaping forward. This provides great prospects for the overseas Chinese residents and students who have come back to work and to study; thus, there are more and more overseas Chinese who return to join in the Socialist construction. In particular, the number of overseas Chinese students who come back to study has been ever increasing. The Party and the People's government, in addition to establishing a number of supplementary schools for overseas Chinese students in Peking, Canton, and Amoy, have set up some universities, secondary schools, and elementary schools, such as the Chi Nan University in Canton and the overseas Chinese middle schools and primary schools in the various districts in Kwangtung Province, to absorb mainly overseas Chinese youth, making it possible for the large number of returned overseas Chinese students not only to attend schools immediately after their return but also to receive adequate and thorough care.

Recently, there arose in some Southeast Asian countries an adverse anti-Chinese current, owing to the instigation on the part of a few of the reactionaries and imperialists, particularly the American imperialists. For the last few months, this adverse current has been developing in Indonesia, so the number of returned overseas Chinese residents and students is very large. The problem of educating the returned overseas students, therefore, has become a special one which requires urgent solution. I would like to report to you, my fellow committee members, some of the situations and problems as I understand them.

It should be pointed out first that the Party and the People's Government are very much concerned with the problem of providing further education for the returned overseas students. Branches of the Overseas Chinese Affairs Commission in the various parts of the country and the personnel who are responsible for receiving and taking care of the returned overseas Chinese have done their practical work very well. I recalled, during the rule of the Peiyang warlords and of the Kuomintang, how difficult it was for the overseas Chinese students like myself to return to the country for further education. The parents were worried when their children came back to the mother country to study since they had to go over the seas; what worried them most was that, under the rule of the reactionary government, the maintenance of public peace and order was poor. After the return, it was not easy to enter a school. What was worse was this: they might be cheated or even kidnapped. Besides, many schools were not properly run; when the students had entered school, they not only learned very little but might even run wild.

Today, we have not only many universities and secondary and primary schools to accommodate them but also many ships to take them back from Southeast Asia. This is something which the overseas Chinese students of twenty or thirty years ago could not possibly imagine. In Canton, I took part in several welcome parties for the overseas Chinese students. Many of them felt the warmth of their mother country the moment they stepped on board the ships which had been sent for them. The food for the three daily meals had been transported from the mother country; when they became sick, there were our own doctors on board to take care of them; when they felt cold, cotton underwear and cotton clothes were provided for them. Within a week after their return, the returned overseas Chinese students by hundreds and by thousands had their accommodations, in accordance with their wishes, distributed among schools in Peking, Canton, and Amoy. In school not only were they taken care of with full attention by their teachers and fellow students with regard to their studies but subsidies were given to those of them who were in financial difficulties. One returned overseas student said that the Party was more considerate and kinder to the returned overseas Chinese students than their own parents.

SEVERAL NOTABLE PROBLEMS CONCERNING FURTHER
EDUCATION FOR RETURNED OVERSEAS CHINESE STUDENTS
IN THE COUNTRY

But it is not utterly without problems for the overseas Chinese
students to come back to the country to study. This can be discussed in three respects: the ways of life, the study of cultural
activities, and the study of politics.

First of all, we must point out that, to the returned overseas
Chinese students, the study of politics is extremely important.
They were born and brought up abroad; they hate very much
the imperialists for their oppression and exploitation of the
peoples of Southeast Asia and the overseas Chinese there. After
their return, since they have long been under the influence of
bourgeois and imperialist thoughts and cultures, they do not understand enough of or have even misunderstood the Party's educational principle of integrating education and productive labor
when they returned to the mother country, which had been
liberated for ten years and which had undergone tremendous
changes. Thus, their ideological education appears to be of particular importance. In the past, the schools for overseas Chinese
students had done a great deal in this respect. Now, the number
of returned overseas Chinese students is increasingly larger and,
since a good many of them were forced to return by the reactionaries abroad, their patriotic sentiments have been greatly stimulated and will promote the solidarity of the overseas Chinese residents and overseas Chinese students. This is a favorable factor in
strengthening their ideological education. I believe that, besides
major and minor political reports, we should pay particular attention to the ideological problems of individual overseas Chinese
students.

With regard to the study activities of cultural activities, problems are comparatively more numerous and more complicated.
We all know that, before the Second World War, the countries
in Southeast Asia were all oppressed by colonialists. The colonialists had always been indifferent to the education of their enslaved
people. When they did run some schools, their only purpose was

to serve the colonialists; it was pure slave education. In the schools they ran, a good many subjects, such as mathematics, physics, and chemistry, were not taught; even when there were taught such subjects, they were only names without meaning or reality. Their purpose was simply to foster low-ranking government officials, or translators, or slaves for foreigners—compradors of import-and-export firms. This and the present education of our mother country are entirely two different lines of education.

As for the schools established by the overseas Chinese themselves, they were greatly restricted. For instance, there began in Thailand thirty years ago various restrictions on Chinese schools. Originally, the Chinese schools used Chinese as the medium of instruction; but gradually restrictions were imposed on them; the Chinese language was taken to be a foreign language and could be taught only five or six hours a week. Teachers were banned from going from China to Thailand. Not only were there no higher Chinese institutions run by overseas Chinese (the Nan Yang University in Singapore was not established until 1950) but even the local governments seldom established higher institutions of learning of their own. There was, therefore, a great shortage of trained teachers. There were many schools employing middle school graduates to teach middle schools. As a result, the level of the students' cultural activities was comparatively low. After returning to the country, these overseas Chinese students would enter supplementary schools; if the period of their making-up course is too short, their foundation can hardly be consolidated; but, if the period of their supplementary course is too long, it may easily make them lose their confidence in their studies.

As to those overseas Chinese students who have learned only foreign languages and are utterly ignorant of Chinese, their problems are more complicated. For instance, some of them have graduated from foreign secondary schools. After they returned to the mother country, they have to study Chinese as beginners, since they are utterly ignorant of the language. This means that they have to start from a primary class or its equivalent. Although they may make every effort to finish both primary and secondary courses within a short time. the twelve-year course (six years of primary course and six years of secondary course) cannot be crammed for completion within two or three years. If the supplementary course runs too long, they easily become overaged students. For instance, if these students learned English originally, are they to be put into the English department of a university? If they originally studied the languages of the various countries of Southeast Asia, are they to be put into the department like the Department of Eastern Languages of Peking University? Whether we should decrease some of their requirements in the university so that they may have more time to study Chinese is a problem worthy of consideration.

Since the various countries of Southeast Asia are in the tropical zone, their daily life is greatly different from that in the interior and particularly the northern part of the country. That they have to bathe thrice a day in Southeast Asia is an example. Although this is a trivial matter in our daily life, it is still a problem to those overseas Chinese students who have just come from the tropic region. These overseas Chinese students who were born or grew up in Southeast Asia seldom or never before came back to the mother country; meanwhile, they who had long been under the influence of bourgeois education and culture, after they returned to the country, feel on the one hand the warmth of the mother country and the infinite kindness and consideration with which the Party and the People's government treat them and on the other feel that the modes of living inside the country are greatly different from those they experienced in Southeast Asia. How to make them adapt themselves to this new society and new life is also a problem worthy of notice.

It should be pointed out that some of the above-mentioned problems, though worthy of attention, are not difficult to solve. I remember, for instance, that last year some returned overseas Chinese students were greatly perturbed in their thinking when they learned that they had to practice labor in the countryside. They said: "We return to the mother country to study, but we do not come back to become 'porters.'" After an explanation of the Party's educational principles by their school authorities, teachers, and fellow students, they not only are willing to work but work energetically. In laboring work there are not a few active elements among the returned students. In studying, there are many who improve quickly. In recent years, the percentage of successful returned students who took part in the entrance examinations of higher institutions of learning was also very high. Therefore, if only the work of their ideological education goes well, they would change quickly and improve quickly.

In short, the returned overseas Chinese residents and students are welcomed by the whole nation, particularly at the time when the great Socialist construction of the mother country is developing in leaps and bounds and when it needs more manpower and more technicians. The more overseas Chinese residents who come back to work and the more overseas Chinese students who come back to study, the better it would be. Although we mentioned above some problems concerning education of the returned overseas students, yet if only their ideological education goes well and politics commands everything, the problems existing in their study of activities and modes of life would be solved easily. We thus believe that this young generation returned to the mother country from overseas would surely in the near future make outstanding achievements on the front of the great Socialist construction.

SOURCE: *Current Background,* No. 627 (Hong Kong: United States Consulate General, July 18, 1960). Originally published in *Jen Min Jih Pao* [People's Daily], April 8, 1960.

The Great Significance of the Operation of Schools by Factories
By T'ao Lu-chia
June 1960

This speech by T'ao Lu-chia, First Secretary of the Chinese Communist Party Shansi Provincial Committee, reflects the regime's awareness of certain criticisms of its program to combine "education with productive labor." In 1958, nationwide plans were put into effect, so that a greater percentage of the students' time would be spent on practical and applied studies. The corollary of this design was for industrial units and factories to establish their own educational systems, which in some cases extended from literacy classes to "university courses." The diffusion of "higher education goals" has thrown the burden of establishing "teaching institutions" onto local authorities as well as on the government departments such as those of "industry, agriculture, forestry, water conservation, building communications, transport, finance, and trade."

Whether or not our industrial and mining enterprises can set up spare-time schools and schools providing employment and study simultaneously and whether or not these schools can foster the good quality of the intellectuals of the working class are matters of importance which the high-speed development of Socialist construction has placed before us.

The establishment of schools by factories is no news to us. Since the liberation, many of the industrial and mining enterprises have set up full-time primary schools for the children of their workers, schools for the elimination of illiteracy among the

360

workers themselves, and technical schools and secondary technical schools providing employment and study simultaneously. But this concept of factories operating schools has gone beyond its old narrow confines and has developed into one where factories serve simultaneously as schools. While producing goods, the factories are fostering men of the Communist order, and this new concept has been prevalent since the great leap forward in 1958. Since then, many of the industrial and mining enterprises have not only been able to set up many spare-time primary schools and secondary schools but have also established many spare-time institutions of higher education and schools providing work and study simultaneously (in the case of big factories, they usually have one school each, and in the case of small schools, they have established joint schools). Some of the large industrial and mining enterprises are able to set up gradually an educational system from full-time primary school to college. At the same time, the Chinhsi Machine Works in Taiyuan and many other advanced factories have reported that it will be entirely possible for the spare-time schools and the schools providing work and study simultaneously to train large numbers of intellectuals of the working class. It is clear, therefore, that the establishment of schools by factories has entered into a new stage of development. In other words, it has become an important component of the cultural revolution that is going on in our country. Obviously, it is a natural tendency for all industrial and mining enterprises to improve the quality of the schools they have set up, especially the spare-time schools that have been established primarily for their workers.

. . . .

Daring efforts have been made in the reform of the school system, lessons, teaching materials, and methods of teaching by the full implementation of the spirit of uninterrupted revolution, the work method of the mass line, and the policy of achieving greater, better, faster, and more economical results. As a result, the factory has found the road towards greater, better, faster, and more economical results. Of course, efforts will have to be continued to achieve perfection. But the conspicuous results that have been achieved in the reforms deal a heavy blow to the section of people

who advocate the operation of schools by factories in a manner
that will produce smaller, worse, slower, and less economical results. The factory has also adopted revolutionary methods in the
solution of the shortage of teachers. In this connection, it has,
aside from employing a number of competent teachers, chosen
from among the workers those who are qualified to teach.

.   .   .   .

It must be pointed out that there are still some persons who are
skeptical of the wisdom of factories operating schools. The trouble
with them is that they do not quite understand the significance
and necessity of carrying out the educational reform. Just what
significance does the educational reform have? In view of the
above facts, it is necessary to state the following points:

(1) The educational reform is the foundation for accelerating
the development of the technical revolution and the constant raising of quality and is also one of the indispensable conditions for
the realization of the continued leap forward in Socialist construction. Industrial and mining enterprises under socialism must
not only turn out the needed products but also foster new persons
of communism. The quality of man directly influences the quality
of products. Thus only when the Communist consciousness and
scientific and cultural levels of the people are constantly raised
will it be possible to bring into being a continued leap forward
in production in the long transition from socialism to communism.

(2) Industrial and mining enterprises are the best place for
the implementation of the policy brought forward by the Central
Committee of the Chinese Communist Party for gearing education
to the needs of the proletarian class and for coördinating education with productive labor. They are the best places for the conduct of the educational revolution on the basis of that educational
policy. If all the industries and mines and even people's communes in villages and cities operate schools and steadily carry out
the educational reform, then it will be possible to bring about a
constant leap forward in the scientific and cultural and Marxist
theoretical levels of the workers. And we shall then be realizing
one of the principal missions which the Central Committee has
asked us to accomplish with greater, better, faster, and more eco-

nomical results—the mission of building up a large army of intellectuals of the proletarian order including technical cadres (the largest percentage), professors, teachers, scientists, journalists, writers, artists, and Marxist theorists.

(3) The Central Committee points out in its resolution concerning the people's communes that the elevation of Communist consciousness, the popularization and improvement of education of the whole people, and the elimination of the difference between manual labor and mental labor are the basic conditions for the transition from socialism to communism. Obviously, sole reliance on the full-time schools established by the State will not lead to the full realization of that goal. We must thoroughly carry out the policy providing for the state, the industrial and mining enterprises, and the people's communes to operate schools and for full-time schools, spare-time schools, and schools providing work and study to be simultaneously established. In other words, we must walk on two legs. We must see that there is a great future for spare-time schools and that, with the elevation of industrial and agricultural skills, the development of industrial and agricultural production, and the shortening of labor hours, the difference between spare-time schools and schools providing for work and study will be eliminated. The spare-time schools and schools providing for work and study are able to do a great deal more work in popularizing education and raising the political consciousness of the workers and peasants than the state-operated full-time schools can. Obviously, they are the only way of turning the workers and peasants into intellectuals. Without this leg in our educational enterprise, it will be impossible to raise the Communist consciousness and moral quality of the people, popularize and improve education, and eliminate the difference between manual labor and mental labor. In other words, it will not be possible to consummate the transition to communism. Of course, in our endeavor to eliminate the difference between manual labor and mental labor, we must have the regular schools operate factories and farms and have the students go regularly to people's communes and industrial and mining enterprises to work there. In this connection, it will be necessary to carry out the policy of

turning intellectuals into laborers. Increasingly successful results have been accomplished in the realization of that policy.

It is clear from the above that as fighters of the Marxist-Leninist order, we must appreciate the great significance in the operation of schools by factories, take the operation of schools by industrial and mining enterprises and people's communes as a task to be accomplished, rely on the whole Party and the whole people to set up different kinds of schools, refrain from limiting the work to a small number of departments, and carry out the educational revolution in accordance with the policy of achieving greater, better, faster, and more economical results, so that the mistake of right opportunism may be avoided.

About 110 years ago, Marx and Engels wrote into the *Communist Manifesto* the great ideal of coördinating education with material production. Lenin wrote at the end of the last century:

Without coördination between the education of the younger generation and productive labor, the ideal of the future society will be unthinkable. Neither teaching and education divorced from productive labor nor education and productive labor if they are not simultaneously carried out will lead to the attainment of the high degree of perfection required by the modern technological levels and scientific knowledge.

Is not this great ideal of Marx, Engels, and Lenin rapidly becoming a fact in our daily life under the illumination of the thought of Mao Tse-tung?

SOURCE: *Survey of China Mainland Press,* No. 2284 (Hong Kong: United States Consulate General, June 24, 1960). Originally published in *Jen Min Jih Pao* [People's Daily,] June 11, 1960.

For additional readings, see Li Fang, "New Phases in Education: Factories Run Schools," *Peking Review,* I, No. 41 (1958), 13–14; and "New Phases in Education: Schools Run by Communes," *ibid.,* No. 44 (1958), 16–17.

Let Us Be Promoters of Teaching Reform
By Yang Hsiu-feng
June 1960

Minister of Education Yang Hsiu-feng, in addressing himself to educational reform, was making his second major pronouncement on the subject in four months. He had in April endorsed a blueprint for the "new educational system" (primary and secondary) proposed by Lu Ting-yi, the Vice-Premier of the State Council and in the following statement expands on the proposals.

It is apparent by his speech that "old ideas" still persisted and that there was need to "prosecute new education vigorously." Yang delivered a polemic against "bourgeois ideas of teaching according to ability" and pinpoints the efficacy of the reforms as "an impressive revolution for the elimination of capitalism and the growth of the proletariat."

The second portion of Yang's speech deals with the necessity for increasing Party leadership, so that greater control and direction can be maintained. The proposed reforms accordingly are dependent on the successful vigilance of the Party activists, as well as the continuing extension of Party influence in schools, colleges, and universities.

The slogan to accompany the reform is perhaps indicative of intention: "In education we shall have not only what others have but what others do not have."

Here, I would like to confine myself to certain problems concerning the teaching reform.

Both the international and internal situations are very good at present. The situation on the educational front is very good, too. Under the impact of the all-round continuous forward leaps in Socialist construction, the upsurge of the ideological-reform movement, with the study of Marxism-Leninism, and the works of Mao Tse-tung as the center, and the cultural revolution, with the elimination of illiteracy and educational revolution as the center, have arrived.

As everyone knows, the old China, under the rule of imperialism and its running dog, Chiang Kai-shek, was not only an extremely poor country but also a country where the proportion of illiterates was large and culture was very backward. Now, such a position has gone forever. Under the leadership of the Party Central Committee and Chairman Mao, the Chinese people are not only transforming the physical outlook of their mother country but also changing rapidly the state of cultural backwardness inherited from the old China. Unprecedented signs of prosperity have appeared in the educational field. Throughout the country, over 300,000,000 persons are studying in schools at all levels or in kindergartens. Millions upon millions of workers and peasants are making strenuous efforts at their study and are on their way to becoming masters of science and culture in our country. The intellectuals, too, are actively taking part in productive labor, trying hard to reform their own world outlook. The broad masses of the people, guided by the Party, are treading along the road when workers and peasants will be converted into intellectuals and vice versa. We must have an ambitious scheme to change thoroughly the "poor and white" outlook, overtake Britain in production output, and overtake all capitalist countries in education.

At present, one of the important characteristics on our educational front is that the educational revolution has penetrated deep into the sphere of teaching. In spring of this year, the Party center issued an appeal for teaching reform which was warmly supported by the broad masses of the people in general and the teachers and students in particular. This shows that appeals made by the Party center are supported by the people. For the past several months, many schools in various parts of the country, under the leadership of the Party committees and the educational administrative departments, have freely mobilized the masses to undertake boldly many experiments of teaching reform. The broad masses of educational workers have exerted great efforts, liberated their thought, and actively plunged themselves into the work of teaching-reform. The results of experiments carried out in many schools show that the general demand put by the Party on the teaching-reform in middle and primary schools (namely, appropriately to reduce the age limit, appropriately to raise the academic standards, appropriately to control the duration of study, and appropriately to increase productive labor) can be met without much difficulty. Now, the various provinces and cities, in the light of their own conditions and concrete arrangements, are carrying out comparatively large experiments in teaching-reform. The mass movement for teaching-reform is being unfolded extensively throughout the country. Under the urge of the technical innovations and technical revolution and the movement for criticizing bourgeois academic thoughts and also under the influence of colleges and secondary specialized schools in the whole nation is also unfolding a teaching-reform movement. We educational workers must have a clear understanding of the new situation of this educational revolution and take the teaching-reform as our present important task of top priority.

.   .   .   .

In the sphere of education, the class struggle between the proletariat and the bourgeoisie for the right of leadership has not ended, except that the forms of the struggle have changed, the battlefield has changed, and the content of the struggle has become more penetrating. Now, the problem of teaching has become the core of the struggle.

As we are all aware, during the past ten years or more since the founding of the state, our educational work, under the leadership of the Party and through the positive efforts made by the broad masses of educational workers, has already changed the old educational system which served the politics and economy of the semifeudal and semicolonial society into a new educational system which serves Socialist revolution and Socialist construction. In particular, the great educational revolution since 1958 has served to renew completely the outlook of our educational enterprise, inducing deep changes in various respects. In the field of teaching work, we once effected a series of readjustments and reforms, and particularly with regard to social science we conducted comparatively thorough criticism of the bourgeois ideas and made brilliant achievements. However, on the whole, in the past our struggle against the bourgeoisie on the educational front was mainly the struggle concerning politics, ideology, educational lines, and policies; in the field of teaching we could only effect localized improvements such as "chopping, replacing, mending, and removing." We were not yet able to carry out the educational revolution thoroughly; we were not yet able to carry out basic revolutionary reforms of the teaching systems, content, and even methods inherited from the old society in accordance with the proletarian educational principles and the world outlook of Marxism-Leninism. Thanks to the great educational revolution since 1958, we have sufficient conditions and the necessity to carry out a basic reform of teaching right now. Our economic foundation has already undergone Socialist transformation, but the bourgeois ideology still exists in the superstructure; economic construction is being carried out with greater, faster, better, and more economical results, but the progress in educational work, in comparison, is still slow and unsatisfactory. As a result, the development and promotion of educational work cannot satisfy the needs of various aspects of Socialist construction. Not only that, but the facts prove that if we do not carry out a revolution in teaching, the bourgeois thought would necessarily retain its dominance in education. At present, the existing educational systems and many contents of teaching in our country are inherited from the old China, but the educational systems and contents of teaching of old China were taken from the capitalist countries, were the products of the capitalist social system, and were established in our country to sell these systems as a means of carrying out their cultural aggression and upbringing the proimperialist social influences. Large quantities of data that came to light in the teaching-reform show that, despite our efforts to carry out reforms continuously and our success in basically eliminating the feudal, comprador, Fascist, and imperialist ideological poisons in the old education, nevertheless some people are still disseminating bourgeois ideas through teaching. If we do not carry out teaching reforms penetratingly, it will be impossible to follow the proletarian educational policy thoroughly and to stamp out thoroughly the political and ideological influence of the bourgeoisie. Hence, the carrying-out of teaching reforms is not only for meeting the needs of Socialist economic construction but, at the same time, also for the purpose of intensifying the educational revolution and the Socialist revolution on the political and ideological fronts in the sphere of education and for the purpose of developing the struggle for the "elimination of capitalism and the growth of the proletariat."

·   ·   ·   ·   ·   ·   ·   ·   ·   ·   ·   ·   ·   ·   ·   ·

"The principle of teaching according to ability" in the educational theory of the bourgeoisie was a most important basis for the people to oppose, criticize, and doubt the teaching reform. Those who support this theory have given up completely the method of analysis, promoted the existing errors and reactionary nature of this principle, and are unmindful of the obstacle which this principle poses to the development of education under Socialist conditions. "The principle of measurement of ability" in the education of the capitalist class is right in one aspect, however, and that is that students should not be required to shoulder an excessively heavy burden, and teaching should be carried out in consideration of the capacity of the students concerned. We should pay attention to this aspect of education. But this principle is wrong and reactionary in another aspect. We know that the bourgeoisie allowed the laboring people only to receive a low education, not a high education. It allowed them only to have sufficient knowledge so that they would not spoil the machines of the capitalists; it did not allow them to have high and profound knowledge. The policy of the bourgeoisie on the education of the laboring people was to promote and retain the "smaller, slower, poorer, and more extensive results" in teaching, in order to reach their aim of protecting their capitalist exploitation system and reactionary rule. "The principle of teaching to ability" also held that "God determines everything" and that teachers could not do anything to help the students; it held that a student was purely a living being and, like any other animal or plant, had no consciousness and initiative. Therefore, such a theory of the capitalist class is essentially a theory of idealism and metaphysics; it is diametrically opposed to dialetical materialism.

Obviously, it is entirely wrong to copy this bourgeois theory and call it "Socialist" educational theory. Those who support the bourgeois "principle of teaching according to ability" often used the reasonable aspect of this principle to oppose teaching-reform. They do not understand that only on the condition of thoroughly criticizing and negating this theory is it possible to absorb the useful elements of it. They do not understand that one of the purposes of our teaching-reform is to control appropriately the period of study so that the students may not waste their time and energy on studying some backward, outdated, and useless subjects. Teaching-reform represents an impressive revolution for the "elimination of capitalism and the growth of the proletariat"; we must thoroughly criticize all reactionary theories which stand in the way of revolution and in the way of the development of education.

Another important means employed by the bourgeois educationists in opposing teaching-reform was to emphasize the peculiarity of education. They maintained that whereas the leap forward was possible in industry and agriculture, it was utterly impossible in education, that whereas production techniques could be innovated continuously, educational systems could not be altered. For this reason, they had all along vigorously opposed the revolutionary reforms of the educational system, particularly with regard to the curricular system. As we all know, when the Peking Normal University broke the system of Euclidean theorems of geometry and set up a new mathematical system on the basis of functions, combinations of figures and forms, and unity of concepts with calculation, strong opposition was voiced in some quarters. This is an example. It should be said that this is a superstition which leads one to worship the curricular system of the bourgeoisie. This viewpoint, the adherents of which thought that the content of teaching and the scientific systems were forever unalterable or thought that there should be only continuous increase in quantity but no forward leaps in quality, was a metaphysical viewpoint in contradiction to Marxism-Leninism.

. . . .

Teaching-reform is an impressive revolution. It is absolutely impossible to fulfill it without Party leadership. Strengthening of Party leadership and insisting on placing politics in command is a basic guarantee for carrying out teaching-reform successfully. Teaching-reform in all schools of all levels should be carried out without exception under the leadership of Party committees at corresponding levels, so that the work of teaching-reform can proceed entirely in accordance with the instructions of the Party. All educational workers should accept Party leadership, subordinate themselves to Party leadership, and resolutely follow the Party's policy on teaching-reform.

In the present school education, the principal battle for the struggle for the "elimination of capitalism and the establishment of the proletariat" will be fought in the field of teaching, and this demands that Party organizations and administrative leadership personnel of all schools should go deep into the teaching work. They must firmly rely on the broad masses of teachers who approve teaching-reform and support them in carrying out bold experiments and fully developing their activism and inventiveness in the course of teaching-reform. We should strive to win over those who basically support teaching-reform but who still have certain misgivings; we should help them to remove their worries, clarify their thought, and raise their understanding. We should, moreover, adopt all practical and effective means to help them to raise their professional levels, overcome the difficulties in teaching, and increase their confidence. We should arrange satisfactorily their employment, and even if changes in employment have to be made, under no circumstances should their wages be cut. Further, the living standards of the teachers should be gradually raised by increasing the collective welfare facilities. Only thus will it be possible to remove misgivings and make them dedicated to the teaching-reform movement with resolve. As regards a small number of people who are opposed to teaching-reform, we should place the facts before them, explain to them the truth, and convince them by means of education. We must employ all resources to coördinate the teachers with more experience with teachers with less experience and teachers with new experience with teachers of old experience, so that, under the leadership of the Party and the guidance of the thought of Mao Tse-tung, they can closely unite and with one will strive to make a success of teaching-reform.

. . . .

Active training and promoting of teachers is a task of vital significance. Through teaching-reform, many great or even basic changes in the curricular systems will take place; we shall have to introduce a great deal of new scientific and technical knowledge in our textbooks; and a number of subjects will have to be gradually popularized. New and higher demands will then be put on the teachers. It is for this reason that we must adopt all possible means to raise the political, cultural, and business levels of the existing teachers, in order to meet promptly the urgent needs of teaching-reform. In the course of training and promoting teachers, it is necessary to insist on putting politics in command, so as to enable the teachers to advance along the path to becoming both red and expert, as directed by the Party.

As regards the method of training, the policy of "walking on two legs" must be put into effect. Long-term training must be coördinated with short-term training. Training of teachers who remain at their posts should be coördinated with the advanced study of teachers who are away from their posts; systematic training should be combined with temporary training made necessary by emergency needs. At the moment, many places are taking steps to promote coöperation and coördination between the higher levels and the lower levels and to take up proportionate responsibility in training the existing teachers. They are building teachers' training schools which will operate full-day sessions or half-day sessions or operate on a spare-time basis. They are holding training classes at regular intervals, organizing lecturers' groups, sponsoring research classes on teaching materials, and broadly launching the activities of mutual-study and mutual-teaching. All these aim at enabling the teachers to teach and study at the same time. "When the tide rises, the boat sails." These measures are very good indeed. Through the adoption of these measures, coupled with the subjective efforts made by the teachers themselves, new academic subjects and new content and methods of teaching will definitely be mastered, and teaching will be satisfactorily performed.

. . . .

Educational administrative departments and schools are required to set up production undertakings, particularly with regard to building, equipment-manufacturing, and paper-making industries. The task of construction of schools of all levels will be very heavy in the future. If we rely solely on the capital construction departments to solve our problems, we would be beset with great difficulties with respect of materials and construction workers, and it would be hard to fulfill the task on schedule, thereby greatly affecting the development of the educational enterprises. For this reason, educational departments must positively create their own conditions to strive to produce their own building materials and have their own designers and construction workers. Educational departments and institutions of higher education must also rely on their own efforts principally to do their work, coöperate with one another, and produce their own latest teaching tools, apparatus, and equipment in large quantities, with a view to achieving self-sufficiency basically within three to five years. Because there is need for the supply of large numbers of textbooks and popular readers wanted by the broad masses of workers and peasants, the use of paper in the field of education has drastically increased during the past several years. In the future, educational administrative departments at all levels and schools which have satisfactory conditions should rely on their own efforts principally to adopt all possible methods to solve their own problems with respect to the use of paper.

It is necessary to change, gradually and by separate groups, schools which operate morning and afternoon sessions into schools of full-day sessions and then into boarding schools. At the moment, some cities, under the favorable situation brought about by the establishment of people's communes, have relied on the masses and dug up all potentialities in changing all "two-sessions" schools into schools of "one session," thereby solving the problems which remained unsolved for many years in the past.

. . . .

In order to become promoters of teaching-reform, we should establish a Marxist-Leninist attitude toward revolution; we should not be afraid of revolution but instead welcome it and on our own initiative promote it. We should have the revolutionary spirit of making inventions boldly and overcoming difficulties courageously. In educational work, we must have such a strong ambition: "We shall have what others have. We shall also have what others do not have." We should break down superstitions, liberate our thought, and coördinate the spirit of carrying out bold experiments with realistic work style, so that we can "appear in the world as a nation with a high level of culture" at an early date. We are treading along a path which was not trodden by our predecessors, and that we will encounter some difficulties in our way is to be expected. We are adequately mentally prepared for any difficulties that confront us and will not be scared by them. With the educational revolution penetrating deep into the sphere of teaching, it is unavoidable that teachers find that the things they learned in the past have become obsolete and that there are many new things which are strange to them. It is certain that they would come across temporary difficulties. However, as long as we persist in study tirelessly, it is not difficult to master all these new things, and new teaching experiences will be acquired. At present, some subjects which are added to ordinary education are not subjects which are difficult to master. Moreover, the Party and government are actively creating the necessary conditions to give the opportunity to the teachers to take up refresher courses. As long as we persist in study and research perseveringly, we believe that most of the teachers will surely be so promoted that they shall be capable of discharging their teaching responsibilities.

Comrades! We must value highly the honor which the Party and the people have conferred on us. We must forever preserve our revolutionary zeal and fully develop the Communist style of daring to think, speak, and act. Let us compete with one another in pushing the cultural revolution to new heights and struggle for the early building of our country into a prosperous and wealthy Socialist country and for the realization of our great and lofty Communist ideals.

Source: *Current Background,* No. 630 (Hong Kong: United States Consulate General, August 8, 1960). Originally published in *Jen Min Jih Pao* [People's Daily], June 15, 1960.

For additional readings, see Lu Ting-yi, "Reform in Educational Work," *Peking Review,* No. 19 (May 10, 1960), 12–20.

All-Out Effort in Cultural Revolution to Promote Education among Worker-Peasant Masses and Labor Performance by Intellectuals

By Lin Feng

June 1960

Lin Feng was a member of the Central Committee of the Chinese Communist Party and Vice-Chairman of the Standing Committee of the National People's Congress when he made this speech to the National Conference of Outstanding Groups and Individuals in Socialist Construction in the Fields of Education, Culture, Health, Physical Culture, and Journalism.

Lin analyzes the development of education and culture during the preceding decade and refers to three "principal" stages of development. The first stage (1949–1952) encompassed reconstruction and the initial reforms in education. The second phase of "postliberation history" (1953–1957) included the transition to socialism and national construction, both exemplified in the first Five-Year Plan. The third stage of development (1958–1961) was premised on "walking with two legs" and the combining of intellectual activity with physical labor.

For education the most interesting point made by Lin relates to the exhortation for wider local interest in establishing educational "units." Provincial and municipal authorities are expected to develop their own institutes of higher education, though under the "unified leadership and centralized planning" of the Central Ministries.

The National Conference of Outstanding Groups and Individuals in Socialist Construction in the Fields of Education, Culture, Health, Physical Culture, and Journalism opens today in Peking, the capital of our great fatherland. This meeting of the

376

elite on the cultural and educational front in our country has been called on an unprecedentedly large scale. Attending this conference are outstanding workers and groups from all areas of our fatherland and from all nationalities and work posts. There are workers, peasants, and people from other social strata; Communist Party members, Young Communist League members, and members of all democratic parties; young intellectuals as well as old intellectuals; and full-time cultural and educational workers as well as spare-time cultural and educational workers.

. . . .

Following the successive political campaigns and the resolute struggle continuously waged against bourgeois ideas, many old intellectuals have discarded, step by step, their former class viewpoint and changed over to the side of the proletariat. Particularly with encouragement from the situation of the great leap forward, they have come out from their own studies and narrow circles and joined the young people and the broad masses of workers and peasants in studying, working, and performing labor, thus contributing their own knowledge and talents in the enthusiastic campaign to build socialism. Just as Comrade Mao Tse-tung said:

Never before have we seen such high spirit, exuberant fighting morale, and strong resolution among the masses of people. The former exploiting classes are now completely drowned in the ocean of the working masses. They must change, even though they have no intention to change. There are, to be sure, those who will remain unchanged till their death, willing to take with them their granite brains to see their god. However, they are of no importance. All the rotten ideas and those other unsuitable parts in the superstructure are dissolving every day. While time is required to clear away completely this rubbish, nevertheless it is beyond doubt that the collapse of these things is certain.

. . . .

Tremendous development has taken place in our country in the various fields of culture and education. In the educational field, over one hundred million illiterate people have become literate. The experiences of wiping out youth illiteracy during a comparatively short period in Wanjung Hsien of Shansi Province by using alphabetic script is an important matter in our country's cultural revolution. The number of students of full-time higher learning institutes has reached more than 810,000—4.2 times that of the highest year, 1947, in old China. The number of students of full-time middle schools and intermediate vocational schools has reached 12.97 million—5.8 times that of the highest year, 1946, in old China. The attendance rate of students at middle schools and spare-time schools of various categories has also developed rapidly. Through the consolidation and development of people's communes in both rural and urban areas, nurseries and kindergartens have been developed rapidly throughout the country.

. . . .

A large and powerful column of red and expert cultural and educational workers of the working class is growing rapidly in our country. At present we have more than seven million regular and some thirty million spare-time cultural and educational workers, and a large number of progressive elements have become members of the Chinese Communist Party. All this testifies to the fact that no capitalist nation is capable of keeping abreast with our country in cultural and educational development both in scale and speed.

. . . .

During the past ten years, the development of our cultural and educational work has gone through three different stages. The Chinese People's Republic was founded in October of 1949. Since then, our country has entered into the stage of Socialist revolution. Following liberation of the entire country, we first confiscated the bureaucratic capital that occupied 80 percent of the capitalist industry and commerce throughout the country.

Between 1949 and 1952, after devoting three years of our time, we successfully completed the work of restoring our national economy, a task inherited from the democratic revolution, in such measures as land reform and the suppression of counterrevolutionaries, etc. In this same period we defeated the frantic attacks launched by the bourgeoisie on the economic front by scoring a triumphant victory in our "three anti" and "five anti" movements and the aggression of U. S. imperialism by scoring a great victory in the "resist America, aid Korea" campaign. In the course of this period, we established our Socialist cultural and educational enterprises and, at the same time, made revolutionary reforms in the cultural and educational organizations taken over from old China and waged a solemn struggle against feudalism, bureaucracy, and imperialism, particularly the remnant forces and political and ideological influences of U. S. imperialism.

U. S. imperialists have always been the archenemies of the Chinese people. They have carried out not only direct military aggressions against our country but also cultural aggressions through culture, education, religion, and other ways, in an effort to create an influence beneficial to their aggressive and colonial policies among the intellectuals. Therefore, the thorough elimination of U. S. imperialism and its influence in politics and ideology in our country is extremely important in our revolution.

Shortly after the founding of our country, we carried out a struggle against the so-called "democratic individualism" and, in the course of the "resist America, aid Korea" campaign, we waged a resolute struggle against the ideology friendly towards the United States, as well as the thinking of worshiping the United States and fearing the United States. These struggles played an important role in fulfilling our democratic revolution, promoting Socialist revolution, and establishing the political dictatorship of the proletariat. This was the first stage of development of our country's cultural and educational work.

In late 1952, the Central Committee of the Chinese Communist Party and Comrade Mao Tse-tung drafted the general line for the period of Socialist transformation, that is, the general line for carrying out Socialist revolution together with Socialist construction. Under the guidance of this general line, in the five years between 1953 and 1957, we basically completed the Socialist transformation of agriculture, the handicraft industry, and capitalist industry and commerce, as well as the Socialist revolution on the economic front. Moreover, we overfulfilled the first five-year economic development plan, which laid the preliminary foundation for industrialization, while scoring decisive victories in our Socialist revolution on the political and ideological fronts.

During this period, coping with the needs for Socialist transformation, we continuously carried out a series of struggles against bourgeois concepts on the cultural and educational front. This was the second stage of development of cultural and educational work in our country.

Under the direct leadership of Comrade Mao Tse-tung and before the Socialist revolution on the economic front reached its upsurge, we began to conduct studies and criticized the "Wu Hsun Biography" and the "Red Chamber," which had disseminated bourgeois thinking among the broad masses, as well as the Hu Feng counterrevolutionary clique and the bourgeois academic views represented by Hu Shih. Through these struggles, the leadership of Marxism-Leninism was greatly strengthened and the bourgeois thinking was defeated, thus creating favorable conditions for bringing about an upsurge in our Socialist revolution on the ideological front.

The Socialist revolution on the economic front in our country was completed in 1956. After making a comprehensive analysis of the basic conflicts in our Socialist society, Comrade Mao Tse-tung put forth the theory for the correct handling of contradictions among the people and the policy for carrying out the policy of "let a hundred flowers bloom and a hundred schools contend" in the literary and art circles. In accordance with Comrade Mao Tse-tung's theories, cultural and educational circles carried out a two-road struggle in the course of the Socialist revolution on the political and ideological fronts and scored decisive victories.

Our country's cultural and educational undertakings are Socialist cultural and educational undertakings, and they are the instruments of the proletariat political dictatorship for educating the people with Communist ideology. Their basic principle is to render services to proletariat politics and to Socialist economic construction. To do this, it is necessary to follow the leadership of the Communist Party.

The struggle between the proletariat and the bourgeoisie in the fields of culture and education and the struggle between the two roads of socialism and capitalism reflect many phases of our work. However, these struggles have long been focused on the basic problem of leadership. Although tremendous success has been achieved on the cultural and educational front since 1957, we were still unable to establish in time a firm leadership of the proletariat in these fields.

Taking advantage of the situation, bourgeois rightists have tried painstakingly to undermine the proletariat on the political and ideological fronts, as well as in the fields of culture and education, by clamoring that "the Party is unable to display leadership over culture and education." For this reason, our struggle with the bourgeoisie on the cultural and educational front for leadership at one time became very acute. As a result of our struggle against the bourgeois rightists and the successful implementation of the rectification campaign, we brought utter defeat to the frantic attacks of the bourgeois rightists by criticizing their various absurd views against the leadership of the Party.

At the same time, a resolute struggle was launched in various phases of the cultural and educational front to refute the bourgeois concepts of "education for education's sake," "culture for culture's sake," and "separation between mental and physical labor" and to implement resolutely the guiding principles of making culture and education serve the politics of the proletariat, as well as other Party policies to be carried out in different stages in the fields of education, culture, journalism, public health, and physical education.

Efforts were also exerted to promote debates on the question of trends in the fields of literature and the arts. Thus were eliminated the bourgeois lines for the development of arts and literature adopted by the reactionary clique represented by Ting Ling and Chen Chi-hsia. Thus were firmly upheld the Socialist lines for the development of literature and arts of the proletariat and the policies of resolutely making literature and arts serve industry, agriculture, and the armed forces and of determinedly disseminating and promoting the coördination of the guiding principle of "let a hundred flowers bloom, eliminate the old, and bring out the new."

As a result of the struggles, an atmosphere of brilliance and prosperity prevails over our undertakings in the fields of literature and the arts. With regard to journalism, a great debate was launched to criticize the so-called "freedom of press" viewpoints of the bourgeoisie, particularly those adopted by the *Wen Hui Pao,* and a great victory was scored. All this has enabled our country's journalism to develop fully its fighting potential within the scope of international and domestic class struggle, thus making it become a more effective instrument for carrying out the propaganda of the proletariat, as well as for disseminating the ideology of Marxism-Leninism and modern scientific and cultural knowledge among the broad masses.

.   .   .   .

In such a large country as ours, with a population of over 600,000,000 and a very backward educational background, it is an immense and arduous task to intellectualize the worker-peasant masses and to help intellectuals acquire the qualities of the working people. Some bourgeois educators once proposed a restriction upon the development of education. They advocated "permission for the state alone to promote education," "permission to promote only one type of school," "permission for experts alone to promote education," and so forth. There were also those who, while also calling for development of education, nevertheless insisted upon following a line for little, slow, poor, and uneconomical achievements. They emphasized the so-called "regular" system of education and pedagogical methods and either ignored or else even disapproved of the bold creation and uninterrupted renovation by the masses in the field of education.

Should we follow these suggestions, it is obvious that it would be a very long period before we could popularize education in our country to intellectualize the worker-peasant masses, provided they did not make it entirely impossible to do so. We have resolutely opposed these erroneous suggestions and followed the policy pointed out by the central authorities of the Chinese Communist Party and Comrade Mao Tse-tung to "walk on both legs" in the educational revolution and have mobilized the whole Party and all people to promote education. By doing so, we have found a way to popularize and elevate the people's education for greater, faster, better, and more economical achievements.

.   .   .   .

Another important task at present on the cultural and educational fronts in China is to apply Marxist-Leninist views in criticizing and correctly evaluating the cultural inheritance of the bourgeoisie. The modern revisionist attitude towards bourgeois cultural inheritance, especially that of the eighteenth and nineteenth centuries, is to take the dregs and throw away the cream, giving away the good and beneficial and advocating the reactionary and passive parts in order to sell revisionist theories and disseminate bourgeois thinking. For this reason, we should apply Marxist-Leninist views in correctly evaluating the cultural inheritance. Contrary to the modern revisionists, our attitude is to absorb the cream and throw away the dregs. An attitude of "study, criticize; study again, criticize again" should be taken towards cultural inheritance.

The policy of "let a hundred flowers bloom and a hundred schools contend" is the steadfast line to be followed in criticizing bourgeois cultural inheritance. There should be full expression of different academic views and step-by-step differentiation between the correct and the incorrect, the genuine and the false. Free competition should be allowed among different sects and styles in literature and arts and among different schools in science and technology. We must make strict distinction between criticism against modern revisionism and debate on the academic problem of inheriting cultures in a critical manner and then adopt correct policies respectively.

The *Communist Manifesto* pointed out that

the Communist revolution is to carry out the most thorough departure from relations of ownership which have been inherited from the past. Therefore, no wonder, during the course of its own development it carries out the most thorough departure from various concepts which have been inherited from the past.

That is to say, for the sake of carrying out communism, it is not only necessary to change the relations of ownership but it is also necessary to thoroughly wipe out all ideological influences of the bourgeoisie and petty bourgeoisie, thus making a basic change in existing ideology.

. . . .

Our cultural and educational work must be so developed as

to meet the needs of economic construction. We must strive, in the second Five-Year Plan period, basically to fulfill the task of wiping out illiteracy among young workers and peasants and basically to popularize primary school education among children of school age. We must strive, in the third Five-Year Plan period, basically to popularize junior high school education and to develop senior high school education, vocational education of high school standards, higher education, spare-time education of various levels and kinds, and education for young children.

In addition to stepping up production, we must continue to intensify the development of nationwide health movements centering on exterminating the four pests, improving public health, and eliminating main diseases; we must fulfill the tasks of pest extermination and disease elimination provided in the national agricultural development program; and we must further carry out mass sports movements to improve the people's physical condition. We must also vigorously develop other cultural and educational undertakings, set up a powerful scientific and technical force and a Marxist-Leninist theoretical force, and exert our best efforts to cultivate new forces. All the people, who are ambitious for the materialization of communism and the development of educational undertakings, should be united to exert their best efforts to rid our country of poverty and blankness, to catch up with Britain in production, and to overtake all capitalist countries in educational undertakings.

For the popularization and improvement of nationwide education, a complete educational system should be established not simply on a nationwide basis. Various localities should also set up their own educational systems according to their own individual needs and circumstances to train needed personnel. Provinces, municipalities, special districts, *hsiens,* and communes should rely mainly on their own efforts in considering their own educational arrangements, gradually establish their own educational systems, and vigorously set up full-time, half-time, and spare-time schools of various categories. Full-time primary schools should be established by people's communes step-by-step to cope with the new situation on the development of culture and education after the establishment of people's communes. In the future, the responsibility for the popularization of primary school education should be gradually transferred to the people's communes in both urban and rural areas. A commune should not only set up and strengthen its own educational system but also develop various cultural, health, and sports undertakings.

. . . .

Educational reforms should also be carried out in our full-time institutes of higher learning. The principle followed in carrying out educational reforms in the institutes of higher learning is not to allow any lowering of student standards in basic knowledge of science but to provide for the raising of their standards and the widening of the range of their study. We should not allow any increase in teacher and student labor but provide for insuring the combining of labor and relaxation. We want to enable students to become experts in one field, while, at the same time, possessing all-round scientific knowledge and ability in labor.

Comrade Mao Tse-tung said: "We will appear in the world as a highly civilized nation." Let us whip up a high tide in the cultural revolution and march forward heroically for the fulfillment of this great target.

SOURCE: *Current Background*, No. 622 (Hong Kong: United States Consulate General, June 28, 1960). Originally published by *New China News Agency*, June 1, 1960.

Another translation of this document is to be found as "Carry Out the Cultural Revolution in a Big Way: Help the Workers and Peasants Become Well Educated and the Intellectuals Become Identical with the Working People" in *The National Conference of Outstanding Groups and Individuals in Socialist Construction in Education, Culture, Health, Physical Culture, and Journalism* (Peking: Foreign Languages Press, 1960), pp. 9–46.

See also Lin Feng, "The Tasks of China's Cultural Revolution," *Peking Review*, III, No. 25 (June 21, 1960), 14–19; and No. 26 (June 28, 1960), 19–25.

For additional reading, see "Educational Training for Worker and Peasant Intellectuals," *Peking Review*, I, No. 12 (1958), 16.

A New System of Teaching English Instituted
by the Peking Institute of Foreign Languages
July 1960

The Peking Institute of Foreign Languages had as its primary responsibility the training of translators, interpreters, and persons linguistically competent for overseas positions or for special research. It is interesting to note that some of the earliest Western schools organized in China during the nineteenth century were partially concerned with the task of training Chinese as competent foreign language specialists. The Peking Institute, in claiming to reduce by a half to a third the time spent in learning English, does not support its press release (below) with sufficient methodological details. Mention is made of a curricular reorganization, the greater use of topical Communist themes for class exercises, speed exercises in reading, and "rush teaching," but details are conspicuously absent. However, there is little reason to doubt the Chinese contention that the pedagogic methods used in teaching English and other languages could be drastically overhauled. During the last five years there have been many improvements in the teaching of foreign languages throughout the world, with which language training specialists in Peking would be familiar. However, it is impossible to evaluate the claims for improvement by the Peking Institute of Foreign Languages on the basis of this overgeneralized article, which claims that spectacular progress has been made in foreign language instruction.

The English Department of the Peking Institute of Foreign Languages has, under the leadership of the Party and the policy of placing politics in command and launching extensive mass movements, initially instituted a new system to teach English

386

with greater, faster, better, and more economical results. The system came as a result of the pedagogic reform effected by the teachers and students of the department with the spirit of uninterrupted revolution immediately after the National Conference of Outstanding Cultural and Educational Workers.

Since the last semester, the English Department of the Peking Institute of Foreign Languages, with a view to bringing about continued leaps forward in pedagogic work, has mobilized the masses further, in checking up the problems existing in teaching work, breaking down the old teaching system, and establishing a new teaching program, which has already achieved initial success in the course of practice.

Under this teaching program, new arrangements have been made for a five-year course of study, accelerating the speed of progress in pedagogic work. The department has already succeeded in making the first-year students rapidly grasp in eight weeks what used to take them one year—the fundamental knowledge of phonetics and sentence construction and a certain number of new words. According to the arrangements made under the new program, the students will be able, within a period of two years, to lay a good foundation of English which used to take three years. The standard of English, both oral and written, of the third-year students will reach the same level as that of the graduates from the five-year course, while the standard of English of the fifth-year students will be the same as that of the present postgraduates.

In keeping with the new program, the department has compiled, on a large scale, textbooks of a comprehensive nature and has translated a great variety of teaching materials, reflecting important current political affairs and the new men and new things emerging from the big leaps forward. For instance, the reports made at the National People's Congress, the reports on the urban communes, articles dealing with the Japanese people's opposition to the Japan–U. S. Military Alliance Treaty, articles on "for the sake of the fifty-one class brothers," and the heroic deeds of Hsü Hsüeh-hue and Liu Wen-hsüeh have all been compiled and prepared in time for use as teaching materials. Three days after the appearance in newspapers of the dispatch, "Chairman Mao Tse-tung's Concern over the Learning of Culture by National Warriors," it was translated into English for teaching in class. Such new teaching materials, on the one hand, serve as education in Communist ideology to the students and, on the other, enlarge the scope of use of the English language. The students learn fast and remember well, and marked results have been obtained.

The new teaching program also calls for particular attention to be given to hearing, speaking, writing, and reading and for equal emphasis on special study and general study, thus changing the past practice, where too much time was given to special study, leaving too little time for general study. After certain adjustments have been made in the time for study, the reading capacity of the students increased by two to four times. Although the time for special study has been reduced, the quality has been greatly improved. As the students read intensively, they consciously observe the way the language is used and absorb the knowledge of it. . . . As to hearing, speaking, and writing, equal emphasis is laid on the three things. Extracurricular activities are organized broadly, in order that the students get far more chances to practice outside class than during class hours.

On the basis of the experiences gained since the great leaps forward, the new teaching program also calls for combination of regular teaching and rush teaching under specific circumstances. Rush teaching is employed to supplement regular teaching, and the students are thus enabled to improve their power of hearing, speaking, writing, and reading, and they achieve the result of breaking through one point for overall advancement. Under the new program, through the use of modern teaching facilities to improve the students' ability to hear, speak, write, and read and their knowledge of phonetics and translation, pedagogical efficiency has been raised as the chance for practice is increased.

Through the various reforms described above, the English Department has witnessed a rapid improvement in the students' standard of English.

Since the close of the National Conference of Outstanding Cultural and Educational Workers, encouraged by the revolutionary spirit of the conference, the teachers and students and the Party branch of the Department are organizing their strength, summing up their experiences, and groping further for the law of teaching English with greater, faster, better, and more economical results. Efforts are being made in compiling a complete set of teaching materials. Modern teaching facilities are put into ever-wider use. A high tide of pedagogic reforms has been swept up. Besides, the Party branch in the Department is grasping one link after another, making plans both for the present and for the future and, in the spirit of uninterrupted revolution, has set forth a preliminary pedagogic and scientific research plan for the next academic year.

Source: *Survey of China Mainland Press,* No. 2312 (Hong Kong: United States Consulate General, August 8, 1960). Originally published in *Kuang Ming Jih Pao,* July 4, 1960.

Several Facts Learned about Teaching-Reform in Higher Institutions of Technology

By the Committee of the Chinese Communist Party
of the Central China Institute of Technology
September 1960

The themes of the "great leap forward," of being "both red and expert," and of "combining labor and education" have had some of their best applications in Chinese technical education. The technical institutes, during their "reorganization or establishment period," after 1952, received a somewhat favored position in the overall expansion of higher educational facilities. The technical universities, however, underwent all the usual national periodic ideological reforms and were fully integrated into the government programs for eliminating the "social" differences or barriers between "mental and physical workers."

Specific reforms during 1960 in technical education included changes in classroom procedures and a better balance between theoretical, practical, and applied studies. Closer relations were to be developed between the neighboring factories and industrial complexes and the technical universities. The Marxist basis of science was to be stressed further and emphasis placed on the so-called "dialetical unity of division and combination of labor," which was opposed to what was described as "overrigid Western specialization." Thus the old "mechanical, materialistic, metaphysical" teaching system was to give way completely to the "new" pedagogy of dialetical materialism.

The Central China Institute of Technology wanted to turn itself, through active construction, into a university of technical revolution, make its courses more compatible with Socialist construction, and bring up for the state "red and expert" construction personnel who would be of use to modern industrial production and advanced technology. Accordingly, at the beginning of April of this year, it selected two of its specialization majors for an experiment in teaching-reform. It did so under the leadership of higher Party committees, while organizing all its faculty members and students to take part in the nationwide movement for technical revolution. Towards the end of June, it again organized them to make a general summing-up of the results of technical revolution and scientific research and, with regard to the experience of the two specialization majors mentioned above, mobilized the masses to unfold teaching-reform in all the other specialization majors as well. The principle adhered to was to accomplish the reform of minor items immediately. Separate teaching plans were drawn up, and the education plans and syllabuses were revised. Foundations were laid for intensification of teaching-reform in the future. We have learned that in teaching-reform it is necessary to carry out the revolution of education and the revolution of thinking simultaneously and to mobilize the masses fully. In addition, we have learned rather thoroughly the following facts about teaching-reform in higher institutions of technology.

Technical revolution provides motive force to teaching-reform; teaching-reform must be combined firmly with technical revolution. Taking part in technical revolution for several months, the faculty members and students of the Central China Institute of Technology not only helped factories and enterprises complete more than seven thousand items of technical innovations, thereby making definite contributions to the development of production, but, what is more important still, borrowed the example of all-people technical revolution in promoting teaching-reform. The thousands and tens of thousands of creations that emerged from the technical revolution broke through the old limits of science and technology and posed a series of new questions with respect to the teaching system and the things to be taught in class. Take the generation and distribution of electricity for instance. Technical revolution had been carried out on a large scale in the electric power industry. As a result of development, the simple electricity transmission lines of old had been replaced by integrated transmission systems serving large areas, and, in the operation of power plants, central control and automation had been realized gradually. This made it necessary for the technical cadres in the electric power industry to know how to tackle practical problems in the operation of power plants, continuous current protection, electrical networks, and high-pressure electricity. Previously, technical cadres trained by the electricity generation and distribution specialization major of the Central China Institute of Technology knew only how to solve problems in the operation of single ordinary power plants and simple transmission lines and did not know how to solve problems in the complex operation of integrated electricity transmission systems. Even less was taught in class about contemporary theories concerning automatic electricity generation and distribution and new techniques. Similar contradictions in the form of incompatibility between the things learned by the students in class and the things they were required to learn by the development of production techniques were also present in all the other specialization majors. As for the incompatibility between the things taught in class and the things actually required to be taught by the situation in modern production and technical revolution, it was an even more extensive phenomenon. Take the radio technique specialization major for instance. In the amplification class, which was one of the three main classes in that specialization major, only 10 percent of textbook space was devoted to contemporary techniques, while the other 90 percent was devoted to old theories concerning the amplification of low-frequency pressure and power amplification, such theories being of the technical standard of the 1930s. The book, *Transmission Equipment,* published in two volumes, had 908 pages in all. But only 153 pages were devoted to the contemporary microwave theory and later discoveries. The book, *Receiving Equipment,* talked about nothing but physical phenomena related to five-tube superheterodyne equipment. Similar but more serious cases were found in the older specialization majors. From the movement for technical revolution, we learned that a certain new technique which used to be considered too advanced for application was being extensively applied to production. In class, however, it was seldom or never taught. On the other hand, certain things which had little or no use in production were still being taught as classics to the students, whose energy and time were thus wasted. As for the characteristics—emphasis on native methods, employment of both native methods and Western methods, and the attempt to obtain better results from the use of native methods than from that of Western methods—of the development of science and technology in our country and the inventions, creations, and rich experience of the laboring people of our country, not a single word was mentioned about them in any technical class. There was thus grave disregard for the actual conditions in China. As a result especially of the appearance of new techniques, new technology, new products, and new materials and the production of many comprehensive marginal sciences, the development of science and technology had entered a historical era of new combination and new division of labor. This made it necessary for a series of changes to be effected in all the specialization majors of the institute as a science school with respect to the things to be learned by the students, the extent of education, the teaching system, and the things to be taught in class. Thus, technical revolution provided motive force to teaching reform, and the faculty members and students taking part in technical revolution became shock forces in the present teaching-reform.

The basic purpose of the present teaching-reform is to abolish the old teaching system founded on idealism and mechanical materialism and to institute a new teaching system under the guidance of Marxism-Leninism. From technical revolution and the many facts exposed by the masses, it was clear that the idealistic, especially the mechanical materialistic, metaphysical concept of the world had gravely affected teaching in all the specialization majors and had become the ideological foundation of the old teaching system. This is shown mainly as follows:

First, exclusive emphasis was laid on the hereditary nature of science, and it was held that the development of science of technology could only be by quantitative change, not qualitative change, and that the old teaching system should not be changed, and, if it had to be changed, the change could only be an increase or decrease in quantity. Thus, many of the specialization majors, though they had introduced certain changes in respect to the courses offered and the things taught in class since their founding had done so, as a rule, by simple addition, following the development of production techniques. There had been little radical change in the courses themselves. Certain outdated and even antiscientific technical theories were still being regarded as the foundations of some specialization majors. Take the old machine-building theory for instance. It was thought that a machine was more "advanced" if it was of a bigger size, more complicated in structure, and made up of a greater number of parts. Bigness and smallness, complexity and simplicity were not regarded as unities of opposites. Nor were they regarded as interchangeable under certain conditions. The theory in question could not account for the many new products created by the masses in the technical revolution which, though small in volume and needing comparatively little material to build, were yet highly efficient and had wide use.

Second, whereas history has shown the development of natural science to be a process of dialectical unity of division and combination of labor, the old teaching system exclusively emphasized the systematization of every branch of science and regarded the division of labor among different branches of science as absolute. Fundamental theory classes, technical fundamental classes, and specialized classes were regarded as separate systems which were not interconnected. In addition, these classes taught their specific laws separately and did not teach anything about the relations between the common character and specific character of different branches of science. This was responsible for the grave signs of disunity, opposition, redundancy, and separation among the classes. For instance, the classes on manufacturing normally taught only the names of products and the ways of processing machine parts. Class was conducted in such a manner that only one product or one processing method was taught during one lesson. In this way, the students could not acquire knowledge about the general laws governing a group of interconnected matters. Besides, a bad influence was exerted over their minds, making them short-sighted, handicapped in many ways, and afraid to create. At the same time, the scope for specialized activities was also kept narrow. This was contrary to the demand for the training of people with one specialization and many kinds of skills.

Third, teaching was organized throughout in accordance with the principle "theory (fundamental classes) to method (technical fundamental classes) to application (specialized classes)" or "theory to theory to practice," which had been in force since the eighteenth century. The laying of technical theoretical foundations and the teaching of specialized subjects were set against each other, with the result that even the third-year students did not understand the scope of their specialization majors or the kinds of specialized knowledge required. In addition, the studies of the students of any year were not combined firmly with the links of the entire courses, with scientific research, or with production. This hindered the satisfactory implementation of the direction of combining theory with practice and was contrary to Marxist epistemology.

Fourth, in the classes, politics and the role of man were neglected, and the purely technical view was cherished to an extremely grave extent. In accordance with that view, the development of productivity was simply a development of technique. While apparently technique and the objective laws of natural science were respected, the idea that politics could not lead science or technology was spread wittingly or unwittingly. This greatly affected the implementation in the field of science and technology of the Party's general line and directives and policies relating to economic construction and technical work.

It was very obvious from the above that the old teaching system had become increasingly restrictive to the improvement of the quality of education, with the result that education in science and technology had become increasingly backward in comparison with the situation. Unless a radical reform was carried out, it would be impossible to plant the red flag of the thought of Mao

Tse-tung in the realm of teaching, to cope with the trend of new combination and new division of labor in science and technology, to institute a new teaching system, or to train "red and expert" technical cadres with one specialization and many kinds of skills with greater, faster, better, and more economical results. That is why we say that the basic purpose of the present teaching-reform is to demolish the old views and the old teaching system and to construct new views and a new teaching system.

Needless to say, the reform of the teaching system is a rather complicated thing and takes time. It is impossible to carry out the reform satisfactorily at the first attempt. In the first place, many different classes are taught in a higher institution, and many of these classes, while inheriting existing knowledge, also have to carry out creation and do a lot of exploring work. In the second place, we cannot tell by one glance what the result of the reform will be and so have to test it in practice. Hence, when carrying out the reform completely, we have to divide our work into stages, consider it from all angles, and start with the more important items. Concerning the measures to be adopted for organizing the reform, we should combine the full mobilization of the masses with the strengthening of leadership, precede the reform of major items with experiments, and test the results of such experiments in practice. Concerning the methods to be employed, we should combine the selective reform of major items with the general reform of minor items.

Unfolding academic criticism and deepening the reform of the things taught in class. In order to carry out teaching-reform thoroughly, it is necessary to unfold academic criticism apart from abolishing the old mechanical materialistic, metaphysical teaching system and instituting a new teaching system under the guidance of dialetical materialism.

As learned from the situation in the mass academic criticism of such fundamental subjects as physics, chemistry, electricity, and mechanics and the fundamental subjects of the various specialization majors, there is a crucial struggle between the two classes and the two world outlooks in the realm of natural science. The existing theoretical foundations of such subjects as theoretical mechanics, physics, thermal engineering, and fundamentals of electrical engineering were laid in the eighteenth and nineteenth centuries, when bourgeois science was at its height. While containing many explicit idealistic and mystical views, these subjects are conspicuously and to a large extent under the influence of the mechanical, materialistic, metaphysical world outlook and methodology. This is shown mainly as follows:

First, the mechanical theory of external causes. Academic criticism has revealed that almost all the theories taught in the various classes are closely connected with Newton's mechanical theory of external causes. A prominent manifestation of this mechanical theory is the attempt to explain higher forms of motion of molecules. Chemical affinity is used to explain composition and decomposition. Even in the study of electricity, which has only been developed recently, the mechanical theory prevails. Maxwell, the "father" of electricity, said, "All the phenomena of an electric coil can be reduced to phenomena of dynamics (that is, fluid mechanics)." Hence, most of the formulas and theorems about the phenomena of electric coils in the class on fundamentals of electrical engineering were transplanted from fluid mechanics. Such a view and method naturally cannot reveal the substance of the phenomena of electric coils. Indeed, just as Engels once said, "They seek refuge in the term 'force' whenever they cannot explain some natural phenomenon."

Second, the exclusive and isolated research method. For instance, in a process of metal cutting, it is necessary to study both the cutting tools used and the internal changes of the objects being cut, to study both cutting with mechanical force and the effect of sound, light, heat, electricity, and chemicals on the cutting process. However, in the class on principles of metal cutting, over which the metaphysical research method was holding sway, a cutting process was regarded as an effect of the mechanical force of the cutting tools used, and so research was carried out exclusively on cutting tools, with the result that a series of erroneous principles were derived concerning the choice of cutting tools and the determination of the quantity of material to be consumed in cutting, and there was no way of explaining theoretically the new achievements in cutting technique. Because such an isolated and exclusive research method was employed, the conclusions drawn under specific conditions were frequently applied to general conditions, and loopholes became obvious when they were tested in the new practice.

Third, complex mathematical and logical inference. The faculty members and students forming the team for criticism of fundamentals of electrical engineering summed up Maxwell's research method in these words: "An attempt to explain the phenomena of electromagnets with assumed fluid motions and pure geometrical ideas." By using such a research method, Maxwell described only certain quantitative relations among the phenomena of electromagnets and did not reveal the substance of the matter. Newton used a similar research method. In his representative work, *The Mathematical Principles of Natural Phenomena,* he wrote that his method was to carry out research on the "inference of mathematical principles from natural phenomena." Such a mathematical formalistic research method can be said to have reached its height in some fields of contemporary theoretical physics. As Engels said in many places, mathematical forms are used to cover up the substance of things.

The predominence of the idealistic and mechanical, materialistic, metaphysical view in natural science is the basic cause of the fact that the teaching system and the things taught in class are backward and antiquated and divorced from the practice of production. It is also the basic cause of smaller, slower, poorer, and less economical results being achieved in teaching. It greatly hinders the further development of science and technology. Today, when social productivity is being highly developed, in order that we may critically inherit the legacy of natural science, plant the red flag of the thought of Mao Tse-tung in the realm of natural science, and thoroughly reform the things taught in class, it is important to examine and revise anew the scientific and technical theories of the past generations or even to reform them radically, so as to free natural science from the fetters of the idealistic and mechanical, materialistic, metaphysical view. This is why we have felt deeply that in order to be able to carry out radical reform of the things taught in class, it is necessary to unfold academic criticism and that it is obviously wrong to consider it unnecessary to make academic criticism in the realm of natural science.

Needless to say, academic criticism in the realm of natural science is a rather complex job. As far as we understand, it is necessary first of all to abolish the "theory of special circumstances" and to put forward the fact clearly that in the realm of natural science, too, it is necessary to regard the thought of Mao Tse-tung as the guide and to study and criticize any theory. Such study and criticism must start with the correct viewpoint and method before we can jump out of the circle of formalistic logic and succeed in criticizing the phenomena first and the substance later on. At the same time, we should scientifically adjudge those things which reflect objective truths under definite conditions. Only thus can we correctly handle the relations between criticism and inheritance. Secondly, in the academic criticism of natural science, too, we should carry out the directive of letting "a hundred flowers blossom together and a hundred schools of thought contend," and adhere to the principle "study, criticism, more study, and more criticism." In addition, in making academic criticism in the realm of natural science, we should conduct extensive investigation on production, collect data, and at the same time make large numbers of reliable experiments. Only thus can we base our criticism on genuinely scientific grounds and make it convincing.

SOURCE: *Survey of China Mainland Press*, No. 2345 (Hong Kong: United States Consulate General, September 26, 1960). Originally published in *Jen Min Jih Pao* [People's Daily], September 13, 1960.

Universities and Colleges Must Properly Help Intellectuals Acquire Qualities of Laboring People
October 1960

A perennial problem of Communist society is either the degree of elimination or extent of integration of social classes within society. Theoretically, the worst of the "old-time" bourgeois intellectuals were "reformed" or removed from their university positions in the early years of the regime. But in fact, they persisted and the "one hundred flowers" campaign of 1956–57 showed the surprising strength of many independent-minded academics. In order totally to eliminate this type of "resurgence," the theoretical doctrines of communism relating to the "combination of labor and education" were invoked and translated into more practical terms. It is anathema to Chinese Communist philosophy that the universities become the breeding ground for a strain of governmental functionary or "cadre" who secures for himself a select status in a new but nonmanual laboring class in Communist society. This document stresses the recurrent theme that "education must be combined with labor" and discusses in general terms the curricular revisions which may make this feasible in higher education. (The immediately preceding document, concerning higher technical education, is much more explicit in explaining how its curricula can be reformed and be brought into line with current Party doctrines.)

Universities and colleges are among the major bases of our country for training intellectuals. The sole target of our country's cultural revolution is to help the masses of workers and peasants become well educated and to mobilize the intellectuals in acquiring the qualities of laboring people. Therefore, in cultivating

400

intellectuals, the universities and colleges should not only help all students to possess specialized knowledge at higher levels but should also assist all students to establish a correct viewpoint and habit of labor by mobilizing them to undergo certain kinds of labor training, in order that each one will be able to set up a comparatively good foundation for transforming himself into a working person.

As a result of implementing the correct policy of combining education with productive labor in the past two years, tremendously penetrating and pleasing changes have taken place in university education in China. A good beginning has been made in helping the intellectuals to acquire the qualities of laboring people. We have set up regular systems and methods for applying the policy of combining education with productive labor in universities and colleges throughout the country. Meanwhile, by successfully implementing the policy of coördinating theories with practice and combining mental labor with physical labor, the students' political consciousness has been raised tremendously, and they have gained a more thorough understanding of the line and policies of the country towards the Socialist revolution and Socialist construction. Profound changes in their ideas and feelings towards labor and the laboring people have been engendered. Their enthusiasm for Socialist construction undertakings has grown higher and higher. They have become more and more enthusiastic in supporting the fatherland, the Party, labor, and the laboring people, and they have gained a deeper understanding of what they have learned from books. They are able to use both their hands and brains and have contributed a great deal to the technical innovations and technical revolution movement. All this has also created a direct impetus to the scientific research and schooling reform of universities and colleges.

The integration of education with productive labor is needed by the Socialist revolution and Socialist construction, for the development of education causes on a larger, faster, better, and more economical scale the building of communism. Integration of education with productive labor aims at eliminating all exploiting classes and systems, as well as the ideological influence of these classes and systems and, at the same time, gradually eliminates the difference between the city and countryside, between workers and peasants, and between mental and manual labor, so as to help the intellectuals to acquire the qualities of laboring people, making labor the first necessity in the people's livelihood. Judging from this target, although our current achievements are tremendous, we have only taken our first step in a long march of tens of thousands of miles.

We must admit that the divorce between education and productive labor originated with class society and dates back several thousands of years. The outcome of the vigorous expansion of the exploiting systems and the strenuous efforts of the exploiting class to utilize the intellectuals by promises of granting profitable government positions to them in the past several thousand years have also tremendously influenced the exploited worker and peasant masses. Moreover, in China, the Socialist revolution has not yet been thoroughly accomplished, either on the economic, the political, or, particularly, on the ideological front.

The development of our country's industry and agriculture cannot reach a high level as long as there are still great differences in educational levels among the masses of people throughout the country. As a result, the remnants of bourgeois rights will survive for a considerable time, and some unreasonable differences will unavoidably linger on in the material treatment of mental and manual labor. Therefore, to realize integration between education and productive labor and to reach the goal of helping intellectuals to acquire the qualities of laboring people, it is necessary to launch a long-term hard struggle.

Through launching repeated educational work, extensive mass movements, and the actual practice by the universities and colleges in the past two years, the concept that education must combine with productive labor has been accepted by the people. However, some persons still hold certain incorrect views about the aims of combining education with productive labor, how to combine them, and how far they should be combined.

For instance, some persons hold that intellectuals would be in an awkward position if the masses of workers and peasants became well educated, while others hold the views that schools can only cultivate intellectuals who are able to perform labor. This shows that they still want to be in a higher position than the workers and peasants and have no intention of eliminating the differences between the intellectuals and the workers and peasants. Such incorrect views also indicate that they still believe that inellectuals are a step higher than the laboring people and that mental labor is a step higher than manual labor. Some persons are only interested in labor training which has a direct bearing on their specialized studies or in certain techniques that they can learn. They fail to pay attention to labor training which has no relations to their specialized studies or to certain techniques which they do not need. Some persons are willing to participate in short-term manual labor but refuse to take part in long-term manual labor. This shows that their aims of labor are to attain more knowledge and techniques for themselves through taking part in labor training and that they have not yet become common laborers.

There is nothing unusual about the existence of such ideas. This is because we cannot eliminate the ideological influence against labor and the laboring people left behind by the exploiting classes several thousands of years ago without a long-term struggle radically to transform such a bourgeois world outlook. Therefore, we must pay special attention to this question and further strengthen our leadership to overcome it. In actual practice, many universities and colleges, with the spirit of continued revolution, are making strenuous efforts to solve the above-mentioned questions. Many colleges have attained certain good experiences, and they are worthy of study.

To enable students to receive more and better education on labor, arrangements should be made by the schools for the students to do two kinds of manual work—work linked with their own specialties and work that has no connection at all with their specialized studies. This is a method of great significance. The old society, after dividing mental labor and manual labor, also made a clear-cut difference between various kinds of labor. Such an ideology still exists in our country today. Some persons have high regard for technical work but look down upon manual work; some persons have high respect for productive labor but despise the manual work of the service trades; some persons are willing to take part in industrial labor in urban areas but are unwilling to work on the agricultural front in the countryside. It must be pointed out here that the participation in manual labor by students whose ideology has not yet been thoroughly reformed aims at enriching their own knowledge and technical capability.

If we only arrange for students to take part in manual work linked with their own specialized studies or arrange for them to take part in manual work linked with their own specialties, it will be impossible for the students to make an overall contact with their manual work and will thereby create great difficulties in eliminating their incorrect ideology towards labor; meanwhile, the students might also get the wrong idea that their participation in labor aims only at enabling them further to elevate their own specialties.

Elevation of the students' study levels is one of the aims of combining education with productive labor, but it is not the only aim. Our demand is first of all to enable all students to experience the ideas and feelings of the laboring people by taking part in manual work. To arrange appropriately for participation in all kinds of labor by students will make it much easier for them fully to understand the real meaning of labor and the actual livelihood of laboring people, thereby establishing for themselves the ideas and feelings of the laboring people.

Many universities and colleges have adopted methods for students to take part in both industrial and agricultural labor. This is a very good method. The old society looked down upon agricultural labor; with regard to the differences between city and countryside, the exploiting classes only paid their attention to the urban areas; with regard to industry and agriculture, the exploiting classes despised agriculture. Speaking of mental labor and manual labor, agricultural labor involved only comparatively heavy manual work; therefore, agricultural labor was extremely discriminated against in the old society. Participation of students in agricultural labor will provide us with favorable conditions for launching an ideological education campaign to gradually eliminate the differences between city and countryside, between workers and peasants, and between mental and manual labor.

We must realize that the construction of our country is based on agriculture. We must enable every student to realize deeply the economic and political significance of agriculture as the foundation and the importance of inculcating a warm love for farm work and a readiness to devote their lives to agriculture and build up socialism in rural areas. Today there still exist the activities of well-to-do middle-class peasants, landlords, and rich peasants in the countryside. Participation of students in farmwork in rural areas will also facilitate them to receive the education of class struggle.

Many universities and colleges have made arrangements for students to work both on the grounds of the colleges and at places outside the colleges. This is also an excellent method. It is necessary to set up more workshops, farms, and service centers on the grounds of the colleges. This will enable us to work out the labor program and ensure the progress of labor among the students. However, proper arrangements for students to work outside the colleges must be made. Only by taking part in certain kinds of labor outside the colleges will it be possible for the students properly to study and understand the correctness of the lines, policies, and principles of national construction; to study thoroughly how to implement these policies and principles, to learn more about and to establish the world outlook of the proletariat, and further to elevate their own political consciousness.

Under the guidance of general educational plans, many universities and colleges have made arrangements for long periods of productive labor and short periods ranging from one year to half a year and to three months. This work style is also very good. Short periods of productive labor are needed, because it is easy for the students to combine the manual work with their own specialties. However, appropriate arrangements for comparatively long periods of productive labor in different colleges can even play a greater role in relation to ideological education.

In 1959, graduates of the Molding Department of Tsinghua

University mapped out a one-year labor plan. The graduates, like workers in our country, have assumed full responsibility to carry out their production work. At the beginning, some students complained that manual work was an obstacle for them in learning more new techniques, and later some students became complacent when they learned a little technique, or even attempted to change their work or stopped learning from the experienced workers. All these ideas originated from individualism and the viewpoint of technique; the students have not yet fully understood the importance of labor and the laboring people, and the significance of combining education with productive labor. Their participation in labor aimed only at learning new techniques; furthermore, they looked upon the laboring people as knowing only a little more of productive techniques than intellectuals. When they made a real effort to carry out production tasks after the university authorities handed over the responsibility of production to them, they gradually realized the great responsibilities and important contributions of the laboring people to national construction and began to enjoy the great pleasure of common labor.

They began to understand the important role of each individual laborer in relation to the entire production, thereby further strengthening their viewpoint of collectivism. They learned that only by constant practice could they make new inventions and further expand the technical revolution campaign in the course of production. They also realized that only by means of gradually learning from the workers and peasants could they see the great significance of the proletarian world outlook. Many good experiences in combining education with productive labor have been accumulated by us. We must make special efforts expeditiously to sum up and study in real earnest these experiences. One of the most important experiences is to put our hands firmly on political and ideological work from the beginning to the end in the course of mobilizing the students to take part in manual work. By so doing, we will be able further to elevate their own sense of participation in labor and reform their ideology. Some persons who held the view that labor itself plays a role of reforming the ideas of men concentrated only on the arrangements for labor and failed to put special stress on ideological and political work. Such views and methods are not correct. We must realize that the important aim of combining education with productive labor is to reform our studies, our ideology, and also our philosophy of life. Ideas alienating people from realities, from labor, and from laboring people, based on individualism, are the result of the ideological influence of the bourgeoisie on the ideological front of intellectuals.

Therefore, in the course of launching ideological and political work among students, special attention must be paid first to the views and deeds of students in actual labor, so that ideological education can be conducted constantly. If a student can improve himself in the ideological field at a comparatively rapid rate, he can also make equal accomplishments in other fields. To neglect work in this aspect will result in the failure to fulfill the aims of combining education with productive labor. Only by putting special stresses on ideological and political work to elevate the students' consciousness of taking part in labor and reforming their own ideology will it be possible for us to speed up the elevation of students' political consciousness and cultural levels and to fulfill the target of transforming intellectuals into working people.

The integration of education with productive labor is vital in improving the quality of teaching, in raising the level of political consciousness, and in converting intellectuals into working people. This has been fully proved by facts in the previous two years. This is only the beginning, and we must continue to struggle to create more and better experiences in this respect so as to enable our universities and colleges to turn out Socialist laboring people in large numbers; people who are red and profoundly expert, able to use both their brains and hands, and imbued with high degrees of political consciousness.

SOURCE: *Current Background,* No. 642 (Hong Kong: United States Consulate General, January 5, 1961). Originally published in *Jen Min Jih Pao* [People's Daily], October 15, 1960.

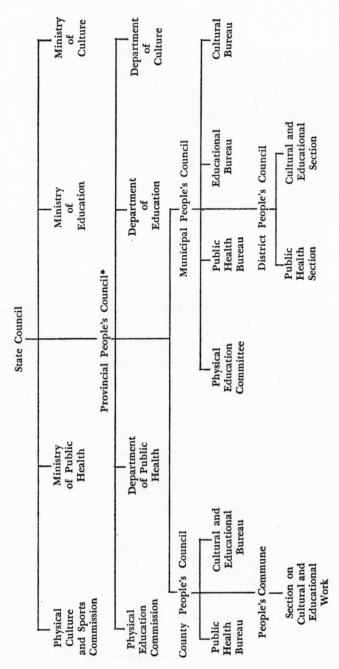

Chinese Communist Government Control of Education in 1960

State Council

Physical Culture and Sports Commission — Ministry of Public Health — Ministry of Education — Ministry of Culture

Provincial People's Council*

Physical Education Commission — Department of Public Health — Department of Education — Department of Culture

Municipal People's Council

Physical Education Committee — Public Health Bureau — Educational Bureau — Cultural Bureau

District People's Council

Public Health Section — Cultural and Educational Section

County People's Council

Public Health Bureau — Cultural and Educational Bureau

People's Commune

Section on Cultural and Educational Work

* Also special municipality people's councils.

SOURCE: Chang-tu Hu, *China: Its People, Its Society, Its Culture* (New Haven, Conn.: HRAF Press, 1960), p. 421.

Chinese Communist Educational System in 1960

Age	Classes							
	5		Research Institutes					
	4							
	3			Universities, Institutes, and Colleges				Red and Expert Colleges
	2	Technical Colleges						
18	1							
17	6	Senior Middle Schools	Vocational Middle (Polytechnic, Normal, and Other) Schools	Short-Term Worker and Peasant Middle Schools	Senior Spare-time Middle Schools 3-4 Years		Red and Expert Middle Schools	
16	5							
15	4							
14	3	Junior Middle Schools			Junior Spare-time Middle Schools 3-4 Years			
13	2							
12	1							
11	6	Primary Schools		Spare-time Primary Schools (No Year Limitation)				
10	5							
9	4							
8	3							
7	2							
6	1							
5		Nurseries and Kindergartens						
4								
3								

SOURCE: Chang-tu Hu, *China: Its People, Its Society, Its Culture* (New Haven, Conn.: HRAF Press, 1960), p. 419.

Bibliography

Bibliographical Note

This bibliography is intended as a general reading guide to supplement the material in the preceding record and documentary collection on Chinese Communist education. Most of the records have further references appended to them which are derived solely from Chinese Communist sources. They stand, therefore, by themselves entirely as a collection of Chinese Communist educational writings or speeches, devoid of non-Communist analysis or interpretation (apart from the few lines of introductory comment). The quality of the record and bibliographical selections is not entirely even, and the English-language material prepared in Peking specifically for worldwide consumption is generally inferior in content, analysis, and self-criticism when compared to the articles on education intended for internal distribution. A check of the source of each record or document will indicate whether the material was intended to be read primarily by a Chinese audience or whether it was to be directed at an international audience. The same caution as to origin must be observed for the bibliography which follows, as it contains references to both Communist and non-Communist publications.

The items listed in the bibliography are, for the most part, directly pertinent to a study of education and culture in Communist China. Although emphasis has been placed on the period from 1950 to 1960, references are not entirely confined to this period or to education *per se*. Several select references are listed which give useful background information on Chinese thought and culture both in the classical and Communist periods. But they are only intended to augment the materials in the record and documentary collection, which more directly relate to Communist Chinese education and are not intended to constitute an up-to-date bibliography.

413

A somewhat neglected source of good, although uneven, information about and analysis of Chinese education before the Communist period can be found in doctoral dissertations. The very large number of Chinese students who undertook graduate study in American universities resulted in a considerable body of research available in the English language. Many of these dissertations were published either in America or in China, and they remain a principal English-language source of educational information for the period between the two World Wars. Since the change of regimes in China in 1949, the number of doctoral dissertations on Chinese education has been reduced significantly. For the student who has patience, energy, and access to these doctoral dissertations, a worthwhile fund of studies both descriptive and analytical is available. However, discrimination in selection is important. The bibliography below includes several doctoral dissertations whose titles bear witness to the wide range of topics covered by graduate student researchers working in the field of Chinese education. A useful research guide to thesis and dissertation material on China can be found in Walter C. Eells's extensive compilation, *American Dissertations on Foreign Education: Doctors' Dissertations and Masters' Theses Written at American Universities and Colleges Concerning Education or Educators in Foreign Countries and Education of Groups of Foreign Birth or Ancestry in the United States, 1884–1958*.[1]

A brief perusal of such standard bibliographical research works as the *Educational Index* or the *Reader's Guide to Periodical Literature* will reveal an extensive and wide variety of English-language references to education and culture in China during the republican period, from 1911 to 1949.

The most thorough, competent, and recent bibliography on Chinese education pertaining directly to the particular period encompassed in this collection of records is in Chang-tu Hu's *China: Its People, Its Society, Its Culture*.[2] It contains over twenty-five major subject bibliographies, each containing carefully selected

1. Washington, D.C.: Committee on International Relations, National Education Association of the United States, 1959. See especially pp. 71–87.
2. New Haven, Conn.: Human Relations Area Files, 1960.

and annotated items of interest to the specialist; several of these will directly interest educators. It may be read in conjunction with Tung-li Yuan's *Economic and Social Development of Modern China: A Bibliographical Guide.*[3] This bibliography is particularly useful for the pre-Communist period, but it is almost devoid of any major reference to educational source material.

The Comparative Education Society in 1960–61 undertook a comprehensive bibliographical collection of reference sheets (mimeographed and distributed by the Comparative Education Center of the School of Education of the University of Chicago) pertinent to education in various countries. The section devoted to Communist Chinese education is particularly useful because of the careful and thorough annotation it contains.

One of the latest bibliographies available on this subject is also afforded by Professor Chang-tu Hu in his *Chinese Education under Communism.*[4] The bibliography in this work is annotated and includes many of the major references to pre-Communist education. *Chinese Education under Communism,* in addition to its most useful bibliography, contains a concise and masterful essay on the development of Chinese education from classical times to the advent of the Communist regime. It is properly complemented by a valuable collection of major documents on Chinese Communist educational philosophy.

The bibliography below does not contain entries derived from the voluminous and detailed sources compiled as English-language translations by the United States Consulate General in Hong Kong. However, many of the selections in the collection of documents have supplementary references obtained from the Consulate's translations. The Consulate's principal publications are thoroughly indexed with cross-references to all the major phases and levels of Communist Chinese education. A researcher utilizing English-language translations of official Communist material would find this source of major importance. In 1950, a press and translation unit was established in the Consulate to develop a

3. New Haven, Conn.: Human Relations Area Files, 1956.
4. New York: Bureau of Publications, Teachers College, Columbia University, 1962.

regular flow of materials on Communist China. The principal English-language translation series of the Consulate are compiled as follows:

(1) *Current Background,* published since June 1950 on an *ad hoc* basis, appearing usually weekly. Each issue focuses on a single aspect of Chinese Communism and is a compilation from various newspaper and periodical articles. Major economic and political conferences are thoroughly documented in the translation, and a chronology of principal developments is presented periodically.

(2) *Survey of China Mainland Press,* published since November 1950. It is the major serial of the translation services issued by the Consulate and covers a carefully selected range of activities in Communist China. The *Survey* carries regularly the main governmental press releases of the *New China News Agency* and of the influential *Jen Min Jih Pao* [People's Daily].

(3) *Extracts from China Mainland Magazines,* published since August 1955 on an *ad hoc* basis, appearing usually weekly. Translations are made in full of periodical articles from various journals such as *Jen Min Chiao Ju* [People's Education], *Hsueh Hsi* [Study], and *Ch'iao Wu Pao* [Overseas Chinese Affairs Journal]. In 1962, *Extracts . . .* became *Selections from China Mainland Magazines.*

(4) *Review of the Hong Kong Chinese Press,* published from 1950 to 1961. It was issued daily and contained résumés of both the pro-Nationalist and pro-Communist press.

Since 1956, *Current Background, Survey of China Mainland Press,* and *Extracts from China Mainland Magazines* have been regularly indexed. The cumulative issues of *Current Background* and *Survey of China Mainland Press* from 1950 to 1955 have recently been indexed, as well.

The Union Research Institute in Hong Kong also engages in translating and compiling English-language studies on various aspects of Chinese communism. The Union Research Institute was first established in Nanking in 1948 and re-established in Hong Kong in January 1951 as a division of the Union Press. The Institute has accumulated a considerable collection of materials concerning Communist China, mostly publications by the Chinese Communists. The materials, covering the entire period since the establishment of the Communist regime, have been minutely classified, microfilmed, and indexed.

URI regularly acquires 95 Chinese newspapers and 228 periodicals from the mainland, Taiwan, and other parts of Asia. Over 3,000,000 classified and indexed clippings are now in its files. These are divided into six basic sections: Political and Social Affairs; Finance and Economics; Education and Culture (including Science and Technology); Military Affairs; Overseas Chinese; and, International Communism. . . .

Its library contains approximately 25,000 books and pamphlets; about eighty percent are from Communist China, and are not readily obtainable in Hong Kong. They include a unique collection of nearly three hundred textbooks published by Chinese Communists for use in primary and high schools on the mainland.

The Institute has produced a valuable English-language publication series, which includes several titles on education, entitled *Communist China Problem Research Series.* In addition, the Institute produces twice weekly a translation service of materials from China mainland regional newspapers which are not generally available. (See *Union Research Service Series.*) The Institute prepares useful monographs on Chinese education and makes available to researchers its index of acquisitions and translations.

A weekly newsletter, the *China News Analysis,* published in Hong Kong since August 1953, has become one of the most valuable sources of analytical information on Communist China. Many of the editions are devoted to educational and related matters.

Still another source of translations containing valuable information on Communist China, including, on occasion, extensive materials on education, are the translation and research reports, issued serially and on an occasional *ad hoc* basis, of the Joint Publications Research Service (JPRS), of Washington, D. C.

A component of the Technical Documentation Center (formerly the Office of Technical Services) of the United States Department of Commerce, the JPRS was established in 1957 to provide a centralized facility to produce translations from open literature for those United States government organizations interested in such materials. The JPRS contracts with private persons to translate or research the materials selected by the various organizations utilizing its services and performs work for federal agencies only. When completed, JPRS translations and research reports are duplicated for distribution to the ordering organizations and, except for scattered items from copyrighted publications, are available to the public either in single-copy sales or on a subscription basis.

One estimate holds that JPRS social science reports account for more than 90 percent of all English-language translations produced for all major fields of social science, including education, sociology, economics, political science, etc.

JPRS reports were first listed in the October 1958 *Monthly Catalog of U. S. Government Publications* and, because no attempt was made to catalog those published prior to that period, plus the fact that some titles (including copyrighted items, which would not have been listed in any case) were inadvertently omitted in the earliest period, all titles have not been listed in that publication. However, with time, gaps in listing have progressively decreased, so that since July 1, 1962, all titles (except copyrighted items) have been listed in the *Monthly Catalog;* since May 1963, all titles have been listed in unbroken numerical sequence.

To date, over 29,000 separate reports have been published, representing highly accurate translations from Russian, Chinese, all of the Eastern European languages, most of the Far Eastern languages, and nearly every other major language. These materials are extremely valuable sources on the current affairs of the countries they concern, making it possible for scholars without the language ability required to read the originals to use them freely in their research. Their scope, moreover, is such that scholars in all fields of learning have recourse to them; somewhat more than half are in the field of social science; the remainder are on scientific and technical subjects.

Social science reports range from atheism to agriculture, from the progress of the Socialist revolution in China to recent military affairs, and from trade and finance to summaries of the provincial press in various countries. In the fields of science, almost every subject is covered, from astronomy to zoölogy, including in some cases abstracts of Soviet and Chinese dissertations in a variety of fields.

A further source for translated materials on Communist China is the *Foreign Broadcast Information Service,* of Washington, D. C., a monitoring service responsible for publishing various reviews of international broadcasts, including *Daily Report: Far East,* made up of translations of current radio broadcasts from China and other Asian countries. It is indexed and available now on microfilm.

The selected bibliography which follows contains a variety of references to Chinese Communist periodicals published originally in English. The reader should be cautioned that the material to be found in these Communist periodicals is intended solely for external consumption, and only rarely does such periodical literature contain articles of substance or thoroughly critical analyses. Such items should be read and contrasted with the translated material published by such sources as the United States Consulate General in Hong Kong and the Joint Publications Research Service. The Chinese Communist publications collected and translated by the Consulate and JPRS are, for the most part, intended only for consumption within China. They often contain interesting and useful Communist self-criticism not evident to the same degree in Communist publications intended purely for foreign readers.

A question sometimes arises as to the scope of the translations and the possibility of overlapping materials emanating from the United States Consulate General in Hong Kong and the Joint Publications Research Service in Washington. It would be difficult to distinguish fully between the work load and types of material translated by these two translation agencies. It is recognized that this may be unavoidable, but efforts are made to minimize such duplication. The United States Consulate in Hong Kong generally concentrates on translations from newspapers and magazines, with only a few translations of books and pamphlets. The JPRS translates from newspapers, magazines, and books in equal measure, and it includes translations from non-Chinese sources (e.g., Russian books on Chinese education, etc.), the latter service not being performed by the Consulate. There is no hard and fast division of labor in handling newspapers and periodicals, but the United States government agencies that engage JPRS to perform translation services are usually careful not to waste resources by having JPRS translate material which is normally forthcoming from the Consulate.

The duplication that does exist (not including normal human error) results from the necessity of both Hong Kong and Washington responding quickly to their respective responsibilities. This frequently creates a situation in which, for example, the JPRS is asked to translate a document for one of the federal agencies in Washington, even though it is felt that the item will certainly be translated in Hong Kong. However, neither Hong Kong nor Washington can wait. While it is realized that duplication must be kept to a minimum, there are times when it might be unsound in the long run from both the economic and operational standpoints to await full and complete coördination of translation requirements between Washington and Hong Kong.

The selected bibliography below falls into two main areas of concentration. The first deals with background material on China, irrespective of historical periods and contains four sections, of which two concern Chinese education up to 1949. These are followed by thirteen sections devoted to China under the Communist regime since 1949. Apart from Section V, which deals with general works on Communist China, the portion of the bibliography covering the Communist period is entirely concerned with various topics related to education. Most of these fall clearly into the area of studies normally considered of direct interest to educators. However, some others, such as those concerning youth and student affairs, language reforms, and literacy campaigns, etc., are also included, as they may have a bearing on any study of education in its ideological and political context.

Readers will note that bibliographical items originating from Chinese Communist sources are listed generally through 1960, although some non-Communist analytical references are listed through 1964. The bibliographical listing of English-language sources of Chinese education, either before or after the advent of the Communist regime, is certainly not exhaustive. But in the absence of other bibliographies devoted exclusively to Chinese Communist education for English readers, it is felt that the listings which follow should be suitable for an introductory study of educational developments in Communist China during the first decade of the regime's existence.

In this bibliography, most Chinese names are given in their original form, i.e.,with the surname first, followed by the given name. Western names are inverted, in the usual bibliographical practice, as are the names of those Chinese who have adopted the Western style. Thus, CHEN PO-TA is alphabetized under C, while Chang-tu Hu is found as HU, CHANG-TU. The absence or presence of the comma indicates whether the name is given in the Chinese or the Western style.

Section I
Bibliography, Reference, and Documentation

"Bibliography of Asian Studies, 1962," *Journal of Asian Studies,* XXII, No. 5 (September 1963).

Bibliography of Social Science Periodicals and Monograph Series: Mainland China, 1949–1960. Washington, D. C.: Government Printing Office, 1961.

CHAN WING-TSIT. *An Outline and an Annotated Bibliography of Chinese Philosophy.* New Haven, Conn.: Far Eastern Publications, 1959.

CHAO KUO-CHUN. *Selected Works in English for a Topical Study of Modern China, 1840–1952.* Cambridge, Mass.: Regional Studies Program on East Asia, Harvard University, 1952.

———. *Source Materials from Communist China,* 3 vols. Cambridge, Mass.: Russian Research Center, Harvard University, 1953.

China: A Selected List of References, 1945–1957. New York: American Institute of Pacific Relations, 1957.

Columbia University Masters' Essays and Doctoral Dissertations on Asia, 1875–1956. New York: Columbia University, the East Asiatic Library, 1957.

DAVIDSON, M. *A List of Published Translations from Chinese into English, French, and German.* 2 parts. Ann Arbor: American Council of Learned Societies, 1952–1957.

EELLS, WALTER CROSBY. *American Dissertations on Foreign Education: Doctors' Dissertations and Masters' Theses Written at American Universities and Colleges Concerning Education or Educators in Foreign Countries and Education of Groups of Foreign Birth or Ancestry in the United States 1884–1958.* Washington: Committee on International Relations, National Education Association of the United States, 1959.

HUCKER, CHARLES O. *China: A Critical Bibliography.* Tucson, Ariz.: University of Arizona Press, 1962.

———. *Chinese History: A Bibliographic Review.* Washington, D. C.: Service Center for Teachers of History, 1958.

422

LINDBECK, JOHN M. H. "Research Materials on Communist China: United States Government Sources," *Journal of Asian Studies,* XVIII, No. 3 (May 1959), 357–363.

A Select Bibliography: Asia, Africa, Eastern Europe, Latin America. New York: American Universities Field Staff, Inc., 1960.

SORICH, RICHARD (ed.). *Contemporary China: A Bibliography of Reports on China Published by the United States Joint Publications Research Service.* [Prepared for the Joint Committee on Contemporary China of the American Council of Learned Societies and the Social Science Research Council.] New York: Readex Microprint Corporation, 1961.

THOMAS, S. B. *Recent Books on China, 1945–51.* New York: Institute of Pacific Relations, 1951.

YUAN TUNG-LI. *Economic and Social Development of Modern China: A Bibliographical Guide.* New Haven, Conn.: Human Relations Area Files, 1956.

Section II
Chinese History, Culture, and Philosophy

BAGCHI, PRABODH CHANDRA. *India and China: A Thousand Years of Cultural Relations.* 2d rev. ed. New York: Philosophical Library 1951.

DEBARY, WILLIAM THEODORE (ed.). *Sources of Chinese Tradition.* New York: Columbia University Press, 1960.

BODDE, G. *China's Cultural Tradition.* New York: Rinehart, 1959.

BRIERE, O. *Fifty Years of Chinese Philosophy (1898–1950).* Translated from the French with additional annotation and bibliography by LAWRENCE G. THOMPSON. London: Allen and Unwin, 1956.

CHAI CH'U. "Chinese Humanism: A Study of Chinese Mentality and Temperament," *Social Research,* XXVI, No. 1 (Spring 1959), 31–46.

―――― and WINBERG CHAI. *The Changing Society of China:* New York: New American Library of World Literature, 1962.

CHEN, WILLIAM JUN-TUNG. "Some Controversies on Chinese Education and Culture." Columbia University doctoral dissertation, 1951.

CHU SHIH-YING. "The Problem of Life and the Problem of Education as Viewed by Ancient Chinese Thinkers: With Constructive Analyses and Suggestions Towards a Philosophy of Education." Harvard University doctoral dissertation, 1926.

CREEL, HERRLEE G. "Chinese Culture and Liberal Education," *Journal of General Education,* XII, No. 1 (January 1959), 29–38.

―――― . *Chinese Thought from Confucius to Mao Tse-tung.* Chicago: University of Chicago Press, 1953.

DANTON, GEORGE H. *The Culture Contacts of the United States and China: The Earliest Sino-American Culture Contacts 1784–1844.* New York: Columbia University Press, 1931.

DAY, CLARENCE BURTON. *The Philosophers of China.* New York: Philosophical Library, 1962.

DENBY, CHARLES. *China and Her People: Being the Observations, Reminiscences, and Conclusions of an American Diplomat.* 2 vols. Boston: L. C. Page & Co., 1906.

424

DICKINSON, G. LOWES. *Letters from a Chinese Official: Being an Eastern View of Western Civilization.* New York: McClure, Phillips & Co., 1906.

FEUERWERKER, ALBERT. *China's Early Industrialization: Sheng Hsuanhuai (1844–1916) and Mandarin Enterprise.* (Harvard East Asian Studies No. 6) Cambridge, Mass.: Harvard University Press, 1961.

FITZGERALD, CHARLES P. *China: A Short Cultural History.* Rev. ed. London: Cresset Press, 1950.

FORKE, ALFRED. *The World Conception of the Chinese: Their Astronomical, Cosmological, and Physico-Philosophical Speculations.* London: Arthur Probsthain, 1925.

FUNG YU-LAN. *A History of Chinese Philosophy.* Translated from the Chinese by DERK BODDE. 2 vols. Princeton, N. J.: Princeton University Press, 1951 (Vol. I), 1953 (Vol. II).

GILES, HERBERT A. *A History of Chinese Literature.* New York: Appleton, 1927.

GOODRICH, L. C., and H. C. FENN. *A Syllabus of the History of Chinese Civilization and Culture.* 6th ed. New York: China Society of America, 1958.

HO PING-TI. *Studies on the Population of China 1368–1953.* Cambridge, Mass.: Harvard University Press, 1959.

HSU, FRANCIS L. K. *Americans and Chinese: Two Ways of Life.* New York: Henry Schuman, 1953.

HU, CHANG-TU. *China: Its People, Its Society, Its Culture.* New Haven, Conn.: HRAF Press, 1960.

LATOURETTE, KENNETH SCOTT. *The Chinese: Their History and Culture.* 3d rev. ed. New York: Macmillan, 1946.

———. *A History of Modern China.* Harmondsworth, Middlesex, England: Penguin Books, 1954.

LEVENSON, JOSEPH RICHMOND. *Confucian China and Its Modern Fate: The Problem of Intellectual Continuity.* Berkeley: University of California Press, 1958.

LIN MOUSHENG. *Men and Ideas: An Informal History of Chinese Political Thought.* New York: John Day, 1942.

LUNG CHIENG-FU. "The Evolution of Chinese Social Thought." University of Southern California doctoral dissertation, 1935.

MIAO CHU-SENG. "The Value of Confucianism for Religious Education in China." University of Chicago doctoral dissertation, 1923.

ROWE, DAVID N. *Modern China: A Brief History.* Princeton, N. J.: D. Van Nostrand, 1959.

TENG SSU-YII. *Research Guide for China's Response to the West.* Cambridge, Mass.: Harvard University Press, 1954.

—— and JOHN K. FAIRBANK. *China's Response to the West.* Cambridge, Mass.: Harvard University Press, 1954.

TSAO WEN-YEN. *The Constitutional Structure of Modern China.* Melbourne, Australia: Melbourne University Press, 1947.

WEBER, MAX. *The Religion of China: Confucianism and Taoism.* Translated and edited by HANS H. GERTH. Glencoe, Ill.: Glencoe Free Press, 1951.

WEI, FRANCIS C. M. *The Spirit of Chinese Culture.* New York: Charles Scribner's Sons, 1947.

WEI, WILSON SHIH-SHENG. "The History of Educational Philosophy in China." New York University doctoral dissertation, 1934.

WILLIAMS, LEA E. *Overseas Chinese Nationalism: The Genesis of the Pan-Chinese Movement in Indonesia, 1900–1916.* Glencoe, Ill.: Glencoe Free Press, 1960.

WILLIAMS, S. WELLS. *A History of China: Being the Historical Chapters from "The Middle Kingdom"* (with a concluding chapter narrating recent events by F. WELLS WILLIAMS). New York: Charles Scribner's Sons, 1901.

——. *Middle Kingdom: A Survey of the Geography, Government, Education, Social Life, Art, Religion of the Chinese Empire and Its Inhabitants.* 2 vols., 3d rev. ed. New York: John Wiley, 1849.

WRIGHT, ARTHUR F. (ed.). *Studies in Chinese Thought.* Chicago: University of Chicago Press, 1953.

WU CHING-TZU. *The Scholars.* Peking: Foreign Languages Press, 1957.

See also:
BRYAN (III) • CHAN (XV) • FAIRBANK (III) • LI (III) • MASATUGU (VII) • NIVISON (VI) • PURCELL (XVII) • SUN YAT-SEN (IV) • TUNG (V)

Section III
Chinese Education: Classical and Imperial

ARNOLD, JULEAN H. "Educational Activity in Foochow, China," in *U.S. Bureau of Education Report, 1907*, I, 191–220.

BERNARD, HENRI. *Matteo Ricci's Scientific Contribution to China.* Translated by EDWARD CHALMERS WERNER. Peiping: Henry Vetch, 1935.

BIGGERSTAF, KNIGHT. *The Earliest Modern Government Schools in China.* Ithaca: Cornell University Press, 1961.

BRUNNERT, H. S., and V. V. HAGELSTORM. *Present Day Political Organization of China.* Translated by A. BELTCHENKO and E. E. MORAN. Shanghai: Kelly and Walsh, Ltd., 1912.

BRYAN, WILLIAM JENNINGS. *Letters to a Chinese Official: Being a Western View of Eastern Civilizations, by William Jennings Bryan.* New York: McClure, Phillips & Co., 1906.

BURTON, MARGARET E. *Education of Women in China.* New York: Fleming H. Revell, 1911.

CHANG CHIH-TUNG. *China's Only Hope: An Appeal by Her Greatest Viceroy, Chang Chih-tung, with the Sanction of the Present Emperor, Kwang Su.* Translated from the Chinese edition by SAMUEL I. WOODBRIDGE; introduction by GRIFFITH JOHN. New York: Fleming H. Revell, 1900.

CHANG, CHUNG-LI. *The Chinese Gentry: Studies on Their Role in Nineteenth-Century Chinese Society.* Seattle: University of Washington Press, 1955.

CHIANG MON-LIN. *A Study in Chinese Principles of Education.* Shanghai: Commercial Press, Ltd., 1924.

"China Proper," pp. 132–133 in *Cyclopedia of Education: A Dictionary of Information for the Use of Teachers, School Officers, Parents, and Others,* ed. HENRY KIDDLE and ALEXANDER J. SCHEM. New York: E. Steiger, 1877.

CH'U, S. Y. "Education and Its Traditions," pp. 599–626 in *The Year Book of Education 1949,* ed. G. B. JEFFERY, et al. London: Evans Bros., Ltd., 1949.

CHU, SAMUEL C. "Chang Chien, Pioneer Industrialist, Educator, and Conservationist of Modern China (1853–1926)." Columbia University doctoral dissertation, 1958.

DOOLITTLE, JUSTUS. *Social Life of the Chinese: With Some Accounts of Their Religious, Governmental, Educational and Business Customs and Opinions.* 2 vols. New York: Harper & Bros., 1865.

DUUS, PETER. "Science and Salvation in China: The Life and Work of W. A. P. Martin," *Papers on China* (Harvard University East Asia Regional Studies Seminars), X (October 1956), 98–141.

FAIRBANK, JOHN KING (ed.). *Chinese Thought and Institutions.* Chicago: University of Chicago Press, 1957.

FRANKE, WOLFGANG. *The Reform and Abolition of the Traditional Chinese Examination System.* Cambridge, Mass.: Distributed by Harvard University Press, 1960.

FRYER, JOHN. *Admission of Chinese Students to American Colleges.* Bulletin No. 2. Washington, D. C.: U.S. Bureau of Education, 1909.

GALT, HOWARD SPILMAN. *The Development of Chinese Educational Theory: The Historical Development of the Theory of Education in China to the Close of the Han Dynasty,* A.D. 220. Shanghai: Commercial Press, Ltd., 1929.

——. *History of Chinese Educational Institutons,* Vol. I, London: Arthur Probsthain, 1951.

——. "Oriental and Occidental Elements in China's Modern Educational System," *Chinese Social and Political Science Review,* XII (1928), 405–425, 627–647; XIII (1929), 12–29.

GILES, HERBERT A. *The Civilization of China.* London: Williams and Norgate, 1911.

HACKETT, ROGER F. "Chinese Students in Japan, 1900–1910," *Papers on China* (Harvard University East Asia Regional Studies Seminars), III (May 1949), 134–169.

HEADLAND, ISAAC T. "Education in China," in *Cyclopedia of Education,* ed. PAUL MONROE. New York: Macmillan, 1911.

HIPPISLEY, ALFRED E. "National Education in China," *The Health Exhibition Literature* (London: Executive Council of the International Health Exhibition and Council of the Society of Arts), XIX (1884), 229–252.

HOH YAM TONG. "The Boxer Indemnity Remissions and Education in China: Being an Historical and Analytical Study of the China Indemnity of 1901 as Remitted to China by the United States of America, Great Britain, France, Belgium, Italy, Soviet Russia, and the Netherlands, and the Applications of these Remissions to Educational and Cultural Purposes, Together with a Chapter on Japan's Use of Her Share 'for Cultural Work in China.'" Columbia University doctoral dissertation, 1933.

HSIAO, THEODORE ENCHENG. *A History of Modern Education in China.* Peking: Peking University Press, 1932; Shanghai: Commercial Press, Ltd., 1935.

HU CHANG HO JIUGOW. "A General Outline on the Reorganization of the Chinese Educational System." New York University doctoral dissertation, 1917.

HU SHIH. *The Development of Logical Methods in Ancient China.* Shanghai: Oriental Book Co., 1922.

KING CHU. "Confucian Tradition," pp. 635–646 in *The Year Book of Education 1951*, ed. J. A. LAUWERYS and N. HANS. London: Evans Bros., Ltd., 1951.

KING, H. E. *The Educational System of China as Recently Reconstructed.* Bulletin No. 15. Washington, D. C.: U. S. Bureau of Education, 1911.

KRACKE, E. A., JR. *Civil Service in Early Sung China 960–1067: With Particular Emphasis on the Development of Controlled Sponsorship to Foster Administrative Responsibility.* Cambridge, Mass.: Harvard University Press, 1953.

KUHN, PHILIP. "T'ao Hsing-chih, 1891–1946: An Educational Reformer," *Papers on China* (Harvard University East Asia Regional Studies Seminars), XIII (December 1959), 163–195.

KUO PING-WEN. *The Chinese System of Public Education.* ("Teachers College Contributions to Education," No. 64.) New York: Teachers College, Columbia University, 1915.

———. "The Effect of the Revolution upon the Educational System of China," *Educational Review*, XLV (May 1913), 457–470.

LEWIS, ROBERT E. *The Educational Conquest of the Far East.* New York: Fleming H. Revell, 1903.

LI AN-CHE. "Buddhist Tradition," pp. 646–654 in *The Year Book of Education 1951*, ed. J. A. LAUWERYS and N. HANS. London: Evans Bros., Ltd., 1951.

MARTIN, W. A. P. *The Chinese: Their Education, Philosophy, and Letters.* New York: Harper & Bros., 1881.

———. *The Lore of Cathay; or, The Intellect of China.* New York: Fleming H. Revell, 1901.

———. *Report on the System of Public Instruction in China*, Circulars of Information No. 1. Washington, D.C.: U. S. Bureau of Education, 1877.

MERRILL, H. F. "The Chinese Student in America," pp. 197–222 in *China and the Far East,* ed. GEORGE H. BLAKESLEE. New York: Thomas Y. Crowell, 1910.

POTT, FRANCIS L. HAWKS. "China's Method of Revising Her Educational System," *Annals of the American Academy of Political and Social Science,* XXXIX (1912), 83–97.

Progress of Western Education in China and Siam. (Accounts forwarded to the Department of State by the United States Minister at Peking and the United State Consul at Bangkok.) Washington, D.C.: U. S. Bureau of Education, 1880.

REINSCH, PAUL SAMUEL. "Cultural Factors in the Chinese Crisis," *Annals of the American Academy of Political and Social Science* XVI (1900), 435–445.

———. *The Intellectual and Political Currents in the Far East.* Boston: Houghton Mifflin, 1911.

SHEFFIELD, D. Z. "The New Learning of China—Its Status and Outlook," pp. 222–244 in *China and the Far East,* ed. GEORGE H. BLAKSLEE. New York: Thomas Y. Crowell, 1910.

SWISHER, EARL. "Chinese Intellectuals and the Western Impact 1838–1900," *Comparative Studies in Society and History,* I, No. 1 (October 1958), 26–37.

WANG, Y. C. "Intellectuals and Society in China 1860–1949," *Comparative Studies in Society and History,* III, No. 4 (July 1961), 395–426.

WILLIAMSON, H. R. *Wang An Shih: A Chinese Statesman and Educationalist.* London: Arthur Probsthain, 1935.

YUNG WING. *My Life in China and America.* New York: Henry Holt, 1909.

See also:
BAGCHI (II) • CHANG CHI-YUN: *Centenary Celebrations* (IV) • CHU (II) • DANTON (II) • DENBY (II) • DICKINSON (II) • FAIRBANK (XV) • FRYER (IV) • GRAYBILL (IV) • KING (IV) • LAMBERTON (IV) • LATOURETTE (IV) • WILLIAM CHENG-CHIAN LEE (XVII) • LUNG (II) • *A Survey of Chinese Students* (IV) • S. WELLS WILLIAMS: *A History of China* (II) • Wu (II)

Section IV
Chinese Education: Modern and Republican

"Anti-foreign education in China," Appendix No. 5 to *The Present Condition of China: With Reference to Circumstances Affecting International Relations and the Good Understanding between Nations upon Which Peace Depends.* (Documents transmitted to the League of Nations, December 10, 1931.) Tokyo: Imperial Japanese Foreign Office, 1932.

Anti-foreign Teachings in New Text Books of China. (Text in English and Japanese.) Tokyo: Sokokusha, c. 1933.

ARNDT, CHRISTIAN OTTOMAR, SEVERIN K. TUROSIENSKI, and TUNG YUEN FONG. *Education in China Today.* (U. S. Office of Education Leaflet No. 69.) Washington, D. C.: U. S. Office of Education, 1944.

"Background: The May Fourth Movement," *Peking Review,* II (April 29, 1959), 31–33.

BATES, M. S. "The Task of Education in China," *Pacific Affairs,* XIX, No. 2 (June 1946), 131–145.

BECKER, C. H. *Educational Problems in the Far and Near East.* London: Oxford University Press, 1933.

BECKER, C. H., P. LANGEVIN, M. FALSKI, and R. H. TAWNEY. *The Reorganization of Education in China.* Paris: League of Nations Institute of Intellectual Co-operation, 1932.

BOROWITZ, ALBERT. "Chiang Monlin: Theory and Practice of Chinese Education 1917–1930," *Papers on China* (Harvard University East Asia Regional Studies Seminars), VIII (February 1954), 107–135.

BUCK, PEARL S. *Tell the People: Talks with James Yen about the Mass Education Movement.* New York: John Day, 1945.

CHANG CHI-YUN. *The Centenary Celebrations of Sino-American Intellectual Friendship.* Taipei: China Culture Publishing Foundation, 1953.

———. "Confucianism and Modern Education in China," *Chinese Culture,* III, No. 2 (October 1960), 101–118.

CHANG JEN-CHI. *Pre-Communist China's Rural School and Community.* Boston: Christopher Publishing House, 1960.

431

CHANG PE-CHIN. "The Administrative Reorganization of the Educational System of a County in China: Based on the Analysis of Cheng Ting-Hsien." Cornell University doctoral dissertation, 1935.

CHANG PENG-CHUN. *Education for Modernization in China: A Search for Criteria of Curriculum-Construction in View of the Transition in National Life, with Special Reference to Secondary Education.* ("Teachers College Contributions to Education," No. 137.) New York: Teachers College, Columbia University, 1923.

CHAO, FREDERICK PU-HSIA. "Education for a Democratic China." Columbia University doctoral dissertation, 1946.

CHEN SIH-KONG. "A Plan for Adult Education in China Based on the Experiences of Major Experiments of Adult Education, the Resources of the Social Conditions in China, and the History of Chinese Education in the Last Eighty Years." Columbia University doctoral dissertation, 1942.

CHEN, THEODORE HSI-EN. "The Educational Crisis in China," *Educational Administration and Supervision*, XXXIV, No. 8, (December 1948), 468–478.

CHEN WEI-LUN. "A Sociological Foundation of Adult Education in China." New York University doctoral dissertation, 1935.

CHENG CHI-PAO. "Public Education," pp. 599–626 in *The Year Book of Education 1949,* ed. G. B. JEFFERY, *et al.* London: Evans Bros., Ltd., 1949.

CHENG, J. CHESTER. "The Educational System in Modern and Contemporary China," pp. 181–194 in *Contemporary China: Economic and Social Studies, Documents, Chronology, Bibliography,* ed. E. STUART KIRBY, Vol. III. Hong Kong: Hong Kong University Press, 1960; London: Oxford University Press, 1960.

CHENG, RONALD YU-SOONG. *The Financing of Public Education in China: A Factual Analysis of Its Major Problems of Reconstruction.* Shanghai: Commercial Press, Ltd., 1935.

CHIANG MONLIN. *Tides from the West: A Chinese Autobiography.* New Haven, Conn.: Yale University Press, 1948.

——— and HOLLINGTON TONG. *Sun Yat-sen on International Co-operation.* Taipei: China Culture Publishing Foundation, 1953.

CHIANG, WEN-HAN. *The Ideological Background of the Chinese Student Movement.* New York: King's Crown Press, 1948.

"Chinese University Degrees," *Quarterly Bulletin of Chinese Bibliography,* II, No. 2 (June 1935), 26.

CHOU FU-CHUAN. "China's Need for Universal Education." Syracuse University doctoral dissertation, 1921.

CHOU WO-MIN. "An Historical and Statistical Survey of the Recent Development of Chinese Education." New York University doctoral dissertation, 1920.

CHOW TSE-TUNG. *The May Fourth Movement: Intellectual Revolution in Modern China.* Cambridge, Mass.: Harvard University Press, 1960.

Christian Education in China: A Study Made by an Educational Commission Representing the Mission Boards Conducting Work in China. New York: Committee of Reference and Counsel of the Foreign Missions Conference of North America, 1922.

CHU PING-CHIEN. "A Proposed Administrative Pattern of the Hsien (County) School System in China." Columbia University doctoral dissertation, 1947.

CHU YU-KUANG. *Some Problems of a National System of Education in China: A Study in the Light of Comparative Education.* Shanghai: Commercial Press, Ltd., 1933.

CHUANG CHAI-HSUAN. *Tendencies Toward a Democratic System of Education in China.* Shanghai: Commercial Press, Ltd., 1922.

CHUNG LU-CHAI. *A History of Democratic Education in Modern China.* Shanghai: Commercial Press, Ltd., 1934.

DEWEY, JOHN. *Letters from China and Japan by John Dewey and Alice Chapman Dewey,* ed. EVELYN DEWEY. New York: Dutton, 1920.

EDMUNDS, CHARLES KEYSER. *Modern Education in China.* Bulletin No. 44. Washington, D. C.: U. S. Bureau of Education, 1919.

"Educational Notes," *Quarterly Bulletin of Chinese Bibliography,* II, No. 1 (March 1935), 2.

FANG TUNG-YUAN. "An Improved Program of Secondary Education in Postwar China." University of Pennsylvania doctoral dissertation, 1947.

FORSTER, LANCELOT. *The New Culture in China.* With an introduction by SIR MICHAEL E. SADLER. New York: Frederick A. Stokes, 1936.

FREYN, HUBERT. *Chinese Education in the War.* Shanghai: Kelly and Walsh, 1940.

FRYER, JOHN. *Report to the Regents of the University of California on the Educational Reform in China* [reprinted from the *University of California Chronicle,* XII, No. 3]. Berkeley: University of California, 1910.

FUGH, PAUL CHEN. "Reconstruction of the Chinese Elementary School Curriculum to Meet Rural Needs of China." Cornell University doctoral dissertation, 1924.

GAGE, BROWNELL. "The American Colleges in the Orient as Exemplified by the College of Yale-in-China." Yale University doctoral dissertation, 1924.

GRAYBILL, HENRY BLAIR. *The Educational Reform in China.* Hong Kong: Kelly and Walsh, 1911.

GREGG, ALICE HENRIETTA. *China and Educational Autonomy: The Changing Role of the Protestant Educational Missionary in China, 1807–1937.* Syracuse, N.Y.: Syracuse University Press, 1946.

GUO, LOIS RUJEN WANG. "A Critique of Proposals for Educational Reconstruction in China." University of Michigan doctoral dissertation, 1944.

HOLDEN, REUBEN ANDRUS. "An Educational Experiment in China: The Story of the Development of Yale-in-China." Yale University doctoral dissertation, 1951.

HSU, JENNIE. "A Study of Certain Problems in the Higher Institutions for Women in China." Columbia University doctoral dissertation, 1931.

HU SHIH. *The Chinese Renaissance.* 2d ed. New York: Paragon Books, 1963.

HUA SHEH. "Youth in Liberated China," *China Digest,* V, No. 4 (December 14, 1948), 11.

HUGHES, E. R. "The Oxford Scheme for Aiding Chinese Universities with Books and Equipment," *Asiatic Review,* XXXVII, No. 129 (January 1941), 114–121.

JUAN KANG-CHENG. "An Educational Program for China in Transition." Columbia University doctoral dissertation, 1940.

KIANG YING-CHENG. "The Geography of Higher Education in China." Columbia University doctoral dissertation, 1955.

KING, HARRY EDWIN. *The Educational System of China as Recently Reconstructed.* Bulletin No. 15. Washington, D. C.: U. S. Bureau of Education, 1911.

KUO PING-WEN. *Higher Education in China.* (*Bulletins on Chinese Education,* Chinese National Association for the Advancement of Education, II, No. 10.) Shanghai: Commercial Press, Ltd., 1923.

LAMBERTON, MARY. *St. John's University, Shanghai, 1879–1951.* New York: United Board for Christian Colleges in China, 1955.

LATOURETTE, KENNETH SCOTT. *A History of Christian Missions in China.* New York: Macmillan, 1929.

LEE, PETER HSING-HSIEN. "A Study of Progressive Christian Education in the Light of the Needs of China." Louisville: Southern Baptist Theological Seminary doctoral dissertation, 1950.

LEFFORGE, ROXY. "Some Guiding Principles for Christian Education in China Today." Boston University doctoral dissertation, 1933.

LEGER, SAMUEL HOWARD. "Education of Christian Ministers in China: A Historical and Critical Study." Columbia University doctoral dissertation, 1925.

LEWIS, IDA BELLE. *The Education of Girls in China.* ("Teachers College Contributions to Education," No. 104.) New York: Bureau of Publications, Teachers College, Columbia University, 1919.

LI CHI-TAO. "The Struggle on the Second Front: Reminiscences of the Shanghai Student Movement during the Third Revolutionary War," *Evergreen: A Magazine of Chinese Youth and Students,* No. 6 (August-September 1961), 15–19; No. 7 (October 1961), 17–20.

LI YUNTIN CHENG. *A Study of the Organization of the American One-Teacher School, with Suggestions for Possible Adaptation to the Chinese Village School.* Shanghai: Chung Hua Book Co., 1929.

LIANG YIN-MEI. "Peiping Teachers Strike for a Full Stomach," *China Digest,* V, No. 2 (November 16, 1948), 12.

LIN YUTANG. "A Berlitz School for Chinese," pp. 73–78 in *Letters of a Chinese Amazon and Wartime Essays.* Shanghai: Commercial Press, Ltd., 1930.

LING HAN-DAH. *A Study of English Textbooks Used in China.* Shanghai: World Book Company, Ltd., 1941.

LOH LING-SU. "The Status of Primary Education in China." University of Chicago doctoral dissertation, 1922.

LUTZ, JESSIE GREGORY. "The Role of the Christian Colleges in Modern China before 1928." Cornell University doctoral dissertation, 1955.

MACNAIR, HARLEY FARNSWORTH (ed.). *Modern Chinese History: Selected Readings; a Collection of Extracts from Various Sources Chosen to Illustrate Some of the Chief Phases of China's International Relations during the Past Hundred Years.* Shanghai: Commercial Press, Ltd., 1927.

MIAO MIN. "Fang Chih-min's Schooldays: Reminiscences of the Revolution," *Evergreen: A Magazine of Chinese Youth and Students,* No. 3 (June 1963), 39–43.

MONROE, PAUL. "Education and Government in China," *Essays in Comparative Education: Republished Papers* (Studies of the International Institute of Teachers College, Columbia University), II (1932), 93–102.

———. "Report on Education in China," *ibid.*, I (1927), 50–87.

———. "Students and Politics in China," *ibid.*, I (1927), 88–96.

O'YANG SIANG. "Reconstruction of Teacher Training in China on the Elementary Level." Ohio State University doctoral dissertation, 1935.

PEAKE, CYRUS HENDERSON. *Nationalism and Education in Modern China.* New York: Columbia University Press, 1932.

POTT, FRANCIS L. HAWKS. "Modern Education," in *China,* ed. H. F. MacNair. Berkeley and Los Angeles: University of California Press, 1946.

PURCELL, V. *Problems of Chinese Education.* London: Kegan Paul, Trench, Trubner and Co., Ltd., 1936.

REES, RONALD. *News From China.* London: Livingstone Press, 1947.

RUGH, ARTHUR DOUGLAS. "American Influence in China's Changing Education." University of Washington doctoral dissertation, 1940.

RUSSELL, BERTRAND. "The Problem of China," in *Education and the Modern World.* New York: W. W. Norton, 1932.

SCOTT, RODERICK. *Fukien Christian University.* New York: United Board for Christian Colleges in China, 1958.

SHEN WEI-CHIH. "The Role of Education in Postwar China." University of Pennsylvania doctoral dissertation, 1948.

SMITH, HAROLD FRED. "Elementary Education in Shantung, China: A Study of the Reorganization of the Curriculum of the Elementary Schools of Rural Shantung and Plans for the Preparation of Teachers for These Schools." Columbia University doctoral dissertation, 1930.

STEIN, GUNTHER. "A People Goes to School," pp. 208–214 in *The Challenge of Red China.* London: Pilot Press, Ltd., 1945.

STUART, JOHN LEIGHTON. *Fifty Years in China: The Memoirs of John Leighton Stuart, Missionary and Ambassador.* New York: Random House, 1954.

SUN HUAI-CHIN. "A Study of Chinese Secondary Education, with a Suggested Program for Reorganization." University of Colorado doctoral dissertation, 1949.

SUN YAT-SEN. *San Min Chu I: The Three Principles of the People.*

Translated by FRANK W. PRICE; ed. L. T. CHEN. Chungking: Ministry of Information of the Republic of China, 1943.

A Survey of Chinese Students in American Universities and Colleges in the Past One Hundred Years. New York: China Institute in America, 1954.

TA CHUNG. "Li Ta-chao and Youth in the Period of May 4th Movement," *Evergreen: A Magazine of Chinese Youth and Students,* No. 3 (April-May 1961), 8–10.

TAI CHEN-HWA. "A Critical Study of the Resolutions of the Chinese Federation of Educational Associations, 1915–1926." Columbia University doctoral dissertation, 1934.

TAN JEN-MEI. "The History of Modern Chinese Secondary Education." University of Pennsylvania doctoral dissertation, 1940.

TAO, L. K. "Unemployment among Intellectual Workers in China," *Chinese Social and Political Science Review,* XIII, No. 3 (July 1929), 251–261.

TENG TA-CHUN. "A Comparative Study of Teacher Education in China, England, France, and the United States." University of Colorado doctoral dissertation, 1950.

TENG TSUI YANG and LEW TIMOTHY TING-FANG (eds.). *Education in China: Papers Contributed by the Members of Committees of the Society for the Study of International Education.* Peking: Society for the Study of International Education, 1923.

TSANG CHIU-SAM. *Nationalism in School Education in China since the Opening of the Twentieth Century.* Hong Kong: South China Morning Post, Ltd., 1933.

TSENG TSO-CHUNG. "Nationalism and Pragmatism in Modern Education, with Special Application to Post-Revolutionary Chinese Conditions." University of Washington doctoral dissertation, 1934.

TWISS, GEORGE RANSOM. *Science and Education in China: A Survey of the Present Status and a Program for Progressive Improvement.* Shanghai: Commercial Press, Ltd., 1925.

WANG CHING. "Recollections of Peking Students' Movement: 'Get Out, U. S. Troops!,' " *Evergreen: A Magazine of Chinese Youth and Students,* No. 6 (October 1962), 26–29.

WANG SHIH-CHIEH. "Education in China," pp. 555–601 in *Year Book of Education 1937,* ed. HARLEY V. USILL. London: Evans Bros., Ltd., 1937.

WANG TUNG-CHI. "Educational Ideas of Dr. Sun Yat-sen." Washington University in St. Louis doctoral dissertation, 1952.

WANG TE-CHUNG. "The Reorganization of Chinese Education to Meet the Needs of the Present Emergency Situation." Cornell University doctoral dissertation, 1939.

WANG TSI-CHANG. *The Youth Movement of China.* New York: New Republic, 1927.

WANG YI-CHU. "Foreign-Educated Chinese, 1872–1948." University of Chicago doctoral dissertation, 1957.

WEI CHO-MIN. *Education in Wartime China.* ("Chungking Pamphlets," No. 7.) Chungking: China Information Publishing Co., 1940.

WINNINGTON, ALAN. "New Challenge to Chinese Students: Background of Student Movement," *China Digest,* V, No. 11 (March 22, 1949), 8–9.

WONG, PEARL HUI. "A Comparative Study of Four Social Movements in China from 1912 to 1942." University of Southern California doctoral dissertation, 1946.

YEH SHENG-TAO. *Schoolmaster Ni Huan-chih.* Translated by A. C. Barnes. Peking: Foreign Languages Press, 1958.

YEN, JAMES Y. C. *How to Educate China's Illiterate Millions for Democracy in a Decade.* (*Bulletins on Chinese Education,* Chinese National Association for the Advancement of Education, II, No. 15.) Shanghai: Commercial Press, Ltd., 1923.

———. *The Mass Education Movement in China.* Shanghai: Commercial Press, Ltd., 1925.

YIN CHI-LING. *The Reconstruction of Modern Educational Organizations in China.* Shanghai: Commercial Press, Ltd., 1924.

See also:

BIGGERSTAF (III) • CHEN (II) • CHIANG (III) • CH'U (III) • CHU (III) • DRUMRIGHT (XVII) • FRANKE (III) • GALT: "Oriental and Occidental Elements" (III) • HACKETT (III) • HSIAO (III) • HU CHANG HO JIUGOW (III) • KUO: *The Chinese System of Public Education* and "The Effect of the Revolution" (III) • MIAO (II) • WANG (III) • WILSON SHIH-SHENG WEI (II) • LEA E. WILLIAMS (II)

Section V
General Survey and Background

AIRD, JOHN S. *The Size, Composition, and Growth of the Population of Mainland China*. Washington, D. C.: U. S. Bureau of the Census, 1961.

BALL, W. MACMAHON. *Nationalism and Communism in East Asia*. Melbourne, Australia: Melbourne University Press, 1953.

BARNETT, A. DOAK. *Communist Economic Strategy: The Rise of Mainland China*. Washington, D.C.: National Planning Association, 1959.

————. "Profile of Red China," *Foreign Policy Reports* (New York: Foreign Policy Association), XXV, No. 19 (February 15, 1950), 230–243.

BODDE, DERK. *Peking Diary: A Year of Revolution*. London: Jonathan Cape, 1951.

BOORMAN, HOWARD L. (ed.). "Contemporary China and the Chinese," *Annals of the American Academy of Political and Social Science*, CCCXXI (1959), *passim*.

————. "The Study of Contemporary Chinese Politics: Some Remarks on Retarded Development," *World Politics*, XII, No. 4 (July 1960), 585–599.

BRANDT, CONRAD, BENJAMIN SCHWARTZ, and JOHN KING FAIRBANK. *A Documentary History of Chinese Communism*. Cambridge, Mass.: Harvard University Press, 1952.

CHANDRASEKHAR, SRIPATI. *China's Population: Census and Vital Statistics*. Hong Kong: Hong Kong University Press, 1959.

CHANG CHI-YUN. *Chinese Culture as a Bulwark Against Communism*. ("China Study Series.") Taipei: Institute of Chinese Culture, 1959.

CHAO KUO-CHUN. *Economic Planning and Organization in Mainland China: A Documentary Study, 1949–1957*. 2 vols. Cambridge, Mass.: Harvard University Press, 1959 (Vol. I); 1960 (Vol. II).

————. *The Mass Organizations in Communist China*. Cambridge, Mass.: Center for International Studies, Massachusetts Institute of Technology, 1953.

439

———. "The National Constitution of Communist China," *Far Eastern Survey*, XXIII, No. 10 (October 1954), 145–151.

CHEN PO-TA. *Stalin and the Chinese Revolution.* Peking: Foreign Languages Press, 1953.

CHEN, THEODORE HSI-EN. *Chinese Communism and the Proletarian-Socialist Revolution.* Los Angeles: University of Southern California Press, 1955.

China in Transition: Selected Articles 1952–1956. Peking: China Reconstructs, 1957.

CHOU EN-LAI. *China and the Asian-African Conference: Documents.* Peking: Foreign Languages Press, 1955.

———. *Report on the Work of the Government.* Peking: Foreign Languages Press, 1959.

CHOW CHING-WEN. *Ten Years of Storm.* New York: Holt, Rinehart and Winston, 1960.

The Common Program and Other Documents of the Plenary Session of the Chinese People's Political Consultative Conference. Peking: Foreign Languages Press, 1950.

DE FRANCIS, JOHN. "National and Minority Policies," *Annals of the American Academy of Political and Social Science,* CCLXXVII (1951), 146–155.

———. *Nationalism and Language Reform in China.* Princeton, N. J.: Princeton University Press, 1950.

"Diploma with Chairman Mao's Autograph: Relics of the Revolution," *Evergreen: A Magazine of Chinese Youth and Students,* No. 4 (June 1961), 12.

Documents of the First Session of the First National People's Congress of the People's Republic of China [1954]. Peking: Foreign Languages Press, 1955.

Economic Development in India and Communist China. (84th Congress, 2d Session, Committee on Foreign Relations, Subcommittee on Technical Assistance Programs, Staff Study No. 6.) Washington, D.C.: Government Printing Office, 1956.

ELEGANT, ROBERT S. *China's Red Masters.* New York: Twayne, 1951.

———. *The Dragon's Seed: Peking and the Overseas Chinese.* New York: St. Martin's Press, 1958.

"The First Decade," *China Quarterly,* No. 1 (January-March 1960), passim.

The First Year of Victory. Peking: Foreign Languages Press, 1951.

FITZGERALD, CHARLES P. *Flood Tide in China.* London: Cresset Press, 1958.

———. *Revolution in China.* London: Cresset Press, 1952.

DE FRANCIS, JOHN. "National and Minority Policies," *Annals of the American Academy of Political and Social Science,* CCLXVII (1951), 146–155.

———. *Nationalism and Language Reform in China.* Princeton, N. J.: Princeton University Press, 1950.

A Guide to New China. Peking: Foreign Languages Press, 1952.

Handbook on People's China. Peking: Foreign Languages Press, 1959.

HO KAN-CHIH. *A History of the Modern Chinese Revolution.* Peking: Foreign Languages Press, 1959.

How the Chinese Reds Hoodwink Visiting Foreigners: Consultation with Mr. Robert Loh. (86th Congress, 2d session; House Committee on Un-American Activities.) Washington, D.C.: Government Printing Office, 1960.

HU CHIAO-MU. *Thirty Years of the Communist Party of China: An Outline History.* Peking: Foreign Languages Press, 1951.

HUNT, R. N. CAREW. *Guide to Communist Jargon.* London: Geoffrey Bles, Ltd., 1957.

"Intellectuals Demand Collective Leadership in China," *Far Eastern Economic Review,* XXIII, No. 1 (July 4, 1957), 9-10.

JOHNSON, HEWLETT. *China's New Creative Age.* New York: International Publishers, 1953.

KIRBY, E. STUART (ed.). *Contemporary China: Economic and Social Studies, Documents, Bibliography, Chronology.* 3 vols. Hong Kong: Hong Kong University Press, and London: Oxford University Press, 1955 (Vol. I), 1956 (Vol. II), 1960 (Vol. III).

KUO PING-CHIA. *China: New Age and New Outlook.* New York: Alfred A. Knopf, 1956.

LACY, CREIGHTON BOUTELLE. "Protestant Missions in Communist China." Yale University doctoral dissertation, 1953.

LI CHO-NIN. *The Statistical System of Communist China.* Berkeley: University of California Press, 1962.

LINDBECK, JOHN M. H. "Communist policy and the Chinese family," *Far Eastern Survey,* XX, No. 14 (July 25, 1951), 137–141.

LINDSAY, MICHAEL. *China and the Cold War: A Study in International Politics.* Melbourne, Australia: Melbourne University Press, 1955.

LING NAI-JUI. "Three Years of Communist Rule in China," *Review of Politics,* XV, No. 1 (January 1953), 3–33.

LIU SHAO-CHI. *The Political Report of the Central Committee of the Communist Party of China to the Eighth National Congress of the Party.* Peking: Foreign Languages Press, 1956.

————. *Report on the Draft Constitution of the People's Republic of China and Constitution of the People's Republic of China.* Peking: Foreign Languages Press, 1954.

LIU SHAW-TONG. *Out of Red China.* New York: Duell, Sloan and Pearce, 1953.

MAO TSE-TUNG. *The Chinese Revolution and the Chinese Communist Party.* (Originally published in 1939.) Rev. ed. Peking: Foreign Languages Press, 1959.

Mao's China: Party Reform Documents, 1942–1944. Translated by BOYD COMPTON. Seattle: University of Washington Press, 1952.

New China Advances to Socialism: A Selection of Speeches Delivered at the Third Session of the First National People's Congress. Peking: Foreign Languages Press, 1956.

New China's Economic Achievements 1949–1952. Peking: Foreign Languages Press, 1952.

NORTH, ROBERT C. *Kuomintang and Chinese Communist Elites.* Stanford: Stanford University Press, 1952.

PALMER, GRETTA. *God's Underground in Asia.* New York: Appleton-Century-Crofts, 1953.

PALMER, NORMAN D., and SHAO CHUAN-LENG. "Organization of the Chinese Communist Party," *Current History,* XXIII, No. 131 (July 1952), 13–19.

People's Communes in China. Peking: Foreign Languages Press, 1958.

Policies toward Nationalities in the People's Republic of China. Peking: Foreign Languages Press, 1953.

Proposals of the Eighth National Congress of the Communist Party of China for the Second Five-Year Plan for Development of [the] National Economy (1958–1962). Peking: Foreign Languages Press, 1956.

"Recent Developments in Communist China," *Current Notes on International Affairs,* XXX, No. 11 (November 1959), 593–596.

ROBINSON, JOAN. *Letters from a Visitor to China.* Cambridge: Students' Bookshop, 1954.

ROSTOW, W. W. *A Comparison of Russian and Chinese Societies under Communism.* Cambridge, Mass.: Center for International Studies, Massachusetts Institute of Technology, 1955.

————, in collaboration with RICHARD W. HATCH, FRANK A. KIERMAN,

Jr., and ALEXANDER ECKSTEIN. *The Prospects for Communist China.* Cambridge. Mass.: M.I.T. Press, 1954.

SCHWARTZ, BENJAMIN I. *China and the Soviet Theory of "People's Democracy."* Cambridge, Mass.: Center for International Studies, Massachusetts Institute of Technology, 1954.

———. *Chinese Communism and the Rise of Mao.* Cambridge, Mass.: Harvard University Press, 1951.

Seven Hundred Million for Peace and Democracy. Peking: Foreign Languages Press, 1950.

SIAO-YU. *Mao Tse-tung and I Were Beggars.* Syracuse, N. Y.: Syracuse University Press, 1959.

Sixth Plenary Session of the Eighth Central Committee of the Communist Party of China. Peking: Foreign Languages Press, 1958.

SNOW, EDGAR. *Red Star over China.* New York: Random House, 1938.

SOONG, CH'ING-LING. "The First Five Years," *China Reconstructs,* IV, No. 1 (January 1955), 2–5.

———. *The Struggle for New China.* Peking: Foreign Languages Press, 1952.

STEINER, H. ARTHUR. *Maoism: A Source Book, Selections from the Writings of Mao Tse-tung.* Berkeley and Los Angeles: University of California Press, 1952.

———. "Report on China," *Annals of the American Academy of Political and Social Science,* CCLXXVII (1951), *passim.*

SUDARIKOV, N. G. "The Creation and Consolidation of the Local Organs of Power in the Chinese People's Republic," *Soviet Press Translations,* VII, No. 4 (February 15, 1952), 99–110.

TANG, PETER S. H. *Communist China Today.* 2 vols. New York: Praeger, 1957 (Vol. I: *Domestic and Foreign Policies*); 1958 (Vol. II: *Chronological and Documentary Supplement*).

———. "Power Struggle in the Chinese Communist Party: The Kao-Jao Purge," *Problems of Communism.* IV, No. 6 (November-December 1955), 18–25.

Ten Glorious Years. Peking: Foreign Languages Press, 1960.

TENG HSIAO-PING. *Report on the Revision of the Constitution of the Communist Party of China.* Peking: Foreign Languages Press, 1956.

Tensions in Communist China: An Analysis of Internal Pressures Generated since 1949. (86th Congress, 1st session; Senate Document No. 66.) Washington, D.C.: Government Printing Office, 1960.

THOMAS, S. B. *Government and Administration in Communist China.*

Rev. ed. New York: International Secretariat, Institute of Pacific Relations, 1955.

———. "Structure and Constitutional Basis of the Chinese People's Republic," *Annals of the American Academy of Political and Social Science,* CCLXXVII (1951), 46–55.

TUNG CHI-MING. *An Outline History of China.* Peking: Foreign Languages Press, 1958.

U. S. DEPARTMENT OF STATE. *United States Relations with China, with Special Reference to the Period 1944–1949.* Based on the files of the Department of State, with an introduction by DEAN ACHESON. (Department of State Publication No. 3573, Far Eastern Series 30.) Washington, D.C.: Government Printing Office, 1949.

VAN DER SPRENKEL, OTTO B., ROBERT GUILLAIN, and MICHAEL LINDSAY. *New China: Three Views.* New York: John Day Company, 1951.

WALKER, RICHARD L. *China under Communism: The First Five Years.* New Haven, Conn.: Yale University Press, 1955.

———. "Guided Tourism in China," *Problems of Communism,* VI, No. 5 (September-October 1957), 31–36.

WILSON, J. TUZO. *One Chinese Moon.* New York: Hill and Wang, 1959.

WITTFOGAL, KARL A. "The Influence of Leninism-Stalinism on China," *Annals of the American Academy of Political and Social Science,* CCLXXVII (1951), 22–34.

———. *Oriental Despotism: A Comparative Study of Total Power.* New Haven, Conn.: Yale University Press, 1957.

YIN, HELEN, and YI-CHANG YIN. *Economic Statistics of Mainland China, 1949–1957.* Cambridge, Mass.: Harvard University Press, 1960.

See also:

BODDE (II) • CHAI: *The Changing Society of China* (II) • Ho (II) • HSIA (XV) • HU (II) • LATOURETTE: *The Chinese* (II) • LEVENSON (II) • ROWE (II)

Section VI
Communist Ideology and Educational Philosophy

"Basic Approach for Linking Theory with Reality in Teaching," in *Education under Party Guidance in Communist China*. (Originally published in *Wen Hui Pao*, Shanghai: July 29, 1959.) Translated in Joint Publications Research Service Doc. 1035, D. C. Regular Series (November 23, 1959).

BOROWITZ, ALBERT. *Fiction in Communist China, 1949–53*. Cambridge, Mass.: Center for International Studies, Massachusetts Institute of Technology, 1954.

CHANG CHIH-CHING. "A Hundred Schools Contend," *China Reconstructs*, VI, No. 1 (January 1957), 7–9.

CHAO CHUNG. *The Communist Program for Literature and Art in China*. (Communist China Problem Research Series.) Hong Kong: Union Research Institute, 1955.

CHEN PO-TA. *Mao Tse-tung on the Chinese Revolution*. Peking: Foreign Languages Press, 1953.

CHEN, THEODORE HSI-EN. "Chinese Communism," in *Contemporary Political Ideologies*, ed. J. S. ROUCEK. New York: Philosophical Library, 1961.

———. "Education for the Chinese Revolution," *Current History*, XXXII, No. 185 (January 1957), 43–48.

CHIEN PO-TSAN. "Some Present Problems in the Teaching of History," in *Articles from the Chinese Communist Periodical, "Hung ch'i."* (Originally published in *Hung ch'i* [Red Flag], Peiping: No. 10, May 16, 1959.) Translated in Joint Publications Research Service Doc. 844, D. C. Regular Series (July 29, 1959).

CHOU YANG. *China's New Literature and Art: Essays and Addresses*. Peking: Foreign Languages Press, 1954.

———. "The Great Debate on the Literary Front," *Peking Review;* [part 1] I, No. 3 (March 18, 1958), 8–11; [part 2] I, No. 4 (March 25, 1958), 12–15.

———. *A Great Debate on the Literary Front*. Peking: Foreign Languages Press, 1958.

———. "The Path of Socialist Literature and Art in China," *Peking*

445

Review, [part 1] III, No. 38 (September 20, 1960), 6–15; [part 2] III, No. 39 (September 27, 1960), 15–24.

DAVID, T. K. "Philosophy in Contemporary China," *Far Eastern Economic Review*, XXIII, No. 2 (July 11, 1957), 35–37.

"A Discussion of the Unitary Character and Complex Nature of Education Work," in *Articles in Chinese Educational Policy*. (Originally published in *Jen Min Jih Pao* [People's Daily], Peking: November 4, 1959.) Translated in Joint Publications Research Service Doc. 1135, D. C. Regular Series (January 22, 1960).

"Education of the Party Members," *China News Analysis* (Hong Kong), No. 24 (February 19, 1954), 3.

"Further Apply the Party Educational Aim," in *Education under Party Guidance in Communist China*. (Speech before Kwantung Conference on Education, originally published in *Nan Fang Jih Pao* [Southern Daily], Canton: May 16, 1959.) Translated in Joint Publications Research Service Doc. 1035, D. C. Regular Series (November 23, 1959).

GOURLAY, WALTER E. *The Chinese Communist Cadre: Key to Political Control*. Cambridge, Mass.: Russian Research Center, Harvard University, 1952.

HSU SHOU-HSUAN. *The Combination of Education with Productive Labor Is the One Correct Road to the Development of the New Man*. (Speech before the Second National People's Congress, second session; originally published in *Jen Min Jih Pao* [People's Daily], Peking: April 12, 1960.) Translated in Joint Publications Research Service Doc. 2775, N. Y. Regular Series (June 3, 1960).

HUANG CHI. "Learning the Party's Educational Aim," in *Translations from China's Political and Sociological Publications*. (Originally published in *Pei Ching Shih Ta Hsueh Pao* [Peking Teacher's College Journal], Peking: No. 1, January 1959.) Translated in Joint Publications Research Service Doc. 909, D. C. Regular Series (September 11, 1959).

LIU SHAO-CH'I. *How to Be a Good Communist*. Peking: Foreign Languages Press, 1951.

———. *On Inner Party Struggle*. Peking: Foreign Languages Press, 1951.

———. *On the Party*. Peking: Foreign Languages Press, 1950.

LO CHI-LAN. "Marxist Education: Millions Study Theory and Philosophy," *Peking Review*, I, No. 26 (August 26, 1958), 10–12.

LU TING-YI. *Education Must Be Combined with Productive Labor*.

Peking: Foreign Languages Press, 1958. See also Lu Ting-yi, "Education Must Be Linked to Productive Work," in *Soviet Education,* I, No. 4 (February 1959), 57–64; (originally translated by V. Z. Klepikov from *Hung ch'i* [Red Flag] for *Sovetskaya Pedagogika,* December 1958). See also "Education Must Be Combined with Productive Labour," *Peking Review,* I, No. 28 (September 9, 1958), 5–12.

———. *Let a Hundred Flowers Blossom: A Hundred Schools of Thought Contend.* (A speech on the policy of the Communist Party of China on art, literature, and science delivered on May 26, 1957.) Peking: Foreign Languages Press, 1958.

MAO TSE-TUNG. "On 'Letting a Hundred Flowers Blossom,' 'Letting a Hundred Schools of Thought Contend,' 'Long Term Co-existence and Mutual Supervision'" (chap. 8) and "The Question of Intellectuals" (chap. 5) in *On the Correct Handling of Contradictions among the People.* Peking: Foreign Languages Press, 1957.

———. *Oppose the Party "Eight-Legged Essay."* Rev. ed. (originally published in 1942). Peking: Foreign Languages Press, 1955.

———. *The Orientation of the Youth Movement.* Rev. ed. (originally published in 1934). Peking: Foreign Languages Press, 1960.

———. *Rectify the Party's Style of Work.* Rev. ed. (originally published in 1942). Peking: Foreign Languages Press, 1955.

———. *Reform Our Study.* Rev. ed. (originally published in 1941). Peking: Foreign Languages Press, 1960.

———. *Talks at the Yenan Forum on Art and Literature.* Rev. ed. (originally published in 1942). Peking: Foreign Languages Press, 1956.

NIVISION, DAVID S. "Communist Ethics and Chinese Tradition," *Journal of Asian Studies,* XVI, No. 1 (November 1956), 51–74.

PAI SHOU-I. "The 'Past' and the 'Present' in the Teaching of History," in *Translations from "Hung ch'i."* (Originally published in *Hung ch'i* [Red Flag], Peiping: No. 11, June 1959.) Translated in Joint Publications Research Service Doc. 872, D. C. Regular Series (August 11, 1959).

PAN TSE-NIEN. "Let's All Learn a Little Philosophy," *Peking Review,* I, No. 12 (May 20, 1958), 11–12.

"Political Leadership Must Be Given Strong Support before the Quality of Teaching Can Be Improved," in *Articles on Chinese Educational Policy.* (Originally published in *Jen Min Jih Pao* [People's Daily], Peking: October 23, 1959.) Translated in Joint

Publications Research Service Doc. 1135, D. C. Regular Series (January 22, 1960).

"Party's Control over Education," *Union Research Service,* VII, No. 24 (April-June 1957) ; IX, No. 10 (October-December 1957) ; XV, Nos. 24 and 26 (April-June 1959).

"Red Ideology in Schools," *Newsletter of the United Nations Association of the Republic of China,* XII, No. 1 (July 1957), 17.

STEINER, H. ARTHUR (ed.). "The Curriculum in Chinese Socialist Education: An Official Bibliography of 'Maoism,' " *Pacific Affairs,* XXXI, No. 3 (September 1958), 286–299.

————. "Ideology and Politics in Communist China," *Annals of the American Academy of Political and Social Science,* CCCXXI (1959), 29–39.

"The Teaching of History," *China News Analysis* (Hong Kong), No. 22 (January 24, 1954), 7.

TU YU-WEN. "Why Workers Study Philosophy," *China Reconstructs,* IX, No. 9 (September 1960), 5–8.

YING, RICHARD. "Harnessing China's Youth to Communism," *Far Eastern Economic Review,* XXV, No. 25 (December 18, 1958), 803–807.

"Youth and the Classics," *China News Analysis* (Hong Kong), No. 233 (June 20, 1958), *passim.*

YUAN PO. "Propaganda Education in Socialism and Communism Must Be Firmly Carried Out in the Cultural Work of the Nationalities," in *Articles from the Chinese Communist Periodical, "Min Tzu Yen Chiu."* (Originally published in *Min Tzu Yen Chiu* [Nationalities Research], Peking: No. 1, January 12, 1959.) Translated in Joint Publications Research Service Doc. 871, D. C. Regular Series (August 14, 1959).

See also:

ANASTASYEVA (VII) • ARENS: "The Impact of Communism" (VII) • BARENDSEN: "Learning, Labor, and Life" and "Planned Reforms" (VIII) • BARNETT (XIII) • BOORMAN: "The Study of Contemporary Chinese Politics" (V) • CHANG LIN-KUAN (VII) • CHAO: *The Mass Organizations* (V) • ANTHONY K. CHEN (VII) • CHEN PO-TA (V) • CHEN (X) • THEODORE HSI-EN CHEN: *Chinese Communism and the Proletarian-Socialist Revolution* (V), "Collective Learning" (IX), "New China: New Texts" (VII), *Thought Reform* (XIII), and "The 'Three Anti' and 'Five Anti' Movements" (XIII) • J. CHESTER

CHENG: "Basic Principles" (VII) and "Half-Work and Half-Study Program" (X) • CHI: *Education for the Proletariat* (VII) • CHIN (XIII) • "Chinese Students off to the Countryside" (XIV) • "Chinese Intellectuals on the Land" (IX) • CHOU (XIII) • SIE PING-TEH and RUGH (XI) • "Communist Attitude towards Intellectuals" (XIII) • "Counter Revolution in Education" (XIII) • CREEL: *Chinese Thought* (II) • "Double Anti Campaign in Education" (XIII) • DRAKE (VII) • "Education Training" (VII) • FRASER (VII, IX, and XIII) • GOLDMAN (IX) • HOUN: "Publications as a Propaganda Medium," *To Change a Nation,* and "Chinese Communist Publication Policy" (XIII) • HOWSE (XIII) • HSIEH (VII) • HU: *Chinese Education under Communism* and "Communist Education" (VII) • HUNT (V) • HUNTER (XIII) • LAMMERS (XIII) • LI FANG: "Why Intellectuals Go to the Countryside" and "Xiafang Intellectuals" (XIII) • LIANG (IX) • LIN FENG (VII) • LINDSAY: "Communist Areas" and *Notes on Educational Problems* (VII) • LING (X) • LIU (XIII) • LU: *Education Must Be Combined with Productive Labor* (VI) • MACFARQUHAR (XIII) • *Mao's China* (V) • "The Meaning of Xiafang" (XIII) • "Mukden Professors" (XIII) • *The National Conference* (VII) • NEWTON: "China's Proletarian Universities" (IX), "China Turns Inward" (VII), "Chinese Universities to Become Proletarian" (IX), and "Philosophers Prefer to Blush Unseen" (XIII) • "The Participation of Cadres" (XIII) • "Philosophers Dig into Life" (XIII) • "Second Year of Xiafang" (XIII) • SNOW (V) • "Social vs. Family Education" (XIII) • STEINER: *Maoism* (V) • T'IEN (VIII) • TSENG CHUN (VII) • WEN CHIA: "At the National Heroes Conference" (VII) • WITTFOGAL: "The Influence of Leninism-Stalinism" and *Oriental Despotism* (V) • WU (VII) • Section XIII, *passim*

Section VII
General Survey of Education

"After-School Study Groups," *China Reconstructs*, VII, No. 10 (October 1958), 34.

ALLEY, REWI. *An Adventure in Creative Education.* Christchurch, New Zealand: Caxton Press, 1959.

———. "At the School Again," *China Reconstructs,* IV, No. 3 (March 1955), 18–20.

ANASTASYEVA, T. N. "The Struggle for a New School and Marxist Education in the Chinese People's Republic at the Present Stage," translated in *Soviet Education,* I, No. 1 (November 1958), 64–71.

ANDREW, GEOFFREY. "China: An Academic Appraisal," *American Scholar* (Summer 1963), p. 383.

ARENS, RICHARD. "Education in Communist China from 1949–1951: The Period of Policy Formation," *Journal of East Asiatic Studies* (University of Manila), V, No. 3 (July 1956), 315–325.

———. "The Impact of Communism on Education in China, 1949–50." University of Chicago doctoral dissertation, 1952.

BARENDSEN, ROBERT D. "Education in China: A Survey," *Problems of Communism,* XIII (July-August 1964), 19–27.

———. "Educational Changes in Chinese Areas," *School Life,* XLIII, No. 1 (September 1960), 19–21, 30.

BENTON, WILLIAM. "Education in Red China," *Saturday Review,* XLIV (July 15, 1961), 46–47, 62–63.

"Big Leap Forward in Education," *Union Research Service,* XVIII, No. 13 (January-March 1960).

BRICKMAN, W. W. "Keeping Informed on Communist Chinese Education," *School and Society,* VII, No. 2156 (June 20, 1959), 322–323.

CHANG CHI-CH'UN. "Develop Education in Our Country Faster and Better," in *Translations from "Hung ch'i."* (Originally published in *Hung ch'i* [Red Flag], Peking: No. 3, February 1, 1960.) Translated in Joint Publications Research Service Doc. 3169, N. Y. Regular Series (April 15, 1960).

CHANG CHIEN. "Schooling for the Millions," *China Reconstructs,* VIII, No. 10 (October 1959), 54–56.

450

CHANG LIN-KUAN. "New Development in Education," *China Reconstructs,* VII, No. 11 (November 1958), 22–24.

CHAO MU-LIANG. "What Teaching the Workers Has Taught Me," *China Reconstructs,* IX, No. 10 (October 1960), 5–8.

CHEN, ANTHONY K. "The Philosophy of Education of Communist China as Applied to Secondary and Higher Education." De Paul University Master's thesis, 1957.

CH'EN LEI-SZU. "Education," pp. 116–131 in *Communist China 1958.* Hong Kong: Union Research Institute, 1959.

CHEN, THEODORE HSI-EN. "Chinese Communist Education: The Three P's," *Far Eastern Survey,* XXIX, No. 6 (June 1960), 86–89.

———. "Communist China's First Decade: Education," *The New Leader,* XLII (May 4, 1959), 16–20.

———. "Education in China," pp. 524–566 in *Comparative Education,* ed. A. H. MOEHLMAN and J. S. ROUCEK. New York: Henry Holt, 1951.

———. "Education under Communism—Remoulding 640,000,000 Chinese," pp. 181–196 in *Education for World Leadership* (1960 Yearbook of the National School Boards Association).

———. "Education and the Economic Failures in Communist China," *Educational Record,* XLIV, No. 4 (October 1963), 348–353.

———. "Education and Propaganda in Communist China," *Annals of the American Academy of Political and Social Science,* CCLXXVII (1951), 135–145.

———. "New China: New Texts," *Current History,* XIX, No. 112 (December 1950), 321–327.

———. New Education in Communist China," *School and Society,* LXXI, No. 1839 (March 18, 1950), 166–169.

———. "New Schools for China," *Current History,* XXII, No. 130 (June 1952), 328–333.

———. "Red Education in China," *Current History,* XIX, No. 107 (July 1950), 14–20.

———. "Salient Characteristics of Education in Communist China," *Education,* LXXVI, No. 6 (February 1956), 360–366.

CHEN YUAN. "My Teaching Life Over the Past Decades," *Evergreen: A Magazine of Chinese Youth and Students,* Nos. 4, 5 [run as single issue] (July 1962), 15–16, 35.

CHENG, J. CHESTER. "Basic Principles Underlying the Chinese Communist Approach to Education," *Information on Education Around the World Series,* No. 51, OE–14034–51. Washington, D. C.: U. S. Office of Education, 1961.

———. "Trends in Chinese Education," *The World Today,* VII, No. 2 (November 1951), 480–488.

CHI TUNG-WEI. "Education," pp. 138–148 in *Communist China 1956.* Hong Kong: Union Research Institute, 1957.

———. *Education for the Proletariat in Communist China.* 2d ed. Hong Kong: Union Research Institute, 1956.

CHIA TAO-HENG. "From City Schools to the Farms," *China Reconstructs,* VII, No. 2 (February 1958), 27–29.

CHIEH KUO-HUI. *Culture and Education in New China.* Peking: Foreign Languages Press, 1951.

"Children's Palace in Shanghai," *China Reconstructs,* III, No. 3 (May-June 1954), 10–11.

CHIN TI. "Students in the Workshop," *China Reconstructs,* VI, No. 4 (April 1957), 6–8.

"The Chinese People's Republic," *Soviet Education,* I, No. 10 (August 1959), 80–81. Reviews of the following books:

Cast Out Distortions of Rightist Elements in the Field of Education. Shanghai: New Knowledge Press, 1958.

CHEN YUAN-KHUEI. *Criticisms of Pragmatic Pedagogy.* Peking: Public Education Press, 1957.

Development of School Education after Creation of the People's Communes. Honan Province: Public Education Department, 1958.

Hoist High the Banner of Communist Education. Peking: Peking Press, 1958.

LO BIN-CHZHI. *Chinese Educators of Modern Times.* Wuchang: People's Press of Hupeh Province, 1958.

The State of Education in Various Countries. Peking: Public Education Press, 1958.

CHOU EN-LAI. "Report on the Work of the Government: Section III, Our Tasks on the Cultural and Educational Fronts," *Peking Review,* II, No. 16 (April 21, 1959), 18–20.

CHOU, KUO-P'ING. "Red China Tackles Its Language Problem," *Harper's Magazine,* CCXIX, No. 1310 (July 1959), 49–54.

CHU, DON-CHEAN (trans.). "Educational, Cultural, and Scientific Plans of Communist China," *School and Society,* LXXXIX, No. 2186 (February 11, 1961), 58–59.

Communist China Digest. Translations in Joint Publications Research Service Doc. 3520, N. Y. Regular Series, No. 19 (July 6, 1960). (Various articles on education—theory, ideological, overseas Chinese, Peking University, agricultural, technical, use of radio broadcasting, originally published in *Hsin Hua Pan Yueh K'an* [New China Semimonthly], Peking: March 27, 1960.)

"Cultural Centres," *China News Analysis* (Hong Kong), No. 13 (November 20, 1953), 5–7.

"Cultural Trends, Spring 1959," *ibid.,* No. 277 (May 22, 1959), *passim.*

"Culture and Education," *ibid.,* No. 32 (April 16, 1954), 7.

Culture and Education in New China. Peking: Foreign Languages Press, 1950.

Culture, Education, and Health in New China. Peking: Foreign Languages Press, 1953.

"Culture in 1953," *China News Analysis* (Hong Kong), No. 20 (January 15, 1954), 2–5.

"Dissemination of Mathematics," *Union Research Service,* XXI, No. 5 (October-December 1960), *passim.*

"Documents from Red China and Russia," *School and Society,* LXXXVII, No. 2156 (June 20, 1959), 313–318.

DOVER, CEDRIC. "Education in China," *United Asia,* VIII, No. 2 (April 1956), 117–119.

DRAKE, F. S. "Principles of Chinese Education," *Far Eastern Economic Review,* XXI, No. 19 (November 1, 1956), 568–569.

"Education" (table showing number of students), *China News Analysis* (Hong Kong), No. 273 (April 24, 1959).

"Education," *Union Research Service,* VII, No. 2 (April-June 1957); XV, No. 26 (April-June 1959); XIX, No. 18 (April-June 1960).

"Education: Every Child Will Go to School," *Peking Review,* I, No. 18 (July 1, 1958), 16.

"Education: In a Nutshell," *ibid.,* II, No. 2 (January 13, 1959), 5.

"Education in China," *Far Eastern Economic Review,* XXII, No. 17 (April 25, 1957), 521.

"Education Leaps in Sinkiang," *Peking Review,* III, No. 30 (July 26, 1960), 5.

"Education Training Worker and Peasant Intellectuals," *ibid.,* I, No. 12 (May 6, 1958), 16.

"Educational Big Leap," *ibid.,* III, No. 7 (February 16, 1960), 5.

"Educational Conferences," *China News Analysis* (Hong Kong), No. 39 (June 11, 1954), 2–6.

"Educational Problems in Peking," *Far Eastern Economic Review*, XVII, No. 25 (December 16, 1954), 783.

"Educational Troubles in China," *ibid.*, XVII, No. 23 (December 2, 1954), 726.

EELLS, WALTER CROSBY. *Communism in Education in Asia, Africa, and the Far Pacific*. Washington, D. C.: American Council on Education, 1954.

"Facts and Figures: The Big Leap in Education," *Peking Review*, I, No. 40 (December 2, 1958), 15–16.

FARRINGTON, B. "Education in the New China," *Journal of Education* (London), LXXXV, No. 1002 (January 1953), 14, 16.

FEI HSIAO-TUNG. "Educating the Educators," *China Weekly Review*, July 29, 1950, p. 157.

FISHER, O. "Education in Communist China," *School and Society*, LXXXVII, No. 2156 (June 20, 1959), 302–305.

FRASER, STEWART E. "Recent Educational Reforms in Communist China," pp. 154–163 in *Melbourne Studies in Education, 1960–61*, ed. E. L. FRENCH. Melbourne, Australia: Melbourne University Press, 1962.

FU LEI. "My Son, Fu Tsung," *China Reconstructs*, VI, No. 4 (April 1957), 9–11.

"Graduation Time," *Peking Review*, II, No. 26 (June 30, 1959), 5.

HALEEM, A. B. A. "Education in China," *Pakistan Horizon*, XIII, No. 4 (1960), 284–299.

HAN TZU. "Teacher of Her People," *China Reconstructs*, V, No. 10 (October 1956), 25–27.

HSIA FANG-YA and KUO-CHUAN KU. "Eradicate the Influence of American Cultural Aggression," *Soviet Press Translations*, No. 6 (July 15, 1951), 396–405.

HSIEH CHIAO-MIN. "The Status of Geography in Communist China," *Geographical Review*, XLIX (October 1959).

HU, CHANG-TU. *Chinese Education under Communism*. ("Classics in Education" No. 7.) New York: Bureau of Publications, Teachers College, Columbia University, 1962.

———. "Communist Education: Theory and Practice," *China Quarterly*, No. 10 (April-June 1962), 84–97.

———. "Recent Trends in Chinese Education," *International Review of Education*, X, No. 1 (1964), 12–21.

HUANG P'EI-CHIH. "Education," pp. 128–137 in *Communist China 1957*. Hong Kong: Union Research Institute, 1958.

I Wo-sheng. "Education," pp. 191–210 in *Communist China 1961,* Vol. II. Hong Kong: Union Research Institute, 1962.

———. "Education in Communist China in 1960," pp. 59–85 in *Communist China 1960,* Vol. I. Hong Kong: Union Research Institute, 1962.

Johnson, Chalmers A. *Communist Policies toward the Intellectual Class.* Hong Kong: Union Research Institute, 1960.

Jones, F. C. "Universities in a Chaotic China," *Universities Review,* XXII, No. 3 (May 1949), 168–175.

———. "Universities under the Harrow," *Universities Review,* XXVI, No. 2 (February 1954), 73–77.

Kierman, Frank A., Jr. *The Chinese Intelligentsia and the Communists.* Cambridge, Mass.: Center for International Studies, Massachusetts Institute of Technology, 1954.

Klepikov, Vladimir Z. "New Curricula of the General Education Schools of China" (translated by Ina Schlesinger), *School and Society,* LXXXVIII, No. 2168 (February 13, 1960), 72–74.

———. "The Preparation of School Reform in China" (translated by A. M. Chabe), *Comparative Education Review,* VII, No. 1 (June 1963), 74–79.

———. "Rules for Pupils in Communist Chinese Elementary Schools" (translated by Ina Schlesinger), *School and Society,* LXXXVIII, No. 2168 (February 13, 1960), 74–75.

Kujal, Bohumir. *Schools, Socialist Education, and Pedagogy in the People's Republic of China.* (Originally published in *Pedagogika,* Prague: VIII, No. 4.) Translated in Joint Publications Research Service Doc. 512, D. C. Regular Series (January 30, 1959).

Kun, Joseph C. "Higher Educational Institutions of Communist China, 1953–1958: A Cumulative List," appendix C to *Selection and Enrollment of Students in Communist Chinese Higher Educational Institutions.* Cambridge, Mass.: Center for International Studies, Massachusetts Institute of Technology, 1961.

———. "Higher Education: Some Problems of Selection and Enrollment," *China Quarterly,* No. 8 (October-December 1961), 135–148.

Lauwerys, J. A. "China," pp. 258–283 in *Communist Education,* ed. Edmund J. King. New York: Bobbs-Merrill, 1963.

———. "China's Educational Expansion: Major Issues of Policy," *London Times Educational Supplement,* No. 2196 (June 21, 1957), 895.

————. "Education in China," *Journal of Education* (London), XC, No. 1064 (March 1958), 97–98.

————. "Problems of Educational Policy in Communist China," *Comparative Education Review*, I, No. 2 (October 1957), 4–6.

"Learning in China," *London Times Educational Supplement*, No. 2194 (June 7, 1957), 816–817.

LI SHU. "The Hui People's Academy," *China Reconstructs*, IV, No. 5 (May 1955), 12–13.

LI SHU-SHENG. "Education for Workers and Peasants," *People's China*, III, No. 6 (1951), 12–14.

LIN EN-CHIN. "Educational Changes in China Since the Establishment of the People's Republic and Some Steps Leading to Them." University of Pennsylvania doctoral dissertation, 1955.

LIN FENG. "The Tasks of China's Cultural Revolution," *Peking Review*, [part 1] III, No. 25 (June 21, 1960), 14–19; [part 2] III, No. 26 (June 28, 1960), 19–23.

LINDSAY, MICHAEL. "Communist Areas [of China]," pp. 621–626 in *Year Book of Education 1949*, ed. G. B. JEFFERY, *et al.* London: Evans Bros., Ltd., 1949.

————. *Notes on Educational Problems in Communist China, 1941–47*, with supplements on 1948–1949 by MARION MENZIES, WILLIAM PAGET, and S. B. THOMAS. New York: International Secretariat, Institute of Pacific Relations, 1950.

LIU K'UN-LIN. "A Brief Discussion of Raising the Quality of Education," in *Translations from Chinese Communist Provincial and City Party Organs.* (Originally published in *Shang-Yu* [Upstream], Canton: No. 23, December 10, 1959.) Translated in Joint Publications Research Service Doc. 2754, N. Y. Regular Series (June 1, 1960).

LIU SHIH. "China's New Educational System," *People's China*, IV, No. 11 (December 11, 1951), 5–8.

————. "Two Years of Advance in People's Education," *ibid.*, No. 7 (October 1, 1951), 32–34.

LU TING-YI. "Education and Culture in New China," *People's China*, I, No. 8 (April 16, 1950), 5–7, 27.

————. "Great Developments in China's Cultural Revolution," *Peking Review*, II, No. 45 (November 10, 1959), 13–16.

————. "Reform in Educational Work," *ibid.*, III, No. 19 (May 10, 1960), 15–20.

MACDOUGALL, COLINA. "The Advancement of Learning," *Far Eastern*

Economic Review, XXXVIII, No. 5 (November 1, 1962), 270.

MASATUGU, KUSUMOTO. "Educational Thought of the People of China," pp. 113–127 in *Year Book of Education 1957,* ed. GEORGE Z. F. BEREDAY and J. A. LAUWERYS. Yonkers-on-Hudson, N. Y.: World Book Co., 1957.

"Mass Cultural Upsurge," *Peking Review,* I, No. 11 (May 13, 1958), 3.

"Model Teacher Kao," *ibid.,* III, No. 37 (September 14, 1960), 5.

MORRISON, ESTHER. "Two Years of Worker-Peasant Education," *Regional Studies 202* (Harvard University East Asia Regional Studies Seminars), 1951–1952.

"Museums in Peking," *Peking Review,* I, No. 10 (May 6, 1958), 15–17.

"A Nation at School," *ibid.,* II, No. 47 (November 24, 1959), 5.

The National Conference of Outstanding Groups and Individuals in Socialist Construction in Education, Culture, Health, Physical Culture, and Journalism. Peking: Foreign Languages Press, 1960.

"New Education," *China News Analysis* (Hong Kong), No. 228 (May 16, 1958).

NEWTON, WYNDHAM. "China Turns Inward for Cultural Inspiration," *Far Eastern Economic Review,* XXV, No. 21 (November 20, 1958), 649–650.

Non-Technical Education in Communist China. (Summaries of articles from Chinese Communist periodicals in 1958 on rightism, counterrevolutionaries, teachers' salaries, physical labor in education, academic discipline, and entry requirements for Shanghai schools.) Joint Publications Research Service Doc. 879, N. Y. Regular Series (November 24, 1958).

"On Psychology," *Union Research Service,* XVI, No. 13 (July-September 1959).

ORLEANS, LEO A. *Professional Manpower and Education in Communist China.* Washington, D. C.: National Science Foundation, 1961.

"Outstanding Workers in Culture and Education Meet," *Peking Review,* III, No. 23 (July 7, 1960), 16–18.

PAN YUEH. "Meeting New Needs in Education," *China Reconstructs,* V, No. 4 (April 1956), 23–26.

———. "A School that Leads the Way," *ibid.,* IV, No. 6 (June 1955), 13–15.

"The Peking Children's Palace," *Evergreen: A Magazine of Chinese Youth and Students,* No. 3 (June 1963), 34–35.

PENG TAO-CHEN. "New China's Libraries," *China Reconstructs,* I, No. 5 (September-October 1952), 44–48.

PRIESTLEY, KENNETH E. "China," pp. 490–512 in *Year Book of Education 1952,* ed. J. A. LAUWERYS and N. HANS. London: Evans Bros., Ltd., 1952.

———. *Education in China.* Hong Kong: Dragonfly Books, 1961.

———. "The People's Republic of China: Communist China," pp. 275–291 in *Comparative Educational Administration,* ed. THEODORE L. RELLER and EDGAR L. MORPET. Englewood Cliffs, N. J.: Prentice Hall, 1962.

"Private Education," *Union Research Service,* II, No. 15 (January-March 1956).

"Professors and Teachers," *ibid.,* IV, No. 24 (July-September 1956); VII, Nos. 9, 20, and 24 (April-June 1957); X, No. 13 (January-March 1958).

"Progress of Education in China," *Far Eastern Economic Review,* XVIII, No. 5 (February 3, 1955), 149–155.

PURCELL, VICTOR W. W. S. "A Peep into a Communist School," *Eastern World,* No. 5 (June 1951), 15–17.

"Revolution in Education," *Peking Review,* I, No. 37 (November 11, 1958), 4.

RUGH, ARTHUR DOUGLAS. "School Custodial Workers in the Schools of Communist China," *School and Society,* LXXXVII, No. 2156 (June 20, 1959), 313.

"School Children," *Union Research Service,* III, No. 2 (April-June 1956); XIII, No. 21 (October-December 1958); XVI, No. 22 (July-September 1958).

"Schools," *ibid.,* V, No. 17 (October-December 1959); VII, No. 4 (April-June 1957).

Selections from Compendium of Laws and Regulations of the People's Republic of China. (Laws, rulings, etc., on the survey of Chinese dialects, promotion of Mandarin, cultural education among handicraft workers, children's reading material, government examinations in institutions of higher learning, physical culture, audio-visual aids in teaching science and technology, sports, and anti-illiteracy work. Originally published in *Chung Hua Jen Min Kung Ho Kuo Fa Kuei Hui Pien,* Peking: Vol. III.) Translated in Joint Publications Research Service Doc. 570, N. Y. Regular Series (July 14, 1958).

"Shanghai Education Flies Forward," in *Education under Party Guidance in Communist China.* (Originally published in *Wen Hui Pao,*

Shanghai: September 19, 1959.) Translated in Joint Publications Research Service Doc. 1035, D. C. Regular Series (November 23, 1959).

"Shanghai Educational Advance," *China Reconstructs,* I, No. 6 (November-December 1952), 37.

SHIH, L. "China's New Educational System," *School and Society,* LXXV, No. 1945 (March 29, 1952).

SIMPSON, R. F. "The Development of Education in Mainland China," *Phi Delta Kappan,* XXXIX, No. 3 (December 1957), 84–93.

"Social Education of Children," *Union Research Service,* XIII, No. 21 (October-December 1958).

"Sports and Physical Training," *ibid.,* IV, No. 17 (July-September 1956).

"Students Quit School," *Newsletter of the United Nations Association of the Republic of China,* IX, No. 6 (June 1956), 9–10.

SUDJONO. "Education in New China," pp. 67–70 in *Glimpses of People's China.* Peking: Foreign Languages Press, 1954.

SUHARDJO. "Culture and Education in People's China," pp. 62–66 in *Glimpses of People's China.* Peking: Foreign Languages Press, 1954.

"Summer Vacations," *China News Analysis* (Hong Kong), No. 51 (September 10, 1954), 6–7.

SUNG JEN-CHIEH. "Education," pp. 136–145 in *Communist China 1955.* Hong Kong: Union Research Institute, 1956.

THOMAS, S. B. "Recent Educational Policy in China," *Pacific Affairs,* XXIII, No. 1 (March 1950), 21–33.

"Too Many Students—Not Enough Schools," *Union Research Service,* VII, No. 4 (April-June 1957), 38–51.

"Training of Personnel for Construction and Promotion of Scientific Research," pp. 176–188 in *First Five-Year Plan for Development of the National Economy of the People's Republic of China in 1953–1957.* Peking: Foreign Languages Press, 1956.

Translations from Communist China's Political and Sociological Publications. (Articles on the place of educational psychology in Communist China originally published in *Jen Min Jih Pao* [People's Daily], Peking: June, July 1959.) Translated in Joint Publications Research Service Doc. 1932, N. Y. Regular Series (October 2, 1959).

Translations of Chinese Communist Articles on Education. (Articles on teaching, spare time teachers; scientific research in schools; combining education with labor; rightism; schools in Kwangtung, Harbin and Fukien, originally published in *Jen Min Jih Pao* [People's Daily], Peking, and *Hsin Hua Pan Yueh K'an* [New China Semi-monthly], Peking: November, December 1959.) Translated in Joint Publications Research Service Doc. 3114, N. Y. Regular Series (March 28, 1960).

Translations of Jen Min Jih Pao Articles on Sociological and Economic Subjects. (Articles on education and labor, spare-time education, specializations, Hunan University, new college of bridge engineering—Hupeh Province . . . ; originally published in *Jen Min Jih Pao* [People's Daily], Peking: April 11, 1960.) Translated in Joint Publications Research Service Doc. 2908, N. Y. Regular Series (June 23, 1960).

TSENG CHAO-LUN. "Training Technicians for Industrialization," *People's China,* No. 8 (April 16, 1954), 11–13.

TSENG CHUN. "Great Accomplishments of Political Theory Education Work in Hupeh Province in the Last Ten Years," in *Chinese Communist Articles on Education.* (Originally published in *Li Lun Chan Hsien* [Theoretical Front], Wu-ch'ang: No. 10, October 10, 1959.) Translated in Joint Publications Research Service Doc. 1165, D. C. Regular Series (February 12, 1960).

"Unhappy Lot of the Teacher in China," *Far Eastern Economic Review,* XVII, No. 10 (September 2, 1954), 294–295.

WANG, CHARLES K. S. *The Control of Teachers in Communist China: A Socio-political Study.* Lackland Air Force Base, Texas: Air Force Personnel and Training Research Center, 1955.

WANG LEH. "Cultural Growth of Minority Peoples," *Peking Review,* II, No. 3 (January 20, 1959), 18–19.

WANG Y-CHU. "The Intelligentsia in Changing China," *Foreign Affairs,* XXXVI, No. 2 (January 1958), 315–329.

WEBER, D. "Education as a Tool of Power: An Analysis of the Schools of Red China Today," *Phi Delta Kappan,* XLI, No. 9 (June 1960), 388–393.

WEN CHIA. "At the National Heroes Conference: People in the Van of the Cultural Revolution," *Peking Review,* III, No. 25 (June 21, 1960), 19–21.

———. "Outstanding Groups in the Cultural Revolution," *ibid.,* No. 27 (July 5, 1960), 19–21.

WEN YEN TSAO. "The Meaning of Chinese Education," *Free World Forum,* II, No. 3 (June 1960), 5–67.

WU PIN. "New Trend in Education," *Peking Review,* I, No. 22 (July 29, 1958), 16–17.

YANG, GLADYS TAYLER. "Books and People," *China Reconstructs,* III, No. 4 (July-August 1954), 44–46.

————. "Education in New China," *China Monthly Review* (July 1953), 84–89.

YANG HSIANG-KWEI. "The First Hundred Schools," *China Reconstructs,* VII, No. 3 (March 1958), 26–29.

YANG HSIU-FENG. *Great Revolution and Great Development in China's Educational Program.* (Originally published in *Jen Min Jih Pao* [People's Daily], Peking: October 8, 1959.) Translated in Joint Publications Research Service Doc. 3019, N. Y. Regular Series (February 26, 1960).

YU CHENG-WEN. "Peking Institute of Physical Education," *Evergreen: A Magazine of Chinese Youth and Students,* No. 5 (October 1963), 39–42.

YU CHI-TUNG. "Three Years of Cultural and Educational Work in the New China," *People's China,* No. 18 (September 17, 1952), 29–35.

See also:

"Basic approach for Linking Theory with Reality" (VI) • BRANDT (V) • CHANG CHI-YUN: "Confucianism and Modern Education" (IV) • CHAO (VI) • CHEN HSUAN-SHAN (IX) • THEODORE HSI-EN CHEN: "Chinese Communism" (VI), "Education and Indoctrination" (XIII), "Science, Scientists, and Politics" (XV), "The Popularization of Higher Education" (IX), and *Teacher Training* (IX) • J. CHESTER CHENG (IV) • *China and Her Youth* (XIV) • *China in Transition* (V) • *China's Youth Marches Forward* (XIV) • *Chinese Youth Enjoys a Happy Life* (XIV) • CHOU (XI) • CHOU: "The Great Debate" and "The Path of Socialist Literature and Art" (VI) • CHU: "The Communes and Their Schools" and "Theories and Practices of the Commune Schools" (XI) • CHUNG (IX) • CREEL: "Chinese Culture" (II) • "A Discussion of the Unitary Character" (VI) • *Further Apply the Party Educational Aim* (VI) • HUANG (VI) • KIANG (IV) • LACY (V) • LI FANG (XI) • LIANG HAN-PING (X) • LO (VI) • MAO: *Talks at the Yenan Forum* (VI) • "New Deal for Students" (XIV) • "Professors Go to School" (XIII) • "The Splendour of Youth" (XIV) • TUNG SHIH-TSIN (XIII) • WILSON (V) • "People's Republic of China" (IX) • YING (VI)

Section VIII
Elementary and Secondary Education

BARENDSEN, ROBERT D. (trans.). "Learning, Labor, and Life in Communist Chinese Schools," *School and Society*, LXXXIX No. 2194 (Summer 1961), 274–276.

———. "Planned Reforms in the Primary and Secondary School System in Communist China," *Information on Education around the World*, No. 45 (August 1960). Washington, D. C.: United States Department of Health, Welfare and Education; Office of Education (Government Printing Office), 1960. (See also "The 1960 Educational Reform," *China Quarterly*, No. 4 (October-December 1960), 55–65.)

CHEN, THEODORE HSI-EN. "Elementary Education in Communist China," *China Quarterly*, No. 10 (April-June 1962), 98–122.

CHEN WEI-PO. "Children Have Fun With Science," *China Reconstructs*, IX, No. 9 (September 1960), 28–30.

Children of China. (A series published at intermittent intervals.) Peking: Chinese People's National Committee for the Defense of Children, 1956, 1957, 1959 (Spring and Autumn), 1960 (Spring).

CHU, S. Y., and CHENG R. YU-SOONG. "Secondary Education in New China," pp. 146–154 in *Year Book of Education 1958*, ed. GEORGE Z. F. BEREDAY and J. A. LAUWERYS. Yonkers-on-Hudson, N. Y.: World Book Co., 1958.

FAN TSIUN-FU. "Success of the Secondary Schools" (translated by INA SCHLESINGER), *School and Society*, LXXXVII, No. 2156 (June 20, 1959), 315–317.

"Floating Schools on the Yangtse," *Peking Review*, II, No. 5 (February 3, 1959), 5.

"From Cradle to Manhood (Nurseries, Kindergarten, Red Scarfs, Morals)," *China News Analysis* (Hong Kong), No. 332 (1960).

GRIMBLE, FREDA. "Children of China," *United Asia*, VIII, No. 2 (April 1956), 102–104.

"In a Peking Primary School," *China Reconstructs*, III, No. 4 (July-August 1954), 37–39.

462

Kuo Lin. "Great Accomplishments in Middle and Elementary Education in the Last Ten Years," in *Chinese Communist Articles on Education*. (Originally published in *Fu Tao Yuan* [Instructor], Peking: No. 10, October 12, 1959.) Translated in Joint Publications Research Service Doc. 1165, D. C. Regular Series (February 12, 1960).

"Ma Hsiao-tsui: Teen-age Teacher," *Peking Review*, I, No. 41 (December 9, 1958), 5.

"Mass Juvenile Education in China," *Far Eastern Economic Review*, XXVI, No. 5 (January 29, 1959), 156–157.

"Middle School in Rapid Course," *China News Analysis* (Hong Kong), No. 39 (June 11, 1954), 7.

"Middle School Teachers," *ibid.*, No. 22 (January 24, 1954), 6.

Novotny, Josef. "A Few Notes . . . [on Chinese Elementary Education; instructional program for elementary schools for the school year 1957–58]," in *A Few Notes on Chinese Elementary Education*. (Originally published in *Komonsky* [Comenius], Prague: LXXXII, No. 4 [April 1958].) Translated in Joint Publications Research Service Doc. 581, D. C. Regular Series (March 9, 1959).

"Parents Protest," *Newsletter of the United Nations Association of the Republic of China*, XII, No. 3 (September 1957), 15.

"Reform of Primary Education," *Union Research Service*, XIX, No. 15 (April-June 1960).

"Reform of Secondary Education," *ibid.*

"Schoolmastering as Hsu Lao Sees It," *Peking Review*, II, No. 29 (July 21, 1959), 5.

"Schools on Wheels," *ibid.*, II, No. 7 (February 17, 1959), 5.

Schuman, Julian. "Peking Primary School: Pioneers New Method," *China Monthly Review* (June 1953), 60–64.

"Secondary Education," *China News Analysis* (Hong Kong), No. 147 (September 7, 1956).

"Shortage of Primary Schools," *ibid.*, No. 8 (October 16, 1953), 6.

Sun Tan-wei. "A Village Nursery—How It Grew," *China Reconstructs*, V, No. 8 (August 1956), 28–29.

T'ien Hsiu-chuan. "Develop the Children to Take Their Turn in the Ranks of Communism," in *Translations of Jen Min Jih Pao: Articles on Education*. (Originally published in *Jen Min Jih Pao* [People's Daily], Peking: April 14, 1960.) Translated in Joint Publications Research Service Doc. 2777, N. Y. Regular Series (June 3, 1960).

"Vicissitudes of Primary Schools," *China News Analysis* (Hong Kong), No. 46 (August 6, 1954), 1–4.

YANG KUANG-TEH. "Growing Boy," *China Reconstructs*, V, No. 6 (June 1956), 24–26.

YEH SHENG-TAO. "Middle and Primary School Textbooks Must Be Reformed," in *Translation of Jen Min Jih Pao: Articles on Education*. (Originally published in *Jen Min Jih Pao* [People's Daily], Peking: April 14, 1960.) Translated in Joint Publications Research Service Doc. 2777, N. Y. Regular Series (June 3, 1960).

See also:

BARENDSEN (XI) • CHANG CHIEN (VII) • CHEN KUANG (XI) • "Education: Every Child Will Go to School" (VII) • HAO (XI) • KAN (X) • "School Children" (VII) • "Schools" (VII)

Section IX
Higher Education

Articles on Education in Communist China. (Originally published in *Kuang Ming Jih Pao* [Illumination Daily], Peking: January 1960.) Translated in Joint Publications Research Service Doc. 3416, N. Y. Regular Series (June 17, 1960).

BELYAYEV, A. I. "The Situation of Higher Education in the People's Republic of China," in *Articles on Higher Education in Communist China.* (Originally published in *Izvestiya Vysshikh Uchebnykh Zavedeniy Tsvetnaya Metallurgiya* [News of Higher Educational Instiutions: Non-ferrous Metallurgy], Moscow: No. 5, 1959.) Translated in Joint Publications Research Service Doc. 1176, D. C. Regular Series (February 19, 1960).

BIGELOW, KARL W. "Some Comparative Reflections on Soviet and Chinese Higher Education," *Comparative Education Review,* IV, No. 3 (February 1961), 169–173.

"Big Leap in Academic Circles," *Peking Review,* II, No. 50 (December 15, 1959), 5.

"Bomb Explodes in College," *Newsletter of the United Nations Association of the Republic of China,* XII, No. 1 (July 1957), 17.

CAMPBELL, SYLVIA. "Reforming the Colleges," *China Monthly Review* (1951), 8–10.

CHANG CHIEN. "More People Go to College," *People's China,* No. 22 (November 16, 1954), 23-25.

———. "360,000 College Graduates in Eight Years," *ibid.,* No. 16 (August 16, 1957), 18–27.

"Changing Tsinghua," *Peking Review,* I, No. 25 (August 19, 1958), 5.

CHEN CHUNG-HSIEN. "Wide Horizons for Students," *China Reconstructs,* III, No. 5 (September-October 1954), 34–36.

CHEN HSUAN-SHAN. "Training Teachers for Middle Schools," *China Reconstructs,* V, No. 9 (September 1956), 18–19.

CHEN, THEODORE HSI-EN. "Collective Learning in Communist China's Universities," *Far Eastern Survey,* XXVI, No. 1 (January 1957), 8–11.

———. "The Popularization of Higher Education in Communist

465

China," *Information on Education around the World,* No. 24, OE-14002 (August 1959). Washington, D.C.: United States Department of Health, Education, and Welfare; Office of Education (Government Printing Office), 1959.

———. *Teacher Training in Communist China* ("Studies in Comparative Education Series," No. OE-14058). Washington, D.C.: United States Office of Education, 1960.

CHENG, J. CHESTER. "Higher Education in Communist China: Some Recent Developments," *The World Today,* XV, No. 1 (January 1959), 38–45.

CHIANG NAN-HSIANG. "A Revolution in Higher Education," *China Reconstructs* VIII, No. 2 (February 1959), 10–13.

CHIANG YIN-EN. "Yenching—the Rebirth of a University," *People's China,* III, No. 10 (May 16, 1951), 19–20.

CHIEN TUAN-SHENG. "New Path for Higher Education," pp. 322–327 in *China in Transition.* Peking: *China Reconstructs,* 1957.

"Chinese Intellectuals on the Land," *Far Eastern Economic Review,* XXIV, No. 19 (May 8, 1958), 581–582.

CHOU PEI-YUAN. "Higher Education with a Noble Purpose," *Women of China,* No. 6 (1959), 20–22.

CHUNG SHIH. *Higher Education in Communist China.* Hong Kong: Union Research Institute, 1953.

"Compulsory Higher Education," *Union Research Service,* IV, No. 14 (July-September 1956).

"Cultural News: 200,000 College Graduates Go to Work," *Evergreen: A Magazine of Chinese Youth and Students,* No. 5 (October 1963), 22.

"Cultural News: 170,000 College Graduates; Graduates of Worker and Peasant Origin," *ibid.,* No. 6 (October 1962), 24–25.

"Facts and Figures: Higher Education in China," *Peking Review,* I, No. 27 (September 2, 1958), 10–11.

"First University in Chinghai," *ibid.,* III, No. 51 (November 20, 1960), 5.

FITZGERALD, CHARLES P. "The Scholar in Present-Day China," *Asiana,* I (1956), 17–23.

FRASER, STEWART E. "Some Aspects of Higher Education in the People's Republic of China." University of Colorado doctoral dissertation, 1961.

GOLDMAN, RENÉ. "Peking University Today," *China Quarterly,* No. 7 (July-September 1961), 101–111.

"Handing on the Torch," *Peking Review,* II, No. 23 (June 9, 1959), 5.

"Higher Education (Types of Higher School, Number of Schools)," *China News Analysis* (Hong Kong), No. 81 (April 29, 1955), 2–7.

"Higher Learning," *ibid.,* No. 292 (September 11, 1959).

HPAIN, Y. H. "China's New University," *China Monthly Review* (August 13, 1959), 206–212.

HSU, IMMANUEL C. Y. "The Reorganization of Higher Education in Communist China, 1949–1961," *China Quarterly,* No. 19 (July-September 1964).

HU, CHANG-TU. "Higher Education in Communist China: Implications for the U.S.," pp. 233-234 in *Current Issues in Education.* National Conference on Higher Education, 1960.

————. "Higher Education in Mainland China," *Comparative Education Review,* IV, No. 3 (February 1961), 159–168.

"Intellectuals and the Party," *Union Research Service,* II, No. 15 (January-March 1956); IV, No. 4 (July-September 1956).

KAO, JACK. "Students on a State Farm," *China Reconstructs,* IV, No. 4 (April 1955), 21–23.

LIANG NIEN. "Tsinghua University: Integrating Education with Productive Labor," *Peking Review,* II, No. 21 (May 26, 1959), 14–16.

LIN WEI-NAN. "Learning to Be an Architect," *China Reconstructs,* VIII, No. 9 (September 1959), 12–14.

LIU SHUI-SHENG (pseud.). "Life in a Chinese University," *Institute of International Education News Bulletin,* XXXVI, No. 6 (February 1961), 20–26.

LIU YI-FANG. "A Mill Girl Goes to College," *China Reconstructs,* IX, No. 5 (May 1960), 16–17.

LU YUN. "Education: a Job for Every College Graduate," *Peking Review,* II, No. 33 (August 13, 1959), 14–15.

"Manpower Distribution and Migration," *China News Analysis* (Hong Kong), No. 95 (August 12, 1955), 1–7.

"The Model University," *ibid.,* No. 9 (October 23, 1953), 6.

"More University Students," *Peking Review,* I, No. 20 (July 15, 1958), 4.

"The New Academic Year in Communist China's Universities," *School and Society,* XC, No. 2207 (March 24, 1962), 147–148.

"New Technology University," *Peking Review,* I, No. 31 (September 30, 1958), 5.

NEWTON, WYNDHAM. "China's Proletarian Universities," *Far Eastern Economic Review*, XXV, No. 29 (November 6, 1958), 577–579.

———. "Chinese Universities to Become Proletarian," *ibid.*, No. 22 (November 27, 1958), 686–688.

"New Way of Writing Text Books," *Peking Review*, I, No. 33 (October 14, 1958), 5.

"On the Mainland Intelligentsia," pp. 1–13 in *Analysis of Current Chinese Communist Problems*. Taiwan: Institute of International Relations, Republic of China, 1963.

P'AN MOU-YUAN. "Great Accomplishments in Educational Reforms at Amoy University in the Last Ten Years," in *Chinese Communist Articles on Education*. (Originally published in *Lun Tan* [Forum], Amoy: No. 5, October 1959.) Translated in Joint Publications Service Doc. 1165, D. C. Regular Series (February 12, 1960).

"Party's Control over Higher Education," *Union Research Service*, IX, No. 10 (October-December 1957); XV, No. 24 (April-June 1959); VIII, No. 26 (January-March 1960).

"The Peking School of Engineering," *People's China*, No. 5 (March 1, 1956), 26.

"People's Republic of China," pp. 227–236 in *The World of Learning, 1963-64*. 14th ed. London: Europa Publications, Ltd., 1963.

"People's University—a New School," *China Monthly Review* (May 1951), 266.

PEPOV, G. N. "Higher Mining Engineering Education in the People's Republic of China," in *Articles on Higher Education in Communist China*. (Originally published in *Izvestiya Vysshikh Uchebnykh Zavedeniy Tsvetnaya Metallurgiya* [News of Higher Educational Institutions: Non-ferrous Metallurgy], Moscow: No. 5, 1959.) Translated in Joint Publications Research Service Doc. 1176, D. C. Regular Series (February 19, 1960).

PIRIE, N. W. "The Academic Sciences in China," *United Asia*, VIII, No. 2 (April 1956), 126–127.

"Premier Chou Visits Tsinghua," *Peking Review*, I, No. 27 (September 2, 1958), 4–5.

"Problems in Higher Education," *Union Research Service*, VII, No. 1 (April-June 1957); IX, No. 19 (October-December 1957).

"Rebuilding China's Universities," *China Monthly Review* (August 1952), 109–113.

"Reforming the Colleges," *ibid.* (January 1951), 8.

"Reform of Higher Education," *Union Research Service*, XXI, No. 9 (October-December 1960).

Ross, D. M. "Higher Education in China," *Universities Review*, XXVI, No. 2 (February 1954), 64–72.

Rugh, Arthur Douglas. "Conduct Standards for Teacher Candidates in the Normal Schools of Communist China," *Teacher Education Quarterly* (State Board of Education, Connecticut), No. 17 (Fall 1959), 27–30.

"The Scandal of Peking University," *China News Analysis*, No. 251 (October 31, 1958), 1–7.

Selected Translations on Education from Kuang Ming Jih Pao. (Originally published October, November, December 1959). Translated in Joint Publications Research Service Doc. 3132, N. Y. Regular Series (April 1, 1960).

Shan Chin. "Tsinghua University: Fifty Years of Great Changes," *Evergreen: A Magazine of Chinese Youth and Students*, No. 4 (June 1961), 22–23.

Shih Ch'eng-chih. *The Status of Science and Education in Communist China: And a Comparison with That in the U.S.S.R.* Hong Kong: Union Research Institute, 1962.

"Students in Higher Education," *Union Research Service*, V, No. 22 (October-December 1956); VIII, No. 8 (July-September 1957); X, No. 13 (January-March 1958); XVIII, No. 26 (January-March 1960); XXI, No. 14 (October-December 1960).

"Subjugation of Intellectuals," *ibid.*, XIV, No. 6 (January-March 1959).

T. T. "The Intellectual in New China," *Problems of Communism*, II, No. 2 (March-April 1953).

"Tan Kah-kee at 82," *China Reconstructs*, IV, No. 6 (June 1955), 20–22.

Ting Hao-chuan. "Peking Normal University—China's Largest Teacher-Training Center," *People's China*, No. 3 (Feburary 1, 1955), 31–34.

Ting Kuang-hsun. "Nanking's New Union Theological Seminary," *China Monthly Review* (July 1953), 11–19.

Tsao Wei-feng. "Reorganization of China's Colleges," *China Monthly Review* (June 1953), 14–21.

Tseng Chao-lun. "Higher Education in New China," *People's China*, No. 12 (June 16, 1953), 6–10.

TSIEN, LILY (trans.). "The New Academic Year in Communist China's Universities," *School and Society,* XC, No. 2207 (March 24, 1962), 147–148.

"Turning a New Page of Life: 162,000 College Graduates to Join in Socialist Construction," *Evergreen Review: A Magazine of Chinese Youth and Students,* No. 6 (August-September 1961), 8–9.

"University Professors," *China News Analysis* (Hong Kong), No. 97 (August 26, 1955), 2–7.

"University Workshop Streamlined," *Peking Review,* II, No. 5 (February 3, 1959), 4–5.

WANG-CHI. *Mainland China Organizations of Higher Learning in Science and Technology and Their Publications: A Selected Guide.* Washington, D.C.: Government Printing Office, 1961.

WANG, PERCY HUNG-FANG. "Higher Education in Communist China." University of Washington Master's thesis, 1953.

WILMOTT, EARL. "New Democracy on the Campus," *China Weekly Review* (July 1, 1950), 77–78.

WONG, JENNINGS L. "Specializations in Higher Technological Education in Communist China," in *Information on Education around the World,* No. 13. Washington, D.C.: U.S. Department of Health, Education and Welfare; Office of Education (Government Printing Office), 1959.

YAO FANG-YING. "Tsinghua University," *People's China,* No. 14 (July 16, 1953), 23–25.

YEN FU-CHING. "Medical Training Today," *China Reconstructs,* VIII, No. 6 (June 1959), 30–32.

See also:

CHEN: "Helping the Chinese Intellectuals" (XIII) • CHI (XV) • *College Students of New China* (XIV) • "Colleges on the Farms" (XI) • "Factory College-Graduates" (X) • FENG (XIII) • GOLDMAN (XIII) • "Graduation Time" (VII) • GUILLAIN (XIII) • HU (XVII) • LI K'UANG-CHIH (XI) • LI KUO-YING (XI) • LI TA (XIII) • LIANG NIEN; "Education" (X) • "On Psychology" (VII) • Orleans (VII) • "Peking's Counter Offensive in Colleges" (XIII) • "Physical Sciences" (XV) • "Problems of Intellectuals" (XIII) • "Professors under Fire" (XIII) • "Reform of Intellectuals" (XIII) • "Rural Universities" (XI) • "Scholar on Mainland under Bitter Attack (XIII) • SCOTT (IV) • TSUI (XIII) • "Unrest in Colleges" (XIV)

Section X
Part-Time and Half-Time Educational Programs

ABE, MUNEMITSU. "Spare-Time Education in Communist China," *China Quarterly*, No. 8 (October-December 1961), 149–159.

BARENDSEN, ROBERT D. *Half-Work, Half-Study Schools in Communist China: Recent Experiments With Self-Supporting Educational Institutions.* Bulletin No. FS5.214, OE14100 (1964). Washington, D.C.: Government Printing Office, 1964.

CHEN TAN. "A Worker-Peasant School," *People's China*, II, No. 4 (August 1950), 22–24.

CHENG, J. CHESTER. "Half-Work and Half-Study Program in Communist China," *History of Education Journal*, IX, No. 4 (Summer 1958), 88–92.

CHENG, K. C. "Part Work; Part Study: Half-day Agricultural School," *Peking Review*, II, No. 13 (March 31, 1959, 14–15.

"Education: Training Worker and Peasant Intellectuals; Spare-Time Education for Workers," *Peking Review*, I, No. 12 (May 20, 1958), 16.

"Factory College Graduates," *ibid.*, III, No. 22 (May 31, 1960), 5.

"First Crop from Spare-Time Colleges," *ibid.*, No. 45 (November 8, 1960), 4.

HARPER, PAUL. *Spare-Time Education for Workers in Communist China.* Bulletin No. 30, OE-14102 (1964). Washington, D.C.: Government Printing Office, 1964.

KAN WEI-CHUNG. "A Middle School Sets Up Workshops," *China Reconstructs*, VIII, No. 4 (April 1959), 13–14.

LI CHIH-WO. "Report on Inspection of Tientsin Half-work Half-study Schools," in *Translations from China's Political and Sociological Publications.* (Originally published in *Pei Ching Shih Ta Hsueh Pao* [Peking Teachers' College Journal], Peking: No. 1, January 1959.) Translated in Joint Publications Research Service Doc. 909, D. C. Regular Series (September 11, 1959).

LI FANG. "Factories Run Schools," *Peking Review*, I, No. 41 (December 9, 1958), 13–14.

471

LIANG HAN-PING. "Merging Factory and School," *China Reconstructs,* VIII, No. 1 (January 1959), 14–16.

LIANG NIEN. "Education: Spare-Time Colleges for Workers," *Peking Review,* III, No. 21 (May 24, 1960), 41–42.

————. "On the Cultural Front: Worker's Spare-Time Education Spurts Ahead," *ibid.,* III, No. 3 (January 19, 1960), 15–16.

LING YANG. "New Phase in Education: Schools Run Factories," *ibid.,* No. 39 (November 25, 1958), 14–16.

"Start Half-Work, Half-Study Schools Everywhere," in *Education under Party Guidance in Communist China.* (Originally published in *Hopeh Jih Pao* [Hopeh Daily], Tientsin: November 8, 1958.) Translated in Joint Publications Research Service Doc. 1035, D. C. Regular Series (November 23, 1959).

WANG TI. "Combining Work and Study" *China Reconstructs,* VII, No. 7 (July 1958), 9–11.

WEN YU. "The New Generation of Skilled Workers," *China Reconstructs,* IX, No. 8 (August 1960), 24–26.

"Work while You Learn," *Peking Review,* I, No. 6 (April 8, 1958), 14–15.

See also:

"After-School Study Groups" (VII) • CHAO (VII) • CHIN (VII) • FU (VII) • "The Peking School of Engineering" (IX)

Section XI
Agricultural and Rural Education

"About Chinese Youth: All-Out Support for Agriculture," *Evergreen: A Magazine of Chinese Youth and Students,* No. 5 (August 1960), 11.

"Adult Education in a Commune," *Peking Review,* II, No. 8 (February 24, 1959), 6.

"Agricultural Schools," *Union Research Service,* XIX, No. 17 (April-June 1960); XX, No. 25 (July-September 1960).

"Art Education: Peasant Art Academies," *Peking Review,* I, No. 39 (November 25, 1958), 21–22.

BARENDSEN, ROBERT D. "The Agricultural Middle School in Communist China," *China Quarterly,* No. 8 (October-December 1961), 106–134.

CHEN KUANG. "Middle Schools for the Countryside," *China Reconstructs,* IX, No. 2 (February 1960), 2–5.

CHEN, THEODORE HSI-EN. "Worker-Peasant Education in China," *Eastern World,* VI, No. 7 (July 1952); continued in VI, No. 8 (August 1952).

CHOU PO. "Adult Education in the Countryside," *China Reconstructs,* IX, No. 7 (July 1960), 29–31.

CHU, DON-CHEAN. "The Communes and Their Schools in China," *News Magazine of the Connecticut Council for the Social Studies,* XXII, No. 4 (June 1963).

———. "The Communes and Their Schools in Communist China," *Journal of Human Relations,* IX, No. 2 (Winter 1961), 265–274.

———. "Theories and Practices of the Commune Schools in Communist China," *News Magazine of the Connecticut Council for the Social Studies,* XXII, No. 1 (May 1962).

"Colleges on the Farms," *Peking Review,* I, No. 33 (October 14, 1958), 5.

"Communes: An Educational Force," *ibid.,* No. 34 (October 21, 1958), 5.

"Education in People's Communes," *Union Research Service,* V, No.

17 (October-December 1956); XIII, No. 21 (October-December 1958); XIV, No. 6 (January-March 1959).

Hao Kuei-yuan. "A Mountain Village Wins Culture," *China Reconstructs,* IX, No. 12 (December 1960), 18–19.

Huang, H. C. "The Village Teacher," *China Monthly Review* (May 1953), 38–42.

Li Fang. "New Phase in Education: Schools Run by Communes," *Peking Review,* I, No. 44 (December 30, 1958), 16–17.

Li K'uang-chih. "Survey of Red and Expert Commune Universities in Honan," in *Translations from China's Political and Sociological Publications.* (Originally published in *Pei Ching Shih Ta Hsueh Pao* [Peking Teachers' College Journal], Peking: No. 1, January 1959.) Translated in Joint Publications Research Service Doc. 909, D. C. Regular Series (September 11, 1959).

Li Kuo-ying. "Young Peasants Go to College," *Evergreen: A Magazine of Chinese Youth and Students,* No. 4 (June 1961), 19–21.

Liang Nien. "In the People's Communes: Schools for the New Type Peasants," *Peking Review,* III, No. 1 (January 5, 1960), 20–21.

―――. "Report from Kiangsu: Agricultural Middle Schools," *ibid.,* II, No. 30 (July 28, 1959), 14–15.

Liao I-fan and Ch'ang Wen-po. "Hu-shui Hsien Sets up Agricultural Colleges to Welcome the Technological Revolution," in *China's Technological Revolution.* (Originally published in *Jen Min Chiao Yu* [People's Education], Peking: Vol. IX, July 1, 1958.) Translated in Joint Publications Research Service Doc. 501, D. C. Regular Series (January 20, 1959).

"Linhsien's School for Peasants," *Peking Review,* I, No. 6 (April 8, 1958), 16.

Lu Ting-yi. "Education: Agricultural Middle School: Second Anniversary," *Peking Review,* III, No. 11 (March 15, 1960), 17-18.

"Peasants Get Secondary Schools," *Peking Review,* III, No. 13 (March 29, 1960), 5.

"The Peasants Study," *ibid.,* II, No. 47 (November 24, 1959), 3.

"Rural Universities," *ibid.,* I, No. 13 (May 27, 1958), 4.

Sie Ping-teh and Douglas Rugh (trans.). "The Commune Experiment in Communist China," *School and Society,* LXXXVIII, No. 2176 (Summer 1960), 301–304.

Sun Chu. "The Farm Taught Me Science," *China Reconstructs,* VIII, No. 11 (November 1959), 34–35.

TAN AI-CHING. "Educated Peasants—a New Concept," *China Reconstructs*, VI, No. 7 (July 1957), 6–8.

See also:
ALLEY: *An Adventure in Creative Education* (VII) • K. C. CHENG (X) • CHIA (VII) • "Education" (X) • MORRISON (VII) • "A Self-Taught Village" (XII) • WANG LEH (VII)

Section XII
Language Reform and Literacy Campaigns

CHANG, BETTY CHANDLER. "Our YWCA Literary Class," *China Monthly Review* (July 1953), 60–65.

CHANG SEN. "National Minorities: Written Languages for All," *Peking Review,* I, No. 37 (November 11, 1958), 16–17.

CHOU YOU-KUANG. "China Gets an Alphabet," *China Reconstructs,* VI, No. 3 (March 1957), 2–4.

CHU, DON-CHEAN. "A Housewife Becomes Literate in Communist China Wang Leng-yun," *School and Society,* XCI, No. 2233 (November 30, 1963).

"Facing Illiteracy," *China News Analysis* (Hong Kong), No. 115 (January 13, 1956).

HU YU-CHIH. "Phonetic Script Helps Literacy," *China Reconstructs,* VIII, No. 8 (August 1959), 25–27.

LI CHIN-HSI. "The Phonetic Alphabet and the Cultural Revolution," in *Translations of Jen Min Jih Pao: Articles on Education.* (Originally published in *Jen Min Jih Pao* [People's Daily], Peking: April 14, 1960.) Translated in Joint Publications Research Service Doc. 2777, N. Y. Regular Series (June 3, 1960).

LI HUI. "Cultural Revolution in Waujung: Phonetic Alphabet— Short Cut to Literacy," *Peking Review,* III, No. 28 (July 12, 1960), 17–19.

LIN HAN-DA. "First Step to Language Reform," *China Reconstructs,* V, No. 1 (January 1956), 21–24.

MA HSUEH-LIANG. "Minority Languages of China," *China Reconstructs,* III, No. 3 (May-June 1954), 37–41.

"The Mute Teacher," *Peking Review,* II, No. 15 (April 14, 1959), 4–5.

"The Phonetic Writing," *China News Analysis* (Hong Kong), No. 85 (May 27, 1955), 2–7.

"Reform of Language and Writing," *ibid.,* No. 108 (November 11, 1955), 6–7.

"Reform of Writing," *ibid.,* No. 32 (April 16, 1954), 6; No. 33 (April 30, 1954), 1–7.

"Reform of Writing (with Tables)," *ibid.*, No. 136 (June 15, 1956).

"A Self-Taught Village," *Peking Review*, III, No. 28 (July 12, 1960), 5.

"A Village Teacher Fights Illiteracy," *China Reconstructs*, I, No. 2 (March-April 1952), 12–13.

WEI CHUEH. "Language Reform: Progress in Popularizing the Phonetic Alphabet," *Peking Review*, I, No. 35 (October 28, 1958), 15–17.

———. "Making Chinese Easier to Learn," *ibid.*, No. 2 (March 11, 1958), 14–16.

"Writing Reform," *China News Analysis* (Hong Kong), No. 183 (May 31, 1957), 4–5.

"Writing Reform," *ibid.*, No. 207 (November 29, 1957), 7.

"Writing Reform," *ibid.*, No. 214 (January 31, 1958), 5–6.

WU PIN. "Heilung Kiang's Victory over Illiteracy," *Peking Review*, I, No. 15 (June 10, 1958), 14–15.

———. "Hsiaochang Township Fights Illiteracy," *ibid.*, No. 7 (April 15, 1958), 11–12.

YANG KWANG-TEH. "A Village Learns to Read," *China Reconstructs*, VI, No. 9 (September 1957), 6–8.

Section XIII
Thought Control and Ideological Reforms
in Education

"Arts as Weapons against U. S. Imperialism," *Evergreen: A Magazine of Chinese Youth and Students*, No. 5 (August 1960), 17–19.

BARNETT, A. DOAK. "Social Controls in Communist China," *Far Eastern Survey*, XXII, No. 5 (April 22, 1953), 45–58.

CHAO CHUNG and I-FAN YANG. *Students in Mainland China*. Hong Kong: Union Research Institute, 1956.

CHEN, THEODORE HSI-EN. "Education and Indoctrination in Red China," *Current History*, XLI, No. 241 (September 1961), 157–163.

———. "Helping the Chinese Intellectuals Help Themselves," *Educational Record*, XXXIV, No. 1 (January 1953), 25–31.

———. "Rectification of Error and the Error of Rectification," *Soviet Survey*, XXIV (April-June 1958), 27–31.

———. *Thought Reform of the Chinese Intellectuals*. Hong Kong: Hong Kong University Press; and London: Oxford University Press, 1960.

———. "The Thought Reform of Intellectuals," *Annal of the American Academy of Political and Social Science*, CCCXXI (1959), 82–89.

———, and SIN-MING CHIU. "Thought Reform in Communist China," *Far Eastern Survey*, XXIV, No. 12 (December 1955) 177–184.

———, and WEN HUI C. CHEN. "The 'Three Anti' and 'Five Anti' Movements in Communist China," *Pacific Affairs*, XXVI, No. 1 (March 1953), 3–23.

CHIN YUEH-LIN. "The 'Hundred Schools' Policy as I See It," *People's China*, No. 12 (June 16, 1957), 10–12.

"Chinese Scientists and Marxism," *Far Eastern Economic Review*, XXIII, No. 22 (November 25, 1957), 675, 683.

CHOU EN-LAI. *Report on the Question of the Intellectuals*. Peking: Foreign Languages Press, 1956.

"Communist Attitude towards Intellectuals," *Union Research Service*, IV, No. 12 (July-September 1956).

478

"Counter Revolution in Education," *ibid.,* I, No. 5 (September 1955-January 1956).

"Double Anti Campaign in Education," *ibid.,* XI, No. 5 (April-June 1958).

Education in Communist China. Translated in Joint Publications Research Service Doc. 514, N.Y. Regular Series (June 23, 1958).

"Education under Attack," *Newsletter of the United Nations Association of the Republic of China,* XII, No. 1 (July 1957), 18.

"Fates of Professors," *ibid.,* IX, No. 3 (March 1956), 9.

FENG TING. "Chinese Intellectuals and Socialism," *People's China,* No. 18 (September 16, 1957), 9–13.

FRASER, STEWART E. "Education and Politics in Red China," *Colorado Quarterly* (Summer 1960), 5–16.

GOLDMAN, RENÉ. "The Rectification Campaign at Peking University," *China Quarterly,* No. 12 (October-December 1962), 138–153.

GUILLAIN, ROBERT. "Red China Seeks New Intellectuals," *New Leader,* XL (March 24, 1958), 14–15.

HOUN, FRANKLIN W. "Publications as a Propaganda Medium in Communist China," *Far Eastern Survey,* XXIX, No. 12 (December 1960), 177–186.

―――. *To Change a Nation: Propaganda and Indoctrination in Communist China.* Glencoe, Ill.: Glencoe Free Press, 1961.

―――, and YUAN-LI WU. "Chinese Communist Publication Policy and Thought Control," *Pacific Spectator,* X (Summer 1956), 282–91.

HOWSE, HUGH. "The Use of Radio in China," *China Quarterly,* No. 2 (April-June 1960), 59–68.

HUNTER, EDWARD. *Brainwashing in Red China: The Calculated Destruction of Men's Minds.* New York: Vanguard Press, 1951.

"Intellectuals," *China News Analysis* (Hong Kong), No. 146 (August 31, 1956), 5–7.

"Intellectuals Sent to Farm," *Newsletter of the United Nations Association of the Republic of China,* XIII, No. 1 (January 1958), 15–16.

ISAACS, HAROLD R. "The Blind Alley of Totalitarianism," *Annals of the American Academy of Political and Social Science,* CCLXXVI (1951) 81–90.

JOHNSON, CHALMERS A. "An Intellectual Weed in the Socialist Garden: The Case of Ch'ien Tuan-sheng," *China Quarterly,* No. 6 (April-June 1961), 29–52.

―――. *Freedom of Thought and Expression in China: Communist*

Policies toward the Intellectual Class. Hong Kong: Union Research Institute, 1959.

LAMMERS, RAYMOND JOHN. "An Analysis of a Representative Sample of Plays Written and Used for Propagandistic Purposes by the Chinese Communists." University of Minnesota doctoral dissertation, 1962.

LI FANG. "Why Intellectuals Go to the Countryside," *Peking Review,* I, No. 4 (March 25, 1958), 8–10.

———. "Xiafang Intellectuals: Back from the Countryside," *Peking Review,* II, No. 6 (February 10, 1959), 10–12.

LI TA. "Concerning the Thought Rehabilitation of University Professors," *Soviet Press Translations,* VII, No. 3 (February 1, 1952), 86–89.

LIFTON, ROBERT J. "Thought Reform of Chinese Intellectuals: A Psychiatric Evaluation," *Journal of Asian Studies,* XVI, No. 1 (November 1956), 75–88.

———. *Thought Reform and the Psychology of Totalism: A Study of "Brainwashing" in China.* New York: W. W. Norton, 1961.

LIU YANG-CHIAO. "Question of Mass Line in Reform of Teaching and Learning," in *Translations of Political Articles from the China Mainland Press.* (Originally published in *Kuang Ming Jih Pao* [Illumination Daily], Peking: October 10, 1958.) Translated in Joint Publications Research Service Doc. 746, D. C. Regular Series (June 3, 1959).

MACFARQUHAR, RODERICK. *The Hundred Flowers Campaign and the Chinese Intellectuals.* New York: Praeger, 1960.

"The Meaning of Xiafang," *Peking Review,* II, No. 2 (January 13, 1959), 5.

"Mood of Students," *China News Analysis* (Hong Kong), No. 168 (February 15, 1957), 4–5.

MU FU-SHENG. *The Wilting of the Hundred Flowers: The Chinese Intelligentsia under Mao.* New York: Praeger, 1962.

"Mukden Professors and the 'Three Evils,'" *Far Eastern Economic Review,* XXIII, No. 14 (October 3, 1957), 422–424.

NEWTON, WYNDHAM. "The Fate of Intellectuals in China," *Far Eastern Economic Review,* XXIII, No. 2 (July 11, 1957), 33–35.

———. "Philosophers Prefer to Blush Unseen," *ibid.,* No. 1 (July 4, 1957), 6–7.

"The Participation of Cadres in Manual Labor," *Peking Review,* II, No. 12 (March 24, 1959), 13–15.

"Peking's Counter Offensive in Colleges," *Far Eastern Economic Review*, XXIII, No. 15 (October 10, 1957), 456–458.

"Peking's Trouble with Soldiers and Students," *ibid.*, XXII, No. 24 (June 13, 1957), 753–754.

"Philosophers Dig into Life," *Peking Review*, I, No. 23 (August 5, 1958), 4.

"Problems of Intellectuals," *Union Research Service*, III, No. 15 (April-June 1959).

"Professors Go to School," *China News Analysis* (Hong Kong), No. 7 (October 9, 1953), 6.

"Professors under Fire," *Newsletter of the United Nations Association of the Republic of China*, XIII, No. 4 (April 1958), 17–18.

"Readers and Reading Matter (U.S.S.R. Literature, Western Classics, Prohibited Books)," *China News Analysis* (Hong Kong), No. 123 (March 9, 1956).

"Rectification Campaign Ends," *Peking Review*, I, No. 26 (August 26, 1958), 4.

"Rectification of Youth in China," *Far Eastern Economic Review*, XXIII, No. 14 (October 3, 1957), 421, 448.

"Reds Tighten Students' Gag," *Newsletter of the United Nations Association of the Republic of China*, XII, No. 4 (October 1957), 15.

"Reform of Intellectuals," *Union Research Service*, I, No. 29 (September 1955); XII, No. 7 (July-September 1958); XV, No. 13 (April-June 1959); XVIII, No. 26 (January-March 1960); XX, No. 11 (July-September 1960).

"Reform of Intellectuals (Chou En-lai)," *China News Analysis* (Hong Kong), No. 120 (February 17, 1956), 3–5.

"Scholar on Mainland under Bitter Attack," *Newsletter of the United Nations Association of the Republic of China*, XVIII, No. 3 (September 1960), 17.

"Second Year of Xiafang," *Peking Review*, II, No. 7 (February 17, 1959), 5.

SHAPERO, SEYMOUR. *Brainwashing: A Partial Bibliography*. Washington, D. C.: American University, Special Operations Research Office, 1958.

SHIH CHUN. "More Contact! Closer Friendship!: The Path of the Chinese Intellectuals," *People's China* (June 16, 1956), 5–7.

"Social vs. Family Education," *Union Research Service*, XII, No. 21 (July-September 1958).

"Storm in the Universities," *China News Analysis* (Hong Kong), No. 195 (September 6, 1957).

"Student Unrest," *Union Research Service,* X, Nos. 13 and 21 (January and March 1958).

"Students Put under Thought Control," *Newsletter of the United Nations Association of the Republic of China,* XII, No. 2 (August 1957), 17–18.

TENG HSIAO-PING. *Report on the Rectification Campaign.* (Third plenary session of the Eighth Central Committee of the Communist Party of China, September 23, 1957.) Peking: Foreign Languages Press, 1957.

TSUI SHU-CHIN. *From Academic Freedom to Brainwashing: The Tragic Ordeal of Professors on the Chinese Mainland.* Taipei, Taiwan: China Culture Publishing Foundation, 1953.

TUNG SHIH-TSIN. *Secret Diary From Red China.* Transcribed from the original work of "Earnest Liu" (pseud.). New York: Bobbs-Merrill, 1961.

WHITING, ALLEN S. "Rewriting Modern History in Communist China: A Review Article," *Far Eastern Survey,* XXIV, No. 11 (November 1955), 173–174.

"Xiafang Cadres Do Their Stuff," *Peking Review,* III, No. 51 (November 20, 1960), 3–4.

"Xiafang Progress Sheet," *ibid.,* No. 46 (November 15, 1960), 3.

YANG I-FAN. *The Case of Hu Feng.* Hong Kong: Union Research Institute, 1956.

YEN, MARIE (pseud.). *The Umbrella Garden: A Picture of Student Life in Red China.* (Originally published as *College Life under the Red Flag.* Hong Kong: Union Press, 1952.) New York: Macmillan, 1954.

See also:

Analysis of Current Chinese Communist Problems (IX) • "Bomb Explodes in College" (IX) • CAMPBELL (IX) • CHANG (VI) • THEODORE HSI-EN CHEN: "Chinese Communist Education" (VII), "Education for the Chinese Revolution" (VI), "Education under Communism" (VII), and "Education and Propaganda" (VII) • CHOW (V) • "Despondency among Communist Youth" (XIV) • "Disillusioned Students" (XIV) • "Education of the Party Members" (VI) • FEI (VII) • "Hanyang Students Revolt" (XIV) • "Intellectuals and the Party" (IX) • JOHNSON (VII) • KASSOF

(XIV) • Kierman (VII) • Kuo (VIII) • Liu Shaw-tong (V) • Lu: *Let a Hundred Flowers Blossom* (VI) • Mao: *On the Correct Handling of Contradictions* (VI) • Gretta Palmer (V) • P'an (IX) • "Parents Protest" (VIII) • "Party's Control over Education" (VI) • "Professors and Teachers" (VII) • "Red Ideology in Schools" (VI) • "Reforming the Colleges" (IX) • "Regimentation of Students" (XIV) • "Social Education of Children" (VII) • Steiner: "The Curriculum in Chinese Socialist Education" and "Ideology and Politics in Communist China" (VI) • "Subjugation of Intellectuals" (IX) • T. T. (IX) • Tang: "Power Struggle" (V) • Tu (VI) • Walker: *China under Communism* (V) Charles K. S. Wang (VII) • Wang Y-chu (VII) • Weber (VII) • Section VI, *passim*

Section XIV
Youth and Student Affairs

CHEN, H. K. "All China Student Congress," *China Digest*, V, No. 9 (February 22, 1949), 10.

China and Her Youth. Peking: All China Youth Federation, Foreign Languages Press, 1959–1960.

"China's Young Men Go Westward," *Far Eastern Economic Review*, XXVI, No. 25 (June 18, 1959), 844–846.

China's Youth Marches Forward. Peking: Foreign Languages Press, 1950.

"Chinese Students off to the Countryside," *Far Eastern Economic Review*, XXIV, No. 23 (June 5, 1958), 713–715.

Chinese Youth Enjoys a Happy Life. Peking: Foreign Languages Press, 1953.

College Students of New China. Peking: Foreign Languages Press, 1958.

"Congress of Militant Youth," *China News Analysis* (Hong Kong), No. 105 (October 21, 1955), 2–5.

"Despondency among Communist Youth," *Far Eastern Economic Review, XXII*, No. 10 (March 7, 1957), 299–300.

"Disillusioned Students," *Newsletter of the United Nations Association of the Republic of China*, XIV, No. 2 (August 1958), 21.

"The Function of the Youth Corps," *China News Analysis* (Hong Kong), No. 9, (October 23, 1953), 2–4.

"Hanyang Students Revolt," *Newsletter of the United Nations Association of the Republic of China*, XII, No. 2 (August 1957), 14.

KASSOF, ALLEN. "The Young Generation and the Communists," *Far Eastern Economic Review*, XXIV, No. 1 (January 2, 1958), 3–7.

"Model Youngsters," *China News Analysis* (Hong Kong), No. 264 (February 13, 1959).

"New Deal for Students," *China Weekly Review*, CXVIII, No. 8 (July 22, 1950), 128.

"Peking Students," *Newsletter of the United Nations Association of the Republic of China*, XII, No. 1 (July 1957), 16–17.

PRINGSHEIM, KLAUS H. "Chinese Communist Youth Leagues," *China*

Quarterly, No. 12 (October-December 1962), 75–91.

"Regimentation of Students," *Union Research Service*, IV, No. 2 (July-September 1956); V, No. 22 (October-December 1956).

"The Splendour of Youth," *Evergreen: A Magazine of Chinese Youth and Students*, No. 5 (October 1963), 14–17.

"The Story of a Youth Corps Member," *China News Analysis* (Hong Kong), No. 259 (January 9, 1959).

"Students' Congress," *Peking Review*, III, No. 7 (February 16, 1960), 5.

"Trials and Tribulations of China's Youth," *Far Eastern Economic Review*, XVIII, No. 4 (January 27, 1955), 118–119.

"Tumult among Red Youths," *Newsletter of the United Nations Association of the Republic of China*, XI, No. 5 (May 1957), 16–17.

"Unrest in Colleges," *ibid.*, No. 3 (March 1957), 16.

WANG CHIH-HSING. "Problems in Work among the Young Pioneers," in *Selected Political and Sociological Translations on Communist China*. (Originally published in *Fu Tao Yuan* [Instructor], Peking: No. 8, August 12, 1959.) Translated in Joint Publications Research Service Doc. 1953, N. Y. Regular Series (October 15, 1959).

YAO FANG-YING. "State Aid for Students," *People's China*, No. 22 (November 16, 1953), 31–34.

Young Builders of Peking. Peking: Foreign Languages Press, 1953.

"Youth: A Problem," *China News Analysis* (Hong Kong), No. 66 (January 7, 1955), 2–7.

See also:

"Afro-Asian Youth Conference" (XVII) • "Afro-Asian Youth Conference Hailed" (XVII) • CHANG CHAO (XVII) • CHAO (XIII) • CHEN CHUNG-HSIEN (IX) • "Children's Palace in Shanghai" (VII) • "Chinese Scientists and Marxism" (XIII) • "I.U.S. Congress in Peking" (XVII) • KAO (IX) • LIU SHUI-SHENG (IX) • "Mood of Students" (XIII) • *Motherland* (XVII) • "Peking Children's Palace" (VII) • "Peking's Trouble with Soldiers and Students" (XIII) • "Rectification of Youth in China" (XIII) • "Reds Tighten Students' Gag" (XIII) • *Resolutions of the 5th I.U.S. Congress* (XVII) • "Storm in the Universities" (XIII) • "Students in Higher Education" (IX) • "Students Put under Thought Control" (XIII) • "Students Quit School" (VII) • "Student Unrest" (XIII) • "The Scandal of Peking University" (IX) • WILMOTT (IX) • YEN (XIII)

Section XV
Educational Aspects of Science, Technology, and Economic Development

"The Academy of Science," *China News Analysis* (Hong Kong), No. 131 (May 11, 1956).

"Atomic Science," *Peking Review*, I, No. 43 (December 23, 1958), 26.

BERNAL, J. D. "Science in China," *United Asia*, VIII, No. 2 (April 1956), 124–133.

——. "Science and Technology in China," *Universities Quarterly*, XI, No. 1 (November 1956), 64–75.

CHAN WING-TSIT. "Neo-Confucianism and Chinese Scientific Thought," *Philosophy East and West*, VI, No. 4 (January 1957), 309–332.

CHANG, ALFRED ZEE. "Scientists in Communist China," *Science*, CXIX, No. 3101 (June 4, 1954), 785–789.

CHEN PIAO. "Young Astronomers at the Purple Mountain Observatory," *Evergreen: A Magazine of Chinese Youth and Students*, No. 6 (October 1962), 20–21.

CHEN, THEODORE HSI-EN. "Science, Scientists, and Politics," in *Sciences in Communist China*, ed. S. H. GOULD. Washington, D. C.: American Association for the Advancement of Science, 1961.

CHENG HSIAO-FENG. "Reinforcement for National Construction," *People's China*, No. 18 (September 16, 1955), 16–18.

CHI TI. "A Promising Student of Science: Tsai Yao-tsu," *Evergreen: A Magazine of Chinese Youth and Students*, No. 1 (February-March 1962), 15–16.

COCHING CHU. "For Long-Term Economic Planning: Scientific Expeditions in China," *Peking Review*, II, No. 52 (Decemberr 29, 1959), 11–14.

——. "What China's Scientists Are Doing," *China Reconstructs*, V, No. 3 (March 1956), 18–22.

DOVER, CEDRIC. "The Use of Biology in China," *United Asia*, VIII, No. 2 (April 1956), 134–136.

FAIRBANK, JOHN KING. "The Influence of Modern Western Science

486

and Technology on Japan and China," *Explorations in Entrepreneurial History,* VII (April 1955), 189–204.

GOULD, SIDNEY H. (ed.). *Sciences in Communist China.* Washington, D. C.: American Association for the Advancement of Science, 1961.

HSIA, RONALD. *Economic Planning in Communist China.* Cambridge, Mass.: Center for International Studies, Massachusetts Institute of Technology, 1953.

IKLE, FRED C. *The Growth of China's Scientific and Technical Manpower.* Santa Monica, Calif.: Rand Corporation, 1957.

KIRBY, E. STUART. "Economic Planning and Policy in Communist China," *International Affairs,* XXXIV, No. 2 (April 1958), 174–183.

KUO MO-JO. "A New Stage in Chinese Science," *People's China,* No. 14 (July 16, 1955), 8–12.

———. "Soviet Scientific Help to China," *ibid.,* No. 15 (August 1, 1956), 8–11.

LI CHOH-MING. "The First Decade, Part 2. Analysis: Economic Development," *China Quarterly,* No. 1 (January-March 1960), 35–50.

LIANG CHUAN. "Technical Revolution: The Concern of All," *Evergreen: A Magazine of Chinese Youth and Students,* No. 5 (August 1960), 20–22.

LING YANG. "Science Sets New Sights," *Peking Review,* I, No. 5 (April 1, 1958), 11–12.

LUZHNAYA, N. P. "Scientific Institutes of the Chinese People's Republic," in *Scientific Institutes of the Chinese People's Republic.* (Academy of Sciences of the Chinese People's Republic and its chemical institutions; originally published in *Zhurnal Neorganicheskoy Khimii* [Journal of Inorganic Chemistry], Moscow: Vol. III, No. 2, 1958.) Translated in Joint Publications Research Service Doc. 2568, N. Y. Regular Series (April 27, 1960).

NEEDHAM, JOSEPH. *Science and Civilization in China.* 3 vols. Cambridge: Cambridge University Press, 1954 (Vol. I), 1956 (Vol. II), 1959 (Vol. III).

"New Stage in China's Atomic Science," *Peking Review,* I, No. 31 (September 30, 1958), 7–8.

NIEH JUNG-CHEN. "The Development of Science and Technology in Our Country over the Last Ten Years," pp. 328–347 in *Ten Glorious Years.* Peking: Foreign Languages Press, 1960.

"Physical Sciences," *Union Research Service,* XIII, No. 19 (October-

December 1958) ; XVIII, No. 12 (January-March 1960) ; XIX, No. 12 (April-June 1960).

"Science Development Accelerated," *Peking Review,* I, No. 31 (September 30, 1958), 4–5.

"Science in China" (the revised version of contributions made to the symposium on "Sciences in Communist China," held in New York in December 1960, sponsored by the American Association for the Advancement of Science), *China Quarterly,* No. 6 (April-June 1961), 91–169.

"Science in Communist China" (a summary of papers presented to the symposium mentioned in the immediately preceding entry), *Scientific American,* CCIV, No. 2 (February 1961), 66–70.

"Sciences and Technology," *Union Research Service,* XXI, No. 26 (October-December 1960).

"Scientific Research," *China News Analysis* (Hong Kong), No. 97 (August 26, 1955), 6–7.

"Scientific Research (Physics, Mathematics, and Geography; Biology and Physical Geography; Technical Sciences; Philosophy and Social Sciences)," *ibid.,* No. 132 (May 18, 1956).

"Scientific Work," *ibid.,* No. 263 (February 6, 1959).

TAN CHO. "Training Technical Cadres for Expanding Local Industry," in *China's Technological Revolution.* (Originally published in *Jen Min Chiao Yu* [People's Education], Peking: Vol. IX, July 1, 1958.) Translated in Joint Publications Research Service Doc. 501, D. C. Regular Series (January 20, 1959).

TAO MENG-HO. "China's New Academia Sinica," *China Monthly Review* (November 1951), 235–239.

"Towards a New Science of Medicine," *China News Analysis* (Hong Kong), No. 269 (March 20, 1959).

"Vintage Year in Science," *Peking Review,* II, No. 2 (January 13, 1959), 4–5.

WOLFSTONE, DANIEL. "China's Research Reactor," *Far Eastern Economic Review,* XXVII, No. 9 (August 27, 1959), 315–317.

See also:

CHAO: *Economic Planning and Organization* (V) • THEODORE HSIEN CHEN: "Education and the Economic Failures" (VII) • CHU (VII) • "Documents from Red China and Russia" (VII) • "Training of Personnel" (VII) • "For a Joint Scientific Advance" (XVI)

• LI (V) • LIAO (XI) • *New China's Economic Achievements 1949–1952* (V) • "New Technology University" (IX) • ORLEANS (VII) • PIRIE (IX) • *Proposals of the Eighth National Congress* (V) • REBINDER (XVI) • *Selected Translations on Education* (IX) • WANG-CHI (IX) • YEN (IX) • YIN (V)

Section XVI
Sino-Soviet Relations and Educational Coöperation

BOORMAN, HOWARD L. "Chronology of Sino-Soviet Relations," *Problems of Communism*, III, No. 3 (May-June 1954), 14–21.

BURTON, ROBERT A. "Stalking the Elusive Chinese in Russia" (American Universities Field Staff Report), *East Asia*, VIII, No. 2 (March 15, 1960).

CHENG PING. "Socialist Solidarity: Sino-Soviet Scientific and Technical Coöperation," *Peking Review*, II, No. 7 (February 17, 1959), 11–13.

CHIN SZU-KÁI. *Communist China's Relations with the Soviet Union 1949–1957*. Hong Kong: Union Research Institute, 1961.

CLUBB, EDMUND O. "Oriental Studies through Soviet Eyes," *Pacific Affairs*, XXXII, No. 3 (September 1959), 306–309.

"For a Joint Scientific Advance," *Peking Review*, II, No. 3 (January 20, 1959), 21.

FRASER, STEWART E. "Notes on Sino-Soviet Educational Co-operation," pp. 36–54 in *Melbourne Studies in Education, 1961–62*, ed. E. L. FRENCH. Melbourne, Australia: Melbourne University Press, 1963.

HAO TO-FU. "Soviet Assistance and the Development of Chinese Economic Reconstruction in the Past Two Years," *Soviet Press Translations*, VII, No. 9 (May 1, 1952), 237–240.

HO TUN-SUN. "Soviet Aid to New China," *China Monthly Review* (May 1953), 50–53.

"In the Field of Scientific and Technical Coöperation," *Peking Review*, I, No. 43 (December 23, 1958), 30.

MAYER, PETER. *Sino-Soviet Relations since the Death of Stalin*. Hong Kong: Union Research Institute, 1962.

NORTH, ROBERT C. *Moscow and the Chinese Communists*. Stanford, Calif.: Stanford University Press, 1952.

"Peking–Moscow (Foreign Student News)," *China News Analysis* (Hong Kong), No. 205 (November 15, 1957).

PLUNKETT, RICHARD L. "China Views Her Russian Tutor," *Far Eastern Survey*, XXII, No. 8 (July 1953), 95–101.

PRIESTLEY, K. E. "The Sino-Soviet Friendship Association," *Pacific Affairs*, XXV, No. 3 (September 1952), 287–292.

REBINDER, P. A., and YE D. SHCHUKIN. "An Example of Scientific Co-operation between the U.S.S.R. and the People's Republic of China," in *Soviet Reports on Scientific Progress in China.* (Originally published in *Vestnik Akademii Nauk S.S.S.R.* [Herald of the Academy of Sciences of the U.S.S.R.], Moscow: No. 10, October 1959.) Translated in Joint Publications Research Service Doc. 3037, N. Y. Regular Series (March 2, 1960).

Report on Inspection of Science and Technology in the Soviet Union and China. (Articles originally published in *Soren Chungoku Gakujutsu Shisatsu Hokoku,* February 25, 1956.) Translated in Joint Publications Research Service Doc. 356, D. C. Regular Series November 14, 1958).

RUBINSTEIN, ALVIN Z. "Scholarship and Cold War in Moscow: The Twenty-fifth International Congress of Orientalists," *Orbis: A Quarterly Journal of World Affairs,* IV, No. 4 (Winter 1961), 467–477.

"Russian Impact on Chinese Culture," *China News Analysis* (Hong Kong), No. 223 (April 11, 1958).

"Russian Influence in 1954," *ibid.,* No. 65 (December 17, 1954), 1–7.

"Russians in the Universities," *ibid.,* No. 14 (November 27, 1953), 6.

SHIH YUAN-CH'ING. *The Relations between Moscow and Peiping.* Taipei: Asian Peoples' Anti-Communist League, 1961.

"Sino-Soviet Scientific Coöperation," *Peking Review,* I, No. 18 (July 1, 1958), 19.

"Sino-Soviet Scientific Coöperation," *ibid.,* No. 37 (November 11, 1958), 21.

"Sino-Soviet Scientific Protocol," *ibid.,* No. 20 (July 15, 1958), 19.

"Sino-Soviet Unity Is Indestructible," *ibid.,* II, No. 7 (February 17, 1959), 6–8.

"Sino-U.S.S.R. Philosophical Relations," *China News Analysis* (Hong Kong), No. 51 (September 10, 1954), 2–3.

SOONG CH'ING-LING. "China's Liberation—Sino-Soviet Friendship—Man's Great Leap into the Future," pp. 105–118 in *Ten Glorious Years.* Peking: Foreign Languages Press, 1960.

"Soviet Experts," *Newsletter of the United Nations Association of the Republic of China,* XIV, No. 2 (August 1958), 19–21.

SUCHKOV, B. I., and B. M. REMENNIKOV. "Soviet Colleges' International Ties—Great Plans for 1960," *Soviet Education,* II, No. 9 (July 1960), 44–46.

TAI YEN-NIEN. "The Soviet People's Aid to China," *People's China,* No. 22 (November 16, 1953), 8–12.

TIKHVINSKIY, S. L. "Soviet Chinese Cultural Ties," in *Ten Years of the People's Republic of China.* (Originally published as *10 [Desyat] Let Kitayskoy Narodnoy Respubliki,* Moscow: 1959.) Translated in Joint Publications Research Service Doc. 2825, N. Y. Regular Series (June 22, 1960).

WHITING, ALLEN B. "Communist China and 'Big Brother,'" *Far Eastern Survey,* XXIV, No. 10 (October 1955), 145–151.

WU YU-CHANG. "Sino-Soviet Friendship and Unity among the Socialist Countries," *People's China,* No. 2 (January 16, 1957), 4–8.

YANG HAI-PO. "Chinese and Soviet Youth Are Forever United," *Evergreen: A Magazine of Chinese Youth and Students,* Nos. 4 and 5 (July 1962), 8–9.

See also:

BIGELOW (IX) • CHANG HSI-JO (XVII) • KUO: "Soviet Scientific Help to China" (XV) • ROSTOW: *A Comparison of Russian and Chinese Societies* (V) • SHIH (IX)

Section XVII
International Relations in Education

"Afro-Asian Youth Conference," *Peking Review*, II, No. 6 (February 10, 1959), 18.

"Afro-Asian Youth Conference Hailed," *ibid.*, No. 7 (February 17, 1959), 19.

BAGCHI, P. C. *India and China: A Thousand Years of Cultural Relations*. Bombay: Hinds Kitab, Ltd., 1950.

CHANG CHAO. "Chinese Youth Forever Stand by Their Latin American Brothers" (speech by the leader of the Chinese Youth Delegation at the first Latin American Youth Congress, in Havana, July 26–August 8, 1961.) *Evergreen: A Magazine of Chinese Youth and Students*, No. 5 (August 1960), 5–7.

CHANG-FAN. "Advance a Step in Implementing the Education Policy of the Party and Improve the Quality of Supplementary Education for Returned Overseas Chinese," in *Selected Political and Sociological Translations on Communist China*. (Originally published in *Chiao Wu Pao* [Overseas Affairs Bulletin], Peking: No. 7, July 20, 1959.) Translated in Joint Publications Research Service Doc. 1953, N. Y. Regular Series (October 15, 1959).

CHANG HSI-JO. "Cultural Relations with Foreign Countries," *Peking Review*, II, No. 21 (May 26, 1959), 6–8.

Chinese Students in the United States, 1948–55: A Study in Government Policy. New York: Committee on Educational Interchange Policy, 1956.

CHOU YANG. "Education of Overseas Chinese," *Far Eastern Economic Review*, XXI, No. 12 (September 20, 1956), 369–371.

CLEWS, JOHN. "The Youth and Communist Student Fronts," *Far Eastern Economic Review*, XXII, No. 18 (May 2, 1957), 549–552.

Communist China in Africa. Taipei: Asian People's Anti-Communist League, 1961.

COUGHLIN, RICHARD J. *Double Identity: The Chinese in Modern Thailand*. Hong Kong: Hong Kong University Press, 1960.

DRUMRIGHT, EVERETT F. "Chinese Students in the United States," *News-*

letter of the United Nations Association of the Republic of China,
XIV, No. 1 (July 1958), 1–5.

"Education: Away from Russia?," *China News Analysis* (Hong Kong),
No. 5 (September 5, 1953), 7.

"Education for Overseas Chinese Students," *Union Research Service,*
XIX, No. 13 (April-June 1960).

FENG CHIA-SHENG. "China and the Arab World," *China Reconstructs,*
IV, No. 4 (April 1955), 24–26.

FONG NG BICKLEEN. *The Chinese in New Zealand: A Study in Assimila-
tion.* Hong Kong: Hong Kong University Press, 1959.

"For Closer Unity of World Students in Struggle against Imperialism:
Peking Students Rally to Celebrate 15th Anniversary of I. U. S.,"
Evergreen: A Magazine of Chinese Youth and Students, No. 8
(December 1961), 10–12, 21.

FRIED, M. H. (ed.). *Colloquium on Overseas Chinese.* New York: Institute of Pacific Relations, 1958.

GUILLEN, NICHOLAS. "My Second Visit to Peking," *China Reconstructs,* III, No. 1 (January, February 1954), 18–19.

HARPER, NORMAN. "Asian Students and Asian Studies in Australia,"
Pacific Affairs, XXXI, No. 1 (March 1958), 54–64.

HEVI, EMMANUEL JOHN. *An African Student in China.* New York:
Praeger, 1964.

HU, CHANG-TU. "Chinese Higher Education and World Affairs," *Teachers College Record,* LXII, No. 5 (February 1961), 356–366.

"I.U.S. Congress in Peking: Students of the World Speak Out," *Peking
Review,* I, No. 30 (September 23, 1958), 16–17.

"I.U.S. Sanatorium for Asian and African Students," *Evergreen: A
Magazine of Chinese Youth and Students,* No. 8 (December 1961),
13.

"Learning English," *China News Analysis* (Hong Kong), No. 264
(February 13, 1959), 6–7.

LEE, ROSE HUM. *The Chinese in the United States of America.* Hong
Kong: Hong Kong University Press, 1960.

LEE, WILLIAM CHENG-CHIAN. "The Opinions of American Professional
Educators about Chinese Education from 1895–1945." University
of California at Los Angeles doctoral dissertation, 1957.

LIU LI-SHEN. "A Student Back from America," *China Reconstructs,*
V, No. 8 (August 1956), 25–27.

LIU YI-FANG. "Foreign Students in China," *China Reconstructs,* VI,
No. 10 (October 1957), 18–20.

Lu Yu-sun. *Programs of Communist China for Overseas Chinese.* Hong Kong: Union Research Institute, 1956.

Ma Ho-ching. "Foreign Students in China," *People's China,* No. 24 (December 16, 1955), 27–30.

Mitchison, Lois. *The Overseas Chinese.* London: The Bodley Head, 1961.

Modern Chinese Reader, Parts 1 & 2, compiled 'by the Chinese Language Special Class for Foreign Students in Peking University. Peking: Epoch Publishing House, Foreign Languages Press, 1958.

Mohammad, Habib. "Two Thousand Years of Friendship," *China Reconstructs,* IV, No. 2 (February 1955), 18–22.

Motherland: Four Overseas Chinese Students Tell the Stories of Their Welcome in China. Hong Kong: Union Press, 1956.

"Premier Chou Speaks to Asian, African, and Latin American Youth," *Peking Review,* III, No. 41 (October 11, 1960), 19–20.

Purcell, Victor W. W. S. *The Chinese in Southeast Asia,* London and New York: Oxford University Press, 1951.

Pye, Lucian W. *Some Observations on the Political Behavior of Overseas Chinese.* Cambridge, Mass: Massachusetts Institute of Technology, 1954.

Resolutions of the 5th I.U.S. Congress; Peking, 4th-14th September, 1958. Prague: International Union of Students, 1959.

"Rich Cultural Exchange Programme," *Peking Review,* II, No. 4 (January 20, 1959), 21. :

Seto Mee Tong. "Lessons of My Life," *China Reconstructs,* III, No. 3 (May-June 1954), 17–20.

"Some Facts on China's Promotion of Peaceful and Friendly Relations with Other Countries and Her Efforts for the Relaxation of International Tension," *Evergreen: A Magazine of Chinese Youth and Students,* No. 2 (April 1962), 8–10.

Su Kai-ming. "Home Town Revisited," *China Reconstructs,* III, No. 6 (November-December 1959), 41–43.

Tan Kah-kee. "Opening Address at the Returned Overseas Chinese Federation Session," *Peking Review,* II, No. 51 (December 22, 1959), 9–12.

"Training the Younger Generation," *Peking Review,* II, No. 23 (June 9, 1959), 4.

"Union of African Students in China Formed," *Evergreen: A Magazine of Chinese Youth and Students,* No. 3 (April-May 1961), 11.

Wang Cheng-shu. "I Am Home Again," *China Reconstructs,* VII, No.

7 (July 1958), 5–7.

WILLIAMS, LEA E. "Nationalistic Indoctrination in the Chinese Minority Schools of Indonesia." *Comparative Education Review,* I, No. 3 (February 1957), 13–17.

WILLMOTT, DONALD E. *The National Status of the Chinese in Indonesia.* Ithaca, N. Y.: Department of Far Eastern Studies, Cornell University, 1956.

"World Youth in Peking," *China Reconstructs,* III, No. 6 (November-December 1954), 16–17.

WU, AITCHEN K. *China and the Soviet Union: A Study of Sino-Soviet Relations.* London: Methuen, 1950.

ZAGORIA, DONALD S. (ed.). "Communist China and the Soviet Bloc," *Annals of the American Academy of Political and Social Science,* CCCXLIX (1963).

See also:

"Arts as Weapons" (XIII) • CHOU: *China and the Asian-African Conference* (V) • ELEGANT: *The Dragon's Seed* (V) • GOLDMAN (IX and XIII) • HSIA (VII) • "In the Field of Scientific and Technical Coöperation" (XVI) • SOONG: "The First Five Years" (V)

Index

Index

Ability, measure of, 369

Academia Sinica, 18, 36, 165–185 *passim;* Yen Chi-ts'u, Director of Technical Science Department, 344; coöperation plan with Soviet Academy of Sciences, 346; *see also* Chinese Academy of Sciences

Academic criticism, development of, 396, 397

Academic problems, overseas Chinese overcome, 353

Academics, 26, 122, 141–146 *passim,* 147–158 *passim,* 159–164 *passim;* confessions of, 104–110 *passim; see also* Intellectuals

Academic standards, reform and improvement of, 367

Academic work, students complain of too much, 255

Academy of Sciences: *see* Academia Sinica; and *see* Chinese Academy of Sciences

Acheson, Dean, 108

Administration, Yenan University courses in, 80

Administrative districts, Military and Political Committee of, 92

Administrative system of Soviet Union adopted, 210

Adult education, 18, 334

Africa, spread of Chinese Communist philosophy to, 241

Agrarian reform, 25, 183

Agricultural affairs, Education Department coöperation in, 89–90

Agricultural chemistry, college entrance examinations for courses in, 319

Agricultural colleges, 28, 134, 319

Agricultural coöperatives, schools to be run by, 297

Agricultural electrification, college entrance examinations for courses in, 319

Agricultural forestry colleges, numbers of, 191

Agricultural machine building, college entrance examinations for courses in, 319

Agricultural mechanization courses, college entrance examinations for courses in, 319

"Agricultural Middle School in Communist China, The," 14n

Agricultural production: intellectuals participate in, 50, 51; great leap forward in, 333; students participate in, 334

Agricultural Science Institute, Soviet Academy of Sciences coöperation with, 346

Agriculture: Border Region lectures given on, 77; Yenan University courses in, 80; courses in, 124; manufacturing combined with, 296; Sino-Soviet coöperation in, 344; industry and arts to serve, 381; social science translations on, 418

"Aid Korea" campaign, 99, 100, 109, 123, 128, 378; *see also* "Resist America" campaign

Aircraft jet technology, new achievements in, 333

All-China Federation of Youths: All-China Federation of Students membership in, 341; constitution of, 341–343; membership, organization, function, powers of, 341–342

All-China Federation of Labor, 22

All-China Federation of Women, 22

All-China Students Federation, 22

Allowances: *see* People's subsidy

All-round development, educational philosophy of, 292

Alphabetic script, literacy campaign utilizing, 377

America, 6, 16, 26, 105, 107, 108, 109, 160, 182; higher educational institutions subsidized by, 98, 99, 100, 101, 102, 105, 106, 110, 210; traditional friendship for China of, 99; severance

Index